MARGINS
of Political
Discourse

SUNY series in Contemporary Continental Philosophy
Dennis J. Schmidt, editor

MARGINS

of Political Discourse

FRED DALLMAYR

State University of New York Press

Published by
State University of New York Press, Albany

© 1989 State University of New York

For information, address State University of New York
Press, State University Plaza, Albany, N.Y., 12246

Library of Congress Cataloging-in-Publication Data

Dallmayr, Fred R. (Fred Reinhard), 1928–
    Margins of political discourse/Fred Dallmayr.
        p.   cm. — (SUNY series in contemporary continental
    philosophy)
    Includes index.
    ISBN 0-7914-0034-4.   ISBN 0-7914-0035-2 (pbk.)
    1. Political science—History—20th century.   2. Philosophy-
    -History—20th century.   I. Title.   II. Series.
    JA83.D353 1989
    320.5'09'04—dc19

                                                                    88-30582
                                                                        CIP

For Mark and Nick
and for Peter Handke in admiration

Quia melius dies una in atriis tuis
quam millia....

Jetzt wär es Zeit, dass Götter träten aus
bewohnten Dingen....
                        Rilke

CONTENTS

Preface   ix

Introduction   xi

1. Polis and Cosmopolis   1

2. Gandhi as Mediator between East and West   22

3. The Discourse and Counter-Discourses of Modernity   39

4. Voegelin's Search for Order   73

5. Postmodernism and Political Order   95

6. Hegemony and Democracy: A Post-Hegelian Perspective   116

7. Rethinking the Hegelian State   137

8. Bloch's Principle of Hope   158

9. Politics of the Kingdom: Pannenberg's Anthropology   183

Appendix: Heidegger, Hölderlin, and Politics   207

Notes   221

Index   259

PREFACE

The present volume assembles *marginalia*—texts written into the margins of other texts and themselves inserted into contexts which I cannot fully plumb or discern. Such writing puts a particular strain on authorial intent. Yet, a brief biographical pointer is perhaps in order. In previous instances, I have used "prefaces" and "introductions" as an opportunity to offer a kind of road map or signpost to readers interested in the author's development. On several such occasions, the phrase *practical ontology* served as such a signpost. Contrasted with an abstract-spectatorial stance, the phrase was meant to underscore the experiential or event-character of thought and practice—particularly the aspect that, far from signaling a willful project, practice involves a combination of doing and enduring, of initiative and response or responsiveness. Differently phrased: practice means participation or engagement in a story whose unfolding plot is not entirely up for invention.

In the meantime, I have found that ontology is often misconstrued foundationally, namely, as a stable grounding or fixed abode—into which human thought and action might blend "naturally" and without labor (so to speak). This construal, of course, is entirely at odds with Heidegger's conception of 'being'—for whom the term always designated an open question or rather *the* question at issue in human life and unable to receive a definitive answer. In an effort to reduce the chances of misunderstanding, I have of late tended to accentuate the indeterminacy of being and the interpretive struggle or contest inevitably involved in a practical ontology or ontological practice (where struggle does not necessarily denote enmity). Margins of political discourse, from this perspective, designate those border-zones or crossroads where attentiveness and creative initiative intersect and where the stakes of meaning and non-meaning, order and disorder have to be continually renegotiated. Participating in this negotiation means to be a marginalist or *Grenzgänger*, a person habituated to crossing back and forth between self and other, between home and abroad.

As in the past, my explorations have been guided by a number of intellectual mentors whose core has not substantially changed; they include Heidegger, Gadamer, Merleau-Ponty, and Derrida. In the present volume, some additional figures have loomed large on my intellectual horizon, particularly Bernhard Waldenfels and Ernesto Laclau. Regarding political thinkers, I have at last found a way of expressing my indebtedness to Eric Voegelin, while carefully sorting out affinities from differences or disagreements. In addition, the volume has given me an opportunity of paying tribute to more distant intellectual and political models or exemplars, above all to Gandhi and Ernst Bloch. As always, mentors of this kind have been augmented or supplemented by a more proximate circle of friends and colleagues—among whom I want to mention here William Connolly, Hwa Yol Jung, Richard Bernstein, Thomas Pantham, John O'Neill, and Drucilla Cornell. Among a still more proximate group of friends (at Notre Dame), I wish to single out such *Grenzgänger* as David Burrell, for his efforts to rekindle a dialogue between Christian, Jewish and Islamic traditions; and Gerald Bruns, for his bridge-building between modern-literary and biblical hermeneutics.

Drawing the circle around me still more closely, I want to thank my loyally supportive family: my wife Ilse and our two children, Dominique and Philip, who during the writing of this volume navigated the currents of college life. The manuscript was typed and retyped with the usual efficiency by Patricia Flanigan. The volume is dedicated, first of all, to two former students: Mark Ishaug, who since has explored the margins between America and Africa; and Nicholas Griffin, who has done the same in the Near East. In the same context I want to recall fondly two other students who crossed borders in the reverse direction: Shrikant Dash from India and Stanley Muschett Ibarra from Central America. The volume is also dedicated to Peter Handke, whose novels and poetry epitomize in a striking contemporary idiom the intersection of immanence and transcendence, of sameness and otherness.

INTRODUCTION

... und *alles Nie-gehörende sei Dein.*
                    Rilke

Our age seems to be haunted by a slippage, a peculiar subterranean dislocation. "In attempting to uncover the deepest strata of Western culture," Michel Foucault wrote some two decades ago, "I am restoring to our silent and apparently immobile soil its rifts, its instability, its flaws; and it is the same ground that is once more stirring under our feet."[1] The instability referred to by Foucault was not merely cultural or literary in kind, but also philosophical and political—and perhaps it required a European to be alert to these combined tremors. Politically, our age is marked by the decentering of the dominant position of European nation-states (and their colonial appendages)—with the contours of a new ordering or centering of the world still hazy or barely perceptible. Philosophically, our age is said to witness the end of metaphysics, that is, of the grand totalizing systems anchored in *logos*, reason or the synthesizing power of subjectivity—systems which again are chiefly of European origin. Yet, neither level shows signs of a simple reversal. Politically, the end of supremacy has by no means cancelled Europe's political legacy—manifest in modern political structures and an array of political doctrines ranging from liberalism to socialism. Similarly, contrary to rash expectations, metaphysics does not simply give way to positivism or empiricism—which, on the contrary, are afflicted by their own malaise. In this situation, philosophy and political reflection are prone to be decentered themselves and deprived of secure moorings. Practitioners in these fields are bound to be "marginals"—not in the sense of aimless drift, but of being "border people" or *Grenzgänger*, inhabiting a peculiar margin or twilight zone in which traditional boundaries are blurred without being erased.

In the present volume, this margin or border-zone is examined on a number of levels and in a variety of contexts. The first and most important context is that of the political constellation emerging in our post-colonial era on a rapidly shrinking globe. Given the advances of technology and the growing interpenetration of economies, our time holds open the prospect of a uniform world-culture, and possibly a uniform world-state, in which all local traditions and cultural differences are relegated to the status of folklore or sentimental nostalgia. There is a long line of philosophical thought buttressing this prospect, a line extending from Stoicism and Hellenistic empires to Enlightenment rationalism and various contemporary forms of universalism or internationalism. The premise underlying this thought is that of the oneness of mankind which, in turn, is predicated on the oneness of human nature or reason and the basic sameness or congruence of human interests. In recent years, this outlook has been challenged by defenders of cultural and political pluralism, and not necessarily from retrospective or restorative motives. Apart from exposing imperialist designs (behind universalist rhetoric) recent pluralists have attacked the 'foundational' metaphysics of universalism: the assumption of the identity of reason and of the sameness or univocity of languages. Moving to the offensive, some anti-foundational writers have reversed traditional categories, replacing reason with radical contingency and reducing human interactions to the relentless contest and power-play of competing discourses or ways of life.[2] Countering both global synthesis and conflictual contestation, this study counsels an alternative perspective, one lodged precariously at the crossroads of *polis* and *cosmopolis*. Taking its bearings from the notion of a 'lateral universalism'—first articulated by Merleau-Ponty—the opening chapter suggests a global ordering bypassing synthesis and reciprocal repulsion in favor of an agonal mutual engagement. What such engagement requires is neither a narrow parochialism nor a bland cosmopolitanism, but rather a widespread *Grenzgängertum* or border-crossing (as a backdrop to prevailing hegemonies).

As it seems to me, a splendid exemplar of such *Grenzgängertum* in our century is Gandhi, both as regards his politics and his intellectual or spiritual life. Politically, Gandhi launched the struggle for independence against European colonialism—while simultaneously adopting or preserving crucial institutional features of that legacy. Seen in a long-range perspective, this struggle served as preamble to a policy of non-alignment, a policy seeking to maintain open spaces in the interstices of competing hegemonial structures. Most importantly, his strategy of non-violent resistance became a beacon of light for oppressed peoples around the world, a beacon eluding or shortchanging the vicious spiral of violence in favor of a struggle for mutual recognition. In terms of Indian politics, Gandhi's name stands for the open interchange of different cultural and religious traditions, including Hindu, Muslim, and Sikh communities—an interchange designed to promote not a melting pot but an agonal pluralism of cultures. The focus of the present volume, however, is on the global dimensions of this pluralism. In this respect, I believe, Gandhi occupies a particularly significant role: namely, as *Grenzgänger* and mediator between East and West. Educated in the best Western schools, Gandhi turned into a relentless critic of the deficiencies of Western modernity—without, however, embracing Hindu traditionalism (an embrace obstructed by his severe attacks on the caste system and other defects of traditional Hinduism). Basically, East and West here are short-hand formulas for opposed ways of life: while the latter term, by and large, stands for an activist culture bent on changing and governing the world, Eastern or Oriental thought has tended to focus on primordial premises or parameters undergirding intentional human designs. As a *karmayogin,* one devoted to the practical pursuit of perfection, Gandhi breached or undercut this cultural bifurcation. His central notion of *satyagraha*—translatable as the "doing of truth"—involved precisely a blending of action and passion, of doing and suffering bypassing assertiveness and fatalism. The same notion reverberates in *ahimsa* or "non-violence," seen as caring engagement even with the enemy.[3]

Problems afflicting Western modernity—or at least the linear pursuit of modernization—have been noted not only by spokesmen of Eastern culture. In fact, a fissure can presently be detected in Western culture itself, a fissure loosely designated by such paired labels as *modernity* versus *postmodernism* or *Enlightenment rationalism* versus *deconstruction.* Actually, the fissure is not of recent origin. As Jürgen Habermas points out, in his *The Philosophical Discourse of Modernity,* Western modernity has been accompanied from the beginning by an internal critique, in the sense that the rationalist optimism of Enlightenment thinkers was supplemented by a counter-discourse or counter-formulation stressing the dialectical character of modernization—a formulation epitomized by the writings of Hegel and his heirs. In more recent times, according to Habermas, this internal critique has given way to a more radical counter- or anti-discourse challenging not the defects of modernity or the Enlightenment but modernity itself and thus championing a perspective of anti-or postmodernism and counter-enlightenment; the chief spokesmen of this outlook, in his presentation, are Nietzsche, Heidegger, Derrida, and Foucault. Taking up the notion of a discourse of modernity, my third chapter questions this pejorative portrayal of postmodernism. Focusing on Nietzsche and Heidegger, I argue for an (at least partial) continuity of their writings with the Hegelian counter-discourse—their greater radicalism being chiefly attributable to the intensification of the ills or predicaments of modernity. Generally speaking, modernity and postmodernism in my view are not two separate periods or antithetical movements but rather moments in an agonal dialogue about the future of Western culture. Seen in this light, postmodernism is not simply an exit or exodus from modernity, but rather an internal rift or tremor—the very rift or flaw alluded to by Foucault in the passage above.[4]

One critic of Western modernity not mentioned in Habermas's book is the political philosopher and historian Eric Voegelin. In the present context, Voegelin deserves attention for a number of reasons. First of all, as an emigrant from his native Austria he was a long-time *Grenzgänger* at the intersection or margins of Continental and American culture. More importantly, the central category of his thought is the Platonic *metaxy* or "in-between," a term designating the crossroads between the mundane-natural and the divine, between immanence and transcendence—or in his words, between "intentionality" and "luminosity," between "thing-reality" and "It-reality." The fourth chapter explores Voegelin's theoretical-metaphysical perspective as outlined in his (posthumously published) *In Search of Order*. The accent is placed on his experiential-participatory ontology and on the tensional structure of the *metaxy*—an outlook resembling in many ways Heidegger's 'fundamental ontology' and also more recent anti-foundational or post-structuralist arguments concerning the ambivalence and multivocity of meaning structures and modes of discourse. My reservations about Voegelin's work have to do with a certain tendency to relax the tensional "between" into a juxtaposition of opposed domains or into a "two-worlds" conception—a bent transforming at least potentially It-reality into a stable grounding of human order (in a manner contravening his own stress on non-polarity and on the indeterminacy of being). Another complaint concerns the one-sidedly pejorative treatment of modernity—under such rubrics as *gnosticism* and *metastatic* revolt—and also the less than even-handed portrayal of major figures of modern thought, from Hegel to Nietzsche and beyond (a portrayal sometimes more acerbic than Habermas's). These and similar concerns, however, are offset in my mind by appreciation of his general anti-dogmatism and his focus on *metaxy* as an experiential and ontological border-zone.[5]

In contemporary thought, the same border-zone has been investigated by a number of (less retrospectively inclined) thinkers, including Merleau-Ponty who thematized the *metaxy* under such labels as *intertwining, chiasm,* and *reversibility.* Following Merleau-Ponty's lead, the German philosopher Waldenfels has used "intertwining" as a gateway to inquiry into the intersection of reason and contingency, of political order and disorder (or non-order). Taking his departure from the "asymmetry" of question and answer in dialogues—the inability of an answer to exhaust or settle a question—Waldenfels draws a parallel with political structures or arrangements, showing that no political structure can fully contain the range of viable possibilities. As he insists in *Order at Twilight*—a study discussed in the fifth chapter—social discourses and interactions can never be stabilized in a definitive synthesis but remain marked by an internal rift or flaw, which is the rift of contingency. Given the asymmetry and indeterminacy of dialogues, human interactions in his view have the character of agonal engagements—which do not coincide with total conflict or mutual repulsion (as this would cancel the nexus of question and response). Silhouetted against the backdrop of "non-order" or the field of the "unordered," attempts at social and political ordering always inhabit a twilight or border-zone *"entre chien et loup"* where meaning and non-meaning, culture and nature intersect. With more specific attention to questions of political power, political theorists Laclau and Mouffe link the contingency of political order with the inevitability of "hegemonic" arrangements—though these arrangements always remain open to contestation. As they argue in *Hegemony and Socialist Strategy* (the topic of the next chapter), politics is basically an "articulated" or creatively constructive practice, one which can never achieve transparent unity but only a precarious blend of concord and dissent. Relying on Hegelian insights, Laclau and Mouffe trace political dissent and antagonism not only to a plurality of possible structures, but to the intersection of positivity and negativity, of presence and absence. With particular reference to democratic theory, they portray democracy as a tensional *metaxy* located between holistic order and polar conflict, between the "logics" of complete identity and pure difference.[6]

The study by Laclau and Mouffe is ·fertile in opening up many new theoretical vistas; in my own case, it assisted the endeavor of rethinking the Hegelian state. The image of Hegel emerging from this endeavor is not that of the spokesman of "identity philosophy" nor that of the defender of a unified "state" guided by bureaucracy seen as "universal class" (or as embodiment of the general will). Instead, Hegelianism here stands for a theory of radical relationism—the kind of relationism depicted in the *Phenomenology of Spirit* as a "bacchantian revel" in which every part or member seeking to isolate itself "immediately dissolves." The seventh chapter examines Hegel's conception of the state as presented in his *Philosophy of Right*, with particular emphasis on the role of *Sittlichkeit* or "ethical life" as human and social bond. In Hegel's portrayal, public *Sittlichkeit* in the modern sense differs from two alternative modes of social interaction: namely, the close-knit and homogeneous "ethical substantiality" characteristic of the ancient *polis*, on the one hand, and on the other, the atomistic individualism and contractarianism typical of *laissez-faire* economics (and acknowledged by Hegel on the level of "civil society"). The chapter also reviews a number of critical rejoinders to Hegel's conception, giving special attention to recent anti-foundational and post-structuralist attacks—above all Lyotard's proposal to replace Hegel's unitary state with social fragmentation and the notion of a common ethical bond with conflictual contestation predicated on the principle of a general agonistics. Countering this reversal of priorities, I advance an alternative view, one which—faithful to the spirit if not the letter of Hegel's teachings—bypasses the antipodes of *Gemeinschaft* and *Gesellschaft* or of social synthesis and separatism: namely, the institutionalization or incorporation of public *Sittlichkeit* in plural, heterogeneous groupings cross-cutting social divisions (or inhabiting the margins of such divisions). No longer enshrined in uniform state structures, I believe, ethical life today can only arise from concrete engagements transgressing social cleavages and decentering all forms of self-enclosure.[7]

One prominent type of enclosure—not readily acknowledged in our time—derives from a complacent secularism and a self-sufficient humanism or anthropocentrism. Abetted by a pervasive anti-metaphysical and agnostic mood, the enclosure is commonly legitimated by the presumed coincidence of modernity and secularization. To unsettle and decenter this presumption, the eighth chapter invokes a resolutely nonconformist study by one of the most notorious *Grenzgänger* of our century: Ernst Bloch's *Principle of Hope* with its celebration of human "anticipatory consciousness" in every form. Apart from outlining a complex and nuanced ontology of the "Not-Yet," Bloch's work offers a panoramic view of the human search for fulfillment or the *summum bonum*, giving broad room particularly to religious visions and yearnings from antiquity to the present. Although detecting in history a trend toward the demythologization and humanization of the divine, Bloch refuses to equate the latter with the progressive sway of secular immanence; on the contrary: precisely to the extent that divine heteronomy is removed, "radical otherness" begins to inhabit human nature itself, thus lending to human yearnings a peculiar depth or mystery. The ultimate goal of religious hopes—the "coming kingdom"—is interpreted here as a *regnum humanum,* but a realm which is itself placed at the margin or "beyond the threshold of previously existing creature, of its anthropology and sociology." In the context of more recent "political theology," a similar perspective has been articulated by Wolfhart Pannenberg in a work stressing the intersection of humanism and faith (titled *Anthropology in a Theological Perspective*). In Pannenbergs view, the coming kingdom is not simply other-worldly—on the model of two-world doctrines—but rather occurs at the crossroads of immanence and transcendence, of *civitas Dei* and *civitas terrena.* The attached Appendix discusses a particular crossroads in Heidegger's intellectual development, namely, the "turning" or *Kehre* from an earlier political aberration to a city of hope or promise—a turning permeated by the mood of mourning.[8]

Exploring margins or border-zones of thought and practice, the chapters and essays collected in this volume cannot themselves coalesce or be aggregated into a unitary doctrine; the themes or arguments of the essays are always profiled against the backdrop of the "unsaid" and inserted into the margins of ongoing experience. To this extent, the chapters emulate the Heideggerian sense of being "underway"; they also reflect the silent vowel in Derrida's *différance*—whose *Margins of Philosophy* served as inspiration for the title of the present volume. As Derrida remarked about the texts assembled in his own study, their combined effect was to raise "the question of the margin," of the line or border separating a text from, and linking it with, a context. In his words, his essays were designed to "interrogate philosophy beyond its meaning," by treating it not as a closed doctrine but as a text inscribed in a broader text—a treatment not only conjuring up the "entire logic of the margin" but also prompting another "reckoning": namely, the realization "that beyond the philosophical text there is not a blank, virgin, empty margin, but another text, a weave of differences of forces without any present center of reference" and that the overt text of philosophy always "overflows and cracks its meaning." Invoking a Hegelian expression, Derrida added that philosophizing means to "cast oneself into the abyss"—or rather into the margin of *Grund* and *Abgrund*—"à corps perdu."[9]

1

POLIS AND COSMOPOLIS

The prospects and perils of our age have reached global proportions. This is due to a host of technological, economic, and cultural-political factors. In the latter sense, ours is the first age ever to give rise to something like a genuinely global history: nations and continents previously hovering in the shadow or on the sidelines of history have stirred from this condition and have become co-shapers and co-definers of the future of mankind. Economically, the spreading of capital markets has for some time eroded traditional national boundaries and fostered the emergence of ever-larger trading zones, partially monitored by multinational organizations. Technologically, the contemporary informational revolution—with its corollaries of tele-communications and jet travel—has tended to reduce the world increasingly to a global village where news from every corner is almost instantly available, at the same rate as the diffusion of technical gadgets is promoting a uniform world culture. While promising and exhilarating in many respects, global tendencies of this kind, however, are fraught with matching dangers—foremost among them the danger of a nuclear holocaust or of the collective self-destruction of the Spaceship Earth. Blending together the promising features of our age, Karl Jaspers at one point anticipated the possibility of a new axial age giving birth to a truly universal civilization in which different cultures would cooperate in shouldering jointly the stewardship of the human race. A generation earlier, however, Friedrich Nietzsche had projected the twentieth century as the arena of an unparalleled battle: namely, the battle for the domination of the globe in which the vastness of the stakes is equaled by the enormity of devastation.[1]

From the vantage of lived experience, the latter prophecy seems to be close to the mark. Without prejudging the dispute between Jaspers and Nietzsche, their disagreement—in my view—points up an important theoretical issue, one which cannot readily be settled by empirical tendencies or statistical forecasts: namely, the question how something like a global city or a cosmopolis can at all be conceived and plausibly articulated. On this point, the history of (Western) philosophy and political thought is not entirely silent, but also not very conclusive. There is a strong universalist streak in Western thought, a streak ranging from the Stoics over the medieval theory of universals to Enlightenment rationalism and beyond. Relying on universal principles and essential definitions, the guiding assumption of those perspectives is that mankind at bottom is (and has always been) one, with cultural diversities constituting at best surface variations on a common theme. Despite its speculative vigor, the defects of this assumption are not hard to detect and have frequently been stated: from nominalism to Romanticism and beyond, critics of universalism have pointed to its high-flown, often tautological abstractness and its aloofness from concrete cultural content. This complaint has been reinforced in our century by language philosophy with its accent on language games and diverse cultural narratives; the latter accent, in turn, has been exacerbated by post-Nietzscheans insisting on the primacy of cultural and political discord or struggle. In the following pages I hope to make some headway in this complex thicket of arguments, focusing chiefly on recent debates. In the first section I intend to discuss versions of universalist approaches from the Stoics to Habermas. The second section explores the particularist (or anti-totalist) challenge to these approaches, emphasizing motifs stretching from Herder to Lyotard. Taking its bearings from (late) hermeneutics and post-structuralism, the concluding part sketches a tentative cross-cultural avenue, in the hope of shedding some theoretical light on the prospect of a global city.

I

In Western thought, universalism or the notion of the oneness of mankind arose first in a philosophically ambitious and politically relevant manner with the Stoics. To be sure, classical Greek philosophy had not been devoid of universal categories (as is evident in Plato's "forms" and Aristotle's teleology); however, in the context of the Greek city-states, these categories retained at best an embryonic and practically circumscribed character—a situation which changed during Hellenism and later with the expansion of the Roman Empire. The founders of Stoicism were Greeks of the post-classical age, but subsequently the center of the school gravitated toward Rome until finally it became a cornerstone of Roman imperial culture. As propounded by a succession of thinkers, a key tenet of Stoicism was the notion of a divine spark or *logos* operative in the universe as a creative potency, a potency in which all human beings were meant to share regardless of race, creed or nationality. Translated as "reason" (or as *ratio et oratio*) this *logos* also functioned as the hidden law governing nature and society alike, and in this capacity it furnished the yardsticks for human behavior and legislation, that is, for rules of practical conduct. In ethical and political terms, the task of a Stoic was to practice citizenship in a given *polis* so that it would be compatible with, and a gateway to, citizenship in a universal "cosmopolis of reason" embracing all mankind. What saved this vision from speculative abstractness was ultimately its linkage with concrete legal institutions and practices. From Cicero to the imperial jurists, persistent efforts were afoot to assimilate the law of reason with the emerging *ius gentium* (law of nations) of the far-flung Empire, in contradistinction to the more restricted civil law of Rome.[2]

To a large extent, the Middle ages remained heir to the Roman legacy of universalism (or the merger of universalism with concrete institutions). Starting roughly with Charlemagne, the Holy Roman Empire kept its spiritual center in Rome or the Roman church while seeking to combine this center politically with loose transnational structures. On a philosophical plane, the medieval theory of universals was a blending of Platonic and Aristotelian essences with the Stoic belief in a rational *logos* governing the cosmos and human thought, a blending which came to serve as backbone to scholastic logic and epistemology. At the same time, in line with the Stoic example, the equation of *logos* and reason was the source of a complex system of rules or norms, and especially of the Thomistic distinction between the "law of nature" (applicable to all mankind) and the "human law" (applicable to a given *polis*). To be sure, rational argument in the Middle Ages tended to be a handmaiden of theology, a circumstance which surfaced in the superimposition of divine and eternal norms on principles of natural reason. To this extent, medieval thought sponsored the idea of a "cosmopolis of faith" as contrasted with Roman or pre-Christian modes of rationalism. As in the case of the Roman precedent, the medieval vision was concretized and rendered partly workable by practical institutional arrangements. Thus, the reception of the Roman law throughout the Continent provided European kingdoms with a semblance of cultural unity, just as feudalism furnished a transnational framework of economic interdependence.[3]

Renaissance and Reformation shattered and relegated to the past Europe's political and spiritual unity—but by no means all universalist aspirations. As has frequently been noted, Renaissance humanism was in many ways affected by Stoic beliefs, especially by the notion of a common or universal human nature. This conception was intensified during the Baroque and Enlightenment periods, chiefly through the assumption—favored by contractarian theorists—of a pristine "state of nature" (outside and prior to social conventions) in which humans are rigorously free and equal and only subject to a universal law of nature (or reason) The latter point, in turn, was corroborated by Enlightenment rationalism from Descartes to Leibniz with its insistence on a universal structure of the human mind giving rise to an absolute, quasi-mathematical form of knowledge (a *mathesis universalis*) valid everywhere irrespective of cultural variations. The metaphysical underpinnings of this kind of rationalism were severely attacked by Kant (and also by Hume). In his three *Critiques* Kant divided reason or rationality into three domains—science, ethics, and art—but without in any way challenging the a priori structure of human consciousness or the possibility of achieving a universally valid, objective type of knowledge. During the nineteenth century, the universalist direction of Enlightenment thought was further pursued by liberal utilitarians and by Marx; however, their hope was grounded less in a common structure of reason than in the globalizing effects of the capitalist market and the advances of modern technology. In contrast to liberal utilitarians, Marxism envisaged a dénouement of social conflicts in the emergence of the proletariat as the 'universal class' embodying the promise of human freedom and equality.[4]

Apart from the continuing effects of these perspectives, twentieth-century thought has engendered its own initiatives in this domain, ranging from the unified science movement (wedded to a universal model of knowledge) to linguistic universalism (stressing syntactical depth structures). Instead of exploring this array of approaches, I want to concentrate here on one prominent example: the modified universalism endorsed in Habermas's "critical theory." This theme has emerged in varying guises and formulations in Habermas's steadily evolving opus—but without damage to a persistant common direction. His epistemological treatise, *Knowledge and Human Interests* (1968), was a concerted assault on logical positivism and its equation of genuine knowledge with that produced by empirical science. However, as one should note, the attack did not call into question the value and objectivity of empirical science but only the restrictedness of the positivist focus: its neglect of historical-hermeneutical knowledge and of critical self-reflection (or ideology critique). Thus, in lieu of the unified science program, *Knowledge and Human Interests* proposed a three-tiered or tripartite model embracing science, hermeneutics and reflection—a model distantly patterned on Kant's three *Critiques;* only a correlation of these three types of cognition, the study claimed, could furnish a truly comprehensive and universal theory of knowledge. In line with the study's title, modes of cognition were linked with underlying interests or motivations, namely, the technical interest in control, the practical interest in understanding, and the emancipatory interest in self-knowledge and free self-realization. These interests, in turn, were presented as universal species dispositions (said to be endowed with a quasi-transcendental status as well as being involved in an historical learning process). As the Appendix of the study asserted, accentuating the universal character of interests and their moorings in both nature and culture: "The achievements of the transcendental subject have their basis in the natural history of the human species. . . . My second thesis is that knowledge equally serves as an instrument and transcends mere (natural) self-preservation." Alerting to the social context of technical, practical, and reflective orientations, the Appendix also affirmed that interests "take form in the medium of labor, language, and power."[5]

The years following publication of *Knowledge and Human Interests* brought several changes in the study's framework. For present purposes, two such modifications were particularly significant: the loosening of the linkage between knowledge and underlying cognitive motivations; and the reassessment of self-reflection particularly when seen as methodological cornerstone of critical social science. In the first rubric—without canceling the linkage entirely—Habermas introduced a crucial distinction or separation between experience and knowledge, between "experiential a priori" and "argumentative a priori" or, more generally, between praxis and discourse. While in ordinary life-praxis, experiences are gathered and integrated into a set of taken-for-granted beliefs, discourses in this scheme bracket or suspend immediate action constraints or ordinary experiences with the sole purpose of permitting the rigorous testing of knowledge claims. Extricated from the opacity of the life-world, discourses function as warrants of the validity and objectivity of cognitive propositions, especially of assertions of empirical 'truth' and normative 'rightness.' Even more dramatic—and pregnant with long-term implications—was the second revision. Distancing himself from the emancipatory model invoked in *Knowledge and Human Interests*, Habermas noted that the model was too closely tailored to therapeutic endeavors to serve properly as paradigm for critical knowledge. Dropping this restriction he prepared a new bifurcation, this time within the emancipatory cognitive domain: namely, the bifurcation between self-reflection and rational reconstruction or, more simply, between critique and reconstructive inquiry. While self-reflection centers on particular life stories or on processes of individual and collective identity formation, rational reconstruction uncovers anonymous rule systems as well as general depth-structures of knowledge and behavior. As leading exemplars of reconstructive inquiry Habermas invoked Wittgenstein's analysis of rule-following, Chomsky's explorations of generative grammar and of universal modes of linguistic competence, and—on a more behavioral level—the findings of developmental psychology (as practiced by Piaget). As he pointed out, it is reconstructive inquiries of this kind which "today step into the place of a (transformed) transcendental philosophy. To the extent that it derives universal rules of a communicative ethics from the basic norms of rational speech, even moral philosophy will establish itself as a reconstructive science."[6]

Both revisions gave direction to Habermas's subsequent investigations. In a prominent manner, the combination of discursive knowledge and reconstructive methodology surfaced in his formulaton of universal pragmatics as a general theory of communication. As he stated in his study on the topic (1976), the task of universal pragmatics is "to identify and reconstruct universal conditions of possible understanding and consensus *(Verständigung)*." Drawing on his conception of discursive validation, Habermas portrayed these conditions as the "validity basis of speech," arguing that (rational) communication necessarily involves basic validity claims—specifically the four claims of factual truth, normative rightness, personal truthfulness, and linguistic comprehensibility. While ordinary exchanges rely on taken-for-granted beliefs, the disruption of direct understanding brings these validity claims to the fore—whose operation can be uncovered through reconstructive analysis. According to Habermas, the latter analysis was not restricted to linguistic depth structures (in Chomsky's sense) nor to the level of general concepts, but could be extended to the pragmatics of speech and communication; universal pragmatic (or formal-pragmatic) inquiry thus supplemented formal semantics and generative grammar. "I would defend the thesis," he wrote, "that not only language *(langue)* but speech too—that is the employment of sentences in utterances—is accessible to formal analysis," in the sense that utterances can be studied "in the methodological attitude of a reconstructive science." Reconstruction in this case aimed at uncovering the depth capacity or "intuitive rule consciousness" of speakers—what Habermas called their "communicative competence." In contrast to the interpretation of meaning contents, and also to individual self-reflection, reconstructive inquiry was said to relate to "pretheoretical knowledge of a general sort" or to "universal capabilities" of speech; to this extent, "what begins as an explication of meaning aims at the reconstruction of species competences." In comparison with a general linguistic or grammatical know-how, universal-pragmatic theory (we read) "postulates a corresponding communicative rule competence, namely, the competence to employ sentences in speech acts. It is further assumed that communicative competence has just as universal a core as linguistic competence."[7]

Seen as a general theory of communication, universal pragmatics was a broad-gauged program buttressing reconstructive endeavors in a variety of fields, including the domains of empirical truth and normative rightness. In line with his earlier anticipation, Habermas soon embarked on the reconstruction of moral philosophy by focusing on the rightness claims implicit in speech acts and their discursive validation. Deviating from non-cognitive and emotivist stances, Habermasian communicative ethics (or discourse ethics) provides a linguistic grounding for categorical standards—standards which are now seen as embedded in communication and amenable to testing in practical discourses. Simultaneously with the analysis of depth assumptions or capabilities, Habermas turned to the reconstruction of developmental (or diachronic) processes—in line with his view that universal competences are both natural (or species endowments) and historically generated. Thus, his study on universal pragmatics was accompanied and succeeded by a number of essays dealing in detail with human cognitive development, with stages of moral consciousness, with the formation of ego identity, and with the progressive maturation of behavioral and linguistic faculties. In large measure, these essays were indebted to psychologists like Piaget and Lawrence Kohlberg; however, the latter's framework was significantly expanded, especially by means of analogies with "phylogenetic" evolution, that is, with the sequential transformation of group life in the course of social development and modernization.[8] Analytical-synchronic and developmental considerations were linked in Habermas's major work of sociological theory: *The Theory of Communicative Action.* The central concept of the study—communicative rationality and action —was basically a restatement of the validity basis of speech, embracing (in contrast to instrumental behavior) the full range of validity claims embedded in communicative exchanges. At the same time, relying in part on Weberian teachings, the study portrayed modernization as a process of societal rationalization along sequential stages of cognitive and normative development. Rationality in both dimensions was said to be not simply a Western-cultural bias but (at least potentially) a universal category. In Habermas's words: "Theory formation is in danger of being limited from the start to a particular, culturally or historically bound perspective—unless fundamental concepts are constructed in such a way that the concept of rationality implicit in them is encompassing and general, that is, satisfies universalistic claims."[9]

II

While captivating in its theoretical élan, Western universalism has always been suspect: both because of its abstractness and its proclivity to ethnocentrism (if not cultural paternalism). Throughout the history of Western thought, assertions of oneness and universal principles have consistently been opposed by perspectives stressing contingency and cultural diversity. Thus, the Stoic doctrine of the *logos* unifying mankind was challenged by a long string of skeptical thinkers—from Carneades to Sextus Empiricus—counseling a more patient and sober concern with concrete detail and particular circumstances. Similarly, the medieval theory of universals did not hold undisputed sway, but was contested with growing intensity by nominalists insisting on the verbal and ultimately vacuous character of universal categories (in comparison with the concrete reality of particulars). During the eighteenth century, Enlightenment rationalism was critiqued by both skeptics and *Sturm-und-Drang* thinkers—the latter precursors of the Romantic movement—questioning the belief in the linear evolution of mankind along the path of growing rationalization. To some extent, Johann Gottlieb Herder—the contemporary of Voltaire—was illustrative of this counterpoint. In his philosophical reflections on the "formation of mankind," Herder emphasized the language- and context-bound quality of human thought and action. In contrast to a uniform evolutionary pattern or telos, history in his view was dispersed or disseminated among diverse peoples, cultures and periods; moreover, these cultures and periods needed to be judged on their own terms rather than being subjected to a general measuring-rod, invariably taken from a later and presumably more advanced vantage. As he wrote: "The enlightened man of the later age—not only does he wish to listen to everything, but he also pretends to be the final synthesis of all voices, mirror of the entire past, and representative of the goal of the entire historical production. The precocious child blasphemes."[10]

From Herder an intellectual line might be drawn—with some caution—over the Romantics and Nietzsche to contemporary expressions of postmodern or anti-foundational thought. With regard to Habermas Richard Rorty has extended his indictment of foundationalism also to the rational (and quasi-Kantian) universalism of critical theory. As he observes in *Philosophy and the Mirror of Nature*, Habermas as well as Karl-Otto Apel have labored to create a new transcendental vista "enabling us to do something like what Kant tried to do," namely, by formulating a "universal pragmatics" or a "transcendental hermeneutics" —efforts which he finds "very suspicious" and misguided. As he adds, the notion that we can overcome positivistic reductions "only by adopting something like Kant's transcendental standpoint seems to me the basic mistake in programs like that of Habermas." Rorty's assessment could be fleshed out by reference to recent developments in scientific theory calling into question the univocal objectivity of scientific inquiry (including reconstructive science). According to a leading spokesman of post-empiricism, Mary Hesse, it has been "sufficiently demonstrated that the language of theoretical science is irreducibly metaphorical and unformalizable and that the logic of science is circular interpretation, reinterpretation and self-correction of data in terms of theory, theory in terms of data."[11] Habermasian universalism, in my view, is particularly flawed from a practical and political perspective. For, if the oneness of mankind is already assured by a priori categories and built-in universal capabilities, what need is there to engage in interaction and transcultural dialogue with a view toward achieving (a measure of) political concord? Theory at this point seems to preempt practice—unless the latter is seen simply as (technical-deductive) implementation of preordained formulas.[12]

Critiquing human oneness, to be sure, can entail different conclusions. In the case of many postmodern or post-foundational thinkers, anti-universalism tends to give rise to a frank endorsement of cultural segregation or separatism. Thus, in several of his writings, Rorty gleefully celebrates his native habitat—North American culture—with its attachment to technology, social engineering, and human mastery of the environment; in contrast to global philosophical schemes, his preference is for local, even parochial narratives and their deliberate continuation. "Whereas Habermas compliments 'bourgeois ideals' by reference to the 'elements of reason' contained in them," he states at one point, "it would be better just to compliment those untheoretical sorts of narrative discourse which make up the political speech of the Western democracies. It would be better to be frankly ethnocentric."[13] In Rorty's case—due to his liberal-pluralistic leanings—ethnocentrism retains a somewhat benign or noncombative flavor—which differentiates his out-look sharply from other, more radical formulations of postmodernism. Partly under the influence of Nietzschean motifs, these formulations construe the exit from universalism as warrant for cultural incompatibility and relentless reciprocal contestation. Once general foundations are removed, all cultural contexts or discourses are said to be radically politicized—in the sense that given contexts reflect political choices or preferences which necessarily are in conflict with competing political frameworks or interpretations. A major representative of conflictual or agonal analysis is Jean-François Lyotard—some of whose works I select to illustrate this version of anti-universalism.

In the English-speaking world, Lyotard first emerged as a spokes-man or standard-bearer of postmodernism through a book whose main epistemological content only obliquely matched its startling title: *The Postmodern Condition: A Report on Knowledge* (of 1979/1984). In con-densed form, the Introduction summarized the thrust of the book's argument. As used in the study, the term *modern* was said to desig-nate any science or knowledge form that legitimates itself through ref-erence to a universal "metadiscourse" or by appealing to "some grand narrative such as the dialectics of spirit, the hermeneutics of meaning, the emancipation of the rational or working subject, or the creation of wealth." By contrast, the term *postmodern* denoted a basic "in-credulity toward metanarratives," an incredulity or skepsis fostered by the contemporary crisis of metaphysics as well as the malaise of the "university institution" erected on metaphysical grounds. What happened as a result of this skepsis, according to Lyotard, was the dismantling of metanarratives and their dispersal into heterogeneous discourses or "clouds of narrative language elements." In lieu of grand unifying schemes, postmodernism tolerates only a "pragmatics of lan-guage particles" arranged in many diverse "language games"—a prag-matics giving rise to institutionalization only "in patches—local determinism." Such localism stands in opposition to the dictates of total systems—governed by efficiency criteria—but also to neo-uni-versalist schemes stressing rational consensus. Turning to the Haber-masian model of communicative agreement, Lyotard insisted: "Such consensus does violence to the heterogeneity of language games. And invention is always born of dissension." Postmodern knowledge, he added, can no longer be accommodated in universalizing frameworks; rather, it "refines our sensitivity to differences and reinforces our ability to tolerate the incommensurable. Its principle is not the expert's homol-ogy, but the inventor's paralogy"—where "paralogy" means a disruption of paradigms.[14]

Congruent with its subtitle, a large portion of *The Postmodern Condition* dealt with changing modes of knowledge or science, and particularly with the computerization of knowledge associated with the contemporary informational revolution. No longer a part of character formation or individual training, Lyotard observed, scientific knowledge in our time has become a marketable commodity and, in fact, the chief force of production in developed countries; to this extent, such knowledge "is already, and will continue to be, a major—perhaps *the* major—stake in the worldwide competition for power." Together with computerization, our age has accentuated another feature of knowledge or cognition: its basically linguistic character, that is, the status of cognitive frameworks as discursive formations or language games. In a manner reminiscent of Habermas—but without universalist ambitions—*The Postmodern Condition* endorsed the primacy of the pragmatics of language: the notion that—far from simply copying an external reality—cognitive statements or assertions should be seen as utterances or speech acts executed in the context of rule-governed linguistic conventions. Deviating from Habermas, the study placed the emphasis of pragmatics less on the 'illocutionary' than the 'perlocutionary' quality of speech: the ability of speakers to parry objections or counter-proposals and ultimately to defeat opponents as part of a competitive struggle or contest. Normally, opponents are other speakers or interlocutors; but even in their absence, there remains "at least one adversary, and a formidable one: the accepted language or connotation." In Lyotard's presentation, every utterance must be seen as a "move" within a game—where "move" signifies a combative strategy or challenge. This, he writes, "brings us to the first principle underlying our method as a whole: to speak is to fight, in the sense of playing, and speech acts fall within the domain of a general agonistics."[15]

The arguments concerning linguistic moves carry over into social and political interactions and ultimately shape the nature of the social bond in our time. According to Lyotard two traditional models or construals of the social bond can be distinguished: the models of integral holism and of binary opposition or conflict. The first model had been inaugurated by the French founders of sociology and was developed by functionalist theorists from Malinowski to Talcott Parsons. In our own time, the same model has been further refined by systems theory and cybernetics—approaches exclusively wedded to operational efficiency. What remained constant throughout these historical variations is the view of society as "a unified totality, a 'unicity'." In opposition to this view, Marxism adopted a dualistic model stressing the class struggle between workers and management. As Lyotard points out, however, the

Marxist alternative has largely lost its salt: either by being coopted in Western welfare societies, or else by being transformed into a functional holism in communist countries. Returning to the notion of linguistic pragmatics, the study reaffirms the centrality of language games— actually a multiplicity of games—which function as the only remaining social bond in a postmodern context. Contrary to the pretense of integral holism or of the grand narratives of the past, our age is said to witness the " 'atomization' of the social into flexible networks of language games"—with each speaker or participant being located at particular "nodal points" of competing communication circuits. Instead of being submerged in social harmony, the "atoms" of society are perceived as operating at the "crossroads of pragmatic relationships" and involved in perpetual moves and countermoves—an interplay which exceeds predictable stimulus-response processes. While reactive responses are no more than programmed effects, genuine countermoves are seen as enhancing displacement in the games and even a disorientation encouraging unexpected moves. "What is needed," Lyotard comments, "if we are to understand social relations in this manner, on whatever scale we choose, is not only a theory of communication but a theory of games which accepts agonistics as a founding principle." Such games approximate a general state of war—but the war is "not without rules."[16]

As the study recognizes, forms of knowledge are not self-sufficient but dependent on some kind of legitimation; typically such legitimation in the past has assumed a narrative cast. Thus, Plato's theory of forms was embedded in a dialogical context, while Cartesian and post-Cartesian thought relied on a mental narrative—the story of the development and clarification of mind. In the wake of the Enlightenment, two major legitimation stories or grand narratives are distinguished in the study: the conception of a dialectic of spirit (or of spirit coming to itself) promulgated by German idealism, and the notion of popular emancipation initiated by the French Revolution and later translated into proletarian emancipation. Both types of stories, in Lyotard's view, have collapsed or lost their plausibility: speculative idealism has been undermined by the proliferation of language games following different rules—an experience first formulated by Nietzsche; regarding popular emancipation, the presumed theory-praxis nexus has been dissolved due to the segregation of denotative and prescriptive language games. In our own time, a new metanarrative has been propounded by cybernetics and systems theory with the accent on technical efficiency or performativity; but the latter principle offers at best a de facto legitimation and can by no means account for itself. As a result, we are faced today with a lack or erosion of general narratives or universal metalanguages and accordingly confined to a multitude of competing narrative accounts. Realization of this situation first dawned in *fin-de-siècle* Vienna, among philosophers and scientists as well as artists: "They carried awareness of and theoretical and artistic responsibility for delegitimation as far as it could be taken." Wittgenstein's accomplishment, in particular, is said to reside in his delineation of the theory of language games without recourse to either grand narratives or sheer performativity: "That is what the postmodern world is all about."[17]

In its conclusion, the study points to various developments in contemporary science, all illustrative of the postmodern situation of polymorphous non-universalism. Contrary to the focus on ultra-stability endemic to systems theory, postmodern science is said to be embarked on a search for instabilities and even the exploration of logical paradoxes. Quantum mechanics and microphysics have shifted the accent from steady, predictable processes to the study of discontinuity and indeterminacy; the same is true of recent mathematical theory with its focus on Brownian movements and the description of reversals or catastrophes in phenomena. Following René Thom, Lyotard sees the catastrophe model as reducing all causal processes to a single one: namely, "conflict, the father of all things according to Heraclitus." What remains at this point are at best "islands of determinism," while catastrophic antagonism is "literally the rule." The lesson to be drawn from these scientific developments is that the "continuous differential equation" has lost its preeminence for contemporary science; instead, by concerning itself with "undecidables, the limits of precise control, ... 'fracta', catastrophes, and pragmatic paradoxes" postmodern science is grasping its own evolution as "discontinuous, catastrophic, nonrectifiable, and paradoxical." After the demise of the grand narratives, the only remaining legitimation of knowledge is one based on paralogy or the transgression of paradigms. In contrast to the consensual model favored by rationalism, Lyotard insists, "it is now dissension that must be emphasized." While paradigmatic research tends to stabilize and domesticate, he states, one must posit "the existence of a power that destabilizes the capacity for explanation, manifested in the promulgation of new norms for understanding" and knowledge.[18]

Lyotard's "dissensual" or combative-agonal approach is fleshed out and amplified in a number of other writings, particularly in *Le Différend* (of 1983)—a complex study to which I can only briefly allude. Elaborating on the study's title, the opening section distinguishes sharply between contest *(différend)* and juridical litigation *(litige)*. "In contrast to a litigation," we read, "an agonal contest is a conflict between (at least) two parties which cannot properly be decided due to the absence of a decision rule applicable to both sides of the argument. The legitimacy of one side does not entail the illegitimacy of the other." If the same decision rule is applied to both sides, the contest is transformed into a litigation—with damaging results for at least one party, and possibly both. As Lyotard adds, the title of the book suggests that "generally there is no universal rule applicable to diverse modes of discourse." As in his previous work, this circumstance is traced to the pragmatics of language games, particularly to the rule-governed character of sentences and discourses. A sentence, he writes, is formed "in accordance with a set or system of rules," and there are several systems of sentence formation. Sentences, in turn, are part of discourses or discursive structures which are equally rule-governed. Here is the linguistic source of agonal contestation. For, sentences belonging to diverse or heterogeneous rule systems "cannot be translated into each other"; they can only be connected in compliance with a given discursive goal. Similarly, the diversity of discursive structures engenders on inter-discursive conflict or contest—one unable to be settled by a higher authority (due to the absence of a universal discourse). According to Lyotard, philosophical reflection emerges precisely at the boundaries of discourses and language games. The aim of his study, he notes, is to convince the reader "that thinking, knowledge, ethics, politics, and being are at stake at the margins between sentences," and to counter the prejudice that there is something like "man" as such or "language" as such. In this sense, the study seeks to make a contribution to "philosophical politics," by bearing witness to contestation.[19]

Philosophical politics of this kind stands in contrast to traditional, non-political metaphysics. The change in outlook is attributed chiefly to the "linguistic turn" in Western thought, a turn accompanied by the "decline of universalistic discourses." In a more personal vein, Lyotard lists as his main sources of inspiration two works (whose combination is certainly uncommon): namely, Kant's *Critique of Judgment* (together with his historical-political writings) and Wittgenstein's *Philosophical Investigations*. Kant's teachings are invoked because of his denial of intellectual intuition, and Wittgenstein because of his pragmatic definition of meaning. Both thinkers, Lyotard states, attest the demise of "universalistic doctrines": their works are "epilogues of modernity and prologues of a significant postmodernity"; thus they prepare the "thought of dispersal" (or the thinking in diaspora) befitting our postmodern context. In line with Kantian initiatives, contestation is opposed to all forms of holism, including intuited universals or substantive-general ideas. As a rule, the study observes, the categories of the whole (or the absolute) cannot characterize objects of cognition; the thesis affirming the opposite "might be called 'totalitarism'." Totalist tendencies are encouraged

by several contemporary frameworks, including cybernetic communication models and also theories of complete rational consensus. In contrast to such synthetizing approaches, agonal contest is said to demarcate a situation of instability where different discursive options are still
open and the outcome hangs in the balance. Properly conceived, politics means the possibility or threat of contestation. In Lyotard's words:
Politics "is not a mode of discourse but rather denotes their multiplication, the diversity of goals and especially the question of their connection. . . . Politics arises from the fact that language is not one language
but sentences, and being not one being but different instances of 'Es
gibt'. It is mere being which is (also) not—one of its names."[20]

III

I do not mean here to question the importance and even profundity of
many of Lyotard's insights—a depth which is unfairly curtailed by my
condensed and selective reading of his texts. My concern is mainly with
certain accents and perhaps overstatements marking these texts, particularly with the heavy accentuation of dissensus and conflict. One
source of my concern is the similarity of Lyotard's arguments with perspectives arising on very different soil: particularly contemporary neo-
utilitarianism and (naturalistic) behavioralism. According to the former,
politics is basically a struggle for advantage among individuals (or
groups), with each participant seeking to maximize interests or benefits
over losses; according to the latter, politics is an arena of power where
the strong invariably dominate the weak. No doubt, Lyotard—like other
post-Nietzscheans—would want to distance himself from these approaches whose premises, he might argue, are still moored in traditional subject-centered (or "logocentric") versions of metaphysics and
thus oblivious of the linguistic turn. On a different level, this is also his
central objection to Habermasian universalism and his model of rational
consensus. Yet, rationalist metaphysics may be more difficult to van-
quish than is often assumed. Generally speaking—and this is my basic
concern or apprehension—metaphysics can scarcely be overcome by
inverting its premises or priorities. Such an inversion (I am afraid) is
manifest at many junctures of Lyotard's work: particularly in the reversal from consensus to dissensus, from paradigm to paralogy, from holism
to dispersion, and from totality to agonal contests. What these reversals
neglect is the complex interlacing of the paired opposites and the
ambivalent status of their meaning. Most importantly, placed in radical
opposition, the terms tend to replicate or mirror each other's defects.
This applies prominently to the (so-called) social bond. In the absence

of mutual—and more than contingent-accidental—relations, the contending parties are liable to lapse into self-centeredness. Differently put: unless contest involves more than combat and mutual repulsion, competing discourses or language games are bound to suffer the very enclosure rightly bemoaned in the case of integral holism.[21]

What these considerations suggest is that universalism and agonistics (or holism and contest) are not mutually exclusive but rather correlated and interlocking vistas—though correlated neither on the level of a priori categories nor that of accidental contacts. Something like this correlation seems to have been involved in the universality claim of hermeneutics as originally formulated by Hans-Georg Gadamer (in 1966). Universality in this case did not denote a complete transparency of understanding predicated on abstract categories of reason; nor, conversely, was it compatible with radical fragmentation. As Gadamer stated in his essay on the topic: "The claim to universality proper to the hermeneutic dimension means this: understanding is tied to language" or a linguistic context, and language is not an abstract "system of signals" nor an anonymous rule structure which could be generalized and computerized. Viewed ontologically, understanding is always context-bound and embedded in a given mode of being fraught with various judgments and prejudgments. According to Gadamer, however, this feature did not vindicate a "linguistic relativism"—because (he wrote) there "cannot be an enclosure in language, not even in one's mother tongue. This we all experience when we learn a foreign language and especially in traveling insofar as we somehow master a foreign idiom." To this extent, every living language had to be viewed as unlimited or "infinite," and it was "entirely erroneous" to derive from the diversity of languages something like a dispersal or fragmentation of understanding. "The opposite is true," Gadamer stated (somewhat exuberantly): "Precisely the experience of the finitude and particularity of our being— a finitude manifest in the diversity of languages—opens the road to the infinite dialogue in the direction of ontological truth" (or the truth "that we are").[22]

The same point was reinforced in Gadamer's rejoinder to Habermas's critique of universal hermeneutics (in 1971). As Gadamer observed at the time in his defense, hermeneutical experience is not the experience of universal meaning or the discernment of a general "plan of reason"—an ambition plausible only *sub specie aeternitatis;* by contrast, hermeneutical inquiry is an "ever renewed attempt to decode the meaning fragments of history, fragments limited by the opaque contingency of reality and especially by the twilight zone in which the future hovers from the vantage of the present." The notion of universal hermeneutics had to be seen in the same subdued light: understanding was universal only in the sense of being an inescapable feature of the human mode of life, a mode articulating itself (in the first instance) in ordinary language and common-sense beliefs—into which even alien or abstracted idioms have ultimately to be translated. Recapitulating arguments advanced in *Truth and Method,* Gadamer presented understanding not so much as a method or a methodologically trained exegesis but rather as the "medium of human social life which, in the last analysis, has the character of a linguistic or dialogical community" (though not one geared to uniform consensus). In this sense, hermeneutics reflected not a universal reason but the plurality of modes of rational argumentation as well as "the pluralism which combines and connects mutually opposed or conflicting elements in society."[23]

In many ways, the path beyond universalism and agonistics had been prepared by Gadamer's teacher, Martin Heidegger. In several of his writings of the interbellum period, Heidegger had articulated a mode of relationship between diverse elements which eluded the alternatives of both coincidence (or synthesis) and radical separation. Thus, the lectures on "The Origin of the Work of Art" (of 1936) differentiated between two dimensions or modalities—namely, 'world' and 'earth'—whose precarious interplay was said to constitute the central trademark of artworks. In this juxtaposition, the term *world* designated the aspect of meaning-disclosure or the "self-disclosing openness" of cultural understanding and of narrative-historical meaning-contexts; the term *earth* by contrast pointed to the aspect of "permanent self-seclusion or sheltering," that is, to the dimension of concealment (of meaning), of non-understanding and non-reason. In Heidegger's presentation, the two modalities were not simply factual domains standing in a relation of causal or functional dependence (which would reduce one to a variable of the other). Most importantly, their interplay in art-works did not yield a facile blend but rather amounted to a strenuous contest or agonal "strife." "In resting upon the earth," he noted, "world strives to surmount the latter; as disclosing openness it cannot endure anything secluded. On the other hand, earth in its mode of sheltering tends to embrace and harbor the world in its own ambience." Yet, strife in this case was not synonymous with hostile collision or mutual repulsion; rather, art-works had the distinctive ability to sustain the strife while raising or lifting the contesting parties into a tensional unity or non-synthetic harmony (that is, a harmony preserving heterogeneity). As the lectures stated: "The work-being of the work consists in the enactment of the strife between world and earth. It is because the strife achieves its culmination in the simplicity of mutual intimacy that this enactment yields the unity of the works. . . . The serene repose of a work at peace with itself reflects the intimacy of the strife."[24]

Heidegger's comments on agonal concord were fleshed out and amplified in his postwar discussion of 'identity and difference' and also in his conception of a complex fourfold constellation *(das Geviert)* combining contest and sympathy. Roughly at the same time, strides in a similar direction were undertaken by another student or successor of Husserlian philosophy: Maurice Merleau-Ponty, especially through his notions of 'intertwining' and 'chiasm'—terms meant to designate the tensional intersection of meaning and non-meaning, of culture and nature, immanence and transcendence, and of self and other. Defining chiasm also as a mode of reversibility—"the finger of the glove that is turned inside out"—Merleau-Ponty saw such an intersection at work particularly in the arena of intersubjective or self-other relations: "In reality there is neither me nor the other as tangible, positive subjectivities. There are two caverns, two opennesses, two stages where something will take place—and which both belong to the same world, to the stage of being." In another context, he extended the perspective of intertwining explicitly to the domain of inter- or cross-cultural relations, coining at that point the suggestive concept of a 'lateral universalism.' Objecting to an abstract type of structuralism concerned with invariant categories, Merleau-Ponty observed: "Even if these invariants exist, even if social science were to find beneath structures a metastructure to which they conformed (as phonology does beneath phonemes), the universal we would thus arrive at could no more be substituted for the particular than general geometry annuls the local truth of Euclidean spatial relations." The antidote or necessary complement to a structuralist focus had to be found in anthropological field work, in lived experience which exposes the analyst to concrete modes of cultural diversity. In this manner a new path opened up to cross-cultural understanding or to "the universal: no longer the overarching universal of a strictly objective method, but a sort of lateral universal which we acquire through ethnological experience and its incessant testing of the self through the other person and the other person through the self."[25]

Merleau-Ponty's intimations of lateral connectedness and agonal reversibility have been further pursued by one of his leading German followers: the philosopher Bernhard Waldenfels. Translating or recasting agonal concord as the problem of the contingent ordering of social life, his *Order at Twilight* portrays social and cross-cultural relations as patterned on the model of agonal dialogue, a model highlighting the inevitable asymmetry between question and answer, challenge and response. Since in dialogues—Waldenfels observes—questions are typi-

cally unprovoked and unpredictable and there usually is room for multiple answers, communicative exchanges cannot be subsumed under
(either deductively or inductively constructed) holistic systems and retain
instead an open-ended, multivocal character. The communicative model
can be extended to concrete social practices and interactions, where it
surfaces as the interplay between "stimulus" (seen as enticement or provocation) and "reaction" (seen as responding action or countermove). "If
it is true," he notes, "that every question opens up a field of possibilities
and thus permits several responses and not only one, then there emerges
a rift between question and reply," between stimulus and response. The
rift here has the nature of an agonal contest—but one which does not
cancel the connectedness of the contending parties. Dialogical exchange
thus implies a "peculiar" kind of correlation: one which "simultaneously
links and separates"; for a given response "may meet the point of a
question—but without thereby exhausting the possibilities and need of
responding." Reflecting this asymmetrical structure, acts of social ordering are never fully transparent but fraught with ambivalence and contingency; far from achieving rational wholeness or consensus, such
ordering requires continuous negotiation and renegotiation of the terms
of interaction. According to Order at Twilight, this fact ultimately derives
from the tensional intertwining of meaning and non-meaning, culture
and nature. Since ordering always presupposes non-order or the backdrop of the unordered—a domain it can never completely eradicate—
social order is bound to inhabit a twilight zone "entre chien et loup"—
just as human thought and existence can never shed traces (in Merleau-
Ponty's terms) of "a pensée sauvage and an etre sauvage."[26]

Among political theorists or philosophers, a similar outlook has
been formulated by Ernesto Laclau and Chantal Mouffe—though with
greater emphasis on hegemonic arrangements or the asymmetrical dis-
tribution of political power. In their presentation, hegemony signifies a
contingent or selective mode of ordering, in sharp contrast to foundational or essentialist political conceptions—conceptions stressing either
an integral holism or the complete segregation (and self-enclosure) of
opposing camps. Generally speaking, politics in their view is an articulated practice or a creatively constructive enterprise, a practice which
can never achieve total rational transparency or logical unity but only a
precarious blend of meaning and non-meaning, of concord and dissent.
Seen as constructive enterprises, political formations only selectively
structure a given social domain without being able to exhaust available
possibilities; differently phrased: discursive orders or practices always
are silhouetted against the horizon of the unordered and unarticulated
or against the broader field of discursivity with its inherent surplus of

meaning. This aspect is the deeper source of social conflict or antagonism. Due to their finite and selective character, political formations
inevitably are in tension with alternative types of ordering. Antagonism, however, results not only from the confrontation of empirical
structures but from the intrinsic contingency of political order as such,
that is, from the built-in limit and negative potency challenging its
positive arrangements. Hegemonic order, in this sense, is located at the
margins not only of meaning and non-meaning, but also of presence
and absence, positivity and negativity. Yet, just as positive structures
can never be fully integrated or stabilized, negativity cannot be synonymous with total opposition (without canceling the ambivalence of political articulation) This is particularly true in the case of democracy.
According to Laclau and Mouffe, democracy cannot be equated with a
holistic system nor with a polar conflict between opposed camps—despite
the persistence of agonal tensions. "Between the logic of complete identity and that of pure difference," they write, "the experience of democracy should consist of the recognition of the multiplicity of social logics
along with the necessity of their (hegemonic) articulation"—an articulation which needs to be "constantly re-created and renegotiated."[27]

The preceding formulations apply primarily to domestic (or intra-
societal) relations—but they can readily be extended to the field of cross-
cultural and international politics. In the latter arena, the vista of an
agonal universalism or a tensional cosmopolis has been articulated by a
number of political thinkers, including Eric Voegelin—though chiefly
with reference to the Hellenistic age. Pondering the difference between
regional or "ecumenic" orders and the idea of a "universal mankind,"
Voegelin presents the former as historical instantiations or anticipations of the universal idea—which in itself remains a symbol or index
of a hidden meaning. "Universal mankind," he writes (in *The Ecumenic
Age*), "is not a society existing in the world, but a symbol" expressing
obliquely the sense of human destiny—in the form of an "eschatological index." On a broader philosophical level, the notion of mankind as
a "calling"—or rather as a reciprocal calling and invocation—has been
expressed by Merleau-Ponty, with specific reference to contemporary
global contacts between East and West. "The relationship between Orient and Occident," he observed, is "not that of ignorance to knowledge
or of non-philosophy to (rational) philosophy; it is much more subtle,
making room on the part of the Orient for all kinds of anticipations and
'prematurations'." Against this background, it is not merely the Orient's
task to learn from the West, but also the Occident's task to reassess itself
by remembering abandoned possibilities. Indian and Chinese thought,
we read, have tried "not so much to dominate existence as to be the

sounding board of our relationship to being"; Western philosophy can learn from this example by seeking to rediscover this relationship and to "estimate the options we have shut ourselves off from in becoming 'Westerners' and perhaps reopen them." As Merleau-Ponty concluded, the unity of mankind is not a bland synthesis but rather "exists in each culture's lateral relations to the others, in the echoes one awakens in the other."[28]

2

GANDHI AS MEDIATOR
BETWEEN EAST AND WEST

Perhaps I should first apologize for the temerity of coming to India to talk about Gandhi.* Surely it is one of the less urgent needs of Indians to have a Westerner lecture them about such an eminently indigenous thinker as Gandhi. Thus, my undertaking from the beginning requires and solicits your kind indulgence—all the more so as I do not pretend to speak as an expert on Indian affairs. My task would be entirely forbidding if the gulf between cultures (or language games) were really as unbridgeable as some linguists claim. As it happens, despite his profound native roots, Gandhi's thought and activities were never of a circumscribed parochial character; without being blandly cosmopolitan, his voice managed to breach all the barriers of nationality, culture, and creed. It certainly penetrated into my own life-world. As far as this presentation is concerned, my approach is prompted not by detached schol-

---

*Prepared for presentation at the conference on "Phenomenology and Indian Philosophy" held at New Delhi in January 1988.

arship nor by the arrogance of expertise, but rather by a deep intellectual and existential fascination and affection; more succinctly put: I am
here not to lecture you but to pay tribute or homage to probably the
greatest figure of the twentieth century—and to one of the most enticing
and exemplary human beings of all times. In my view, Gandhi was and
remains a source of immense ferment unsettling all kinds of (intellectual and political) complacency. Intellectually, he came closest to being
a modern-day Socrates, a gadfly challenging ingrained habits and
unleashing new vistas; but transgressing philosophical boundaries,
Socratism in his case was amplified by the democratic fervor of a Gramsci
and the all-embracing caring and compassion of a Mother Teresa. Albert
Einstein was quite correct (I think) when he noted that generations to
come "will scarcely believe that such a one as this, ever in flesh and
blood, walked upon this earth."[1]

Clearly, paying tribute to a man of this stature would be un-
manageable in the absence of prudent self-limitation. In the case of
Gandhi, the student or reader is quickly humbled by the vastness and
complexity of his life-work, and also by the sheer bulk of his writings—
many of them originally penned in languages not ordinarily familiar
to a Western audience. In the latter respect, access has recently been
immensely improved or facilitated by the endeavors of Raghavan Iyer,
particularly by his collection in three volumes of the central *Moral
and Political Writings of Mahatma Gandhi*, a collection which ably
supplements his earlier study on Gandhi's "moral and political thought."[2]
My own understanding of Gandhi is greatly indebted to Iyer's publications—and also to the writings of some Indian friends and colleagues,
including Bhikhu Parekh, Thomas Pantham, and Ashis Nandi. Apart
from hewing to readily accessible materials, my comments in the following shall be limited or circumscribed in another, more important
sense: bracketing concretely political activities or achievements—which
made Gandhi the "father" of Indian independence—I want to concentrate on the Socratic or quasi-Socratic quality of his thought, that is, his
capacity for unsettling traditional dividing lines and dichotomies,
including (above all) the polarity between East and West. Taking for
granted the absence of a Gandhian philosophical "system" (a point frequently noted), I want to indicate how precisely this non-system places
him at crucial junctures of contemporary philosophical developments
(and of contemporary politics as well). After exploring briefly the East-
West bifurcation and its role in Gandhi's life and thought, I shall turn
to some of his key concepts or teachings in an effort to highlight both
their intrinsic merits and their relevance as a meeting-ground of present-
day Western and Indian philosophy.

I

In seeking to portray Gandhi as a mediator between cultures, I enter the treacherous terrain of overly general speculation. Beyond their purely geographical significance, East and West stand for broad cultural conglomerates nearly impervious to concrete inquiry. As a result, my observations here must be very cautious and tentative—without succumbing to complete skepsis. Fortunately, my task is aided by Gandhi himself who frequently spoke of "the West" seen as a counter-term to Indian and (more broadly) Oriental culture. Thus, already an essay of 1905 referred to an "Oriental Ideal of Truth" as manifest chiefly in classical Indian texts. Reacting to Lord Curzon's claim that "the highest ideal of truth is to a large extent a Western conception," Gandhi recommended to the then Viceroy of India a number of passages "from Oriental scriptures and epics and other religious and ethical works" in an attempt to induce him to "withdraw his baseless and offensive imputations." While countering in this instance Western conceit, Gandhi did not perceive the distinction entirely as a matter of bias. In fact, pursuing the theme, an editorial of 1929 accentuated the difference into a specifically Western and non-Western "choice": "Today the superficial glamour of the West dazzles us, and we mistake for progress the giddy dance which engages us from day to day. . . . If we are to be saved and are to make a substantial contribution to the world's progress, ours must emphatically and predominantly be the way of peace."[3]

    To be sure, these comments do not really settle the issue at hand: the distinction between cultures, between East and West. Perhaps, one strategy to make headway in this area is to probe further the dispute raised by Lord Curzon. Presumably, in labeling *truth* a Western conception, Curzon was thinking of truth as an epistemological category, as the product or outcome of a process of empirical testing and argumentative validation. By contrast, the scriptural passages invoked by Gandhi present truth as a primordial grounding, as an ontological matrix in which all modes of testing and argumentation are already inscribed or embedded. In the first instance, truth signifies an achievement or the result of a deliberate investigative enterprise; in the second case, it designates the precondition (though not merely the abstract condition of possibility) of cognition. Elaborating somewhat boldly—perhaps rashly —on this distinction, one might say that Eastern culture (traditionally) thematizes primordial and more-or-less timeless underpinnings of thought and action while Western culture accentuates purposive modes of inquiry and practical human designs. Still more rashly formulated, the East adumbrates cosmic-maternal (or else maternal-paternal) structures or principles in comparison with the West's infatuation with masculine initiative and active innovation. Against this background, Marx's dictum that philosophy in the past has merely interpreted the world while the real task is to *change* it appears as a quintessentially Western statement—moreover as a statement which merely captures a tendency operative in Western philosophy for a long time (at the latest since Bacon's equation of knowledge and power).[4]

Treated as antipodes, both cultural traditions have their intrinsic strengths, but also their readily apparent drawbacks. When stylized into rigid and immutable codes, ontological structures can degenerate into fatalistic constraints stifling human self-reflection and concerned engagement; on the other hand, divorced from broader frameworks the focus on initiative can turn into a recipe for human self-glorification and unlimited mastery over nature. While, in the one case, ontology gives way to objectivism and reification, counter-ontology in the other case spawns arrogance and the boundless pursuit of the will to power. As a Western-educated Indian, Gandhi may be said to have bypassed the defects of both cultures while enhancing their respective strengths through careful mediation and cross-fertilization. Although a devoted reader of classical Indian texts and a partisan of ontological truth *(satya)*, Gandhi spent his life engaged in practical and political endeavors— endeavors which, without renouncing truth, exposed the latter forever to the test of concrete experience. While not shunning or deprecating meditative exercises, his overall orientation was in the direction of practical wisdom or of the practical pursuit of perfection, that is, in the direction of *karma yoga*—which is not the same as mindless activism. Although a faithful Hindu in many ways, he resolutely opposed the traditional Indian caste structure—or at least its modern-day effects— by embracing the cause of the poorest and outcaste sections of society, the *Harijans*, whom he called lovingly the "children of God."

A good example of Gandhi's unorthodox or in-between position can be found in his attitude toward *moksha* or personal salvation. In traditional Indian thought, *moksha* signified the ultimate and highest human good or aim, the aim of spiritual freedom and redemption. As Iyer observes, this aim could in principle be pursued over two distinct paths: the path of *pravritti* or involvement, and that of *nivritti*, meaning withdrawal or disengagement. While the first path emphasized the pursuit of perfection through active engagement and suffering with and for others, the second path stressed abstinence, retreat, and the discontinuance of worldly acts or projects. Over the centuries the first path tended to atrophy in India, with the result that *moksha* became increasingly identified with personal salvation, with an individual escape route from mundane and social reality; the preferred means of reaching this exit were individual penances and private ascesis. Against this background, Gandhi's turn to praxis unsettled established traditions by excavating or reviving a nearly forgotten strand. In Iyer's words, "the Gandhian emphasis on *karma yoga*, on *pravritti*, as the necessary (and not merely a legitimate) means to *moksha*, was a blow" to traditional salvationism—but a blow which did not sacrifice the traditional goal itself. As Gandhi affirmed in the preface to his autobiography, the aim of all his strivings was *moksha* or self-perfection: "I live, move, and have my being in pursuit of this goal. All that I do by way of speaking and writing, and all my ventures in the political field, are directed to this same end." However, instead of restricting himself to private deliverance, Gandhi regarded his social and political work as an integral part of emancipation or of the task of freeing himself from spurious bondage; differently put: inner and outer modes of liberation were for him not strictly segregated. Although a crucial goal, personal salvation in his eyes was impossible without engagement or *pravritti* on the side of the poor, without active co-suffering and sacrifice in the midst of society. According to another passage: "I am striving for the kingdom of heaven, which is spiritual deliverance. For me the road to salvation lies through incessant toil in the service of my country and of my humanity. I want to identify myself with everything that lives; in the language of the *Gita*, I want to live in peace with both friend and foe."[5]

II

The notion of mediation might suggest a weak compromise or (more grandly) a Hegelian kind of synthesis—which would surely be beside the point. Perhaps a better way of approaching Gandhi is by emphasizing the topological quality of mediation, that is, the in-between character of his status at the crossroads of cultures. Seen from this angle, rather than representing an amalgam, Gandhi emerges as a figure critically inhabiting the margins of cultures—one employing his marginality precisely in order to tease out novel ways of cultural interaction or of reciprocal challenge and response. In this sense, Gandhi occupied the position of a gateway or threshold between cultures, a threshold which links and separates at the same time. From the side of Indian traditionalists, Gandhi was frequently accused of being too strongly Westernized, for having exchanged inherited native beliefs for alien customs and thought-patterns. Undeniably, a good part of his life—perhaps as much as a third—was spent either abroad or else in Indian jails (and thus at the inner margins of his native country). From 1888 until 1891 he received

legal training in London, and from 1893 until 1914 he lived with inter-
ruptions in South Africa organizing the struggle of Asians against the
Apartheid regime. Until 1912 he wore European dress, and he undoubt-
edly absorbed much of European culture during these formative years
of his life. Yet, although not completely hostile or dismissive, his attitude toward Western civilization was always distant and oblique—as
befits a figure who was never part of mainstream European society but
always exposed to its seamy and exploitative underside.

Gandhi's critical attitude toward the West surfaced eloquently in
an early book he wrote during a voyage from South Africa to England,
called *Hind Swaraj* (translated as *Indian Home Rule*). From beginning
to end, the book was a sustained and even passionate indictment of the
Western way of life, especially of its rampant materialism and the growing commercialization of all facets of existence; in the words of its author,
the book was meant to be "a severe condemnation of modern civilization." Although extreme in some of its formulations, *Hind Swaraj* was
not simply a polemical tract. Devotees of Western modernization would
do well to read the book periodically in order to appreciate more fully
the effects of modernity on its victims (and even on its proponents). In
its spirited attack on modern civilization, *Hind Swaraj* was reminiscent
of the early Rousseau—although the immediate inspiration came more
from Tolstoy than the French thinker. Together with Tolstoy and Rousseau, Gandhi saw the chief source of modern ills in possessivism and
the amassing of material wealth, a possessivism accelerated and intensified by capitalism and industrialization; in his own words, wedded to
"the multiplication of wants and machinery contrived to supply them"
modernity reduces man to a "cog" in his self-created machine or
mechanized mode of production. In order to satisfy the multiple wants
unleashed by this process, Western society resorts increasingly to the
mastery and exploitation of human and natural resources, a mastery
enhanced by technical or technological contrivances. Exploitation of
resources in turn is only one facet of a pervasive system of domination,
a system glaringly manifest in domestic and international displays of
violence. Students of Western philosophy can hardly fail to detect in
this indictment affinities with the Heideggerian critique of technological 'enframing' *(Gestell)*—as well as with Marxist denunciations of class
divisions and colonial or imperialist ventures.[6]

Gandhi's critical posture extended from modern ills to some of the
proposed Western remedies or antidotes, including Marxism. Although
deeply committed to improving the lot of the masses and especially
their poorest sections, he throughout his life remained distant from
Marxist teachings and programs. His main reservations in this respect

had to do with Marxism's focus on economic materialism and its pro-
pensity to violence (or totalitarian rule). Regarding the tendency toward
reductionism he observed in the later part of his life: "The Marxist
regards thought, as it were, as a 'secretion of the brain' and the mind
'a reflex of the material environment.' I cannot accept that." Rebuking
in particular the economic determinism endorsed or encouraged by
(orthodox) Marxism, he observed at another point: "I do not consider
economic factors to be the source of all evils in the world. Nor is it
correct to trace the origin of all wars to economic causes." While clearly
a source of irritation, however, economism as a doctrine was not at the
heart of Gandhi's complaint; what troubled him was not so much the
theory as rather the practical consequences or implications of a materi-
alist outlook: its proclivity to foster and reinforce the instrumental and
domineering features of Western civilization. As Iyer comments perceptively, referring to the shared faith in material progress: "Gandhi was
the first thinker to see clearly what was common to European capitalism and communist Russia. He easily extended his attack on modern
civilization, the gospel of material progress and the glorification of violence to cover Soviet civilization as well as capitalist countries." Violence in this context encompasses the technological mastery of natural
resources; but it also—and more directly—points to revolutionary force
as a primary means of social change. To quote Iyer again: "In 1946,
when asked about Marx, he (Gandhi) said that he had a high regard for
Marx's great industry and acumen, but he could not share the view that
the use of violence could usher in non-violence."[7]

In more general terms, Gandhi occupied a marginal or oblique
position to central pillars of Western thought—above all to the tradition
of rationalist metaphysics. Although a lucid and clear-minded thinker
and a fervent devotee of truth (I shall return to this point), he never
gave himself over completely to Western rationalism—or what today is
frequently called "logocentrism"—preferring instead a precarious balance between critical judgment and prejudgment, between reason and
faith. Following Pascal's lead—but in a completely non-sentimental and
non-Romantic manner—he juxtaposed to logical reasoning a broader
raison du coeur, that is, an openness of the mind to the concrete nuances
of pre-reflective experience. The practice of non-violence (ahimsa), in
particular, was to him "a matter not of the intellect but of the heart,"
that is, a matter primarily of pre-cognitive sensibility and compassion
and only subsidiarily an ethical principle. Commenting on this issue
Gandhi observed at one point to Mahadev Desai: "Mere logic sometimes leads to wrong conclusions and is disastrous in results. This is not
the fault of logic, but all the data needed in order to arrive at a proper

conclusion are not available at all times. . . . Therefore the heart, that is devotion, faith and knowledge grounded in experience are invested with greater importance. Logic is a matter of mere intelligence which cannot apprehend things that are clear as crystal to the heart."[8] Statements of this kind, one needs to emphasize, should not be seen as indicative of a lapse into irrationalism or a blind obscurantism. In the case of Gandhi, "faith" and "devotion" carry no tinge of sectarian intolerance: someone who sacrificed his life in attempting to reconcile religions is clearly exempt from the charge of harboring a rigid parochialism.

III

Given Gandhi's criticisms of modernity and Western modes of life and thought, the temptation is strong to banish him entirely from Western culture and to treat him as an Eastern—and more narrowly a Hindu—traditionalist. Clearly, nothing has imprinted itself more vividly on the Western mind than Gandhi's external appearance: the image of a small, ascetic figure dressed in native garb. Even to otherwise enlightened observers, his abandonment of European dress around 1912 appeared often as an affront to modern standards and even to codes of common decency. Most well-known and notorious in this respect is Winston Churchill's derision of the "half-naked fakir" and his objection to the "nauseating" and "humiliating" dress worn by Gandhi during negotiations with the British Viceroy and during visits to Buckingham Palace. Slurs and objections of this kind, however, were not restricted to Western politicians and colonialists; in less overt or offensive form, similar sentiments were shared by fellow-Indians imbued with Western education and attached to modernization. As Lala Lajput Rai candidly observed at one point: "Such of his countrymen as have drunk deep from the fountains of European history and European politics and who have developed a deep love for European manners and European culture, neither understand nor like him. In their eyes he is a barbarian, a visionary and a dreamer."[9]

Yet, exiling Gandhi from the West does not provide him with a safe abode. While uncomfortable in a modern Western setting, he was too much of a marginalist—or a "transcendent eccentric" (in A. K. Saran's terms)—to fit neatly into his native culture or into Hindu traditionalism. Basically, Eastern or Hindu tradition was for him not a fixed doctrine or theory which one could passively embrace and memorize routinely; instead of ossifying or reifying tradition he was constantly bent on recapturing or retrieving its spirit in the living present. Bhikhu Parekh has reported in detail on Gandhi's difficult encounters and persistent frustrations with Hindu traditionalists. Pointing to the tension between Brahmanic or elitist Hinduism and popular or ritualized Hinduism, he emphasizes Gandhi's critique of both variants: "In his view, each was self-centered and lacked social conscience and commitment. While he could understand the attitude of the illiterate masses, he could not understand the crass indifference of the elite to the vast social and economic injustices of their society, the acute poverty of the masses, the condition of women, the inhuman practice of untouchability and the indignity and humiliation of hundreds of years of foreign rule." Parekh also alerts to Gandhi's subtle way of reading sacred Hindu texts—to which he felt deeply drawn—and of giving them a novel meaning in line with practical contemporary needs: "He began by accepting such fundamental premises of Hinduism as the *Brahman* alone is real, *moksha* consists in becoming one with it and that the *Brahman* is manifested in all living beings, especially men. However, he radically reinterpreted these premises and drew novel conclusions: He argued that since the *Brahman* was manifested in all living beings, especially men, to become one with it meant becoming one with all living beings, especially men. ... To become one with all men was to share their suffering and dedicate oneself to its alleviation and elimination, to suffer and struggle with them, in a word, to serve them."[10]

The most severe dispute between Gandhi and Hindu traditionalists arose over the issue of untouchability—a dispute which remained unresolved (and perhaps unresolvable) on a purely theoretical level. With regard to this issue, Hindu scholars could readily point to Vedic passages and time-honored doctrines elevating untouchability to an unquestionable (and thus itself untouchable) status. To quote Parekh again: Hindu traditionalists disputed that Gandhi's views "represented the spirit" of Hindu scriptures or "denied that untouchability was necessarily incompatible with them. Although many of them were reluctant to say so openly, they did not hesitate to imply that he was too much under the influence of Christianity, had lived abroad too long and had too little knowledge of Sanskrit to understand and interpret Hinduism. They questioned his right to interpret Hinduism and to call himself a Hindu." The conflict reached a peak in the drawn-out debate between Gandhi and the Brahmins in Travancore, a place where untouchables had traditionally been barred from passing through a road near the temple. After a non-violent campaign against the practice proved fruitless, Gandhi decided to visit Travancore himself to confront the Brahmins, offering them at the end three compromises: namely, a referendum among high-caste Hindus of the area, arbitration, and a critical examination of pertinent sacred texts by scholars in Benares. When all three notions were rejected, Gandhi nearly despaired of the possibility of theoretical persuasion—turning instead with renewed vigor to a life of personal example (in line with his interpretation of Hinduism). The "little-noticed debate with the gentle but fanatical Brahmins," Parekh comments, "contains the most frustrating exchanges, and deserves to be read by everyone interested in studying the intensity" of entrenched interests.[11]

Untouchability was only one—though the most prominent and glaring—of numerous drawbacks or dilemmas besetting traditional Indian society and its political fabric. This is not the place to explore in detail all the facets of this legacy. As it happens, Parekh has given a useful summary of the central features of the "Hindu tradition of political thought" and its impact on social life. As he notes, the Hindu political tradition was "basically inegalitarian" in that it made caste "the basis not only of society but also of the polity, and integrated it into its very structure." Furthermore, the tradition was "largely uncritical and apologetic of the established social order" in the sense that Hindu political thinkers "justified (or rather simply took for granted) the caste system, the caste-based conception of *dharma* (moral duty), the largely fatalist concept of *karma*, the degradation of the Sudras and the slaves." On all these and related features of the tradition Gandhi's life-work mounted a concerted assault or a sustained immanent critique. A brief juxtaposition of the respective postures reveals a profound tension or agonal relationship: "Hinduism had a weak social conscience; he infused in it a strong sense of social justice. . . . For centuries Hindus had lived with the practice of untouchability; Gandhi declared war on it and shook its very roots. For centuries women had occupied a low position in Hindu society; Gandhi brought thousands of them into public life, gave them high social and political visibility and made them an equal and integral part of Indian public life. The upper strata of Hindu society had treated the peasant with scorn for a long time; Gandhi placed him at the center of the political stage and gave him an unprecedented political and cultural presence."[12]

Still, it bears repeating: Gandhi's critique was an immanent one and not simply that of an anti-traditional modernizer. His agonal relationship involved a creative struggle with the tradition and not merely its rejection; on a deeper level his assault was a sign of genuine loyalty (akin to the loyalty affirmed by Socrates after his trial and conviction).[13] This loyalty was to his native land and to the spirit of Hinduism—but a Hinduism purged of all traces of fatalism, blind superstition, or fanatical sectarianism. Reinterpreted as a call to serve mankind, Hinduism was in effect a synonym for non-domineering praxis—pointing to a level where all religions intersect and mutually sustain each other. As Gandhi himself stated in 1921, in a passage poignantly capturing his ecumenic approach: "Hinduism is not an exclusive religion. In it there is room for the worship of all the prophets of the world. . . . (It) tells everyone to worship God according to his own faith or dharma, and so it lives at peace with all the religions." His tolerant ecumenicism was particularly important in a country like India, marked by a complex interlacing of multiple religious and cultural legacies. Just as his general outlook revealed a precarious blending of reason and faith, Gandhi's Hinduism reflected a tensional interplay of many of the major world religions. In the words of Raghavan Iyer: "No Hindu since Ram Mohan Roy was as eager as Gandhi to respond to the *Koran,* and even Roy did not stress, as much as Gandhi did, Jain and Buddhist notions. Even as a Hindu, Gandhi was a Vedantin as well as a Vaishnava—a Vedantin in his transcendental monism and a Vaishnava in his faith in the grace of God as a person."[14] Yet, one should recognize that his affinity with Buddhism opened Gandhi up to transpersonal or non-theistic modes of belief. In the end, his ultimate appeal was to "truth" or *satya,* that is, to a level of being or reality located beyond theism and non-theism.

IV

It was through a creative reinterpretation of the past that Gandhi arrived at some distinctive trademarks of his thought—including the notions of *satyagraha, ahimsa, swadeshi,* and *swaraj.* Much has been written about these notions and their social and political implications; my comments have to be very brief. In my view, one of Gandhi's most seminal contributions to social and political thought is the notion of *satyagraha,* literally translated as firm adherence to or concrete enactment of truth. At a first glance, the term seems to suggest simply the deductive application of fixed principles (or the derivation of praxis from theory); but this misses the point. As previously indicated, *satya* or truth for Gandhi was not merely an epistemological category but an expression laden with ontological and experiential significance. As Gandhi himself stated at one point: "The word *satya* (truth) is derived from *sat,* which means being. And nothing is or exists in reality except truth." Seen in an ontological light, *satya* could by no means be reduced to an epistemic principle or a target of cognitive analysis (a construal violating its primacy over subject-object relations). How little truth denoted an epistemic doctrine is evident from Gandhi's autobiography which he entitled *The Story of My Experiments with Truth.* The open-ended character of his approach to truth is clearly reflected in a passage from this autobiography which reads: "I worship God as truth only. I have not yet found Him, but I am seeking after Him. . . . But as long as I have not realized this absolute truth, I must hold by the relative truth as I have conceived it; that relative truth must meanwhile be my beacon, my shield and buckler." Moreover, it seems that relative truth was for Gandhi not merely a temporary stop-gap but an integral reflection of the reality of being. "It has been my experience," he wrote in another context, "that I am always true from my point of view and often wrong from the point of view of my honest critics. I know that we are both right from our respective points of view. . . . I very much like the doctrine of the manyness of reality. It is this doctrine that has taught me to judge a Mussulman from his own standpoint and a Christian from his."[15]

Emphasizing the doing rather than the cognition of truth, *satyagraha* belongs basically to the vocabulary of praxis or practical philosophy. However, one should note the peculiar character of praxis or action in this case. Contrary to the prevalent Western focus on purposive or intentional activity, Gandhian *satyagraha* involves an action or praxis dislodged from purposive designs or a subjective will to power. In formulating this notion, Gandhi sought to capture the essence of *karma yoga* as presented in the *Bhagavadgita*, that is, a mode of living and acting aloof from self-aggrandizement and from any attachment to the fruits of action. As Albert Schweitzer has perceptively written: "The *Bhagavadgita* continued what the Buddha began. . . . The supreme inactivity it teaches is when one performs actions as if one did not perform them," that is, without any desire or even concern for reward.[16] In a sense, Gandhian *satyagraha* anticipated contemporary (post-structuralist) discussions about the "end of man" or the "decentering of the subject"—expressions which are sometimes (but erroneously) interpreted as simple warrants for passivity. On a different plane, the unselfish doing of truth resonates with religious modes of self-surrender and particularly with the Christian notion of *kenosis* or self-emptying—a notion which Gandhi explicitly invoked in a letter of 1947. "Do not even worry how I am faring or what I am doing here," he stated. "If I succeed in emptying myself utterly, God will possess me. Then I know that everything will come true, but it is a serious question when I shall have reduced myself to zero. Think of 'I' and 'O' in juxtaposition and you have the whole problem of life in two signs."[17]

As a decentered or deflated mode of conduct, *satyagraha* is located at the intersection of action and non-action or else of doing and suffering (or passion). It is mainly for this reason that Gandhian doing of truth was closely linked with the notion of *tapas* or "self-suffering." Self-emptying and exposure to otherness is bound to be a difficult and painful process; the same is true of shouldering the consequences of one's actions (without seeking to reap their benefits). An example of the latter kind is the practice of civil disobedience. As Gandhi observed in 1921: "In civil disobedience the resister suffers the consequences of disobedience. This was what Daniel did when he disobeyed the laws of the Medes and Persians. This is what John Bunyan did, and this is what the *ryots* have done in India from time immemorial. . . . Violence is the law of the beast in us; self-suffering, i.e., civil resistance, is the law of the man in us." However, *tapas* in Gandhi's view was not restricted to civil disobedience but extended to all forms of genuine action and counteraction. In effect, as he said a few years later, *satyagraha* itself was ultimately an "argument of suffering," a practice which assumed that "the hardest heart and grossest ignorance must disappear before the rising sun of suffering without anger and without malice." Seen in this light, *satyagraha* was not merely a mode of argumentation or rational persuasion—although it could follow the path of persuasion and would normally rely on this path before resorting to alternate forms of action. Here we arrive again at the combination or precarious interlacing of reason and sensibility in Gandhi's thought, reflected now in the linkage of truth and suffering. As Thomas Pantham points out: While persuasion through reasoning is an important avenue, "*satyagraha* recognizes the limits of reason in resolving fundamental social, religious, political or ideological conflicts, in which a rational consensus may not be easily or quickly forthcoming. . . . It is the assumption of *satyagrahi* that when reasoning fails to move the head, the argument of suffering by the *satyagrahis* helps move the heart of the oppressors or opponents. Self-suffering, moreover, is the truth-serving alternative to the truth-denying method of inflicting violence on others."[18]

The last comments bring into view the importance of non-violence or *ahimsa*—a notion closely allied with the Gandhian doing of truth. Given its decentered or dispossessed character, *satyagraha* is at odds with strategies of mastery or domination—strategies which always involve violence of some sort. While not equating social interaction with an abstract-rational discourse, Gandhi insisted on preserving the human face of social and political life—that is, on differentiating the social agon from destructive violence. Moreover, ahimsa in Gandhi's treatment meant not merely an abstinence from inflicting injury but a more positive attempt to extricate the doing of truth from prevailing systems or frameworks of domination. As he stated in 1916: "In its *negative* form it *(ahimsa)* means not injuring any living being whether by body or mind. . . . In its *positive* form, *ahimsa* means the largest love, the greatest charity. If I am a follower of *ahimsa*, I must love my enemy or a stranger to me as I would my wrong-doing father or son. This active *ahimsa* necessarily includes truth and fearlessness."[19] The active mode of *ahimsa* as an attempted exit from prevailing forms of domination has been eloquently stressed by Ashis Nandi (partly in opposition to Frantz Fanon's belief in the "cleansing role" of violence). *Ahimsa*, Nandi writes, "recognizes that the meek are blessed only if they are authentically innocent and not pseudo-innocents accepting the values of an oppressive system for secondary psychological gains. Gandhi acted as if he was aware that non-synergic systems, driven by zero-sum competition and search for power, control and masculinity, force the victims of oppression to internalize the norms of the system. . . . So his concept of non-cooperation set a different goal for the victims: he stressed that the aim of the oppressed should be not to become a first class citizen in the world of oppression instead of a second or third class one, but to become the citizen of an alternative world where he can hope to win back his human authenticity."[20]

While seeking to elude the tentacles of violence, Gandhi remained aware of the role of power in social and political life; but power, in his view, was to be exercised not for the sake of controlling others but rather for purposes of self-control and of a kind of mutual empowerment bypassing domination. This view was at the root of his notions of *swaraj* (self-rule) and *swadeshi* (self-reliance)—terms which underscored not arbitrary selfishness but the responsible harnessing of resources and capabilities. The accent on "self" in these terms, incidentally, should not be construed in a narrowly private or individualistic sense. Occasionally, Gandhi has been presented as a radical individualist and even a Romantic anarchist—a portrayal assimilating him too neatly to Western liberal formulas. In light of his decentered posture, individualism in his case was not so much a compact doctrine as rather an antidote or counterpoint to collectivism—that is, a synonym for responsible freedom (in a public space). As he wrote at one point, in discussing democracy: "I value individual freedom, but you must not forget that man is essentially a social being. . . . Unrestricted individualism is the law of the beast of the jungle. We have learnt to strike a mean between individual freedom and social restraint."[21] Gandhi's non-doctrinaire position in this regard is reflected in his close association of *swaraj* with *sarvodaya* (meaning general or communal welfare); it is also revealed in the idea of *ashrams*—an aspect often neglected or de-emphasized in discussions of Gandhi's thought (Iyer's admirable study makes only scant reference to it). As instituted and maintained by Gandhi, *ashrams* were communal settings of concrete character-formation devoted both to self-reliance and unselfish *satyagraha*. Most importantly, *ashrams* were experimental counter-models to the established Indian caste system. As Gandhi reported about the *ashram* near Ahmedabad: "No servants were engaged; therefore cooking, sanitation, fetching water—everything was attended to by the Ashramites. Truth and other observances were obligatory on them all. Distinctions of caste were not observed. Untouchability had not only no place in the Ashram, but its eradication from Hindu society was one of our principal objectives. Emancipation of women from some customary bonds was insisted upon from the first; therefore women in the Ashram enjoy full freedom. Then again it was an Ashram rule that persons following a particular faith should have the same feeling for followers of other faiths as for their co-religionists."[22]

V

Having reviewed some of the *leitmotifs* of Gandhi's thought, I want to return to my starting point: his role as mediator between East and West. As should be clear from the preceding discussion, mediation in this case cannot be equated with a patchwork or eclectic amalgam—for a simple reason: cultural traditions are not finished products or artifacts which can be mixed or reassembled in a wilful fashion. Instead of offering a facile synthesis, Gandhi preferred to inhabit the margins of entrenched cultures, seeking to energize their lacunae and untapped possibilities. In the case of Hindu tradition, his effort was directed at recovering its living core from beneath the growth of empty rituals and the pretense of speculative doctrines. In the case of Western civilization, he appealed to its hidden spiritual or humanist strands as an antidote to the modern fascination with mastery and domination. Yet, the tenor of his endeavor was less strident in the first case than in the second—due to an obvious real-life discrepancy: While Hindu tradition (and Eastern culture in general) is increasingly under attack and forced to retreat into an enclave, Western civilization is on the verge of successfully encircling the globe and of levelling cultural differences into a technological universalism.

This discrepancy readily accounts for Gandhi's more outspoken and persistent critique of modern Western thought patterns and modes of life. In 1909, shortly before the publication of *Hind Swaraj*, Gandhi presented a talk in London specifically devoted to the topic "East and West." Downplaying the contrast on a deeper cultural or spiritual level, the talk placed the onus squarely on the domineering possessiveness of Western modernity. "There is no impossible barrier," he said, "between East and West. There is no such thing as Western or European civilization, but there is a modern civilization which is purely material." Taking the offensive, Gandhi in another context appealed to the West to cure its modern ills by turning to "true civilization" seen as the doing of truth. "What may be hoped for," he wrote, "is that Europe on account of her fine and scientific intellect will realize the obvious and retrace her steps, and from the demoralizing industrialism she will find a way out." Such a change of course, he added, would not necessarily lead back to the "old absolute simplicity"; but it would involve a redefinition of priorities and a subordination of "brute and material force" to *satyagraha.* Easily the most eloquent and moving comments on the East-West theme are to be found in a speech titled "The Message of Asia" which Gandhi delivered at the Asian Relations Conference in New Delhi in April of 1947, just prior to India's gaining of independence. "What I want you to understand," Gandhi said at the time, "is the message of Asia. It is not to be learnt through the Western spectacles or by imitating the atom bomb. If you want to give a message to the West, it must be the message of love and the message of truth. I want you to go away with the thought that Asia has to conquer the West through love and truth. I do not want merely to appeal to your heads; I want to capture your hearts."[23]

As a Westerner, perhaps I am permitted to readdress the East-West issue in a more Western-philosophical idiom. As it happens, developments have been afoot in Western thought during this century which point at least obliquely in the direction of the Gandhian mediation. In the context of political theory, the East-West topic has been sensitively probed by Leo Strauss—significantly in the course of a discussion of "Heideggerian existentialism." At the end of World War II, Strauss notes, the center of gravity in a global or planetary sense shifted from Europe to America and Soviet Russia—both eminently technological societies in Heidegger's view. This shift ushered in the prospect of a "planetary night" or rather nightmare: namely, "the victory of an ever more completely urbanized, ever more completely technological West over the whole planet—complete levelling and uniformity regardless of whether it is brought about by iron compulsion or by soapy advertisement of the output of mass production." What was needed to counter or remedy this situation, in Strauss's account, was a recollection of the roots of technology in Western rationalism, and of the roots of the latter in classical Greek philosophy. Western rationalism seeks to gain an understanding of reality—or of the structure of being—by concentrating on what is directly "present-at-hand" or "ready-to-hand"; that means, its focus is on what is accessible to cognitive analysis, what is "at the disposal of man" and thus provides the basis for "human mastery of the whole." However, Western rationalism depends ultimately itself on non-rational assumptions, that is, on something it "cannot master." Therefore, a more adequate approach to being may be intimated by the view "that *to be* means to be elusive or to be a mystery. This is the Eastern understanding of being; hence there is no will to master in the East. We can hope beyond technological world society . . . only if we become capable of learning from the East." Such learning, in turn, is only possible through an internal transformation or *metanoia* of Western culture. "The West," Strauss concludes, "has first to recover within itself that which would make possible a meeting of West and East. The West has to recover within itself its own deepest roots which antedate its rationalism, which in a way antedate the separation of West and East."[24]

In light of these observations it becomes clear that Gandhi's mediation is not of parochial stature nor restricted to a particular phase of Indian history; in fact, its real significance is only beginning to emerge. Far from being a peculiar Third World phenomenon, Gandhi's life-work is a guidepost or beacon of light for East and West alike, a guidepost pointing toward an alternate cosmopolis or future world society. The futurist relevance of the Gandhian legacy has been aptly pinpointed by Nandi as involving the ascendancy of an "alternate perspective" over technological domination. Projecting this legacy forward, he observes, does not amount to "synthesizing or aggregating different civilizational visions of the future. Rather, it is a matter of admitting that while each civilization must find its own authentic vision of the future . . . , neither is conceivable without admitting the *experience of co-suffering* which has now brought some of the major civilizations of the world close to each other. It is this co-suffering which makes the idea of cultural closeness something more than the chilling concept of One World which nineteenth-century European optimism popularized and promoted to the status of a dogma." Nandi also invokes Gandhi's own conception of a future utopia—a conception highlighted by the vision of *ramarajya,* that is, the earthly kingdom of God or the community of genuine doers of truth. The same vision, one might add, forms an integral part also of Iyer's notion of parapolitics, a term denoting the continuous rethinking and experimental testing of the "frontiers of conventional politics." Using Western terminology, Iyer renders *ramarajya* as an ongoing quest beyond the claims of "class and race, sect and creed": namely as "the continual, if incomplete, incarnation of *civitas Dei* into an unfinished *civitas humana,* in the midst of earthly cities where 'ignorant armies clash by night'."[25]

3

THE DISCOURSE AND COUNTER-DISCOURSES OF MODERNITY

The status of modern project is strongly contested today; under such summary labels as *modernism* versus *postmodernism* or *enlightenment* versus *deconstruction* champions and critics of the project are embroiled in lively skirmishes both inside and outside of academia. Unfortunately, the salience of the issues is not often reflected in the character of exchanges: more than other contemporary topics the themes of modernity and post-modernity tend to be submerged in trendiness and facile rhetoric. Only rarely does literature devoted to these themes rise above the plane of broad manifestoes or petty polemics; Jürgen Habermas's *The Philosophical Discourse of Modernity* is clearly such an exception. First published in 1985, the study lends substance and focus to otherwise often diffuse debates; moving beyond surface changes and technical gadgets it locates the core issues of modernity on the level of philosophy—more specifically of an ongoing philosophical discourse. From Habermas's perspective, modernity is intimately linked with the central aspirations of Reformation and Enlightenment: the aspirations of cognitive rationality, moral autonomy, and social-political self-determination. Accentuating this linkage means to underscore the stakes involved in current discussions. For, profiled against the backdrop of heteronomy and caprice, how can one blandly dismiss modernity's gains? On the other hand, given the lengthening shadows cast by anthropocentrism and technical prowess, how can one blithely endorse these gains without naiveté or callousness?

One of the chief merits of Habermas's study is the treatment of modernity not as a platform or doctrine but as a discourse or conversation—a conversation made up of different protagonists or voices and stretching over successive historical periods. In Habermas's presentation, the discourse was inaugurated by Enlightenment thinkers from Descartes to Voltaire and first crystallized in the rationalist theories of Kant and Fichte. In Kantian thought, he notes, modernity meant basically the progressive refinement of consciousness and subjectivity, specifically the segregation of reason into the domains of science, ethical freedom, and aesthetic judgment—a segregation apparently achieved without costs or charring effects. Neglect of these costs soon led to dissent or insurgency within modern discourse, in the sense that the *cantus firmus* of analytical rationalism was joined by the supplementary or counter-discourse of rational synthesis—an insurgency which found its chief voice in Hegel's system. Countering the divisions and cleavages *(Entzweiungen)* resulting from modernity, Hegel—without abandoning the modern project—sought to reconcile the dichotomies of "nature and spirit, sensuality and reason, *Verstand* and *Vernunft*, theoretical and practical reason, judgment and imagination, finitude and infinity, knowledge and faith."[1] While praising Hegel's philosophical élan, Habermas finds Hegel's insurgency flawed and ultimately unsuccessful—mainly because of its subjectivist moorings and its excessively theoretical-contemplative character. During the nineteenth century, the Hegelian legacy was continued by the opposing camps of "Young Hegelians" and "Right Hegelians": the first devoted to the implementation of reason on the basis of praxis or productivity, and the second to the maintenance of objective rational structures as embedded in state, economy or technology. As opposed to these internal modulations of modernity, the study shifts attention at this point to another, more radical insurgency or anti-discourse *(Sonderdiskurs)*—one seeking not so much to modify as to cancel the modern project and whose diverse articulations take up the bulk of the volume. The instigator of this radical stance was Nietszche who, in the study, figures as the turning point or as the "turn-table" *(Drehscheibe)* ushering in the move from modernity to postmodernism. As in Hegel's case, Nietzsche's legacy is said to have been continued by two opposing (but also interdependent) camps: one pursuing a more skeptical and quasi-scientific approach, the other attempting an ontological or quasi-ontological reversal of modernity. The chief representatives of the first camp are Bataille, Lacan and Focault; those of the second camp Heidegger and Derrida.[2]

To be sure, the preceding synopsis does not do full justice to the complexity of the study, particularly to its many sidelines and repeated interludes or excursions; nevertheless, it captures (I believe) the chief strands and counter-strands of the modern discourse (and anti-discourse) as seen by Habermas. It cannot be my ambition in the present context to recapitulate and discuss all the facets of this discursive or conversational fabric; such an effort would require the format of a full-length commentary or counter-study. At this point I propose to examine three central episodes in the study's historical scenario, episodes connected with the names of Hegel, Nietzsche, and Heidegger. The choice of these thinkers seems justified by their role in Habermas's narrative: while Hegel inaugurated the modern discourse in its broad multidimensionality, Nietzsche marks the dividing line between modernity and postmodernism (or between discourse and anti-discourse); Heidegger finally can be seen as (arguably) the leading philosophical representative of a post-Nietzschean perspective. Following a review of these episodes I shall critically assess Habermas's own model of communicative rationality as developed in the study's concluding chapters—with the intent of providing an alternative interpretation of the modern project and of the conversational structure of the discourse of modernity.[3]

I

Renaissance and Reformation (together with the discovery of the New World) heralded an implicit break with the classical and medieval past; but the notion of a distinctly modern period emerged only slowly in the aftermath of these events. According to Habermas, it was left to Hegel to grasp the philosophical meaning and import of the modern project. Hegel, he writes, was "the first philosopher to develop a clear conception of modernity." Although anticipated dimly by Enlightenment thinkers from Descartes to Kant, it was only toward the end of the eighteenth century that "the problem of the *self-understanding* of modernity became so acute that Hegel could perceive it *as* a philosophical problem and moreover as *the basic problem* of his philosophy." Together with his philosophical precursors, Hegel located the core of modernity in the principle of subjectivity—a principle which carried for him mainly the connotations of individualism, critical-rational competence, and autonomy of action. The same principle had already been succinctly pinpointed by Kant who treated subjectivity as the foundation of the segregated modern domains of science, (categorical) ethics, and expressive art. Kant, we read, "put in place of the substantial rationality bequeathed by metaphysics the notion of a reason differentiated into separate moments whose unity has merely formal character; he distinguished the faculties of practical reason and judgment from theoretical cognition end assigned to each moment its own place." Yet, while pursuing his analytical task, Kant did not grasp the differentiation of reason as a problem, nor the separation of modern value spheres as division or a source of divisiveness *(Entzweiung);* consequently he also ignored the synthetic need emerging from his analysis. Here was precisely the *motif* of Hegel's insurgency: while accepting the principle of subjectivity he recognized both its emancipatory potential and its ambivalence. In Habermas's words, the principle "explained for him simultaneously the superiority of the modern world and its crisis character, in the sense that it represents both a world of progress and of alienated spirit. For this reason the first attempt to conceptualize the modern era was at the same time a critique of modernity."[4]

In the chapter devoted to Hegel, Habermas traces the successive stages of his insurgency within the confines of Enlightenment disourse. As he notes, the initial impulses of his synthetic efforts can be traced back to critical or "crisis experiences" of the young Hegel himself, experiences which nurtured his conviction "that reason must be marshalled as conciliatory power against the divided positivities of his age." Turning first to Hegel's early (especially his theological) writings, Habermas points to a certain Romantic or mythopoetic version of reconciliation which Hegel shared with Schelling and Hölderlin, his friends in the Tübingen seminary. Countering both the orthodoxy of positive (or established) religion and the abstractness of Enlightenment ideas, these writings appealed to a purified public faith or civil religiosity as the bond tying together and reconciling the conflicting segments of society. Only when represented in public festivals and cults and linked with myths engaging heart and phantasy—Hegel argued at the time—could a religiously mediated reason "permeate the entire fabric of the state." The same writings also spoke of a "nexus of guilt" or a "causality of fate" as the driving motor propelling a reconciliation of criminally severed relationships, a motor revealing the injury inflicted on others ultimately as self-injury. According to the study, Hegel "opposed to the abstract laws of morality the very different rule mechanism of a concrete nexus of guilt generated by the sundering of a prior ethical totality *(sittliche Totalität)*"; by suffering the consequences of his action the criminal comes to recognize in the injured alien existence "his own repudiated nature." Shifting from narrative to critique, Habermas at this point challenges the character of the invoked totality or social bond: both in the case of civil religion and of the nexus of guilt, he argues, reconciliation relies on premodern life-forms which the process of modernization necessarily leaves behind. "For the fated reconciliation of a divided modernity," he writes, "Hegel presupposes an ethical totality which is not germane to modern conditions but rather is *borrowed* from the idealized past of early Christian communities and the Greek *polis*"; yet, modernity had gained its self-understanding precisely through "a reflection which bars the systematic regress to such exemplary traditions."[5]

Similar or related dilemmas—dilemmas soon recognized by Hegel himself—beset another early or transitional work in his intellectual development: the so-called oldest system program formulated in Frankfurt and still under the influence of Schelling and Hölderlin. In that program, the function of reconciliation was attributed to art or artistic-poetic imagination. "Rational religion," the study comments, "was presumed to yield to *art* in order to develop into a popular religion; the monotheism of reason and heart was to ally itself with the polytheism of imagination to produce an (aesthetic) mythology of ideas." As Habermas observes, this program was clearly reminiscent of Schiller's letters on the "aesthetic education of mankind" (of 1795), and it was retained in Schelling's transcendental idealism and in Hölderlin's works to the end. According to Habermas's narrative, however, Hegel quickly abandoned this outlook as an insufficient remedy for modern ills and divisions. Given that modernity is based on subjectivity and critical reflection, only philosophical reason or thought—a thought moving within subjective reflection and beyond it—could accomplish the hoped-for reconciliation and subdue the pitfalls of a solipsistic or domineering subjectivism. This insight, Habermas argues, was the crucial steppingstone to Hegel's notion of "absolute spirit." If modern advances are to be taken seriously and yet to be corrected, he writes, "reason must indeed be construed as self-relation of a subject, but now as a reflection which does not simply impose itself on otherness through the pure force of subjectivity but rather as one which has its essence and motor only in the effort to oppose all finite absolutisms and to overcame all encountered positivities." In contrast to static metaphysical conceptions of the past, the absolute spirit in Hegel's treatment consisted "purely in the process of the relation of finitude and infinity and thus in the consuming activity of self-discovery"; moving beyond the level of substances and fragmented subjects, the absolute is construed "solely as the mediating process of an unconditionally self-productive self-relation." In this manner, Habermas concludes, Hegel utilized the philosophy of subjectivity "with the aim of overcoming a subject-centered reason; with this move the mature Hegel can criticize the defects of modernity without appealing to any *other* premise than the immanent-modern principle of subjectivity."[6]

The self-transcendence of modernity encapsulated in the absolute spirit is replicated, in somewhat different guise, on the level of objective spirit, and especially in the theory of the modern state. Turning to the *Philosophy of Right* (and earlier preparatory writings), Habermas finds Hegel's main contribution in his formulation of the notion of civil society as a domain differentiated from, and mediating between, family and state; civil society in this context meant a mode of association governed by private interest and market exchanges. In formulating this notion and juxtaposing it to the state, Hegel took account both of the advances of modernity and its divisive effects. In Habermas's words, the issue confronting Hegel was "how civil society could be conceived not only as a *sphere of decay* of substantive ethics but in its negativity at the same time as a *necessary moment* of ethics *(Sittlichkeit)*. He took his departure from the premise that the classical ideal of the *polis* cannot be restored in the context of modern, depoliticized social life; on the other hand, he maintained the idea of an ethical totality which he had thematized earlier under the rubric of popular religion." By separating and simultaneously linking society and state (embodying the objective spirit), Hegel's *Philosophy of Right* promoted a self-transcendence of modernity under modern auspices; in opposing both a homogeneous *polis* and an unlimited sway of private interests, the work set itself apart "from restorative philosophies of the state as well as from rational natural law" (in the Enlightenment sense). To quote Hegel himself: "The idea of the modern state has this strength and depth that it allows the principle of subjectivity to unfold to the extreme of self-sustained individual separateness while simultaneously guiding the principle back into substantive unity and maintaining the latter within itself."[7]

Having thus outlined Hegel's mature position as reflected in the notions of absolute and objective spirit, Habermas immediately proceeds to criticize this position for failing to solve modern predicaments. Two (related) reasons are given for this failure. Although having previously applauded Hegel's firm adherence to the modern principle, Habermas now takes him to task for remaining hostage to a self-enclosed subjectivity unable to perform a synthetic function. "With the notion of the absolute (spirit)," we read, "Hegel regresses behind the intuitions of his youth: he conceives the overcoming of subjectivity only within the limits of the philosophy of the subject."[8] By claiming the power of synthesis for absolute reason or subjectivity Hegel is said to have feigned reconciliation by a slight-of-hand: "He would have had to demonstrate, rather than merely presuppose that (absolute) reason— which is more than abstract *Verstand—can* strictly reconcile or unify those divisions which reason also must discursively disassemble." The same defect is said to be operative in the objective spirit as represented in the Hegelian state. According to Habermas, the state is unable on the face of it to unify or reassemble the divisions of modern social and political life. Such a solution can be assumed only on the supposition of "an absolute which is construed after the model of the self-relation of a cognitive subject." Only when the absolute is conceived as pure or infinite subjectivity, he writes, "can the moments of universality and particularity be thought to be reconciled in the confines of a monological self-knowledge; in the concrete universal (of the state) universal subjectivity thus takes precedence over the individual subject. In the domain of ethical life, this construction yields the priority of the *higher subjectivity of the state* over the subjective freedom of individuals."[9]

The second line of critique takes its aim not so much at self-enclosed subjectivity, but at the presumed abstractness or aloofness of Hegelian thought: the tendency of objective and absolute spirit to become the objects of passive contemplation removed from participation in the actual world process. Retired into itself or into its own absoluteness, Hegelian *Vernunft* is claimed to accomplish at best a *"partial* reconciliation"— namely, within the confines of philosophy but divorced from the shared beliefs of public religiosity which, in his early writings, were meant to link sense and reason, the common people and philosophers. Restricted to its own concerns, Hegelian philosophy—according to Habermas— "ultimately robbed present actuality of its salience, destroyed its intrinsic interest and denied its promise for self-critical renewal." Only latent in his early works, this tendency to passivity is said to surface strongly in Hegel's later system, including his *Philosophy of Right.* At this point his thought no longer criticized existing reality but only sought to "grasp reality as it is." This "muffling of critique" was a close corollary of the "devaluation of actuality" by philosophy; thus, "the conceptually defined modernity permits the Stoic retreat from itself." As remedy for Hegel's failings, Habermas's study proposes a different model of reconciliation or of the "mediation of the universal and the particular": it is the model of communicative interaction (well-known from his other writings). Instead of subordinating the freedom of individuals to the "higher subjectivity of the state," this model relies on the *"higher intersubjectivity of an uncoerced will formation* within a communication community obeying the need for cooperation." Rather than appealing to the power of *Vernunft,* synthesis here derives from the "universality of an uncoerced consensus achieved between free and equal individuals."[10]

Habermas's reprimands clearly call for a critical response or rejoinder (which I can attempt here only in sharply condensed form). As it seems to me, Habermas's interpretation is lopsided both on the level of certain historical nuances and with respect to key Hegelian concepts. Regarding the former, I find the division between the young and the mature Hegel—or between a Romantic, mythopoetic outlook and a later pure rationalism—vastly exaggerated if not mythopoetic in turn. In my own reading, Hegel never abandoned his early views on ethical totality in his later works, nor did he dismiss the notions of public religiosity, the nexus of guilt or the function of art as emblems of an ethical-social bond; he simply proceeded to reformulate these notions in accordance with the needs of his overall system. Like Plato he always maintained the correlation of truth, goodness, and beauty, and also the linkage of reason and faith (as is evident in the triad of art, religion and philosophy on the level of absolute spirit).[11] This leads me to more important conceptual issues. Habermas chides Hegel's *Vernunft* for remaining locked in a self-contained subjectivity and even in "the confines of monological self-knowledge." Moreover, absolute reason or subjectivity is presented as a "consuming activity of self-discovery" and as an "unconditionally self-productive self-relation." At the same time, however, Hegelian spirit is treated as a detached realm in itself, as a passively contemplated "objective reason." Now clearly *Vernunft* cannot be both (that is, ceaseless activity and passivity); in my view it is actually neither. As it seems to me, by stressing self-production Habermas injects into subjectivity a Fichtean flavor of self-constitution. More pointedly: the combination of consuming activity and self-production gives to *Vernunft* a "Young Hegelian" cast—the cast of a praxis philosophy relying on self-realization and productivity (which the study elsewhere takes great pains to disavow). On the other hand, the treatment of spirit as an objective realm amenable to contemplation carries overtones of "Right Hegelianism"—a perspective which, as the study indicates, was always bent on transforming *Vernunft* into a set of abstract and heteronomous rational precepts.

To a large extent, Habermas's Hegel chapter thus oscillates precariously between subjective and objective reason, between action and passivity (or else between Left and Right Hegelian vistas). Under the pressure of these opposing trends, Hegel's philosophy is liable to be torn asunder. To restore its unity requires more than patchwork; what is needed, I believe, is an appreciation of fact that Hegel's 'spirit' (like other key concepts) is a metaphysical or ontological category—and not a partisan idea available for direct political utilization. As such a category, idea or spirit is not simply a subjective capacity (a capacity of self-production) nor an objective rational principle, but rather a dimension presupposed by both and in which both are finally again reconciled. As is well known, the course of Hegelian philosophy leads from subjective over objective to absolute spirit, or else from simple consciousness over mediated self-consciousness to a consciousness of self-consciousness. On one level, this course is described in the *Phenomenology of Spirit* as a path of experience—where experience means neither subjective constitution nor passive endurance. More importantly, the dimension of absolute spirit is not a domain produced or constituted as the outcome of a process of self-production (nor is it externally imposed); rather, it is always already presupposed in the movement of thought, permeating the path of experience from beginning to end. As in the case of all great thinkers, Hegel's philosophizing moved in a circle—not a narrowly self-contained circle but one whose spirals meant to embrace everything. This aspect of Hegel's thought has been eloquently articulated by Heidegger (in his lectures on the *Phenomenology of Spirit*). "The conclusion of the work," he writes, "has not moved away from its beginning but is a return to it. *The ending is only the transformed beginning which thereby has arrived at itself.* This means, however: the standpoint of the understanding and re-enacting reader is from beginning to end, and from the end to the beginning the same—that of absolute reason, of a knowledge which confronts the absolute."[12]

My point here is not to vindicate Hegel's vocabulary or his foundational view of subjectivity. Philosophical developments in our century have amply illustrated the close linkage which always exists between consciousness (or subjectivity) and the unconscious, between enlightenment and processes of darkening or occlusion, between revealment and concealment. My point is simply that no path can possibly be charted beyond Hegel by shortchanging the depth of his insights. Regarding the remedial course proposed in Habermas's study, one can reasonably doubt its viability. In pitting the interest and subjective freedom of individuals against the ethical life of the state, Habermas basically invokes Kierkegaardian and Young Hegelian arguments in favor of particularity and concrete-individual praxis. From Hegel's perspective, however, individuals removed from public-ethical life are precisely unfree since freedom is genuinely a public category (and ultimately a synonym for spirit or idea). By presenting the public sphere as deriving from cooperative "will-formation" and the consensus reached between "free and equal" individuals, Habermas's proposal harkens back to the contractarian tradition—a tradition strongly rebuked in *Philosophy of Right.* If the public realm is reduced or subordinated to society (or the sum of associated individuals), Hegel writes, "and if its specific end is defined as the security and protection of property and individual freedom, then the interest of the individuals as such becomes the ultimate end of their association, and hence membership in the state something optional. But the state's relation to the individual is quite different: since the former is objective spirit, it is only as a member that the individual gains concrete objectivity, genuine individuality, and ethical life."[13] To the extent that—to elude contractarian premises—Habermas stresses the rationality of cooperative will-formation (reflected in an ideal speech community), he merely appeals to a regulative principle which, in Hegel's terms, remains on the level of an abstract philosophy of reflection. On the other hand, if escape from contractarianism is sought in a concrete life-world, recourse is taken to the same un- or pre-reflective traditions which were chided in Hegel's early writings. Even when not returning to the *cantus firmus* of Enlightenment rationalism, Habermas's proposal thus retains at best the *disjecta membra* of Hegelian philosophy.

II

According to the study, Hegel did not only inaugurate the modern philosophical discourse, focused on the critical self-understanding of modernity; he also specified the rules in terms of which this discursive theme could be modified or transformed—the rules of the dialectic of enlightenment. During much of the nineteenth century, the broad parameters of these rules were maintained by the opposing schools of thought which cast the lot over Hegel's complex legacy.[14] A radical challenge to these parameters arose only in the later part of the last century, and chiefly in Nietzsche's work. While Young and Right Hegelians were rehearsing or playing out the radical and conservative strands in Hegel's thought, Habermas observes, Nietzsche decided to "unmask the dramaturgy of the entire plot in which both parties—the representatives of revolution and of reaction—play their roles." In unmasking the structure of the plot, Nietzsche is also said to have challenged its basic thematic content: the themes of reason and enlightenment. Nietzsche's work, we read, relates to the tradition of reason as a whole "in the same manner as the Young Hegelians related to reason's sublimations: reason now is nothing else but power or the perverted will to power which reason only serves to disguise." In this manner, Nietzsche initiated not only a moderate counterpoint or counter-discourse within the confines of Hegelian parameters but rather a radical anti-discourse no longer obeying the rules of the dialectic of enlightenment. Nietzsche, the study affirms, "wants to bolt the framework of occidental rationalism which still was binding for the opposing Left and Right Hegelian factions. Continued subsequently in two versions by Heidegger and Bataille, this anti-humanism constitutes the real challenge to the discourse of modernity."15

While setting off Nietzsche sharply against preceding perspectives, Habermas also acknowledges a certain linkage with earlier, Young Hegelian arguments, a linkage evident particularly in the rebellious-insurgent tenor of his thought. Pointing to the second *Untimely Meditation* ("On the Use and Disadvantage of History for Life"), the study emphasizes Nietzsche's assault on a sterile antiquarianism and a passively contemplative outlook. Against an education relying on a purely "antiquarian historiography," we read, Nietzsche "marshals the spirit of modernity in a similar manner as did the Young Hegelians against the objectivism of Hegel's philosophy of history." The affinity, however, was only limited and superficial. While the praxis-orientation of Hegel's heirs was still tied to the dialectic of enlightenment, Nietzsche bid farewell to the Hegelian tradition and to modern rationality as such. In Habermas's words: "Nietzsche uses the ladder of historical reason only in order to discard it in the end and to take his stand in myth as the otherness of reason." To be sure, given his anti-antiquarian stance, Nietzsche's departure from modern enlightenment does not simply mean a return or regression to a mythical past, but rather carries a utopian-futuristic cast. In contrast to purely restorative vistas, his opus depicted the future as "the only horizon for the revival of mythical tradition. . . . This *utopian* posture—oriented toward a *coming* God—distinguishes Nietzsche's undertaking from the reactionary motto 'Back to the origins'." In his futuristic leanings, Nietzsche is said to have pushed modernity toward postmodernism—a circumstance reflected in his treatment of modern art ("which in its most subjectivist expressions carries modernity to the extreme") as the medium linking past and future, utopia and myth. The chief protagonist of this linkage was for the young Nietzsche Richard Wagner with his vision of art as a quasi-religious festival. Thus, an "aesthetically renewed mythology" was meant to dissolve the blockages or divisions of industrial society, and modern consciousnes was to be "opened to archaic experiences."16

As Habermas recognizes, Nietzsche's vision was not entirely unprecedented, but could be traced broadly to aesthetic views held earlier by Schiller as well as the young Hegel and his friends. In Hegel's early writings and in Schelling's *System of Transcendental Idealism,* he notes, art was granted a mythopoetic quality and assigned a power of synthesis and reconciliation exceeding the competence of a dissecting or analytical reason. This aesthetic outlook was intensified and radicalized by

Romanticism—particularly by Schlegel and Hölderlin who connected the mythopoetic quality of art with quasi-messianic hopes for a historical renewal, hopes which increasingly moved away from Enlightenment rationalism. Schlegel, Habermas asserts, "conceives the new mythology no longer as a sensual manifestation of reason, as an aesthetic expression of ideas which thus would fuse with the interests of the people"; rather, segregating it from theoretical and practical reason he sees art alone as the avenue of renewal. In this manner, modernity is dislodged and confronted "with the 'primordial chaos' as the otherness of reason." A key theme in early Romanticist literature was the figure of Dionysus, "the god of intoxication, madness and ceaseless transformation." According to ancient myth, Dionysus was an expelled or banished but also an expected or coming god—a feature which could nurture quasi-messianic sentiments. In Hölderlin's presentation, Dionysus was an alien or "foreign god," a mythical figure whose absence nourished hopes for a transfigured return—in a manner loosely parallel to Christian hopes for a Second Coming of Christ. While thus tracing the historical lineage of a mythopoetic aesthetics, Habermas immediately differentiates Nietzsche from these Romantic precedents. Despite a common allegiance to Dionysus, the dividing line from Romanticism is said to reside in Nietzsche's anti-Christian sentiments which somehow are linked with his radical anti-Enlightenment posture or anti-rationalism. The key to Nietzsche's departure from Romanticism, Habermas asserts, lies in the "nexus of Dionysus and Christ" which permeated Romantic poetry: "This identification of the intoxicated wine-god with the Christian savior-god was possible only because Romantic messianism aimed at a *rejuvenation* of, not a *farewell* from occidental culture. The new mythology was meant to restore a lost solidarity, not to deny the emancipation" progressively accomplished in that culture—as was Nietzsche's goal.[17]

The line separating Nietzsche from Romanticism was also the source of his rift with Wagner, focused on the latter's Christian proclivities. Wagner, we read, "remained tied to the Romantic nexus of Dionysus and Christ; as little as the Romantics did he regard Dionysus as the demi-god capable of releasing mankind from the curse of identity, of invalidating the principle of individuation, and thus of unleashing polymorphous chaos against the unity of the transcendental God or *anomie* against lawfulness." As opposed to the moderate stance of Wagner and the Romantics, Nietzsche is said to have plunged himself head-long into Dionysian frenzy and also into an irrational, boundless subjectivism. As Habermas affirms, Nietzsche's conception of the Dionysian element involved an "intensification of subjectivism to the point of total self-oblivion"—an oblivion shattering "the categories of reasonable thought and action and the norms of everyday life." In fact, Nietzschean aesthetics or what he called the "aesthetic phenomenon" was predicated on the single-minded "preoccupation of a decentered subjectivity with itself, a subjectivity extricated from the normal conventions of perception and action." This retreat into subjectivism is a central feature of Habermas's critical indictment, a theme which is reiterated in a number of variations. On one level, the retreat was a crucial motive of Nietzsche's break with Enlightenment traditions. What Nietzsche initiated, we are told, was a "total rejection of a nihilistically deflated modernity"; in his work "the critique of modernity renounced for the first time its emancipatory content." In contrast with Enlightenment aspirations Nietzsche is said to have conjured up the "experiences of self-disclosure of a subjectivity removed from all limiting rules of cognition and instrumental activity, from all imperatives of utility and ethics"—experiences, moreover, which were retrojected into an "archaic past." On another level, the same retreat surfaced in the notion of the "will to power," to the extent that the notion pointed to "subjective power claims of valuations disguised behind universal validity claims."[18]

Closely allied with the charge of subjectivism, in Habermas's indictment, is Nietzsche's presumed irrationalism or his abandonment of rational standards—particularly the standards erected by modern epistemology and ethics. According to the study, Nietzsche "continued the Romantic purge of aesthetics of all cognitive and moral ingredients"; on the level of aesthetic experience "a Dionysian reality is immunized by a 'hiatus of oblivion' against the domains of theoretical cognition and moral action, against the world of everyday life." By segregating itself from these domains Nietzsche's perspective was constrained to drift irremediably into the sphere of a "metaphysically sublimated irrationalism"—a sphere in which subjective-aesthetic preferences overwhelm and absorb both empirical and moral considerations. As Habermas insists, however, removed from rational standards Nietzsche's perspective was ultimately unable to legitimate itself, with the result that the metaphysics (or aesthetics) of the will to power lacked a philosophical warrant. Nietzsche, he asserts, "owes his power-focused concept of modernity to a debunking critique of reason which places itself outside the horizons of reason." While suggestive in many ways, such a debunking operation is self-defeating in the end. Moving beyond a modern aesthetics of "taste," Nietzsche can no longer "justify the standards of aesthetic judgment" because of his decision "to transpose aesthetic experiences into an archaic past" and to separate the critical faculty of art appreciation from its moorings in "rational argumentation" or a procedurally unified rationality. As a result, treated as "gateway to the Dionysian realm," aesthetics is "hypostatized into the otherness of reason."[19]

As in Hegel's case, Habermas's reading of Nietzsche calls for a critical reply. Given the broad range of the indictment, several points or facets need to be considered in turn. One point has to do with Nietzsche's alleged break with his Romantic and classicist precursors, deriving from his anti-Christian stance—an argument which strikes me as odd (if not in poor taste) in the case of an author whose own defense of modernity and rationalization tends to reduce religion largely to a relic of the past. As was true for some of his precursors, one needs to distinguish, I believe, between Nietzsche's attitude toward official (or positive) Christianity and toward the person of its founder (for whom he consistently voiced praise); moreover, someone who signed his last writings alternatively or simultaneously as "The Crucified" and "Dionysus" can hardly be accused of having sundered the nexus of Dionysus and Christ.[20] More important in the present context is the presumed plunge into Dionysian frenzy and rampant subjectivism. On the face of it, the latter charge is again odd or curious—given that subjectivity is treated as the basic principle of modernity. For, how can Nietzsche have been the instigator of a radical exit or exodus from modern discourse, and simultaneously been mired in an undiluted subjectivity (and thus an undiluted modernism)? The charge, however, is blunted and rendered obscure by Habermas's own presentation. As indicated, Nietzsche is said to be addicted to a subjectivity removed from normal, everyday conventions; at the same time, his conception of Dionysus is portrayed as an "intensification of subjectivism (or the subjective) to the point of total self-oblivion" or self-abandonment, "Only when the subject *loses* itself," Habermas writes, the door opens to "the world of the unforeseen and completely surprising, the domain of aesthetic appearances." Another passage presents as Nietzsche's exit route from modernity the "sundering of the principle of individuation"—a claim which follows on the heels of a sentence underscoring his subjectivism. But is subjectivity enhanced through self-oblivion? Can Nietzsche have unleashed "polymorphous chaos" and *anomie*—and simultaneously have worshipped the modern ego? The same dilemma besets the treatment of the will to power—which Habermas at one point links with "subjective power claims" and, at another, with a "trans-subjective will" revealing "anonymous processes of domination."[21]

The preceding point is closely connected with Nietzsche's Dionysian leanings or the status of Dionysus in his work. As it seems to me, Habermas's stress on untamed frenzy is vastly excessive and neglects the tensional and multidimensional character of Nietzsche's thought.

Even and particularly *The Birth of Tragedy*—a youthful and (in his own admission) somewhat Romantic-effusive work—did not simply glorify irrational chaos, but rather culminated in a paean on Attic tragedy seen as combination and reconciliation of Dionysus and Apollo. In Nietzsche's portrayal, the former appeared as a symbol of nondifferentiation, of an "original oneness of nature," while Apollo was the god of moderation and insight, representing the "principle of individuation." Reacting against classicist construals of antiquity (emphasizing "quiet grandeur"), *The Birth of Tragedy* clearly sought to recapture and reinvigorate the Dionysian dimension of Greek culture—but without neglecting the need for artistic form and aesthetic sublimation. Pointedly the work distinguished the Greek celebrations of Dionysus from their wilder, barbarian counterparts. In the barbarian festivals, Nietzsche wrote, the central trait was a complete "promiscuity overriding every form of tribal law," an unleashing of "all the savage urges of the mind until they reached that paroxism of lust and cruelty which has always struck me as the 'witches' cauldron' *par excellence.*" In opposition to these wild excesses, "what kept Greece safe was the proud, imposing image of Apollo who, in holding up the head of Gorgon to these brutal and grotesque Dionysian forces, subdued them." As Nietzsche added, this "act of pacification" represented "the most important event in the history of Greek ritual": for only now did it become possible "to speak of nature's celebrating an *aesthetic* triumph; only now has the absorption of the *principium individuations* become an aesthetic event."[22]

In my view, Nietzsche never abandoned nor revoked this complex-tensional outlook—a circumstance which foils any attempt at a univocal interpretation (either as a simple modernist or as a Romantic regressing to an archaic past). This continuity is reflected in his self-description or projection as an artistic Socrates and also in his ambivalence toward reason or rationality throughout his life. Although decrying an abstract or lifeless Socratism, Nietzsche never renounced philosophical reason nor his (ambivalent) admiration for Socrates. What he opposed in traditional rationalism was chiefly a high-flown essentialism or foundationalism—the pretense of being able to absorb concrete, multilayered experience into uniform concepts or unchanging categories. Turning against self-styled rationalists, his *Twilight of the Idols* attacked their blatant "Egypticism": "They think that they show their respect for a topic when they dehistoricize it, *sub specie aeterni*—they turn it into a mummy. All that philosophers have handled for thousands of years have been concept-mummies; nothing real has escaped their grasp alive." Against conceptual abstractions Nietzsche pitted the endeavor of concrete inquiry—an inquiry he did not disdain to call "science" (despite his aversion to a reductive scientism or naturalism): "Today we possess science precisely to the extent to which we have decided to accept the testimony of the senses—to the extent to which we sharpen or strengthen them and have learned to think through them." This attitude toward reason and science also colored his estimate of modernity and modern enlightenment. As is well documented, Nietzsche opposed obscurantism in every form, especially the obscurantism spreading during the Bismarck era. Noting the danger of a regressive atavism or shallow Romanticism, *The Dawn* observed that—far from being the monopoly of reactionaries—the study of history and interest in the past had fortunately "changed their nature one fine day and now soar with the broadest wings past their old conjurers and upward, as new and stronger geniuses of that very Enlightenment against which they were conjured up. This Enlightenment we must now advance further."[23]

Broadly speaking, Nietzsche's thought is the very reverse of dogmatism or a fixed message or doctrine—a doctrine which necessarily would mutilate real life. This anti-dogmatism is a recurrent theme in all his writings, most notably in *The Joyful Science* where we read: "We, however, we others who thirst for reason, want to look our experiences as straight in the eye as if they represented a scientific experiment—hour after hour, day after day. We want ourselves to be our experiments and guinea pigs." Wedded to this experimentalism, Nietzsche's thought militated against received formulas or answers, remaining always open to new vistas—an openness scarcely evident in the reviewed study. Although broadly endorsing the notion of "fallibilism," Habermas fails to question (or treat as questionable) modern rationalism or his own model of rational discourse. Presumably armed with truth, Habermas hurls at Nietzsche the charges of subjectivism, nihilism, and irrationalism—labels which (though I consider them incorrect) *might* well designate the legitimate outcome of sustained inquiry, rather than being signs of corruption. For who or what method can safeguard thinking in advance to preclude this outcome? A case in point is Nietzsche's aesthetics which Habermas takes to task for eluding the standards of theoretical and practical reason. But where is it established that these standards are applicable to, or binding on, art? Which doctrine secures the primacy of epistemology and ethics? In light of recent developments in the philosophy of science, can one not plausibly argue that some kind of creative or artful inventiveness is presupposed even in the rule-governed domains of science and ethical discourse? And if such inventiveness is treated not as a marginal gloss but as constitutive feature, how can one fault Nietzsche for pursuing the implications of this insight—rather than returning to the *terra firma* of (realist) epistemology?

As it seems to me, his genealogical ventures are evidence of this fearless and relentless quest, as are his (posthumously collected) fragments on the "will to power as knowledge" and the "will to power as art."[24] Far from being a renegade, Nietzsche in these and related areas (I believe) steadfastly advanced the discourse of modernity.

III

As noted before, Habermas treats Nietzsche as the turn-table or hiatus separating defenders of modern reason from champions of postmodernism and counter-enlightenment. In the postmodernist camp, his study differentiates in turn between two camps: one attached to Nietzsche's genealogical method as well as his Dionysian zest, the other concerned with his broader metaphysical ruminations. The founder of the first camp was Georges Bataille, the poet or *écrivain* of human excess. In the case of Bataille, we are told, Nietzsche's legacy inspired an attempted regress to a lost oneness accomplished through an "eruption of anti-rational elements, a consuming act of self-immolation"; Dionysian frenzy here took the form of an orgiastic revelry manifesting itself "in play, dance, and intoxication just as much as in those sentiments—mingling horror and lust—which are triggered by destruction and the confrontation with suffering and violent death." The chief spokesman of the second camp was Heidegger with his focus on Nietzschean metaphysics. "The goal," Habermas writes, "that Nietzsche pursued through his total, all-embracing critique of ideology—this goal Heidegger seeks to reach through an immanent destruction of occidental metaphysics. . . . In doing so Heidegger faces the task of putting philosophy into the place" occupied by art in Nietzsche's work. In treating the latter explicitly as a philosopher, Heidegger's exegesis assigns or reassigns to philosophy the function ceded by Romanticism to art—the function of synthesis or reconciliation "countermanding the divisions of modernity." What links the two camps, in Habermas's view, is their common anti-rationalism. Both Bataille and Heidegger, he says, "want to perform a radical critique of reason which attacks the roots of critique itself." While Heidegger aimed his critique at the objectivist character of science, Bataille concentrated on modern instrumental rationality and efficiency. In both instances, the "totalizing" thrust of critique catapulted thought toward an "otherness" entirely outside the bonds of reason: "While reason is defined as calculating control and utilization, its otherness can only be characterized negatively as the completely non-controllable and unusable—as a medium which the subject can reach only by transgressing and abandoning itself as subject."[25]

The study's Heidegger chapter offers initially a broad overview, recapitulating general themes involved in his turn to metaphysics or a critique of metaphysics. Four main themes are accentuated at this point. The first theme is Heidegger's commitment to philosophy, that is, his effort to reinstitute philosophy into the position "from which it had been expelled by Young Hegelian criticism." A direct corollary of this reinvigoration was his emphasis on "ontological pre-understanding" as the dimension pre-forming the particular ideas and perspectives of a given society or culture. For Heidegger, this dimension was in the past commonly articulated by metaphysics, with the result that changes in pre-understanding furnished clues for the history of metaphysics. In modern times—and this is the second theme—metaphysics has progressively buttressed or taken the form of a defense of technology. Based on the philosophy of subjectivity inaugurated by Descartes, modernity has increasingly given rise to calculating rationality, instrumental control of nature, and finally to an all-out "struggle for control of the earth." This expanding sway of technology has ushered in a crisis in our time—the third theme. As in the case of Nietzsche, countering this crisis requires recollection of a distant past—but in a non-antiquarian sense and with an eye to the future. Following Hölderlin, Heidegger views our period as marked by traces of an "exiled god" whose absence presages a possible return. In metaphysical language, this absence denotes the withdrawal or oblivion of being—a withdrawal fostering an ontological (not merely psychological) need for recovery. As a guidepost to recovery, Heidegger's later writings appeal to a recollective or "anamnetic" mode of thinking, transgressing the bounds of calculating reason—the fourth theme. Using the notion of "ontological difference" as a guiding thread, we read, Heidegger's work claims access to a "cognitive competence located beyond the pale of (traditional) self-reflection and discursive reasoning."[26]

In an effort to retrace the steps leading to Heidegger's later writings, the study turns attention to his early *magnum opus, Being and Time* (of 1927). As Habermas recognizes, the work formed a watershed in twentieth-century attempts to transgress the bounds of the "philosophy of consciousness" (or subjectivity). Heidegger confronted the task, he writes, of "overcoming or supplanting the concept of transcendental subjectivity—dominant since Kant—without cancelling the wealth of differentiations" generated by Husserl's phenomenology. In trying to surpass the subjectivist legacy, Heidegger performed an ontological turn—while at the same time maintaining the transcendental project of a reflective clarification of the conditions of possibility of human *Dasein* or "being-in-the-world." In Habermas's portrayal, the opening chapter

of *Being and Time* introduced three crucial innovations paving the way
to a "fundamental ontology." The first step involved an ontological
interpretation of transcendental inquiry or epistemology. Instead of
relying (with Kant) on the a priori categories of consciousness, Heidegger
at this point appealed to the domain of "ontological pre-understanding"
as the matrix underlying different cognitive and practical pursuits.
This pre-understanding surfaces, we read, "when we probe *behind* the
categorial structure of things supplied by a (scientifically informed)
transcendental philosophy. The analysis of pre-understanding yields
those structures of the life-world or 'being-in-the-world' Heidegger
calls 'existentials'." The second step has to do with the interpretive or
hermeneutical cast of pre-understanding, a cast modifying or under-
cutting the straightforward, intentional inspection of phenomena. In contrast to Husserl's focus on perception and direct description, Heidegger's
"hermeneutical phenomenology" shifted the accent to textual (or quasi-
textual) exegesis. In a third step, this ontological-hermeneutical outlook was applied to the analysis of *Dasein*, construed as that mode of
being concerned essentially with the understanding of "its own being"
and its possibilities. These three steps together—and especially the notion
of pre-understanding thematized in them—are said to have enabled
Heidegger finally to articulate the "key concept of his fundamental
ontology": the concept of "world." In his usage, "world" signifies a non-
objective and nonobjectifiable background of experience which is "always
already" assumed by subjects relating to objects: "For it is not the subject that establishes a relation to something in the world, it is the world
which initially furnishes the context of pre-understanding in which
beings can be encountered." Several different modes of encountering
and "caring" about beings were distinguished in *Being and Time*—all
of them nurtured by a pre-understood world seen as "referential context" *(Bewandtniszusammenhang)*.[27]

Having thus restated the underlying motivation and general tenor
of *Being and Time*, Habermas quickly faults the work for a basic inconsistency vitiating its ontological turn. This inconsistency is said to
emerge in the analysis of *Dasein* or the "who of *Dasein*"; in dealing
with this question—and especially with "authentic" *Dasein* and "being-
toward-death"—Heidegger allegedly lapsed back into a Kierkegaardian
subjectivism (if not a hopeless solipsism). Although initially having
reconstructed the "philosophy of the subject" in favor of an underlying
"referential context," Heidegger subsequently "succumbed again to the
conceptual constraints of subjective philosophizing: for the solipsistically
construed *Dasein* reeoccupies the position of transcendental subjectivity." Departing from traditional idealism, it is true, *Being and Time*

ascribed to subjectivity an active potency: in exploring its possibilities, *Dasein* performed a "Fichtean act (of self-constitution) transfigured into a global project." In more general terms (and despite this activist stance), Heidegger's early work—according to Habermas—remained a prisoner of the philosophy of consciousness, particularly in its Husserlian form. Contrary to Mead and the later Wittengenstein (but in conformity with Husserl) Heidegger never eluded "the traditional privileging of theoretical cognition, of constative language-use, and of the validity claim of propositional truth"—thus paying tribute to "the *foundationalism* of the philosophy of consciousness." In the pages of *Being and Time,* this indebtedness to the past manifested itself in many forms, particularly in an incipient objectivism giving priority to (realist) epistemology: "Regardless of whether primacy is accorded to the question of being or of knowledge, in both cases explanatory inquiry is monopolized by a cognitive world-relation, by constative speech, theoretical reason and propositional truth. This ontological-epistemological primacy of knowable beings levels the complexity of world-relations—evident in the plurality of illocutionary modes of natural languages—in favor of *one* privileged relation to the 'objective world'. This latter relation governs even human praxis: instrumental activity, that is, the monological pursuit of goals, is seen as primary mode of action."[28]

Heidegger's later *Kehre* is attributed (at least in part) to an awareness of these predicaments, to the realization that *Being and Time* had ended in the "cul-de-sac of subjectivity." As remedy the *Kehre* initiated a radical reversal or inversion: namely, the turn from subjectivism to a passive celebration of being. While *Being and Time*—we read—had sponsored "the decisionism of an empty resoluteness," Heidegger's later philosopby counseled "the submissiveness of an equally empty readiness for surrender" (to being). According to Habermas, this counsel carried not only metaphysical but practical-political implications. In treating being as a mode of historical happening, he writes, Heidegger stylized historical events and social conditions into "an unimpregnable ontological destiny *(Seinsgeschick)*." The recommendation of surrender (to being) thus had the practical "perlocutionary effect of inducing a diffuse readiness to obedience toward an auratic, but indefinite authority," that is, toward the edicts of "pseudo-sacra1 powers." In producing this effect, Heidegger's later works militate against a central pillar of modernity or the modern discourse: the autonomy of human thought and action. In Habermas's presentation, the turn to being and its destiny sponsored a "training or socialization *(Einüburg)* in a new heteronomy"; Heidegger's critique of modern reason accordingly culminated in a "radical, but substantively empty change of attitude—away from autonomy and toward a devotion to being." Accentuating this feature the study indicts the later work not only of anti-modernism but of an illiberal anti-humanism: "Heidegger rejects the existential-ontological concept of freedom. . . . *Dasein* now submits to the authority of an uncontrollable meaning of being and renounces the will to self-assertion suspect of subjectivism." As reinforcing (if not actually dominant) motive of Heidegger's *Kehre*, the concluding section of the chapter points to his political debacle, that is, his rectorship under the Nazi regime (in 1933-34). Heidegger, we read, "interprets the falseness of the movement in which he had been embroiled, not in terms of subjective responsibility or an existential abdication to 'the They' *(das Man)*, but as an objective lack or failure of truth. . . . This gives rise to the history of being."[29]

Among the thinkers discussed in the study, the treatment of Heidegger is easily the least favorable (or most polemical). Given the broad sweep of the indictment, it seems desirable to disassemble the various charges. Before entering into substantive questions, one may wish to register reservations about the manner Heidegger is first introduced, namely, in conjunction with Georges Bataille. Being presented as an ally or accomplice of the *écrivain* of excess is unlikely to gain friends for Heidegger among right-minded people averse to irrationalism. More substantive (and hardly congruent with the preceding complicity) is the portrayal of Heidegger as a philosopher, that is, as a thinker bent on reinvigorating philosophy and on reinstituting it in the place occupied by art in Nietzsche's writings. I shall not dwell here on the propriety of this move in light of the presumed expulsion of philosophy by Young Hegelian criticism (given that the latter was itself only a strand in Hegelian, that is, modern-philosophical discourse). More important is the juxtaposition with Nietzsche. While Nietzsche had previously been chided for tearing art out of its broader philosophical context — its nexus with truth and goodness — Heidegger is now taken to task for adhering to a classicist aesthetics and for being unable to appreciate the autonomy or separateness of modern art. Quite apart from the fact that I consider the classicist label erroneous, the juxtaposition places both Nietzsche and Heidegger in a no-win position — with either option being tainted with anti-modernism.[30] Heidegger's portrayal as a philosopher, incidentally, collides also with the heavy emphasis placed on political motives animating his later *Kehre* (I shall return to this point). To the extent that Habermas accords great weight if not actually precedence to those motives, the inner movement of Heidegger's thought clearly had a more psychological or ideological rather than philosophical character.[31]

On a philosophical plane, the most serious issues have to do with the interpretation of *Being and Time* as well as Heidegger's later opus.

As indicated, Habermas regards *Being and Time* as an effort to break out of the confines of modern, Cartesian-type philosophizing—but an effort thwarted by Heidegger's relapse into the cul-de-sac of subjectivity. This relapse is said to have spawned a Kierkegaardian existentialism, a Fichtean activism, and also a privileging of (realist) epistemology focused on the objective world. In my view, these charges are highly dubious, both singly and in conjunction. First of all, one should concede, of course, a certain transcendental flavor of *Being and Time*—the study's attempt to continue inquiry into "conditions of possibility" on an ontological level. This aspect, however—which Heidegger repeatedly admitted (and which was a cause of subsequent reformulations)—is a far cry from a lapse into subjectivism, let alone solipsism. The section on the who of *Dasein*—on which the study focuses—points in the very oppositive direction from a Kierkegaardian or Fichtean self-centeredness. The common-sense assumption, Heidegger writes there, that the who of *Dasein* is I (or me), should not stand in the way of further ontological inquiry: for, "we might discover that the 'who of everyday *Dasein*' is precisely *not* I myself" or the "ego of subjective acts." As he adds, the ontological elucidation of being-in-the-world shows that "there is not initially and never ever a mere subject or I without a world. And in the same manner and finally there exists just as little an isolated I without the others." Construed as being-in-the-world, *Dasein* necessarily (or ontologically) and not merely accidentally relates to the world comprising objects, utensils and fellow-beings, and cares about these modalities of being in different ways. Authentic *Dasein* does not mean a cancelling of the hyphens or retreat into selfhood, but rather a *Dasein* that genuinely cares about and cultivates its connections, instead of relating to the world in thoughtless indifference. Even being-toward-death does not negate *Dasein's* connectedness—but only a spurious mutual identification or reciprocal manipulation.[32]

The worldliness of *Dasein* also entails its inter-human linkage, an aspect thematized in *Being and Time* under the label of *co-being* or *being-with (Mitsein)*. In Habermas's account, Heidegger's subjectivist moorings preclude genuine access to intersubjectivity (and especially to communicative interaction in Habermas's sense). Although recognizing that co-being is introduced as a "constitutive trait of being-in-the-world," he charges that the "primacy of intersubjectivity" escapes a conceptual structure "held hostage to the solipsism of Husserlian phenomenology." In a closely parallel fashion, subject-centered *Dasein* is said to "constitute co-being" just as the "transcendental ego" constitutes intersubjectivity in Husserl's theory. This argument is barely intelligible; for, how can co-being be a "constitutive trait" of being-in-the world and yet at the same time be constituted by *Dasein* (which is itself defined by Heidegger as being-in-the-world)? As *Being and Time* repeatedly insists, the ontological construal of being-in-the-world implies that world is "always a world already shared with others: the world of *Dasein* is a *co-world;* being-in signifies a *co-being* with others."[33] The lopsidedness of exegesis on this level is matched by the incongruence of the alleged outcome of *Being and Time:* its return to traditional epistemology privileging the objective world. As will be recalled, Habermas's rehearsal of the opening chapter of the book stressed precisely the non-objective and non-objectifiable character of world seen as a "meaning-disclosing" horizon. World in this sense, he writes, is "always already presupposed by subjects relating cognitively or practically to objects"; consequently, cognitive or practical acts performed in an "objectifying attitude" (or relating to an objective world) can be grasped as derivative modes of a comprehensive life-world and its modalities of being-in-the world. These statements are plainly contradicted by the subsequent summation which speaks of the "ontological-epistemological primacy of (objective) beings as knowable," of the "*one* privileged relation to the objective world," and even of instrumental activity as "primary form of action." But why should Heidegger be blamed for this contradiction?

The cogency of interpretation is equally doubtful with regard to Heidegger's later opus. First a few additional words on the political context of the *Kehre.* There can be no doubt (in my mind) that Heidegger's involvement in 1933 was an egregious mistakes and calamity; I see no need here to compete in professions of anti-fascism. I question, however, the claim that he never addressed his political mistakes "in a *single* sentence"—a claim which is disavowed by his many system-critical remarks during the Nazi regime and by his repeated attempts to account for his behavior afterwards.[34] These accounts, it is true, were never written in a properly contrite or submissive spirit—which may be regrettable and a source of irritation for many. I only note that this same stubborn non-submissiveness accords ill with the claimed reversal initiated by the *Kehre,* namely the turn from autonomy to passive surrender. Although having first criticized the subjectivism of *Being and Time,* Habermas proceeds to rebuke Heidegger's *Kehre* for abandoning or renouncing subjective responsibility in favor of a blind devotion to being or the destiny of being *(Seinsgeschick).* As mentioned before, the *Kehre* is said to separate the earlier decisionism of an empty resoluteness from the later submissiveness of an equally empty readiness for surrender. Little imagination is required to see a simple dualism operative in this shift: namely, the dualism of subjectivism versus objectivism, or activity versus passivity. The same dualism was present in the earlier treatment of Hegel—which (as I tried to show) alternated precariously between a Young Hegelian exegesis focused on subjective praxis, and a Right Hegelian approach stressing passive contemplation. As in all such dualisms, however, the contrasting terms presuppose each other.

Regarding Heidegger's *Kehre,* I would question first of all the abruptness or radicalness of the change. As is well known, *Being and Time* from its opening pages addressed itself to the question of being—although (in Heidegger's admission) the question was not yet properly focused at that juncture. His subsequent works show a progressive intensification of ontological inquiry, but in a manner which never simply discards earlier formulations. Regarding the meaning or status of being, Habermas offers a number of curious and often contradictory assertions. Commenting on the notion of ontological difference he claims: "Heidegger separates Being—which has always been viewed as the Being of beings—from beings"; thus segregated from beings and rendered "quasi-autonmous," the "hypostatized Being can assume the role of Dionysus." Somewhat later, hermeneutical phenomenology is presented as a movement from surface to depth, toward a "Being which is disguised or obstructed by beings." As can readily be seen, segregated into polar components ontological difference is reabsorbed into traditional metaphysical categories (the antitheses of essence and appearance, universals and particulars)—thereby nullifying Heidegger's critique of metaphysics; as the latter has repeatedly observed (not least in his *Identity and Difference*), ontological inquiry probes precisely the being of beings as a mode of differential belonging.[35] Returning to Habermas: the separation of being and its blockage or obstruction by beings would seem to preclude a direct access to being—a conclusion which plainly conflicts with a subsequent passage affirming the opposite. Referring to the temporal but "undialectical" character of Heidegger's ontology, the study asserts that "as in the case of metaphysics" being is for Heidegger "the absolutely immediate or unmediated." Whether seen as pure immediacy or as separate entity, being has the character of external positivity—which leads to Habermas's most serious charge: namely, Heidegger's denial of freedom in favor of heteronomy. Although confidently stated and reiterated, the charge is also the most spurious—given the centrality of freedom in Heidegger's entire philosophy. As in the case of Hegel's spirit or idea, being for Heidegger was essentially a synonym for freedom (although not for arbitrary willfulnsss).[36]

The charge of heteronomy is closely allied with the presumed lapse into counter-enlightenment and anti-rationalism: by abandoning autonomy ontological thought is also said to step beyond the bounds of reason. In turning toward being and its destiny, Habermas writes, Heidegger's opus assumes "a cognitive stance or competence *beyond* the pale of self-reflection, beyond discursive reasoning as such." The recollective or essential thinking practiced and recommended in his work allegedly is hostile "to all empirical and normative questions which can be treated scientifically and historically or discussed in argumentative form." In the end, ontological thinking is said to submerge in an irrational intuitionism or mysticism. The vehemence of these claims again does not buttress their plausibility. For, what are Heidegger's numerous writings in this area—from *What is Metaphysics?* to *What is Called Thinking?* and beyond—if not strings of arguments trying to make sense to readers—although not on the level of calculative-analytical rationality (or *Verstand*). And how can this rationality be corrected if every step beyond its confines is immediately branded as irrational or mystical? The latter charge, incidentally, has been addressed long ago by Heidegger himself, in his lectures on Hegel's *Phenomenology of Spirit* (of 1930). "It is becoming customary now," he remarked, "to label my philosophy as 'mysticism'. It is equally superfluous and pointless to counter this charge. . . . Not logical—hence mystical; not *ratio*—hence irrational. In this manner one only shows that one has not yet faced up to the question why and with what justification being *(on)* is related to *logos* (or *ratio*)."[37] Habermas's remedy for Heidegger's mysticism is a return to propositional truth and pragmatic efficiency—the same outlook he had castigated as outcome of *Being and Time*. Like Nietzsche's radical critique of reason, he writes, Heidegger's turn to being and its destiny involves an "*uprooting of propositional truth* and a devaluation of discursive thought." Despite the role of world and language as horizons of meaning-constitution, the actual functioning of sentences is said to depend not on this horizon but on the "inner-worldly success of praxis" relating to factual conditions; far from antedating and enabling cognitive-factual truth, the horizon of world (or being) is actually governed by this truth and its cognitive standards.[38]

IV

In its concluding chapters the study recapitulates central themes of the preceding discussions, mainly in an effort to profile or set the stage for Habermas's own proposal (of communicative interaction). Returning to his narrative, Habermas recalls the Enlightment *cantus firmus* epitomized by Kant, and also the emerging counter-discourse stressing the intrinsic costs of modernity. What united proponents of this counter-discourse from Schiller to Schelling and Hegel, he notes, was "the intent of revising the Enlightenment with the means provided by the latter itself." Pointing to the cleavages or divisions *(Entzweiungen)* of modernity, Hegel in particular invoked the power of synthesis lodged in a totalizing *Vernunft* or absolute spirit. With diverse accents, the strands of the counter-discourse were continued by Young Hegelians stressing rational praxis and Right Hegelians extolling abstract principles. Starting with Nietzsche, however, the modern discourse and its counter-discourse were disrupted in favor of a totalizing critique of reason; exiting from the dialectic of enlightenment, Nietzsche and his heirs dismiss or brush aside "that nearly two hundred year old counter-discourse implicit in modernity itself." At this point Habermas turns to his own preferred remedy or exit route from the dilemmas of modern subjectivity: the shift from the philosophy of consciousness to the paradigm of communicative reason and interaction. In contrast to a purely subject-centered stance the latter paradigm, in his presentation, conceives "intersubjective under-standing and consensus as the *telos* implicit in linguistic communica-tion"; constitutive for the paradigm is "the performative attitude of participants in interactions who coordinate their action plans by reaching mutual consensus on something in the world." By relying on human interaction, the communicative model is said to correct the basic limi-tation of modern subjectivity (or logocentrism): its exclusive focus on the objective world, that is, its tendency to reduce "the relation of man and world to a cognitive dimension, namely, to a relation to the world of (objective) beings as a whole." Most importantly, the model returns to and reinscribes itself within the modern philosophical discourse: "Instead of transgressing or overreaching modernity, it resumes the counter-discourse inherent in modernity, extricating the latter from the hopeless confrontation between Hegel and Nietzsche."[39]

I shall not dwell here extensively on the details of Habermas's proposal or presumed paradigm shift (which has repeatedly been done in the literature). Instead I wish to alert to some quandaries besetting the proposal and its relation to the modern discourse. First of all, one cannot fail to notice the geographical and intellectual restrictedness of this discourse: as portrayed in the study, its chief protagonists or voices are German (with French thinkers mainly continuing or amplifying German initiatives—such as Bataille vis-à-vis Nietzsche, or Derrida vis-à-vis Heidegger). What is chiefly missing is the contribution of Anglo-Saxon thought to modernity—which is hardly negligible. Thus, one misses the legacy of British skepticism and empiricism from Bacon over Berke-ley and Hume to Russell; equally absent is English utilitarianism and neo-utilitarianism which, as an alternative to Hegel, construed civil society as a conglomerate of individual interests. The most important gap, in my view, however, is the neglect of the contractarian tradition from Hobbes to Locke (and later refined by Rousseau and Kant) in which the communicative model was largely prefigured. Contractarian thinkers, as one may recall, derived the commonwealth or the state precisely from the agreement or consensus of free and equal individuals. Generally speaking, modern philosophy (with a few exceptions) was by no means subjectivist in a solipsistic manner—one which would have contested the existence of outer nature or of other subjects; on the contrary, it was the recognized plurality of diverse subjects or individuals which raised the problem of public order and peaceful coexistence (to be met through general agreement). On the same level, it is simply not the case—as Habermas suggests—that modern thought was one-sidedly focused on cognition or a one-world relation (namely, to the so-called objective world). Under the rubric of natural law, modern philosophy created an elaborate system of normative standards which—on a par with the ideal speech community—were meant to regulate human interactions. In a similar vein, modernity has been no stranger to intimate self-disclosure—as manifested in literature from Pascal's *Pensées* to Rousseau's *Confessions*.

The most obvious precursor of the communicative model is Kantian rationalism. In his three *Critiques,* Kant thematized precisely the different world-relations emphasized by the model: a cognitive-theoretical access to the external world; a practical grasp of normative standards governing human interactions; and an expressive self-relation manifest in art and aesthetics. As Habermas himself states (in a previously cited passage), Kant replaced the substantive reason of the past by a conception of rationality "differentiated into separate moments," a concept segregating "practical reason and the critique of judgment from theoretical cognition." These separate moments provided the underpinnings to the cultural value spheres emerging in modernity: those of science, ethics, and art—the same spheres, Habermas says, which Hegel grasped as manifestations of the principle of subjectivity. While modern science disenchants nature, thus liberating the subject from ignorance, modern ethics is grounded in individual autonomy, and modern art in subjective self-expression. Despite the claimed exit from subjectivity, the same spheres or dimensions clearly resurface in Habermas's model with its various divisions or tripartions—particularly the divisions between truth, rightness, and truthfulness (on the level of validity claims); between constative, regulative, and expressive utterances (on the level of speech acts); and between objective, social, and subjective worlds (on the level of world-relations). In light of this intrinsic continuity, one can reasonably doubt the asserted paradigm shift—away from subject- or ego-centered reason—given that the various dimensions of the model all pay homage to the same centering (being classifiable respectively into subject-object, subject-subject, and subject-to-itself relationships). In his study, Habermas repeatedly contests this continuity—but in formulations which confirm the linkage. Contrary to the privileged position of cognitive subjectivity, the communicative paradigm is said to support a different, performative relation of *subjects:* "When ego performs a speech act and *alter* responds, both enter into an interpersonal relation"; at this point ego is enabled "to relate to himself from the perspective of *alter* as a participant in an interaction." Similarly, criticizing Heidegger's notion of being-in-the-world, the study presents communicative interaction as anchored in "the structures of linguistic intersubjectivity" and sustained by "the same medium in which subjects capable of speech and action reach agreement on something in the world."⁴⁰

To be sure, Kantian rationalism is not simply translatable into communicative interaction. What separates the two modes of reasoning is primarily Habermas's reliance on language and also on the dimension of the life-world seen as matrix overarching segregated value spheres. Relying in part on Wittgensteinian *motifs,* Habermas portrays the paradigm shift of his approach also as a linguistic turn—from a straightforward philosophy of consciousness to the conception of a linguistically nurtured or mediated thought and action. This turn is invoked in the study as the chief dividing line from past forms of rationalism, including Kant's 'purism of reason.' "There is no such thing," we read, "as a pure reason only subsequently clothed in linguistic garments. Rather, reason is from the beginning an incarnate reason enmeshed in contexts of communicative action and in structures of the life-world." As an incarnate faculty embroiled in real-life situations, reason cannot simply soar above or cancel space and time, but is always somehow in-the-world. Similarly, given the linguistic character of reason—its inability to be denuded of language—there cannot be a pure or purely rational language, but only an interlacing or tensional mixture of opacity and clarity, of real and ideal elements of discourse. Despite the radicalness of these and similar formulations, however, their import is sharply curtailed in the study: countermanding his ostensible break with Kantian purism, Habermas quickly retreats to the *terra firma* of rational epistemology. His theory of value spheres and corresponding validity claims is entirely erected on this ground; so are the parameters of modern discourse as drawn in the study. Apprehensive of the specter of contextualism, his approach basically disaggregates the claimed mixture of elements. Despite the essentially incarnate (and impure) character of reason, pure rationality continues to serve as yardstick of opague or real elements— in a manner relegating the latter to a level of imperfection or inferiority with which we may have to "make do."⁴¹ Obviously, it is only on the assumption of a pure or non-contextual language that a universal pragmatics can be formulated; similarly, it is only by discounting the concrete differences among individuals and the multivocity of speech that ego can be assumed to recognize himself "in the perspective of *alter*" to reach an ideal consensus. More generally, only traditional epistemology provides the basis for subordinating the meaning-disclosing potency of world (or language) to factual or pragmatic claims—as was done in the Heidegger chapter. Returning to the latter issue, Habermas insists that "meaning must *(darf)* not absorb validity," adding that "it is only the prior *conditions* of the validity of statements which change with changing meaning-horizons—but the latter must in turn be *confirmed* through experience and the contact with things encountered in a given horizon."[42]

The same ambivalence affects the status of the life-world. Recapitulating arguments advanced on other occasions, the study depicts the life-world as a background context not directly available to inspection or control. In communicating about something in the world, Habermas writes, speakers and hearers "move within the horizon of a common life-world" which remains "in their backs as an indivisible holistic foil." As a background matrix, the life-world operates "pre-reflectively" and can "only be perceived *a tergo*"; from the "frontal perspective of communicatively acting subjects the always 'co-present' life-world escapes thematization." Another passage speaks of the life-world as "equivalent to the power of synthesis ascribed by subject-centered philosophy to consciousness as such." These and similar formulations do not prevent Habermas, however, from distancing the life-world to a target of analysis and rational reconstruction—an operation basically bracketing its *a tergo* potency (and reducing it to a pliant "resource"). "We need a *theoretically constituted* perspective," he states, "in order to perceive communicative action as the medium through which the life-world as a whole is reproduced."[43] What emerges from this perspective are formal-pragmatic schemata capturing the general "structures of the life-world" stripped of variable contents. The main structures pinpointed in the study (and elsewhere) are "culture," "society," and "personality"— domains which in turn undergird the tripartition of modern value spheres (science, ethics, and self-expression) and corresponding validity claims (truth, rightness, and truthfulness). Although first introduced as a simple change of perspective, the distinction of life-world and formal structures quickly acquires broader historical connotations, in the sense that modernization involves the growing segregation of value spheres from pre-reflective moorings. According to Habermas, the difference between life-world and (communicative) rationality cannot be bridged or reconciled in modernity; on the contrary, the difference is steadily intensified to the degree that the reproduction of the life-world "no longer merely *passes* through the medium of communicative action but *results* from the interpretive accomplishments of actors." To the extent that taken-for-granted modes of consensus are replaced by cooperatively achieved agreement, "*concrete* life-forms and *general* structures of the life-world *move apart*."[44]

Pursuing the modernization theme, Habermas at this juncture projects a future scenario in which the life-world as *vis a tergo* is progressively replaced by formal structures—to the point where pre-reflective existence is virtually absorbed into conscious-rational designs. On the level of culture, the scenario entails the exchange of traditional beliefs for formal modes of argumentation; on the level of society, habitual behavior gives way to universal principles of ethics, while personality proceeds from receptiveness to self-constructed modes of identity. Although presented as a "thought experiment," the scenario is said to reflect the "factual development" of modern life-worlds, namely, the growing "abstraction of general life-world structures" from traditional contents. Recasting this trend as a story of emancipation, the study anticipates these (idealized) goal- or end-points: "for culture, a condition of permanent revision of reflectively liquefied traditions; for society, the dependence of legitimate order on formal-discursive procedures of legislation and norm-validation; for personality, a condition of hazardous self-steering of a highly abstract ego-identity." In line with this development, life-worlds are no longer replenished unconsciously or pre-reflectively; rather, their reproduction relies essentially on cognitive critique, ethical universalism, and "extremely individualized" forms of socialization. Having sketched this emancipatory vision, Habermas— almost abruptly—recoils from its implicit utopianism. Noticing the affinity of his scenario with Enlightenment ideals and especially with Kant's purism of reason, he redirects attention to the life-world and its role of securing "the continuity of meaning-contexts." Despite modernity's steady turn to abstract-formal structures (of thought and speech), tribute is again paid to ordinary-language communication; despite the trend toward extreme individualization, identity is said to be possible only within a "universal community." Yet, this tribute in turn is almost instantly qualified (if not revoked). In a developmental sense, the life-world is portrayed as recalcitrant to complete formalization or structural differentiation; in fact, its interactive and communicative potential is said to be of limited or "low elasticity"—too limited for purposes of effective rationalization. It is as an antidote or corrective to this deficiency that Habermas in the end resorts to a dualistic scheme: the scheme of the progressive uncoupling and tensional correlation of "system" and life-world, where "system" refers to relatively abstract modes of action coordination capable of "unburdening" the life-world of various social tasks or functions.[45]

Given the reduced or tenuous status of the life-world—its progressive subordination to formal structures and system imperatives—the claimed nexus of Habermas's model and Hegelian discourse (or counter-discourse) is hard to perceive. This nexus is reasserted at several points. "The theory of communicative action," Habermas states, "can reconstruct Hegel's concept of an ethical life-context (without relying on consciousness-centered premises)"; like Hegel in his early writings on guilt and punishment the theory is "guided by an intuition expressible in Old-Testament terms as follows: the unrest of real-life conditions nurtures an ambivalence deriving from the dialectic of treason and revenge." In other passages, however, Hegelian echoes are muffled if not entirely canceled. Elaborating on the difference of life-world and formal structures, the study insists that the contrast eludes Hegelian notions of totality and synthesis. In pronounced form, the same is true of the uncoupling of system and life-world in the process of modernization. In his conception of a "divided ethical totality," we read, Hegel (like Marx later) underestimated the "autonomous logic" *(Eigensinn)* of system domains, their tendency to extricate themselves from intersubjective relations in a manner cancelling "structural analogies" with the life-world. Apart from the charges of irrationalism and anti-humanism, the heirs of Nietzsche are also specifically indicted for failing to accept modern value spheres and their segregation from the life-world. What had been granted to Hegel—to complain about the cleavages *(Entzweiungen)* of modernity—becomes a source of rebuke in the case of Nietzscheans. In fact, from Habermas's perspective, the divisions of modernity "must not *per se* be viewed as symptomatic pathologies of a subject-centered reason." While Hegel had still been credited with perceiving both the advances and the "crisis character" of modern life, modernization in Habermas's presentation is no longer intrinsically crisis-prone but only subject to contingent (and essentially remediable) imbalances or derailments. The chief type of imbalance is an "excessive" ascendancy of system imperatives or a certain "preponderance of economic and bureaucratic, and more generally cognitive-instrumental modes of rationality."[46]

If Habermas's Hegelian credentials are dubious, the summary expulsion of Nietzscheans from modernity is even less plausible. In fact, parallels can readily be detected between central Nietzschean *motifs* and Hegel's counter-discourse. As recognized in the study, Hegel and his Tübingen friends subscribed to a strongly imaginative or mytho-poetic conception of synthesis or reconciliation (with nature and fellow-humans); among Romantic writers, this outlook was blended with the

mythic fable of Dionysus, the figure of the absent and expected god—
a theme prominently continued by Nietzsche and Heidegger (and
other post-Nietzscheans). More generally, if modern discourse means
a process of relentless self-scrutiny—a scrutiny extending (as the study
says) to the "sphere of the ephemeral or impermanent"—then Nietzsche
and his heirs would seem to be prime exemplars of modernity (rather
than anti-modernism). Nowhere have the presuppositions and underpinnings of modernity itself be more thoroughly and critically explored
than in the Nietzschean camp. Nowhere also has more attention been
given to the effects of modern divisions and cleavages *(Entzweiungen)*
—that is, to the intrinsic ambivalence or crisis character of modern
times. To be sure, such attention may seem exorbitant to more sanguine
observers for whom modernity, as an "unfinished project," merely requires completion; Hegel's counter-discourse must have seemed equally
lopsided to Enlightenment rationalists.[47] As it happens, the crisis features of modernity have hardly lessened since Hegel's time; the catastrophes of our age attest to the opposite. Against this background, the
extremism of some Nietzschean and post-Nietzschean formulations may
be viewed as a response to the increased hazards or hardships of modern
life, that is, as expression of a concrete suffering—a suffering which
Habermas's study only meets with condescending irony. If, as Hegel
thought, ethical reconciliation is possible only on the basis of a deeply
felt (or suffered) nexus of guilt, then Nietzschean counter-discourse may
have a profound ethical significance—as a counterpoint to the optimism and divisiveness of technological mastery and as signpost to a
different life-form.

Needless to say, Nietzschean and post-Nietzschean discourse does
not simply coincide with Hegel's. Like Habermas, spokesmen of this
legacy have sought an exit route from the principle of modernity; however, instead of simply multiplying subjects, they have challenged the
underlying ontological assumption: the possibility of thinking together
in one category (subjectivity or spirit) the conflicting elements of sameness and otherness, identity and non-identity. This challenge is evident
in Nietzsche's attack on Platonism or Platonic ideas, in Heidegger's critique of metaphysics, and in Derrida's notion of *différance.* Yet, jointly
or singly, these moves do not sponsor a simple reversal or an embrace of
antithesis (in lieu of Hegelian synthesis). In his study, Habermas
distinguishes between two models of reason: an "inclusive" model epitomized in Hegel's synthetic *Vernunft,* and an "exclusive" model in which
otherness is banished entirely from reason. The two types are also
described respectively as *Entzweiungsmodell* where cleavages are ultimately reconciled within reason, and *Ausgrenzungsmodell* which insists

on irremediable conflict. By appealing to being, heteronomy or power, post-Nietzscheans are said to rely on elements "*outside* the horizon of reason" (an exclusive strategy)—and thus to lapse into irrationalism.[48] It is easy to see, however, that the mentioned distinction only reflects traditional metaphysical antimonies: the antimonies between inside and outside, immanence and transcendence. A major thrust of Nietzschean discourse (in the broad sense) has been precisely to unsettle these polar oppositions—that is, to give an account of difference which is neither purely inclusive (synthetic) nor exclusive (antithetical). Here is a source of the genuine intellectual excitement of this discourse, an excitement which is not due to a bland rejection of reason, but to the attempt to rethink its meaning and explore the peculiar interlacing of reason and non-reason, positivity and negativity (or real and ideal elements).

Habermas's study shows little sense for this excitement. With a stern and commanding gesture, Nietzsche and his heirs are exiled or banished from the province of reason—a province seemingly entrusted to Habermas's custody. This banishment, however, exacts a price. With his exclusionary policy Habermas inadvertently lends credence to the claim of some Nietzscheans (especially Foucault) that every discourse, including rational discourse, harbors a principle of exclusion, thus attesting to the intrusion of power (or the interlacing of *pouvoir/savoir*). According to the same Nietzscheans, moreover, discourses also betray a certain doctrinaire bias—by favoring certain kinds of arguments over others. In Habermas's study, the favored argument or perspective is clearly the communicative model of reason. In fact, the model is held in reserve from the opening pages of the study and finally unveiled, in the concluding chapters, as the correct solution of modern predicaments. All the participants of the modern discourse—from Hegel to Heidegger and Foucault—are chided for having missed the correct answer, although some came closer to the mark than others. While approximating the solution briefly during his Jena period, Hegel failed to follow the proper path by resorting to absolute spirit—a failure replicated later by Marx in his reliance on labor. Thus, already at this early juncture or crossroads, modern discourse is said to have taken the wrong turn. The mistake was compounded by Nietzsche and his heirs. In the case of Heidegger, a lecture of 1939 is singled out for showing some promising signs—a promise subsequently foiled by Heidegger's ontological leanings. In sum, all or most of the thinkers discussed in the study at some point stood before "an alternative they did not select": the alternative of the communicative model—which, compared with past fumblings, represents the more solid and "reliable solution" and the proper corrective to the philosophy of consciousness.[49]

In my view, the notion of solution is not only alien to philosophical inquiry but also hostile to communicative discourse—since it implies a conclusion or terminal point of discussions. My reservations, however, extend from the form of presentation to the character of the proposed answer—to the degree that it is meant to remedy or redress modern ills. In Habermas's account, the remedy—if one is needed at all—consists mostly in a quasi-mechanical balancing act: the coupling and uncoupling of system and life-world (with the life-world increasingly shrinking into an enclave among modern-rational structures and systemic units). Little or no substantive changes seem required to accomplish this task or to correct pathological trends. As the study repeatedly affirms, individualization (even in extreme forms) is a pliant corollary of socialization and community life, occasioning few if any frictions—an assumption which is belied by massive collisions in Western societies between private interests and the common good.[50] As it seems to me, modern cleavages (Entzweiungen) and pathologies exceed the capacities of a balancing mechanism. In light of rampantly possessive lifestyles and the predatory thrust of technology, exiting from subjectivity involves more than procedural adjustments: namely, a substantive paradigm shift opening the subject to its otherness. Just as philosophical inquiry implies at some point a turning-about or periagoge (thematized by Plato as "a kind of dying"), this opening demands an experiential turn-about or transformation of individual life, that is, a process of character-formation. Contrary to Habermas's futuristic scenario (the prospect of entirely self-constructed identities), such character-formation or taming of egocentrism can only happen in the context of concrete historical communities—though not necessarily communities bent on self-enclosure or collective modes of solipsism. Neither narrowly communal nor subsumable under abstract principles, the nature of transformative community-life or co-being has been pinpointed by another post-Nietzschean, Derrida, in these terms: "A community of questioning therefore, within that fragile moment when the question is not yet determined enough for the hypocrisy of an answer. . . . A community of the question about the possibility of the question."[51]

4

VOEGELIN'S SEARCH FOR ORDER

Quam dilecta. . . .

The torrent of recent publications contains a small gem which has not sufficiently been noticed perhaps by philosophers and political theorists: Eric Voegelin's *In Search of Order*. Posthumously published, the slender volume constitutes a fitting epitaph to the author's life-long intellectual journey and pilgrim's progress. As is well known, Voegelin's sprawling opus ranged over the fields of philosophy, politics, anthropology, and history (to mention just a few); probably his most celebrated work so far had been the multi-volume *Order and History* which recounted the history of order from the dawn of mankind to the ecumenic age and which has justly been acclaimed as a classic of philosophical historiography in our time. *In Search of Order* serves as sequel and capstone to this *magnum opus*—with a twist. The unsuspecting and hurried reader might have expected the volume to yield a final summation, a definitive statement of the author's position regarding order.

Yet, as it stands, the volume is a torso and offers no complete doctrine—which aptly matches the author's steadily growing conviction of the unending and unfinishable character of his quest (and of any genuine inquiry). In the words of Ellis Sandoz who introduces the volume:

> The fact that the quest of order is an unfinished story as told by Voegelin is most fitting; for, as he insisted, neither reality nor philosophy can be reduced to a system. Thus, the form of the present work can be said to symbolize Voegelin's philosophical vision of history and comprehensive reality as an unfinished tale, one told by God in the reflective language of spiritually gifted men and women open to the mystery of truth.[1]

While revealing as an epitaph, however, the new volume has more than autobiographical significance. Generally speaking, Voegelin's writings cannot narrowly be tied to authorial intent—because of the broader mystery of truth in which inquiry proceeds. The reason that, for him, philosophy could not be reduced to a system was not resignation or some penchant for obscurantism, but rather the fact that philosophical reflection occurs in a larger historical and ontological framework which can never be exhaustively stated in propositional form. As a participatory act, reflection could not be limited to neutral description but always carried moral-political and broadly existential connotations. There can be little doubt that Voegelin's entire opus was an outgrowth of a response to the perceived agonies of our age, as experienced from the vantage of a reflective participant. In heightened form, this is also true of *In Search of Order* whose dense formulations and efforts at symbolization are designed to have both diagnostic and therapeutic relevance. A Voegelin himself states in the opening pages: "The book is meant to be read"—namely as "an event in a vast social field of thought and language, of writing and reading about matters which the members of the field believe to be of concern for their existence in truth." The book would basically be pointless unless it had a function or bearing "in a communion of existential concern."[2] In the following I shall first give a condensed synopsis of some of the main themes discussed in the volume. Next, I intend to highlight aspects of the book which seem to me particularly intriguing or fruitful in the context of contemporary discussions in philosophy and political thought. By way of conclusion I shall voice some general questions or reservations—questions which, I believe, are in tune with Voegelin's concerns and especially with his emphasis on the open-ended and unfinishable quality of reflective endeavors.

I

In Search of Order is broadly divided into two parts: the first part dealing with general philosophical themes, the second carrying a more
historical-recollective character. The first chapter opens with a basic
philosophical problem, namely, the problem of the "beginning" or
"arché" in any reflective endeavor—which raises immediately all the
issues concerning the relation between whole and part, foreground and
background, text and context. Drawing on some of his earlier investigations, Voegelin phrases the issues in terms of the status of consciousness
vis-à-vis reality, a status he finds paradoxical or ambivalent because it
can assume essentially two forms. On the one hand, he writes, "we
speak of consciousness as a something located in human beings in their
bodily existence. In relation to this concretely embodied consciousness
reality assumes the position of an object intended" or of an "external
thingness" juxtaposed to an intending consciousness. On the other hand,
embodied consciousness is itself part of a certain reality—no longer of
external thingness but of a background reality which enables consciousness to function; in this second sense, we read, reality is "not an object
of consciousness but the something in which consciousness occurs as an
event of participation between partners in the community of being."
The duality of relations leads Voegelin to the formulation of two types
of reality, namely "thing-reality" and "It-reality," and two modes of consciousness called "intentionality" and "luminosity" respectively. As used
in the phrase It-reality, the term "it" has not so much ontic-empirical as
rather ontological significance: it involves that "mysterious 'it' that also
occurs in everyday language in such phrases as 'it rains'." The entire
distinction between modes of reality and of consciousness can also be
seen as a subject-predicate exchange, in the sense that "reality moves
from the position of an intended object to that of a subject, while the
consciousness of the human subject intending objects moves to the position of a predicative event in the subject 'reality' as it becomes luminous
for its truth."[3]
   In the following, the preceding duality is further expanded and
complicated by the addition of language—which yields the triple structure of "consciousness-reality-language" as general framework guiding
the volume's inquiries. As Voegelin observes, language can be apprehended either as an empirical body of signs or else as a creative agency
bestowing meaning on the world. "Words and their meanings," he writes,
"are just as much part of the reality to which they refer as the being
things are partners in the comprehending reality; language participates
in the paradox of a quest that lets reality become luminous for its truth

by pursuing truth as a thing intended." The ambivalent character of language is reflected in the distinction between "concept" and "symbol" and, more generally, in the differentiation between scientific explanation and understanding or between the natural-mathematical sciences and the humanities. According to Voegelin, neither of the two types of disciplines can claim to capture the complete truth. The representatives of both types, he notes "are right in their pursuit of truth as long as they confine themselves to areas of reality in which the structures of their preference predominate"; but they are "wrong when they engage in magic dreams of a truth that can be reached by concentrating exclusively on either the intentionality of conceptualizing science or the luminosity of mythic and revelatory symbols."[4]

In trying to illustrate the complex structure of his approach and particularly the paradox of beginnings, Voegelin turns to the creation story as told in *Genesis* I. Reflecting on the role of language in that story ("And God said: Let there be light"), he notes that the spoken word here is "more than a mere sign signifying something"; rather, language is endowed with a creative potency or power which "evokes structures in reality by naming them." This power, in turn, is ascribed to God or to the breath or spirit of God (or rather of a plural divinity, *elohim*) — which is a symbolization of the underlying It-reality enabling the world to be. This underlying reality, we are told, is "symbolized as the strong movement of a spiritual consciousness, imposing form on a formless and non-forming countermovement, as the tension between a pneumatic, formative force and an at least passively resistant counterforce." Thus, when penning the first lines of their text, the authors of *Genesis* I "were conscious of beginning an act of participation in the mysterious Beginning of the It." Cognizant of the difficulties of biblical exegesis, Voegelin immediately seeks to ward off certain "conventional misunderstandings" hampering access to the text. First of all, the symbolism of the creation story must in his view not be "psychologized" or misread as an "anthropomorphism," that is, as "the projection of a human into a divine consciousness" — which would vitiate or muffle the role of the invoked It-reality in the story. More important, the creative happening engendered by the It-reality should be seen as a language-event, as the deed of the "pneumatic word," and not as the simple imposition of a subjective idea on a formless matter construed in terms of thing-reality. In Voegelin's account, the formless waste alluded to in the story was neither a thing nor a mere no-thing: it was not a "thing" if the term denotes "any structure experienced as real in post-creational reality"; it was not nothing, for in this case no "creative evocation of something" would be feasible. Instead of designating an external matter, the formless waste rather preserved the notion of an "originally (co-)generating maternal reality"; probably linked with the "Babylonian *tiamat*," the creation story evoked "the mythic meaning of feminine productivity in the act of generation.⁵

According to Voegelin, the creative beginning recounted in *Genesis* I was not a one-time happening but reverberates through human history seen as experiential openness to the "command of the pneumatic word." As in his earlier writings, he distinguishes between a series of spiritual "epiphanies" throughout history, ranging from *Genesis* over the patriarchs to the prophets, from Taoist, Hindu and Buddhist teachings to Greek philosophy and Christianity—each with its distinct and more or less highly differentiated symbolization of the creative event. Typically, new modes of symbolization are reactions to prevalent but decaying or decayed symbol systems and efforts to provide more elaborate or nuanced expression for the meaning structure of an age. "The quest for truth," we read, "is a movement of resistance to the prevalent disorder: it is an effort to attune the concretely disordered existence again to the truth of the It-reality, an attempt to create a new social field of existential order in competition with the fields whose claim to truth has become doubtful." If the attempt is successful in finding symbols which adequately capture "the newly differentiated experience of order," it may then become the beginning and leavening spirit of "a new social field." In large measure, Voegelin adds, the success of this endeavor depends on the ability of the new symbolization to express the "common sense" of a period, that is, its ability to speak not in a distant-alien idiom but with an "authority commonly present in everybody's consciousness": "The appeal will be no more than a private opinion unless the questioner finds in the course of his quest the word *(logos)* that indeed speaks what is common *(xynon)* to the order of man's existence as a partner in the comprehending reality; only if the questioner speaks the common *logos* of reality can he evoke a truly public order."⁶

Attunement to and recovery of pneumatic meaning is not simply an act of human invention or fabrication; but neither is it an external intervention cancelling human participation. According to Voegelin, this participatory aspect is captured in the Platonic notion of the *metaxy* or of the "between-status" of spiritual life. The search for meaning and truth, he notes, "can be a true story only if the questioner participates existentially in the comprehending story told by the It through its creative epiphany of structure." *Metaxy* in this context means the tensional balance between human and divine reality and also between ordinary temporality and eternity; in this sense, Plato came to symbolize ordinary time as "the moving *eikon* of eternity." Precariously lodged at the intersection of immanence and transcendence, *metaxy* signals—in

Voegelin's words—"an eruption of order within time in response to an irruption of order from the beyond of time." In Platonic thought, this "beyond of time" was portrayed as a divine-immortal sphere, as the "*epekeina* of all being things *(ta onta)*" or as the formative *nous*. In human life and especially in the philosopher's quest for truth, this sphere manifests itself as a "formative force" or as the experienced disclosure or "*Parousia* of the formative It-reality in all things"—a disclosure imposing on ordinary temporality the dimension of "divine presence." As Voegelin cautions, the Platonic notion should not itself be turned into a rigid doctrine, since it is only one of different historical ways of symbolizing the creative event. Still, while recognizing a "plurality" of possible stories and quests, the volume does not endorse a simple historicism or historical relativism. Instead, the different historical formulations are seen as variations on a common theme or as distinct "episodes" occurring within the "same comprehending It-story." Thus, the diversity of historical experience can be grasped and understood "as a field of languages, intelligibly symbolizing the truth of reality in conformity with the recognizable structure of the complex."[7]

Although open to human participation, the beyond of time cannot or must not become the target of human manipulation or control; where It-reality is instrumentalized or reduced to thingness, the road is open to disorder and deformation—as history amply attests. In Voegelin's account, the millennial quest for order and truth is offset and paralleled by a constant counterpull: namely, the temptation "to deform the Beyond and its formative *Parousia*" by corrupting the beyond into a tool and its *parousia* into the "imposition of a definite form on reality." Throughout history, this temptation occurs in different guises. On the level of historical speculation, deformation takes the shape of a unilinear history assumed to culminate or reach its *telos* in the writer's conception—a type extending "from the Sumerian king-list to Hegel's imperial speculation." Where the assumption prevails that the divine beyond can he directly implemented in a given historical context, we are in the presence of what Voegelin calls "metastatic speculation"—an ideological outlook which (he says) has remained a constant down to "the metastatic faith-movements of the twentieth century." Where political crisis or calamity becomes particularly pronounced, metastatic belief gives way to "apocalyptic" thought which expects disorder of catastrophic magnitude to be "ended by divine intervention." Where such intervention is not forthcoming, apocalyptic thought in turn is supplemented or replaced by gnosticism, that is, a perspective which construes the state of the world or the cosmos as the result of a corruption or "psychodramatic fall" in the beyond, a condition to be reversed through human action based on a special "pneumatic understanding *(gnosis)*." Thus, alongside the search for truth and the attunement to its order, there runs through the centuries a "diversified history of untruth and disorder"—and even a story of "increasingly conscious resistance to beginnings" (as initiated by the It-reality). In conformity with this antagonism, Voegelin distinguishes between "resistance to truth" and "agreement or disagreement about the optimal symbolization of truth" and similarly between "resisters" or "deformers," on the one hand, and searching or "questioning thinkers," on the other. An extreme case of resistance is "revolt" or rebellion against the *metaxy*, a revolt directed either at "abolishing reality altogether and escaping into the Beyond" or at "forcing the order of the Beyond into reality"—the latter alternative being the preference of modern gnostics.[8]

Both the search for truth and resistance against it are experiential occurrences in consciousness nurtured by the power of imagination. According to Voegelin, imagination is not solely a human faculty but part of the larger *metaxy* or of the consciousness-reality-language framework; in this sense one may say that "through the imaginative power of man the It-reality moves imaginatively toward its truth." Ultimately, the difference between genuine search and resistance can be traced to the stance adopted by consciousness and its imaginative strivings: a stance which is either self-assertive and anthropocentric or else reflectively seasoned, that is, marked by "reflective distance" and by "remembrance" or recollection of the structure of the *metaxy*. In Platonic thought, the attitude of reflectively distancing remembrance was symbolized as *anamnesis;* on the other hand, forgetfulness or oblivion of being was expressed by the symbol *anoia,* conventionally translated as "folly." The man or resister afflicted with *anoia*—or with the Ciceronian *morbus animi*—is one who does not recall his role as a "partner in the community of being" and as a consequence transforms his searching participation into sheer "self-assertion." Against this background, imagination assumes the status of a "third dimension" of consciousness (alongside intentionality and luminosity) manifesting itself either in reflective remembrance or oblivion. As Voegelin writes: "When a thinker, whatever his motives may be, forgets his role as a partner of being," he "can deform the remembered assertive power of imagination in his quest imaginatively into the sole power of truth. Imaginative remembrance of the process, the remembrance intended by Plato, implies the potential of imaginative oblivion."[9]

The second part of the volume is an excursus in the history of philosophical thought, with the focus initially being placed on German idealism. In Voegelin's account, German philosophy of the time was in large measure a countermove to the "deformation of consciousness" brought about by traditional metaphysics and especially by the habit of thinking "in terms of thing-reality"—a habit reinforced by the success of modern natural science and its (partial) legitimation through Kant. As an antidote to this deformation, German thought—starting with Fichte's "System of Science"—turned to the constitutive role of consciousness, and particularly to the transcendental self-constitution and self-identification of the "I" through an act of "intellectual intuition." In this manner, Voegelin notes, consciousness was essentially cast in the mode of intentionality—to the virtual exclusion of its existential-ontological underpinnings; eclipsing the structure of the *metaxy*, a "nonparticipatory" type of intentionalism tended to usurp the "authority of participatory consciousness." As he reminds us, this usurpation was part of a larger historical upheaval manifesting itself concretely in the American, French, and Dutch revolutions; endorsing this upheaval, German philosophy derived much of its élan from the sense of "participating in a world-historic revolution of consciousness." What emerged from this revolutionary ferment was a speculative outlook emphasizing subjectivity and subjective self-constitution—an outlook commonly called "ego philosophy" or "identity philosophy," and which from Voegelin's vantage is a new and aggravated type of self-assertive deformation. In his words: "A solidly detailed, historically knowledgeable, comprehensive attack on symbols that have lost their meaning" succumbed in German thought to deformation "through the desire to dominate in the mode of thing-reality over the experience recovered." His own category of "reflective distance" is introduced precisely in order to distinguish his approach from the "symbolism of reflective identity" favored by German idealist philosophy.[10]

The most glaring example of "identitarian" deformation, in Voegelin's view, was Hegel, to whom a long section of the volume is devoted. Relying mainly on the "Preface" and "Introduction" to the *Phenomenology of Spirit*, Voegelin castigates Hegel's replacement of existential tension by the attempted construction of a "scientific system" and his substitution of "absolute knowledge" for "love of knowledge." What these changes signaled, he states, was basically the "abolition of philosophy" accomplished through the exclusion of the "experience of existential consciousness, of existence in the tension of the *metaxy*." This exclusion casts its shadow also on Hegel's dialectic of consciousness, especially on the movement from "first order" to "second order" objects (as outlined in the "Introduction"). As Voegelin comments: "The new object does not arise as a new external object, but through a 'turning around of consciousness' "—a turning or *Umkehrung* which Hegel also describes as "our addition" *(unsere Zutat)*. While recognizing a broad affinity between this turning and Plato's *periagoge* (of the prisoner in the cave), the volume denounces Hegel's description as basically vitiating the affinity: If we look "for the light shining from the Beyond that forces, directly or through a mediator, the prisoner to turn, we receive instead the information that the *periagoge* is *unsere Zutat,* our addition or addendum. The *periagoge* is not an assertive response but a self-assertive action." By excluding the higher light Hegel is said to rely only on "natural" consciousness or on *"natürliche Erkenntnis* in its deformative application to the It-reality." While assertively taking charge or control of the *periagoge,* Hegel's account is claimed to transform or "transmogrify" the light from beyond into a mere external compulsion, into "a *Notwendigkeit,* a necessity that operates behind the back of the prisoners' consciousness and forces 'us' to produce one propositionally deformed, intentionalist shadow in the Cave after another." Seen from this angle, Hegel's presentation in the *Phenomenology* emerges as "so unbelievably grotesque that one hardly dares to put it into plain language: Plato's work of a lifetime in exploring the experience of the quest, of its human-divine movements and countermovements . . . —this overwhelmingly conscious drama of the quest, this reality of consciousness and its luminous symbolization in a philosopher's existence, is excluded from the 'experience of consciousness' and relegated to an unconscious 'necessity' behind Plato's back."[11]

In seeking to explain Hegel's idealist deformation or "imaginative oblivion," Voegelin returns to the progressive-revolutionary climate of his age, particularly to the "modern, Protestant principle" of placing the "world of intellect into one's own mind"—a principle which, in Hegel's case, contained or comprehended a variety of "hermetic, apocalyptic, gnostic, and Neoplatonic strands" of speculation. What was at the core of this mixture of strands was basically a "paracletic eschatology," namely, the vision of "a descent of the Spirit that will achieve what the Petrine and Pauline Christianities have not achieved: the ultimately salvational *Parousia* of the Beyond in this world"—a vision congruent with the self-assertive and activist mentality of modernity. In turn, what stands behind this modernist mentality is the steady obfuscation and oblivion of the divine sphere, the reduction of the term *God* to a "senseless sound"—a reduction which is the quintessence of modern agnosticism and the "authoritative expression of the God-is-dead movement that characterizes a period of Western modernity (now lasting for about three hundred years)." In Hegel's thought, the situation was complicated by his frequent references to *parousia* and the quasi-divine character ascribed to absolute knowledge—although, according to Voegelin,

parousia here was "libidinously deformed by Hegel's self-assertive speculation." More importantly, Hegel's identitarian outlook obscured the
role of remembrance and reflective distance by seeking to bring everything into actual cognitive grasp. As a result—we are told—insight into
the paradoxic structure of reality and history was "self-assertively
deformed into a 'thing' to be mastered"; similarly, the distancing remembrance opening the historical horizon became "the instrument of its
closure through the pretense that everything worth remembering about
the process of truth in reality had been remembered."[12]

In an effort to correct or reverse Hegel's deformed speculations, the
volume journeys back to earlier historical phases where the search for
truth can still be encountered in its "original, undeformed" shape—the
first stop being Hesiod's *Theogony*. In the opening lines of his poem,
Hesiod invokes and praises the Heliconian Muses as the divine mediators of the truth about reality as a whole. In Voegelin's words: "The poet
experiences the truth of reality as a divine Beyond, not to be grasped by
intentional consciousness in its *Ansich*, but to be mediated through the
Parousia of the Muses"; to this extent, truth is presented as an "existential, revelatory event" located in the *metaxy* of divine-human encounter.
As the daughters of Mnemosyne (remembrance) from her union with
Zeus, the Muses trace their origin to the Olympian or rather "Jovian
Beyond," and their task is to serve as mnemonic markers, reminding the
Olympians of their divinity. In Hesiod's usage, remembrance does not
recollect a dead past but a living presence encompassing past and future.
Basically, recollection here recalls the "presence of the Beyond" as it is
experienced and gains "the reality of its *Parousia* in the language of the
gods." As Voegelin indicates, however, Hesiod's poem was precariously
lodged at the edge of god-talk; pushing to the limit of available symbolization, he showed that "there are no gods without a Beyond of the
gods." Differently phrased: Hesiod's symbols were still "compactly
divine," without sufficiently distinguishing the experiential *parousia*
of the gods from "its Beyond" (despite hints pointing in this direction). Steps toward more nuanced differentiation were undertaken by
pre-Socratic thinkers and especially by Parmenides, the "self-described
knowing man *(eidos phos)*." In the Parmenidean attack on the Homeric-
Hesiodian legacy, Voegelin notes, the "divine Beyond as the eternal Now"
begins to become articulate on its own, while the "being" that was
previously predicated of all things *(ta onta)* turns into a "Being" which
is non-synonymous with things. Despite a lingering compactness of his
language, Parmenides had become aware of "the paradox of consciousness, of the tension between intentionality and luminosity, between
thing-reality and It-reality, as well as the complex of consciousness-

reality-language in its integrality." Hesitations and inadequacies of pre-Socratic thought were finally outstripped by "Socrates-Plato" with his fully differentiated symbolism of "*Nous*-in-*Psyche*-in-*Soma*," a symbolism combining and reconciling the eternal "beyond" with temporal "becoming" or "non-genetic being" with "non-being genesis" (the two poles being further supplemented by the third category of *"chora"* or space).[13]

The concluding section of the study is devoted to a detailed exegesis of Plato's *Timaeus* and its complex symbolization of reality and the cosmos. Pointing to the tensional character of the *metaxy*, Voegelin comments that in the *Timaeus* "reality is experienced as a tensional oneness in which the poles of the tension carry different weights of reality, while the tension between the poles has its own weight of constancy." He also notes certain "linguistic difficulties" arising from the tensional structure of the symbolization, difficulties which could (and to some extent did) induce Plato to resort to second-order and third-order formulations or metadiscourses in order to counter ontic reification or doctrinal congealment of his symbols. A case in point is the notion of space or *chora* indicating the "unsensed" framework in which all beings appear. Narrowly or reductively construed, the notion seems to impose on all reality, including the framework itself, the "mode of thingness." In Voegelin's view, however, this construal has to be completely rejected, for "it would transform luminous symbols, as they emerge from tensional experiences, into intentionalist concepts referring to objects," thereby destroying the "paradoxic structure" of the symbolization. Following Plato, Voegelin interprets space not as a thingly structure but as an attribute of "cosmos" which, as a non-thing and as the *"periechon* of all things," makes room for space and all its thingly ingredients. This, however, does not entirely resolve the issue of space, since the quest for truth, guided by It-reality, also is supposed to take "place" somewhere and in some sense. At this point, the volume takes recourse to the imagery of a journey in which thing-reality and its beyond are linked at least metaphorically. "The quest for truth as an event in cosmic reality," we read, "appears to be ultimately the 'place' at which reality reveals itself in its structural complexity of thing-reality and It-reality. The event of the quest is the 'place' at which the bodily located consciousness of man experiences itself both in its thingly existence, that is, as moving in the thingly tensions of order-disorder, and in its visionary existence, as a movement toward an unflawed order beyond the order that is flawed by the disorder of things."[14]

II

Having journeyed with Voegelin through the pages of his final book, the reader will not easily put it aside. Congruent with the tenor of a

participatory ontology, the study offers not an abstract doctrine but a
kind of experiential encounter—whose urgency and transformative quality steadily intensifies in the concluding discussion of the *Timaeus*.
Meant for posthumous reading, the reference to the "mysterious movement" from an "It-reality through thing-reality toward a Beyond of
things" acquires touching biographical connotations—quite apart from
showing an uncommon sensitivity for the depth of Plato's ontological
speculation. Generally speaking, the interpretation of *Timaeus* confirms
Voegelin as one of the finest and most subtle students of Plato in our
time—a distinction amply documented already in some of his earlier
writings on Greek thought. The analysis of the *metaxy* as a tensional
structure of order-disorder can readily be seen to have crucial philosophical as well as political-theoretical implications. Yet, beyond attesting to his exegetic competence, *In Search of Order* reveals Voegelin
as an important speculative thinker in his own right—as is evident in
his own efforts at symbolization which, in some cases, transgress the
Platonic model in their differentiated nuances. Voegelin is quite explicit
about the need to go beyond a mere replication of time-honored teachings. As he says at one point in the text, the problems surrounding the
"middle" are "not exhausted by the (Platonic) symbolism of the *metaxy*";
the reason for this fact is the continuing character of the creation story,
the aspect that "the middle in which we begin as Western philosophers
toward the end of the twentieth century, is not the middle in which the
authors of *Genesis* had to begin their story about 500 B.C., nor is it the
middle in which Plato developed his symbolism."[15]

In the context of contemporary philosophical discussions, Voegelin's
stance toward past formulations or traditional teachings might be called
"deconstructive"—although the term would hardly have found his favor.
Picking up another contemporary expression, his conception of a tensional structure devoid of linear beginnings can be described as non- or
"anti-foundational," in the sense of not being rooted in a substantive
arché or a constitutive subjectivity. This anti-foundational quality is
particularly evident in the concluding pages of the study devoted to the
question of final moorings. Might the Platonic "demiurge," Voegelin
asks, be viewed as the Archimedean point through which the tensional
structure of the *metaxy* could come to rest or reach its fulfillment?
Rejecting this option he insists that the demiurge is "not an absolute
either"; for his action is "experienced and symbolized as a complex of
tensions between formative, noetic order and non-formative space,
between a demiurgic will to create order and the 'necessary' obstacle of
chora that limits the creative will to thingness." Another way of suspend-
ing the tension and reaching stability might be found in the intimate

correlation and mutual inherence of the tensional poles of being and becoming, of *nous* and *chora*. Plato at one point considers this possibility, when he likens *nous* to the formative source or "father" of reality and becoming to its "mother"—so that the resolution of the tension might be found in their mutual offspring *(to ekgonos)*. Again, however, this symbolism provides no stable foundation because the offspring is precisely the witness and participating exemplar of the tensional *metaxy:* "Man, as part of the offspring, experiences himself not in a state of terminal paralysis but of existential movement, responsively inclined to the pull from either of the two poles"—where the polar dimensions include the "thingly Beyond" of the *chora* and the "divine Beyond" of the *nous*.[16]

The absence of foundations is closely related with Voegelin's distrust of closed philosophical systems and finished doctrines (especially doctrines nurtured by ideological-political ambitions). In this respect, his work follows in the footsteps of Bergson's rejection of closed in favor of open societies and worldviews, and more generally of existentialist deprecations of philosophical closure. In the new volume (and elsewhere), the distrust extends explicitly to theology seen as a doctrine about God or the gods. "All the gods," he writes in the section on Plato, "have to live under the pressure of a divine Beyond that endows them with their divine life while threatening to let them die from their compactness." Moreover, this tensional pressure is portrayed as a "constant in the history of revelation: neither will the gods disappear, nor will the Beyond let them live in peace." These and similar statements are likely to antagonize religious fundamentalists or literalists hostile to reflective distance—as happened in the case of earlier passages (such as the provocative phrase in *The New Science of Politics* that "uncertainty is the very essence of Christianity"). As Sandoz judiciously remarks: "That there is anything uncertain about their faith came as unwelcome news to dogmatic Christians who reacted angrily to the suggestion, both in 1953 and on later similar occasions." By pursuing the path of reflective meditation, Voegelin is liable to place himself on the wrong side not only of political ideologues and fanatics but also of religious dogmas and philosophical schools of thought. In the midst of the intense "dogmatomachy" of our age, Sandoz adds, Voegelin's attempt to recapture reflectively the experiential parameters of civilization made him in varying degrees "the adversary of all parties bent on success in the power struggle and the butt of their uncomprehending and uncaring obloquy when he would not be recruited to their causes."[17]

Distrust of foundations or foundational truth-claims, however, does not place Voegelin into the camp of agnostics or value-free empiricists.

Ever since his vindication of metaphysics in *The New Science of Politics*, Voegelin's work has stood as a challenge and counterpoint to all forms of positivism, reductive immanentism, and anthropocentrism. In fact, his emphasis on transcendence and the Beyond sometimes approximates his writing to contemporary counter-discourses stressing rupture, radical decentering, and alterity or heterology. Some passages in the new volume evoke the thought of Emmanuel Levinas—a writer not cited in its pages—particularly his conception of the imperative "call" of otherness. "The experiences of divine, formative presence," Voegelin writes, "are events in the *metaxy* of existence, and the symbols engendered by the *Parousia* express divine reality as an *irruption* of ordering force from the Beyond into the existential struggle for order." On other occasions, the volume's formulations carry overtones of negative or dialectical theology—though without any fixed doctrinal commitments. This is especially the case in the distinction between the divine Beyond and its manifestation or *Parousia* in experience. "The imaginative language of the gods," we read, "can express the presence of reality beyond its presence, but the symbolized *Parousia* of the Beyond does not dissolve the Beyond into its *Parousia* in the experienced tension." Thus, even when the divine reveals itself in symbols or in living encounters, "it remains the unrevealed divine reality beyond its revelation."[18]

Philosophically, Voegelin's arguments sometimes bear a resemblance to the depth exegesis articulated and practiced by Ricoeur and also to Gadamer's ontological hermeneutics. In many respects, however, his outlook seems to parallel most closely aspects of Heideggerian thought, especially the fundamental ontology expounded in *Being and Time*—though there are no signs of overt influence. Distinctly Heideggerian is the critique or decentering of subjective intentionality and the portrayal of human existence (or *Dasein*) as participant in the disclosure of being. Already the opening pages of *Order and History* developed this broadly existentialist theme, in opposition to purely spectatorial or epistemological postures. "Man, in his existence," we read there, "participates in being"—and this not in an optional manner as if it were an engagement "he could as well leave alone"; instead, "man's partnership in being is the essence of his existence, and this essence depends on the whole, of which existence is a part." Despite its traditional vocabulary (essence-existence), the passage evokes Heidegger's claim that *Dasein* is that mode of being for which 'being' is the central question. Similarly evocative are references to the "anxiety of existence" and the attack, in a later volume of *Order and History*, on the "subject-object dichotomy" which is said to be "modeled after the cognitive relation between man and things in the external world" but does not apply to the "event of an 'experience-articulating-itself'." Other themes familiar from *Being and Time* are the notion of historicity and the proposal of a destructive reading of traditional doctrines, predicated on the recurrent need for resymbolization of decaying symbol systems. Regarding the former notion, *In Search of Order* points to the close correlation of modes of temporality in the course of ontological participation : "The participatory story, if remembered in the present of existence, expands into the story of its past and future as the story of the relation between its 'presents'. .... I suspect that the much-discussed problem of 'historicity' has found, in Hesiod's Remembrance, an analytical symbol difficult to improve upon."[19]

Affinities or resonances of this kind, however, are not restricted to the period of *Being and Time*, but extend to later Heideggerian themes. Thus. the comments on Hesiod and Parmenides recall Heidegger's rehabilitation of poetic thinking and his exegesis of pre-Socratic texts—although for Voegelin Plato remains the paradigmatic classical philosopher. The story of Western metaphysics from Parmenides and Plato to the present is presented by Voegelin largely as a move from participation to self-assertion or from participatory to activist consciousness—an account which resonates with Heidegger's focus on the growing prominence of subjectivity and human technological mastery over nature. In light of the so-called overcoming of metaphysics, the observations in the new volume on the development of philosophy from Plato to Leibniz and beyond deserve careful attention and scrutiny. Equally suggestive and worth pondering are passages carrying overtones of an ontic-ontological difference—as, for instance, the statement that the *metaxy* expresses the experience of existence as located at the intersection or in the Between of thing-reality and Beyond-reality. Particularly striking are formulations reminiscent of some of Heidegger's later key thoughts, such as the 'fourfold' *(Geviert)* and the 'appropriative event' *(Ereignis)*. Thus, reflecting on the Platonic categories of *Nous-Psyche-Soma* and Being-Becoming-Space and their mutual interconnections, Voegelin notes that "we might arrive at tetradic complexes." At another point, the same conclusion is reached with regard to a particular feature of the structure of consciousness-reality-language which in some way "forces us to think in the mode of thingness," this feature being the "third, or fourth, 'kind of being', that is, the *chora,* space." The construal of the cosmic creation story in terms of a pre-ontological happening or "gift" letting the world be *("Es gibt")* is intimated in Voegelin's comments on the "comprehending symbolism of a Beyond, the *epekeina*" and on a "cosmic reality in which the quest for the truth of its order is an event."[20]

In my view, some of the most intriguing and thought provoking passages in the volume have to do with the character and status of language in the broader context of the *metaxy*. Attacking the fashionable reduction of language to an informational system or an instrument of communication Voegelin—as indicated—embeds language in the structural complex of consciousness-reality-language. "There is no autonomous, non-paradoxic language," he insists, "ready to be used by man as a system of signs when he wants to refer to the paradoxic structure of reality and consciousness." Like human existence language shares instead in the precarious quest for truth which yields luminosity but not univocal cognitive propositions. At a later point in the study the ambivalent status of language is said to be lodged at the crossroads of the sayable and the unsayable, of speech and silence. In the pursuit of truth, we read, the questioner's language reveals itself as "the paradoxic event of the ineffable becoming effable. This tension of effable-ineffable is the paradox in the structure of meditative language that cannot be dissolved by a speculative metalanguage." In its own way, language testifies to the intersection of the divine and the human, to the *metaxy* of immanent experience and its beyond: "In reflective distance, the questioner experiences his speech as the divine silence breaking creatively forth in the imaginative word that will illuminate the quest as the questioner's movement of return to the ineffable silence." In an unpublished manuscript entitled "The Beginning and the Beyond"—written some time before *In Search of Order*—Voegelin underscores the non-instrumental character of language and its irreducibly revelatory quality. After commenting on successive historical symbolizations of spiritual epiphanies, the manuscript arrives at a notion startling in the context of contemporary linguistics: namely, that of "the sacrality of a language in which the truth of divine reality becomes articulate."[21]

III

Having outlined some of the strengths and promising vistas of Voegelin's study, I need to add some qualifying remarks or afterthoughts—remarks intended not so much as stark objections than as questions or apprehensions congruent with the author's questioning disposition. First of all, in a minor key, I note issues of terminology or the chosen vocabulary. Here I find puzzling mainly the centrality assigned to consciousness in a work championing ontological participation. Given the prevalent usage of the term, this centrality seems to insert the study into the context of the modern philosophy of consciousness (or of subjectivity)—an outcome antithetical to Voegelin's ontological concerns and (partially) forestalled by the distinction between intentionality and luminosity. Regarding the latter distinction, additional qualifying comments are in order. It is not so much from the vantage of a concretely embodied consciousness that reality assumes the quality of thingness or of an object intended but rather from that of a transcendental consciousness (in Husserl's sense). Conversely, the insertion of embodiment into an on-going happening does not yield a reductive empiricism, nor a new transindividual reality of which consciousness would be a predicative event. In these and other respects, Voegelin still seems to me too closely wedded to the subject-object dualism and its analogues or corollaries. Terminologically confusing along similar lines may be the distinction between thing-reality and It-reality—particularly in view of Martin Buber's well-known juxtaposition of 'I-Thou' and 'I-It' relations (where It has the character of thingness). Moreover, used in tandem with the stability of the thing-world, it-reality readily acquires unwarranted connotations of compactness (a point to which I shall return).[22]

What surfaces behind these terminological quandaries is a more troublesome issue beleaguering *In Search of Order* (and all of Voegelin's work): namely, the bent to think in dualities and (occasionally) to distend the tensional *metaxy* in favor of self-contained polarities. Dualisms of various sorts are a recurrent feature in the volume, as has repeatedly been noted before. Thus, in addition to the opposition between thing-reality and It-reality, we find the dichotomies of things and non-things, of intentionality and luminosity, of narrative and event, of order and disorder, immanence and transcendence, thinkers and resisters. To be sure, recourse to dualities is not by itself problematic; however, to maintain a tensional structure the poles of the structure must somehow interact or interpenetrate—which militates against their strict conceptual segregation. A case in point is the relation between things and non-things. For, if It-reality is not simply populated by non-things (or nothing) and if it is supposed to manifest itself somehow in the thing-world, then thing-reality itself cannot simply be composed of reified objects—a consideration which throws into jeopardy the received conception of things or at least raises thinghood into a question. This state of affairs is obliquely recognized by Voegelin when he refers to Plato's argument "that 'the divine' cannot be discerned by itself alone; there is no participation in 'the divine' but through the exploration of the 'things' in which it is discerned as formatively present." To which Voegelin adds ambiguously: "The thing-pole of the ultimate mystery, thus, is not itself a 'thing' but a tensional kind of being, responsive to noetic order but imposing the mode of thingness on the Cosmos." Generally speaking, the volume would have benefitted from a more explicit discussion of things and non-things, of presence and absence in their relation to different levels of reality. Short of this, one would have wished the author to adhere more rigorously to his own insight that "none of the single tensions, or any of their poles, is an absolute entity given to an external observer."[23]

These observations are directly relevant to the distinction between intentionality and luminosity, where the former relates to intended objects or things; they also affect the opposition between narrative and event—where narrative (obscurely) "refers to reality intended in the mode of thingness." Easily the most crucial, but also the most difficult and problem-laden distinctions are those juxtaposing order and disorder, truth and untruth, immanence and transcendence. Ever since the time of his earlier writings, Voegelin has tended to identify modernity with secularization and the latter with a progressive immanentism of world-views. Reacting against the "immanentization of the eschaton," he stated in a letter of 1943 explicitly that the "decisive problems of philosophy" are "problems of transcendence"—a view he maintained through the years. While valuable as an antidote to positivism, however, deprecation of immanence is fraught with quandaries. If Plato's argument (cited above) is correct that the divine cannot be discerned separately but only through its formative presence in the world or the cosmos, then the dividing line between immanence and transcendence becomes blurred, giving way to a peculiar intersection. Differently phrased: formative presence or *parousia* must and can only happen on the level of immanence—where the latter is no longer simply the opposite of transcendence. Again, this state of affairs is acknowledged by Voegelin in some passages—which, however, tend to remain on the level of *obiter dicta*. Thus, although repeatedly referring to "external" things or to the "body" as an entity in the "external world," he admits at one point that terms like "external" or "transcendent" only make sense in connection with something "internal" or "immanent." "Such terms as immanent and transcendent, external and internal, this world and the other world, and so forth," he writes, "do not denote objects or their properties but are the language indices arising from the *Metaxy* in the event of its becoming luminous for the comprehensive reality, its structure and dynamics. The terms are exegetic, not descriptive."[24]

These considerations also seem to apply to the opposition between order and disorder, truth and untruth, and likewise between (truthful) thinkers and resisters. By its very title, *In Search of Order* tends to place a premium on order or orderliness in contradistinction to disorder, chaos or anarchy. This preference was still more prevalent in earlier volumes of *Order and History*, guided by the assumption that the history of order could be traced through clear developmental stages of symbolization (an assumption later seen as too simplistic). Even the new volume at points endorses a simple dichotomous scheme of preferences. "The quest for truth," we read, "is a movement of resistance to the prevalent disorder; it is an effort to attune the concretely disordered existence again to the truth of the It-reality." At other points, however, the complexity of the quest and the non-doctrinal status of truth disturb or disorient the preferential hierarchy. As Voegelin notes in his comments on the *Timaeus*, the "paradox of order-disorder" seems to attach to "existence in the mode of thingness." But, he adds, "if it attaches to thingness, can there be an order of 'things' free of disorder? Or would the establishment of true order require the abolition of things?" The same disturbance affects the binary opposition of truth and untruth—where the quest for the former implies resistance to the latter—making room instead for a closer correlation of "formative truth and deformative untruth," as Voegelin admits in one instance. Clearly, if passages of this kind are taken seriously, doubts arise regarding the clear-cut bifurcation between questioners and "deformers" (or resisters) or between "resistance to truth," on the one hand, and "agreement or disagreement about the optimal symbolization of truth experienced," on the other. Struck by the polemical tone of the distinction, the reader may wonder apprehensively whether queries addressed at *In Search of Order* are liable to be branded a sign of resistance or else be admitted as legitimate questions in a broadly structured Socratic dialogue.[25]

The issue of order and disorder, of formation and deformation, is closely connected with the general philosophical problem of unity and multiplicity, of sameness and otherness—a problem which is at the heart of Plato's *Timaeus*. Not unexpectedly, the privileging of order over disorder is matched here by a similar set of priorities. In Voegelin's presentation, order is largely the work of the It-reality, of the attunement of "disordered existence" to the truth of the beyond. Although recognizing the latter's non-thingly status—its non-identity with any specifiable entity—the volume basically endorses the oneness of cosmos and order (thus encouraging at least implicitly its congealment into a stable-univocal ground). The notion of a possible plurality of It-stories is blandly dismissed as "senseless," with the argument that we experience only one "comprehending reality" beyond the mode of thingness. At another point, the Platonic cosmos is explicitly construed as unitary or holistic. "The paradigm of the *zoon*, of the living order of reality, is One," we read. "The phantasy of multiple 'worlds' is incompatible with the experience of the It-reality and, inversely, a reality which engenders a consciousness of itself both intentional and luminous can be only One.

Accordingly, the Platonic cosmos is described as *monogenes*, a perfect reflection of the *monosis* of the divine paradigm. Statements to this effect do not prevent Voegelin from introducing important qualifications, such as the qualifying remark that the oneness at issue here is "not numerical, but the experienced oneness of existential tension." More crucially, he observes, oneness should not be confused with monotheism in a theological-doctrinal sense. "Can this oneness of divine reality, revealed by the *fides* of the one, comprehending cosmos," he asks, "be truly symbolized by a numerically One God ... ? Can the problem indeed be reduced to the generally accepted, numerical cliché of 'monotheism' and 'polytheism'? Would the numerical cliché not reduce the One God to the same rank as his more compact, many confreres and expose him to the same noetic questioning of his divinity as the others?" These considerations lead Voegelin to ponder a possible tension in the divine, a distinction between the "god of the Beginning" and the "god of the End"—and ultimately to the thought of "an *Ungrund*, or a *Gottheit* beyond the God of dogmatic theology."[26]

Paralleling Plato's *Timaeus*, Voegelin's volume (despite its incompleteness) represents a unified-holistic structure—whose individual facets or details need to be viewed in light of its broader metaphysical-ontological concerns. One such facet which deserves at least brief attention is the treatment of prominent philosophers and leading figures in the history of ideas. In view of the numerous affinities noted above, the cursory allusion to Heidegger in the text—stressing his National-Socialist episode—seems unhelpful as well as ungenerous. Heidegger's thought, one should add, is placed by Voegelin in tandem with Marxian materialism or economism, with both variants being classified as overt deformations of truth: both the former's nationalist populism and Marx's reliance on *Produktionsverhältnisse* are portrayed as mere "games played with the symbol 'Being'," after that symbol had lost its status in the *metaxy*. By comparison, however, references to Marx are more hostile and vituperative. Among the followers of Hegel, particularly the Left Hegelians, we are told, imaginary speculation progressively took the place of experiential reflection; in the end, questions concerning "the structure of the speculator's own consciousness" and concerning "the truth it embodied" were shunned and even prohibited: "This last requirement, necessary to protect the speculative efforts against all-too-obvious questions, was raised to the rank of an explicit postulate by Karl Marx." The passage is not further elucidated in the text. However, the reader is familiar with the so-called postulate under the label of the *prohibition of questions* (by Marx), a claim articulated by Voegelin in some of his earlier writings. Unfortunately, the alleged prohibition is backed up there only by reference to a passage in *Economic and Philosophical Manuscripts*—a passage which does not in any way curtail or prohibit questioning but rather suggests that concrete questioning is possible only in the context of an existing world, not from an external Archimedean point (a view not too alien to a participatory ontology). As it seems to me, the claimed prohibition marks a descent into ideological polemics, into the very dogmatomachy from which Voegelin otherwise seeks to rescue us so valiantly.[27]

Among modern philosophers, none is discussed more extensively and also less judiciously (I believe) than Hegel. Perhaps it is the very proximity between Hegelian dialectics and the history of order which prompts critical distantiation in this case. My concern here is not to vindicate Hegelian philosophy in all respects, but only to caution against a simplified or reductive exegesis. Clearly, some of Voegelin's points are well taken, and deserve to be pondered by friends and critics of Hegel alike. This is particularly true of the project of absolute historical knowledge, a project in which every context or horizon would become rationally transparent and amenable to propositional formulation. As Voegelin observes, Hegel went astray in construing being as a subject that "unfolds its substance in the historical process 'dialectically' until it reaches its *eschaton*, its end, in fully articulate conceptualization of its self-consciousness." With a focus on language, a similar argument can be made: that the effable-ineffable tension resists being resolved through a speculative metalanguage "of the kind by which Hegel wanted to dissolve the paradoxic 'identity of identity and non-identity'." Beyond this absolutist and metalinguistic bent, however, Hegel's philosophy is too richly nuanced and circumspect to succumb readily to critical charges, especially charges of a polemical sort. Thus, the charge of an oblivion of remembrance seems farfetched in the case of a thinker whose image of philosophical reflection was the "owl of Minerva." Similarly, the linkage of Hegel with the later death-of-God movement strikes me as implausible—given the metaphysical structure of his thought which has rightly been described as an "onto-theology." (The phrase *senseless sound* occurs in a passage narrowly tailored to questions of concept-formation.) The linkage with modern agnosticism is particularly puzzling in view of the simultaneous ascription to Hegel of a variety of speculative-pneumatic traits, including Protestant, neo-Platonic and gnostic leanings—the last term being most liberally used throughout the text (so liberally, in fact, as to obstruct careful exegesis).[28]

Easily the most dubious or questionable passages of the text occur in the section dealing with Hegel's *Phenomenology of Spirit*. According to Voegelin, Hegel was guilty of immanentizing human experience and

of restricting the latter to "*natürliche Erkenntnis* in its deformative application to the It-reality"—a restriction which perverted *periagoge* into a
product of self-assertive action; simultaneously (and not very consistently), *periagoge* or *Umkehrung* is also said to be the work of external
compulsion, of a necessity operating beyond the range of consciousness.
These claims, I believe, are untenable both singly and in combination.
The stress on *natürliche Erkenntnis*, first of all, neglects that Hegel's
Phenomenology portrays the path of experience as leading from "natural" to "real" or "absolute" consciousness, both stages or dimensions
being modes of human consciousness. As depicted by Hegel, this path of
experience—far from being smooth (or immanent)—is arduous and
punctuated by a rupture; for this reason the path is also called a "path
of despair" or a *via dolorosa* (and "real" consciousness the "golgotha" of
experience). The rupture is thematized by Hegel as a "turning around
of consciousness" or *Umkehrung*, and the latter is termed "our addition" *(unsere Zutat)*—not because it can be fabricated self-assertively,
but because it cannot happen without our participation (a participation
which consists precisely not in self-assertion, but in a kind of "letting-be,"
namely, in letting the *parousia* occur). At the same time, what propels
or compels the *Umkehrung* is not some external power—and certainly
not the unconscious force suggested by Voegelin (in a truly grotesque
interpretation)—but the movement of real or absolute consciousness as
it affects and undermines self-certainty, that is, the complacency of
natürliche Erkenntnis. As Heidegger writes, in his own exegesis of Hegel's
"Introduction": "Our contribution wills the will of the absolute." Thus,
"the reversal of consciousness does not add to the absolute any self-
assertive supplement on our part. Rather, it restores us to our nature or
being which consists in our standing in the *parousia* of the absolute."
To which he adds: "If the reversal as our contribution is the fulfillment
of our essential relation to the absoluteness of the absolute, *then our
being belongs itself into the parousia of the absolute*."[29]

5

POSTMODERNISM AND POLITICAL ORDER

... auch noch im kommendsten Wind
atmen wir Abschied.

Rilke

Discussions of contemporary Western culture sometimes carry the flavor of a postscript or epitaph. Adopting the dispassionate stance of the ethnologist or archaeologist, observers occasionally survey Western traditions like the remnants of the *forum Romanum*. To some extent, the archaeological posture is reflected in the adopted terminology—especially in the flurry of hyphenated or composite terms from post-structuralism and post-metaphysics to post-industrial society and postmodernism. Taken in a literal sense, these composite terms suggest a temporal exit from or leap beyond inherited intellectual frameworks and socio-cultural ways of life. Thus, post-metaphysics (or the overcoming of metaphysics) is sometimes heralded as inaugurating the end of philosophical reflec-

tion, just as post-humanism has been greeted as marking the disappearance or definite "end of man" (in the Western sense). In a similar manner,
postmodernism—defined as farewell from the guiding metanarratives
of the past—appears as a radical alternative or antipode to the central
characteristics of modernity, including the features of analytical rationality, ethical-political responsibility, and the rule of law; couched in
Nietzschean vocabulary, the term signals (or seems to signal) a move
from Apollonian sobriety and order to a Dionysian delight in spontaneity and anarchical chaos. Recoiling from the intellectual and political
perils of this move, defenders of modernity—foremost among them
Jürgen Habermas—have been quick to denounce postmodernism as a
synonym for irrationality and nihilism and, in any case, as incompatible with the standards of the modern discourse.[1]

Seen as a simple epilogue or aftermath, postmodernism curiously
cancels itself or vanishes from view: inserted into a temporal sequence
or periodization, the term still pays homage to a (modernist) theory of
progress (or else a theory of regress and decay). As it seems to me, one of
the chief requisites for grasping its meaning is to extricate the term
from a linear progression of phases and to view it as expression of simul-
taneity or an intersection of elements.[2] Instead of designating a serial
succession or juxtaposition, postmodernism under these auspices signals rather an event or disturbance within modernity itself—an event
which has the earmarks of a quasi-spatial topology: rather than heralding
a new annex or structural addition, postmodernism resembles more the
discovery of a forgotten chamber or hidden staircase within a rambling
architectural structure (which is the structure of modernity). Far from
denoting—as Habermas claims—a simple transit from rationality and
responsibility to irrationalism, the prefix *post* has the significance more
of a dash or incision (or wound), pointing to the non-rational side or
component of rationality, to the unknown (or unknowable) within the
known. From this perspective, the relation between reason and unreason—
and also between modernity and postmodernism—has the character neither of coincidence nor of antithesis and simple negation, but rather of
a chiasm or threshold—an elusive margin or boundary penetrable from
both sides. In the present pages, I want to explore this aspect by concentrating on a contemporary thinker who is pre-eminently a thinker of the
margin or threshold: the German philosopher and social theorist Bernhard Waldenfels, and especially on his recently published book *Order at
Twilight (Ordnung im Zwielicht).*[3]

In the case of Waldenfels, marginality is not simply a topical
concern: in the context of German philosophy, his thinking has always
moved along the margins of mainstream traditions, including the tra-

ditions of neo-Kantianism and neo-Hegelianism. One of his chief sources of inspiration has been Husserlian phenomenology—a legacy nearly extinct in postwar Germany due to the interlude of fascism and the emigration of many phenomenologists to America. Within the confines of Husserl's corpus, Waldenfels has been attracted mainly to the later writings, that is, to the Husserl of the life-world (as articulated in *The Crisis of European Sciences*)—a concept destined to erode or marginalize the centrality of consciousness or subjectivity in modern thought. Next to the Husserlian opus, Waldenfels has been a keen and persistent student (and also translator) of the writings of Merleau-Ponty, the French phenomenologist whose later works revolved entirely around the notions of chiasm and a non-synthetic intertwining (of reason and non-reason, of visible and invisible). During the last decade, Waldenfels' inquiries have broadened beyond these phenomenological moorings in the direction of French post-structuralism and post-hermeneutics (or deconstruction)—a Francophile move which stands in marked contrast to the pervasive neglect of recent French perspectives in German academic philosophy. My presentation here will proceed in three steps. In a first section, I intend to give a condensed overview of Waldenfels' writings in a chronological sequence. The second section shall offer a synopsis of the main themes and arguments developed in *Order at Twilight*. By way of conclusion I shall finally venture some comments and critical afterthoughts, mainly in an effort to highlight or profile further the postmodern features of Waldenfels work.[4]

I

"Notre rapport avec le vrai passe par les autres"—this phrase from Merleau-Ponty stands as motto over Waldenfels' first major publication of 1971, entitled *The In-Between Realm of Dialogue (Das Zwischenreich des Dialogs)*. Printed as part of the prestigious "Phaenomenologica" series, the study was a broad-gauged and rigorous scrutiny of intersubjectivity or intersubjective relations from a phenomenological vantage, matching both in depth and coverage comparable studies by Theunissen and Schutz.[5] As indicated by the study's subtitle—"Social-Philosophical Investigations Inspired by Husserl"—Waldenfels' approach at the time was still strongly indebted to Husserl's framework while simultaneously seeking to overcome the "egological" (or egocentric) restrictions present in transcendental phenomenology. The linkage with Husserl was evident in the reliance on "intentional analysis" or the description and explication of experienced meaning—although such description was amplified or modified through attention to the historical genesis of meaning

contents. The linkage was also preserved in the details of the adopted methodology, particularly in the continued use of "bracketing" or *epoché*—a device which was now curtailed to the domain of intersubjective experience (bypassing the return to an absolutely "primordial" and "originary" selfhood). In general terms, Waldenfels' attitude toward Husserl was marked both by loyalty and dissent: that is, by faithfulness to Husserl's guiding intentions coupled with caveats regarding their actual implementation. Seeking to pinpoint this ambivalence, the study distinguished between a "consistent" and a "broken" (or porous) interpretation, the former wedded to the doctrinal unity of a work, the latter attentive to its incoherences and as-yet unexplored vistas. Opting for the second alternative, Waldenfels noted (in a revealing passage): "One does no favor to a philosopher by insisting at all costs on the internal consistency of his work; for, not infrequently, it is the weak and porous passages which keep a work alive by adumbrating a surplus of possibilities.[6]

In Waldenfels' view, a porous approach was particularly pertinent in the domain of intersubjectivity, especially to the extent that the latter was conceived as concrete "co-presence" or cohabitation mediated through embodiment and linguistic communication. In line with the status of humans as "in-between beings," the intersubjective realm required an open-ended or "intermediary" mode of analysis—a mode "equally far removed from a stance of pure interiority as from that of pure exteriority." In pursuing its inquiry, the study sought to differentiate itself from a number of competing perspectives: including the (orthodox) Husserlian strategy of subjective constitution; the sociological levelling of interaction into "inauthentic" role-playing or habitual performance; and the stylization of intersubjectivity into a unique personal encounter (after the model of Buber's 'I-Thou' relation). Deviating from these perspectives, Waldenfels took his departure from a "bipolar event," that is, from the "equal primordiality" of I and other (or ego and alter)—an event couched in terms broad enough to encompass both everyday and personalized relations. The unifying feature of the event was a common purpose or goal jointly pursued by participants and reciprocally endorsed through communication or dialogue. In his words: The theme of interaction is "an actual goal which claims us as jointly intended"; thus there arises "a *co-activity* against the background of a shared life which includes others as co-subjects" and in which dialogue functions as *"living medium."* Successive chapters of the study dealt with different modalities of co-presence or co-activity, ranging from "indirect" everyday interactions over personalized face-to-face contacts to the disruption of common endeavors through mutual antagonism and struggle —a disruption which still preserves its dialogical moorings in the need for mutual recognition and thus keeps open the path to reconciliation.[7]

In the years following the study on dialogue, Waldenfels wrote a number of essays or papers dealing from varying angles and with growing intensity with the intermediary or in-between status of human experience. In 1980 these essays were collected in a volume entitled *The Ambit of Behavior (Der Spielraum des Verhaltens)* which offered a glimpse into the author's evolving perspective or his thinking *en route*. In the title of the study, Waldenfels deliberately invoked the terminology of behavioral psychology—while radically transforming its meaning. In its traditional usage, "behavior" referred to empirically observable and measurable stimulus-response processes—a focus which prompted phenomenologists to retreat into the private-internal sphere of consciousness and intentionality. As Waldenfels noted, however, this bifurcation had been eroded in recent decades under the combined impact of such trends as Gestalt psychology, interactionism, and structuralist language philosophy. As a result of these developments, behavioral and social psychology had increasingly decided to make room "for the subjective digestion and transformation of stimuli, for the transcription of situations, and for the self-interpretation of speakers and actors." Conversely, philosophers had proceeded "to place 'consciousness' in the lower case, to treat it adjectivally and thus to reintegrate it into concrete behavior." What emerged from these converging tendencies was an "intermediary or mediating space *(Vermittlungsraum)* which escapes the old dualisms of inside and outside and of private and public domains." The new situation was particularly challenging and promising for phenomenological research—provided the latter was seen as open-ended inquiry and not merely as "an arsenal of fundamental doctrines or methodological devices." Referring to its complex intersection with structuralism, hermeneutics, critical theory, and Marxism, Waldenfels affirmed that "one cannot speak today of phenomenology without also mentioning these points of contact, because it is here—in the dialogue with spokesmen of other perspectives— . . . that phenomenology must prove its continued vibrancy and its ability to escape the peril of exegetic scholasticism."[8]

While the earlier work still carried distinct Husserlian overtones, *The Ambit of Behavior* showed the strong imprint of Merleau-Ponty as well as structural linguistics and semiotics. The opening chapter offered a detailed analysis of Merleau-Ponty's theory of human embodiment seen as our mode of insertion both in nature and the social world. Relying on Merleau-Ponty's insights, the chapter sketched a notion of human behavior located on an intermediary or in-between level, a level "where inside and outside interpenetrate and which forestalls the retreat into pure consciousness just as much as it does the reduction to physical mechanisms." The focus on embodied behavior was bound to affect and modify the phenomenological concern with intentional meaning: namely, by shifting the accent to concrete ongoing experience construed as both constituting and constituted, an outlook liable to restore to mundane things their "efficacy and recalcitrancy" vis-à-vis intentional designs. Embodied behavior, in Waldenfels' presentation, was closely linked with linguistic interaction and social communication. Drawing on structuralist and semiotic motifs, the study outlined a view of communication which tightly correlated performative speech with linguistic structures and anonymous language games—in a manner which countered the streamlining of language into a conveyer belt of intended meanings, thereby restoring to communication its ambivalence and density of texture. Attention to the rich, generative multivalence of language placed Waldenfels at odds with recent critical theory, especially with Habermas's notions of an ideal speech situation and of a communicative ethics governed by universal or universalizable norms. Summarizing the guiding themes of his study, Waldenfels singled out these: "selectivity and limited generalizability of intentional designs; differences which resist initial or final synthesis; . . . peculiar connections which are neither arbitrary nor necessary in character; conflicts which cannot simply be removed by rational arguments; shadows which do not adumbrate a future light; open modes of rationality which do not merely explicate what is but intimate novel surprises."[9]

By the time the discussed volume appeared, Waldenfels was already making resolute strides in the direction of French structuralism and post-structuralism, strides which were bound to loosen even further his ties with Husserl and the traditional philosophy of consciousness. A major expression of this incipient turn was his book on *Phenomenology in France (Phänomenologie in Frankreich)* published in 1983—a work which, in its broad erudition and subtle exegesis, constitutes a major access route to French philosophical developments in our century (at least for non-French readers). Noting the resistance frequently encountered by French ideas abroad, Waldenfels subtly shifted the burden of proof: "If newer texts from France sometimes seem all-too mysterious to foreign readers," he wrote, "this may be due to the fact that the receiving antennae or resonance fields are too narrow or unelastic." According to the study, a major and perhaps *the* dominant strand in twentieth-century French thought has been phenomenology—a circumstance which enabled the phenomenological movement to survive and find new fertile soil after its banishment from Nazi Germany. In tracing the development of the French variant, the opening chapter of the study offered a detailed account of the "phase of reception," a phase during which phenomenology was "naturalized" in France and in which it had to accommodate itself to a number of competing perspectives, including the Cartesian, the Hegelian, and the Marxist traditions. The bulk of the study was then devoted to the "productive phase" of the movement, that is, the formulation of powerful indigenous vistas, including Sartre's philosophy of 'radical freedom,' Merleau-Ponty's ontology of 'incarnate meaning,' Levinas's treatment of ethics as 'first philosophy' and Ricoeur's textual and symbolic hermeneutics. Following an overview of the repercussions of phenomenology in the human sciences—from historiography to psychology and psychoanalysis—the book concluded with a discussion of contemporary trends, especially the challenges posed for phenomenology by structuralist and post-structuralist arguments.[10]

For present purposes, the most revealing passages of the study are contained in Waldenfels' concluding comments. In retrospect, he observes, the entire development of French phenomenology can be seen as a steadily intensifying critique and erosion of the foundational status of consciousness and intentionality. This critique was already inaugurated in the early works of Sartre and Merleau-Ponty: "The transformation of transcendental into existential phenomenology meant a growing *concretization of the subject;* with this transfer of the center of reference the *contingency of any mundane and social order* comes to the fore." However, the implications of this contingency were not fully pursued at the time; even Merleau-Ponty's notion of embodiment involved only a "half hearted" decentering of the subject. For "is the body only the heir of transcendental subjectivity, or is it rather the threshold of a complex structure, of a rule-governed process and a dynamic which really dislocates the centered subject?" Contrary to popular misconceptions, Waldenfels views structuralism basically as a further deepening or radicalization of tendencies latent in phenomenology during recent decades. "In contrast to all anti-phenomenological slogans," he writes, "one can plausibly claim that the newer theories achieve their greatest density or power wherever their spokesmen maintain the link with phenomenology—instead of succumbing to a renewed scientism of fixed codes or else to the pure spontaneity of desire." The link with phenomenology was particularly pertinent with regard to the so-called obsolescence or end of man. According to Waldenfels, this end referred validly to man as the fountain of certainty, as the foundational warrant of intellectual and social order. Instead of inaugurating anarchic chaos, however, anti-foundationalism rather demanded renewed reflection on the viability of contingent order. "An order which is no longer solely constituted by consciousness," we read, "requires a *transformation of the subject*—in the sense that 'man' is no longer . . . the carrier of meaning, and order is no longer a meaning obeying subjective intentions."[11]

A first sustained effort to explore these implications—that is, the problem of contingent order—can be found in a study of 1985 entitled *In the Web of the Life-World (In den Netzen der Lebenswelt)*. From different angles the essays collected in the volume all revolved around the status of the life-world seen as a contingently structured order—but an order not equivalent to randomness. As befitted the theme, the study took its point of departure from formulations contained in Husserl's later writings—formulations which, while probing beneath the objectivism of scientific knowledge, portrayed the life-world basically as a source of meaning unifying in a rationally intelligible manner different cognitive and practical pursuits. Questioning this portrayal, Waldenfels pointed to the diversity of historical and cultural practices and also to the internal porousness of life-forms—features which no longer permit their subsumption under a "unified teleology of reason." In lieu of traditional totalizing aspirations, reason on the life-world level disaggregates into concrete "meaning fields" and discontinuous rationalities—thus bringing into view the groundlessness or "abyss of meaning," though not in the sense of a simple irrationalism but of a concretization of reason attentive to the need of the continuing production and reproduction of order: "What is needed here is a preservation of differences, a tolerance for ambiguities, and at the same time a resistance to forced unity." From Husserl the path of the study led to Merleau-Ponty and his peculiar interlacing of meaning and structure. Alerting again to the internal tensions in Merleau-Ponty's posture, Waldenfels observed: "It is instructive to see how—after initial ambiguities deriving from a not fully abandoned philosophy of consciousness—phenomenology is radicalized in this case: the impact of the *être brut* or *être sauvage* pushes the phenomenology of the life-world toward its limits or margins." What happens at this limit is a disjuncture of meaning, a process "akin to what Foucault labeled *dispersion* and Derrida called *dissémination*."[12]

The second part of the study turned to the crucial issue of the rules or regulations governing the life-world, and also to the status of the life-world as source of practical-ethical norms. Reviewing Peter Winch's sociological theory (partly inspired by Wittgenstein), Waldenfels insisted on the open-ended character of social rules—the fact that rules can never be exhaustively specified, thus leaving room for something "unruled" and also for the productive change of rules. "There is something unregulated or untamed in the visible," he wrote, "just as the invisible and the unsayable are located not beyond the pale of the seen or said but inside them. . . . In every cultural work or cultural process there is a reservoir of the raw, unformed or undeveloped—a *sens sauvage* which does not simply wait for, nor retreat from rationalization, but keeps the process alive." Referring specifically to Habermas's theory of rationalization, Waldenfels criticized the privilege accorded in that theory to global rational structures or universal rational principles. Opposing Habermas's reduction of the life-world to a "preamble" of reason, the study appealed instead to the concrete or "material rationality" embedded in life-worlds or the variable "order of things"—an "embodied" and "multivalent" reason reflected in a "web or network of heterogeneous, yet variously linked, not mutually exclusive but intersecting fields of rationality." Regarding practical-ethical norms, Waldenfels pitted against the critique or exegesis of existing norms the aspect of the ongoing genesis or generation of norms, a genesis which is accomplished not by fiat but through concrete agonal struggles both within and between life-worlds—and especially through the encounter between the rule-governed and the unruled, between the normal and the abnormal, between the orderly and the extraordinary. The latter contest pointed again to the *sens sauvage* and to the margins of the life-world—a domain explored in the concluding portion of the study. Viewed from its margins, we read, the life-world appears as "an unfinished order which leaves room for otherness, for the extraordinary." Correspondingly, a non-global critique would be one attentive to the margins of experience—"the margins: that means the unsaid and unsayable within the said, the undone and undoable in what is done, the unregulated and unfamiliar in the regulated and familiar, the uncanny in everyday life."[13]

II

Order at Twilight develops further and pulls together many of the themes announced in the previous writings. Pensive in character and elegantly written, the study ponders anew the problem of a contingent human order, an order precariously lodged at the intersection of reason and non-reason, of culture and nature, of *sens commun* and *sens sauvage.* Taking his cues from a French expression for "twilight," Waldenfels portrays the threshold between nature and culture as an in-between space *"entre chien et loup,"* a space which is the peculiar habitat of human order—given that such order "never completely escapes its origins" and that thinking and being always retain "traces of a *pensée sauvage* and an *être sauvage."* What the study seeks to delineate is not a return to primitivism or a lapse into chaos, but rather the contours of a fragile "twilight order which enables by disabling, which delimits by excluding, and forms by deforming." In venturing into this terrain,

Waldenfels consciously leaves behind the customary precincts of Enlightenment thought as an affirmative conception of modernity—in the direction of an uncharted and exploratory postmodernism. "With the defenders of a 'broken' or fragmented modernity," he writes, "I share the view that the great, solid and all-embracing orders of the past are the work of an extravagant and domineering dream of reason which the modern subject seeks to recapture in vain."[14]

The opening chapter explores more closely the character of "order" and its location at the margin or threshold. Following classical definitions, order is portrayed as a "regulated or rule-governed (that is, non-arbitrary) correlation" of elements. Deviation from this correlation can take two forms: either violation of rules within a given order, or else externality to the rule system itself. In Waldenfels' words: "We must distinguish between the 'disordered' or disorderly in the sense of a rule violation governed by the binary matrix of an order, and a rule-less or unruled dimension on the other side of order which we may call the 'unordered'." Order from this perspective is always an act of ordering something rule-less or unordered. This ordering act can be performed by the cosmos itself (governed by a divine Chronos) or else it has to be the work of man—which happens, in Plato's terms, whenever "man is put on his own feet." With the emergence of man, a rift is opened between nature and culture, between the fixed constraints of the natural universe and the open-ended possibilities of human intervention. This rift, Waldenfels observes, cannot simply be bridged by evolutionary theory or the notion of a close-knit "chain of being," since already the first man was not merely a peculiar ape but an "undetermined animal"—an indeterminacy or ambivalence which increased with the development of language. Borrowing from Walter Benjamin, the chapter describes the rift as a "threshold" *(Schwelle)*—which is not a dividing line but rather a zone in which one can linger and which is interpenetrable from both sides; threshold experiences, we are told, permit exposure to otherness without merger or synthesis, thus maintaining an "asymmetry" between here and there. Building on the threshold image, Waldenfels proposes a mode of human or social ordering which is neither naturally preordained nor categorically superimposed in a totalizing fashion—a mode which is patterned on the structure of dialogue or the interchange of question and answer. Since in such an interchange questions are unplanned and there is usually room for multiple answers, dialogical ordering resists inductive or deductive closure, retaining instead the character of asymmetry and possible disjuncture. Acts of ordering, from this vantage, can be seen as "selective" (though not unsolicited) answers or responses in an agonal-dialogical exchange. Extending this argument from linguistic exchanges to concrete social interactions, Waldenfels arrives at the notion of a "responsive rationality" designating the type of order arising selectively from reciprocal challenges and provocations.[15]

The notion of selectivity gives rise in the second chapter to a review of different ways of patterning or arranging human relations. The starting point is the thesis, familiar from Wittgenstein, that words and deeds are contextually structured—with the result that, sequentially viewed, words insert themselves into speech patterns and deeds into narrative plots. On a synchronic level, Waldenfels adopts from Gestalt psychology and social phenomenology the concept of "field" as a structured correlation of elements. "Field," he writes, "is an internally structured, flexibly delimited domain of experience whose margins and coordinates point to varying internal positions; cognate terms are 'scene,' 'stage,' 'framework' (Goffman), or 'social space' (Bourdieu)." What is crucial is the distinction of "field" from empty space-time schemata of classical physics and also from a cosmic space-time order (grounded in nature). Within a field, elements are patterned selectively so as to give rise to prominent or dominant "themes"—a patterning that obeys not so much universal-rational criteria as rather considerations of importance, significance or "relevance." Instead of simply being a function of subjective interests or preferences, relevance has itself a contextual origin, in the sense that a theme may gain prominence by relating to a given background or to other competing themes. The accentuation or thematization of elements in a field regularly leads to the marginalization of other features—a process which can have serious social-political consequences. Moreover, the foregrounding of themes is closely connected with the structuring of "meaning" in a field, more specifically with the elevation of some elements to a general or generic significance through a process of "typification." "The *type*," we read, "is a temporalized essence. . . . The emergence of margins through thematization corresponds to the rise of the a-typical through typification." Turning from description to questions of evaluation, Waldenfels juxtaposes the standard of importance or "relevance" *(Wichtigkeit)* to the standard of moral "rightness" or correctness *(Richtigkeit)*—the former marked by attention to contingency, the latter by its strictly binary character. As he points out, the rigor of this binary opposition increases as one moves from ordinary everyday behavior to ethical and legal conduct—with the dualism of normality and abnormality giving way to the pair conventional/unconventional and finally lawful/unlawful. In every instance, standards are an expression of selectivity or selective ordering, an ordering restricting the range of possibilities and creating "between yardstick *(ought)* and ability *(can)* a rift akin to the asymmetry between challenge and response."[16]

Seeking to profile his approach further, Waldenfels in the following contrasts contingent-selective ordering with two alternative conceptions which have played a central role in traditional philosophy: the alternatives of a naturally ordered cosmos and of a universal order of reason (or imposed by reason). In the first conception—prevalent in antiquity and especially in classical Greek philosophy—the cosmos functions as a total frame of relevance to which all questions of right behavior are traced and subordinated. Relevance, Waldenfels notes, is "elevated here to the status of a *relevance per se* which coincides with goodness" and which reflects a "substantive or material rationality" inherent in nature. From this vantage, all elements are an integral part of the cosmic whole—an order which does not acknowledge competing patterns alongside itself but only the stark antithesis of chaos or disorder. The guiding yardstick of this order is proportional justice—the arrangement of equal and unequal parts—which is itself rooted in nature, specifically human nature. Various types of cosmic holism are discussed in the study, ranging from the purely contemplative stance of philosophers over the "lived holism" of traditional societies to the fabricated unity of totalitarianism. The second conception—prevalent in modern times—replaces the assumption of cosmic harmony with the formulation of universal-rational standards of rightness; the framework of "cosmic *disposition* gives way to an ordering through *practical imperatives.*" In this case, holism is achieved not on the basis of nature but through the generalization or universalization of rules and norms; rationally binding are those norms which are applicable to "all possible contexts and all possible agents." What is selectively excluded or marginalized by imperatives is not an a-cosmic chaos but the broad domain of the particular, subjective, and contingent—and above all, the dimension of concrete frames of relevance and their genesis. As Waldenfels adds, critiquing these two conceptions of order does not necessarily mean an endorsement of arbitrariness or of prevailing factual arrangements. Although all orders have a factual-positive side, positivity itself is selectively generated. The same consideration applies to the aspect of power—which is endemic to, though not synonymous with social order. The problem of reason and power (or of *pouvoir/savoir*) emerges, we read, "because our acting and speaking is a response to challenges"—in a context which is itself selectively structured and never fully or sufficiently grounded.[17]

The issue of grounding leads Waldenfels to an inquiry into the role of the subject as ultimate source or warrant of ordering processes. As he points out, reliance on such a role is a thoroughly modern phenomenon—unknown to the Greeks for whom the soul was simply a microcosm or a mirror reflecting the larger cosmic harmony. It was the erosion of this cosmic view which led to the search for a new grounding, that is, for a genuine *"hypokeimenon"* or *"subjectum"*—and which terminated in the conception of the human subject as the "epicenter" of the world. To serve in this capacity, the subject was cleansed of contingent particularity and stylized to an absolute *"ego cogito"* in the case of Descartes and, in Kant's case, to a pure or transcendental consciousness as warrant of cognition and as the author of 'pure acts' or acts deriving from 'noumenal freedom.' While appealing in its humanist pathos—Waldenfels notes—modern subjectivity had a number of dubious consequences, especially the rise of binary oppositions isolating the subject. Thus, the focus on pure or free acts led to the division between "action" and "passion" or passivity—the latter seen not as a reservoir of experiences but as simple limitation of activity. More importantly, subjectivity gave rise to the bifurcation between the "own" and the alien or between sameness and otherness; three types of otherness in particular were marginalized in modern thought: "the child, the savage, and the madman or fool." Marginalization in this context occurred on different levels: philosophically, "logocentrism" purged the system of ideas while, in practical terms, "egocentrism" legitimated possessivism and domination. According to Waldenfels, subjectivity cannot shoulder the role assigned to it in modernity: the infinite task" of grounding collides with the "finite means" available to subjects. Marshalling the resources of phenomenology, Waldenfels steers a course between action and passion, autonomy and heteronomy, agency and structure; Merleau-Ponty's notion of 'intercorporeity,' in particular, serves to reconnect sameness and otherness—without erasing their differences in a uniform blend. Instead of serving as secure anchor, the subject at this point figures at best as an intersection between same and other—and, in Freudian terminology, as the crossroads between 'id' and 'super-ego,' between *logos* and *pathos*.[18]

Absence of natural or transcendental grounding does not mean randomness or a complete lack of standards or yardsticks. As Waldenfels insists, however, such standards can be found (if at all) only in the ordering process itself or in close connection with it. In an effort to pinpoint the status of standards, the study differentiates between the genesis and the maintenance of order, that is, between creative or "productive" and "reproductive" processes or events. While, in an existing order, actions are measured against an established rule, genesis always involves a process of standardization or "measure-giving" *(Massgeben)*. In an emerging order, measures or standards arise simultaneously with the experiences they measure and thus may be called "operative standards" *(Masswerk)*; by contrast, established rules are detached from ongoing events and function as "measuring rods" *(Masstäbe)*. The functioning of standards differs in the two cases. Concrete operative standards play the role of "exemplars" or "paradigmata" which can be imitated or approximated to a greater or lesser extent; abstractly general rules, on the other hand, have the status of norms or precepts which yield binary effects (compliance/non-compliance). Both the genesis and the total framework of an order cannot be judged by internal rules—since this ignores the latter's production. Genesis itself, however—and this is a crucial point—escapes randomness since it does not proceed whimsically but in the mode of agonal responsiveness, where responses are triggered by "key" or "threshold events" modifying the parameters of experience. In the struggle between emergent and existing order, newness appears as "deformation" of established forms or as "deviation" from governing rules. Yet, innovation does not merely silence or push aside the past, but involves a creative struggle with tradition—thus bypassing the alternatives of traditionalism and modernism; by the same token, newness does not mean a radical fresh start, but rather immersion in a beginning which is always already taking place. Akin to the artist's work, the production of order from this perspective steers precariously between making and finding, between invention and discovery.[19]

By way of conclusion, Waldenfels returns to the conception of order as an ordering of the "un-ordered" or "un-ruled." This un-ordered, he emphasizes now, is not a primeval origin, but rather a continuing possibility constantly accompanying and transcending a given order. Every event or phenomenon in an order, he writes, occurs in a "broken form," in the sense that it is "simultaneously present and absent, itself and other, here and elsewhere": if it were completely present and itself, it could entirely blend into the order; if it were completely absent and other, it would not be a source of disturbance. This brokenness or ambivalence is ultimately due to the agonal structure of challenge and response, where the challenge or provocation always exceeds the response which remains selective in character. Thus a rift or rupture opens inside the dialogical exchange—though a rift which both links and separates. As Waldenfels points out, the un-ordered exceeds or transgresses a given order not simply by negating its arrangements but by inhabiting its margins. Just as the alien is the other side of the coin or the same the "extra-" or "super-ordinary" functions as the *"dehors"* of the ordinary or orderly— not as a vague "nowhere" or utopia, but rather as an "atopia arising from confrontation with a heterotopia." By the same token, transgression of order does not denote a complete exodus from all finite constraints, but rather a questioning of existing limits or boundaries—without a leap beyond (into dis-order or regression). What happens in transgression is not a denial of meaning but the unleashing of multivocity, of the 'polymorphism of wild being' (in Merleau-Ponty's terms)—exemplified in Surrealist adventures, in carnivalesque interludes, in laughter and tears. Philosophical reflection is not untouched by this dispersal. Instead of occupying a foundational or metaposition extricated from ambivalence, the philosopher commenting on these issues remains poised at the threshold; a marginal activity, reflection questions and unsettles existing discourses "like salt which does not replace but seasons meals."[20]

III

As should have emerged even from this condensed synopsis, *Order at Twilight* is a richly textured and challenging work—precisely in the sense of the challenge or provocation animating agonal dialogue. Like a provocative question, the study stirs up crucial issues in contemporary philosophical and social-theoretical discussions—including the issue of the status of philosophical discourse itself. In probing these issues, the book shuns definitive answers in favor of selective responses and tentative guideposts. Waldenfels' presentation does not proceed in a linear fashion—the manner of traditional philosophical argumentation; without lapsing into aphoristic fragmentation, the chapters of the study are arranged more like the movements of a musical suite, with each movement elaborating in a different key and with different accents on the theme of contingent order. In the following I want to lift up some of the most striking and philosophically innovative or constructive features of the study, and finally end with some critical glosses.

As indicated, one of the study's central motifs is that of agonal dialogue—a notion peculiarly blending communication and conflict. In centerstaging this notion, Waldenfels stakes out a position in ongoing disputes regarding intersubjectivity and social relations: a position lodged somewhere between, or at the crossroads of, a communicative rationalism stressing consensus and versions of post-structuralism extolling discord. In seeking to exit from traditional holistic frameworks, Waldenfels turns to horizontal modes of correlation and thus is led to see dialogue *(Gespräch)* as a structuring device of contingent order. However, countering harmonizing or consensual conceptions, the study accentuates the asymmetry between question and answer, between speaking and hearing—an asymmetry dramatically underscored by terms like "rupture" or "rift" *(Riss)* and "leap" *(Sprung)*. "If it is true," we read, "that every question opens up a field of possibilities and thus permits several responses and not only one, then there emerges a rift between question and reply. ... This rift pinpoints an insuperable 'And' of a peculiar kind, one which simultaneously links and separates; for a

given answer may meet the point of a question—but without thereby exhausting the possibilities and need of responding." As Waldenfels adds,
this rift or hiatus has the character of a threshold which both connects and
separates different domains of experience and which constitutes the space
or topology of the in-between where interlocution and interaction can
occur. Punctuated by a threshold, the relation between question and
answer or between domains of experience is not transitive or continuous:
"What lies between one 'province of meaning' and another is a leap, and
the hesitation on the threshold is precisely a hesitation before the leap."[21]

The motif of agonal exchange is applied beyond speech to the field
of practice or social interaction. Social and political theorists will find
particularly intriguing Waldenfels' reformulation or revamping of action theory—from an intentionalist model toward a more genuinely
"interactive" view. For purposes of capturing agonal exchanges, he
observes, traditional action theory offers little or no assistance—regardless
of whether action is seen as embedded in cosmic or anthropological
teleologies or whether (in more recent versions) psychological striving
and normative standards are segregated and only loosely juxtaposed.
Despite variations of detail, the basic structure of action theory has remained "remarkably homogeneous" from Aristotle over Hume and Kant
to the present; the central ingredients of the structure are these: the agent
"posits, discovers or pursues a goal," employs for this aim certain instruments or means, and takes into account concrete contexts, opportunities
and needs as well as the general framework of existing conventions or
norms. From this vantage, actions can be assessed in terms of their success
or efficiency, that is, their ability to reach a given goal or purpose; in
addition, they can be evaluated on the basis of their normative correctness
or their conformity with prevailing rules or standards. Approached in
this manner, action is absorbed into a comprehensive matrix of criteria:
"what is *objectively* given or achieved is differentiated from what is
subjectively wanted or intended, and both from what is *transsubjectively*
demanded"—with each facet being subject to binary judgments (efficient/
inefficient, need-fulfilling/need-frustrating, normatively correct/incor-
rect). Whatever escapes this threefold matrix of "efficiency, need and
norm," Waldenfels objects, "is in a radical sense *irrelevant*, indifferent,
a matter of accident, whim or discretion." Thus, between instinct and
reason, between need satisfaction and norm compliance, "between necessity from below and from above no room is left for an otherness which
could challenge or provoke us." Since everything that we encounter is
already captured by pre-established categories or criteria, "nothing really
happens *between the own and the alien*, for coordinated individual
actions do not yet constitute inter-action."[22]

In trying to elude traditional schemata, Waldenfels enlists the terms *stimulus* and *response*—but assigns to them an agonal-existential meaning rescuing them from the shallow determinism of behaviorist psychology. As he notes, the term *stimulus* covers a broad range of nuances and shadings, extending from impulse and inducement over attraction, enticement or allurement to exhortation, challenge and provocation. Once stimulus is allowed to regain the quality of allure or enticement, and affect the connotation of affection, the stimulus-reaction scheme begins to approximate the pattern of agonal exchange, that is, the asymmetrical relation of question and answer, of challenge and response. In Waldenfels' words, a stimulus resembles a dialogical question in its enticing but non-constraining quality; in Leibnizian terminology, a stimulus *"inclinat, non necessitat"* or, in Kant's formulation, it "affects but does not determine" human will. Thus, as in the case of interlocution, a rupture or rift opens up in the relation between action and reaction or responding action. The former—the triggering or initiating action—can be seen as an event or occurrence which "invites or prompts a certain behavior and points it in certain directions," but without definitively pre-empting future possibilities. On the other hand, a responding action is akin to a dialogical reply in that it links up with or takes its cues from a preceding statement—but does so in a selective and non-exhaustive manner. Departing from traditional categories or criteria, an agonal conception brings into view different ways of assessing actions and reactions—such as whether and to which extent a reaction matches or "meets" a given challenge, whether and to what degree available opportunities have been explored, and the like. Generally speaking, agonal exchange does not yield a stable concordance but only a continuous negotiation and renegotiation of the terms of interaction, always on a concrete, contextualized level. Following Merleau-Ponty, Waldenfels speaks in this respect of an "agonal bodily engagement or confrontation *(leibliche Auseinandersetzung)*."[23]

The accent on reciprocal engagement dislodges the primacy of intentionality characteristic of traditional action theory. Without being erased or yielding to determinism, subjective intentions occupy a subordinate or subsidiary place vis-à-vis concrete learning experiences (prompted through encounter with otherness). Highlighting the non-intentional quality of these experiences, Waldenfels refers in this context to interactive or interlocutionary events, that is, happenings which occur in the in-between space between challenge and response. In the case of direct confrontations he even uses the term "in-between event" *(Zwischenereignis)*, an expression accentuating even further this intermediary topology. "As in-between event," he writes, "I regard an occurrence or happening which takes its cues from something else, namely by responding to the latter's enticement or claim"—though not in a definitive or exhaustive fashion. The decentering of intentionality has as a corollary the erosion or weakening of traditional dichotomies, particularly the dualism of activity and passivity, of doing and suffering; since action participates in an ongoing event, doing always has an aspect of enduring. In Waldenfels' words: "The dualism becomes spurious at least at the point where action and passion demarcate an event which is seen first from the angle of the agent committing an act and next from that of the 'patient' to whom something is done. This one-sided input-output model leaves no room for question and answer and for the interlacing of statement and counter-statement." In modern (post-Cartesian) metaphysics, the dualism was typically invoked to buttress the priority of subjectivity over external phenomena, that is, the status of the agent as spontaneous author or causal instigator of purposive actions and social projects or programs.[24]

The linkage of action and passion finds a parallel in the correlation of past and future, tradition and innovation. According to Waldenfels, the event-character of history militates both against a placid traditionalism and against a total futurism or utopianism. In both instances, agonal engagement is suspended: in the first case by objectifying and stabilizing the past (or stylizing it into an unfolding meaning); in the second by extolling a newness unhinged from actual challenges or provocations. As he writes: "One can identify truth with the legacy of forefathers or else with the achievements of future generations. In the one case the old is endorsed as the old, in the other the new as the new; there we are under the sway of custom, here under the sway of fashion or (less ephemerally) of modernism." However, neither the old nor the new, neither the past nor the future can provide an ultimate or foundational warrant for contingent order. As Waldenfels adds, we can elude the stalemate of traditionalists and anti-traditionalists (or modernists) once we view tradition and innovation not under the auspices of legitimation or stabilization, but from the vantage of the ongoing agonal production or genesis of order. At this point, tradition emerges as "something with which we wrestle or labor, either for the sake of transformation and renewal, or for the sake of continuation and preservation"; even revolutionary rupture, as a mode of labor, pays its tribute to tradition or the past. What rescues engagement with the past from mere traditionalism is the absence of a linear evolution and also the existence of a plurality of traditions and of a plurality of emergent orders. On the other hand, innovation is not a purely spontaneous new beginning or *creatio continua*. The latter alternative is ruled out by the fact that innovation is embedded in an event-like process, a happening in which primeval beginnings (or *Urproduktion*) are already absorbed and dispersed into diverse modes of renewal. Since the process of ordering "has always already started," we read, "every invention assumes aspects of a recollection, every creation features of a re-creation. ... The presupposed *Urproduktion* belongs to a prehistory which cannot be located on the temporal axis of earlier and later: it is a dawn which happens not earlier but *now;* which does not belong to an infantile past but is a process of constant renewal in which newness erupts *'as on the first day'.*"[25]

As can readily be seen, the focus on event involves a critique of traditional teleologies and a Hegelian philosophy of history (as well as a Hegelianized hermeneutics). As Waldenfels emphasizes, the new is not a negation of the old, just as the alien is not the antithesis of the own but rather its implication or penumbra. And "instead of negating anything, a penumbra is something which is co-experienced and which changes or vanishes with the same experience; a synthesis is not in sight." In addition to Hegelian idealism, *Order at Twilight* also critiques modern rationalism, including Habermas's communicative variant. With or without explicit reference, the study is over long stretches an agonal engagement or confrontation *(Auseinandersetzung)* with the Habermasian perspective. Thus, commenting on the difference between normative correctness and relevance, Waldenfels observes that the exclusive privileging of the former "tends to place the twilight of order into an artificial light expunging the genesis of order and its constraints." Similarly, with regard to speaking and acting, the neglect or de-emphasis of significance is said to leave a blind spot in the theoretical analysis of these phenomena or practices; in particular, a communicative action theory concentrating on validity claims "necessarily bypasses the temporal character (of speech and action) and misjudges the weights imposed on speaking and acting as temporal events." Turning to the segregation of modern value spheres—science, ethics and art—Waldenfels remonstrates against the bracketing of the genesis of cognitive-epistemological and moral-practical orders: "To the extent that productive imagination plays a role here, we can speak of the relevance of art which calls for a *poetics* of knowing and doing." This resurgence of art vis-à-vis validity claims, however, does not signal a simple lapse into randomness or anarchic spontaneity—as is evident from the study's careful distantiation of regression and a (Bataille-like) celebration of excess: "Tempting is this figure of *sacrifice* in total self-abandon—where it finally matters no longer who sacrifices whom. Once we reached this stage of complete amoralism, we would not only have exited from ethics but also from the interplay of challenge and response which sustains every transgression."[26]

The preceding comments shed light on the ethical dimension of order. As Waldenfels seeks to make clear, the alternative to an abstract moralism or normativism is not simply amoralism or nihilism—a bifurcation sometimes suggested by moral cognitivists and non-cognitivists alike. From an agonal perspective, it is important to avoid this as well as other traditional dualisms, including the dualism between description and prescription, between "mere" conventions and absolute moral imperatives. What this polarity ignores or obscures is the broad range of human moral behavior which neither coincides with formal yardsticks nor with purely factual or causally induced reactions. Against this background, *Order at Twilight* adumbrates the terrain of a post-Hegelian type of *Sittlichkeit*, that is, of living ethical practices which are binding though contingent (and thus defy the alternatives of absolutism and relativism). According to Waldenfels, Aristotle himself did not simply equate goodness with tradition or with "what is inherited from the past *(patrion)*; like the German *'Gewohnheit,'* the Greek *ethos* has to do with a proper 'inhabiting' or dwelling *(Wohnen)*." Even Max Weber recognized a kind of living ethos or ethics which is more than factual-empirical custom. Basically, the "more" of ethos involves the concrete instantiation of agonal alertness or responsiveness, the "incarnate" exemplification of goodness in the sense of responsive engagement. Through habituation—in the sense of a proper "inhabiting" of agonal space—ethos promotes an incarnation or "embodiment of order" or (in Bourdieu's terms) an "incorporation of structures" which can be reduced neither to mechanical processes nor to the application of abstract rules; in a peculiarly post-Hegelian sense, moral practices find expression in ethical "corporations" (as concrete exemplars)—an embodiment which does not cancel contingency. Without serving as mere receptacles of norms, moral practices cannot pretend to a permanent instantiation of reason.[27]

While deeply impressed by, and attracted to, Waldenfels' perspective, I cannot refrain from voicing some reservations or critical concerns. A main concern has to do with an occasional resurfacing of dichotomous schemes or formulations—which otherwise are shunned or circumvented in his work. A case in point is the linkage of ethics and ethos. As it seems to me, the portrayal of ethos as a mode of habituation or inhabiting casts doubt on the accentuation (and occasional privileging) of rupture and rift —at least to the extent that these terms denote disaffection or disengagement. More generally, I am troubled by the juxtaposition or opposition of the production of new order and the reproduction of existing order, of standards which are measure-giving and those which are measure-taking, of the domains of the ordered and the unordered (or disordered). Precisely to the degree that order is always simultaneously present and absent, always both here and elsewhere, the relation between the preceding terms cannot be one of strict contrast or opposition, but only one of mutual implication or a shifting alignment—resembling again more a threshold which bridges and divides. A related qualm has to do with an incipient anthropocentrism manifest in the confrontation between man and nature. Clearly, once "man" or the modern subject is decentered or stripped of foundational status, the distance between a contingent ordering of phenomena and open-ended cosmological views (stressing intimation or approximation) begins to narrow. Although nature as such may be inaccessible—and appeal to it a doctrinaire imposition (Gewaltakt)—agonal responsiveness would seem to imply willingness to accept at least some cues or hints from nature in a manner linking invention and discovery in this domain as well.[28] On all these points, I believe, *Order at Twilight* might have benefited from closer attention to Heidegger's arguments or formulations—which occupy in the work a somewhat subsidiary or marginal place. While no thinker can claim a monopoly of terms or concepts, expressions like event (Ereignis), threshold (Schwelle) and rupture (Riss) carry such distinctly Heideggerian resonances that readers might have welcomed exploration of this background.

Perhaps, many of the above qualms can be stilled or removed if the focus is shifted from the contrast of order and non-order to the dimension of the extra-ordinary—the closing and culminating theme of the study. What renders the contrast troubling is the association of non-order with caprice, willful disengagement or self-centeredness—which would not so much strengthen as rather cripple openness toward the alien or toward otherness. Probably it is a consideration of this kind which lies behind Waldenfels' sharp distinction between transgression and regression and behind his insistence that "a transgression which is controlled or engineered would not really transgress but only transplant boundaries; for this reason, boundary transgression always implies self-transgression (or a transgression of the subject)."[29] From the vantage of such self-transgression, non-order involves not so much a violation or disregard of interpersonal or social obligations but rather their overfulfillment in an exemplary display of largesse—a display harkening back to the biblical injunction "if someone asks you for a loaf give him two instead." The extra-ordinary against this background is a synonym less for whimsical idiosyncracy as for a latent but untapped potential or possibility—the possibility not simply of shifting from one order to the next but of transgressing order itself by inhabiting its margins. What looms at these margins, or in the twilight of order, is not an unbounded non-place or utopia but rather a promise or prospect: that of superabundance in the midst of finitude and contingency.

6

HEGEMONY AND DEMOCRACY:
A POST-HEGELIAN PERSPECTIVE

Post-structuralism and deconstruction frequently are seen as mere academic trends, soon to be replaced or outdated by newer fashions. This view is reinforced by their prominent role in literary criticism and aesthetics—fields notoriously prone to quick fluctuations of taste. In application to politics and political theory, deconstruction often appears as little more than a mode of escapism, an attempt at verbal obfuscation oblivious of concrete social contexts and power constellations. Against this background, the work of Ernesto Laclau and Chantal Mouffe offers an invigorating breath of fresh air: brushing aside academic cobwebs their writings—most notably *Hegemony and Socialist Strategy: Towards a Radical Democratic Politics* (of 1985)[1]—relentlessly and almost passionately probe the implications of deconstruction and anti-foundationalism for political life. Unpretentiously stated (and thus shunning notoriety), their arguments touch at the core of contemporary political and philosophical concerns. For from indulging in facile rhetoric, the study on hegemony is the outcome of rigorous and sustained intellectual labor, a labor only barely concealed in an array of succinct and lucid theoretical formulations. Countering their association with escapism or a simple-minded anarchism, the book demonstrates the relevance of post-structural or deconstructive themes for the theoretical grasp of liberalism and socialism, and particularly for the future of democratic politics.

From the vantage of Laclau and Mouffe, the relevance of deconstruction manifests itself prominently or with special virulence in the context of socialist thought (as part and parcel of the so-called crisis of Marxism). As they observe in their "Introduction": "Left-wing thought today stands at a crossroads. The 'evident truths' of the past ... have been seriously challenged by an avalanche of historical mutations which have riven the ground on which those truths were constituted." Apart from a host of social and political changes the authors appeal to more subtle intellectual dislocations, especially the effects of post-metaphysics with its attack on stable foundations: "What is now in crisis is a whole conception of socialism which rests upon the ontological centrality of the working class, upon the role of the Revolution (with a capital 'r'), as the founding moment in the transition from one type of society to another, and upon the illusory prospect of a perfectly unitary and homogeneous collective will that will render pointless the moment of politics." According to Laclau and Mouffe, it is the "plural and multifarious character" of contemporary social struggles—together with their theoretical repercussions—which have undermined the "Jacobin imaginary" present in foundationalist Marxism, and especially the "monist aspiration" of that doctrine to capture "the essence or underlying meaning of History." In turning to the concept of hegemony, the study seeks to do more than add a further refinement or "complementary" twist to traditional essentialism: instead, the aim is to initiate a paradigmatic shift reverberating through the entire set of categories and providing a new "anchorage" from which contemporary social struggles are *"thinkable in their specificity."*[2] In the following I shall first recapitulate briefly some of the main themes or arguments presented in *Hegemony and Socialist Strategy.* Subsequently, I shall lift up for closer scrutiny several of the chief theoretical innovations of the study in order to conclude finally with some critical observations or afterthoughts.

I

Congruent with its paradigmatic ambition, the study opens with a backward glance at the history of Marxist or socialist discourse and, more specifically, with a detailed genealogy of the concept of hegemony. As the authors emphasize, the concept entered Marxist discourse initially as a stop-gap measure or as a mere supplement designed to patch up evolutionary anomalies. In their words, hegemony made its first appearance not as the "majestic unfolding of an identity" but in "response to a crisis": to this extent, genealogical inquiry resembles the "archaeology of a silence" (in Foucault's sense). To illustrate the context of the concept's emergence, the opening chapter points to the dilemmas of Rosa Luxemburg as they are revealed in her book on the mass strike. In that work, Luxemburg recognized the fragmentation of the working class as a necessary structural effect of advancing capitalism; at the same time, however, the prospect of revolutionary struggle was ascribed not to the operation of economic laws but to the spontaneous constitution of class unity through the medium of symbolic action. It was the fissure implicit in this argument which called and made room for a supplementary category curbing the reign of economic necessity. Initially, to be sure, this opening collided head-on with the dominant Marxist model of the time, a framework spelled out and summarized in Karl Kautsky's commentary on the Erfurt Program (of 1892). According to the Kautskian text, Marxism was an essentialist doctrine predicated on the indissoluble "unity of theory, history and strategy." The latter unity or totality, in turn, was based on a number of related features or assumptions—among them, that the structure of industrial society was increasingly simplified in the direction of class conflict; that the two chief classes were differentiated in their essence or by nature due to their diverse status in the mode of production; and that the dénouement of class struggle was intelligible as resolution of prior contradictions. It was only at the end of the Bismarck era, with the rise of organized capitalism, that the flaws of the essentialist model began to surface. What made itself felt at this point, we read, was a "new awareness of the opacity of the social, of the complexities and resistances of an increasingly organized capitalism; and the fragmentation of the different positions of social agents which, according to the classical paradigm, should have been united."[3]

Reactions to these changes were halting and only slowly affected the structure of traditional premises. Laclau and Mouffe discuss three immediate responses to the perceived crisis of Marxism: the establishment of "Marxist orthodoxy," the formulation of a "revisionist" approach by Bernstein, and Sorel's "revolutionary syndicalism." Marxist orthodoxy, in their presentation, involves the ascendancy or privileging of abstract theory over concrete social struggles and also over the political practice of social democratic parties. Divergences from theoretical postulates were treated either as deceptive appearances or surface phenomena or else as marginal contingencies unable to alter the predicted course of events: namely, the ascendancy of a unified proletariat under the leadership of the workers' party. Only occasionally—especially in the cases of Labriola and Austro-Marxism—did orthodoxy grant some space to autonomous political initiative but without proceeding to integrate such initiative within the overall theoretical framework. The issue of the relation of politics and economics, or of superstructure and base, was the central motif underlying Bernstein's revisionist approach—a position which insisted that the fragmentation or division of the working class in advanced capitalism could be remedied only through concrete political intervention. While introducing a breach between politics and economics, however, revisionism never questioned the class-based character of political action or of the workers' party; moreover, Bernstein's Kantian leanings fostered a dualism between the realm of freedom (anchored in the autonomy of ethical subjects) and the determinism of economic laws—a gulf only precariously bridged by the notion of social "evolution" *(Entwicklung)*. Moving beyond a simple juxtaposition of domains, revolutionary syndicalism as advocated by Sorel attempted for the first time to conceptualize social autonomy, that is, to "think the specificity of that 'logic of contingency'" on which "a field of totalizing effects is reconstituted." Pursuing this path, Sorel was led to replace economic class unity with more amorphous social "blocs" held together by ideological devices; the chief device was the syndicalist myth of the "general strike"—a myth serving as the "point of condensation for proletarian identity, constituted on the basis of the dispersion of subject positions."[4]

A corollary of these reactions to social fragmentation was the emergence of the concept of hegemony as the site of a new or ascending political logic. In orthodox discourse the concept occupied only a marginal place, as a marker for theoretically undigested events. In the writings of Plekhanov and Axelrod, for example, hegemony designated the multiple (economic and political) tasks imposed on the Russian proletariat as a result of economic backwardness. According to the authors, hegemonic relations at this point merely "*supplement* class relations. Using a distinction of Saussure's, we could say that hegemonic relations are always facts of *parole,* while class relations are facts of *langue.*" The reduction to supplementary status was still operative in Leninism, and especially in the Leninist formula of a "class alliance" cemented under the leadership of a proletarian "vanguard" party. Due to the "ontological centrality" assigned to the proletariat, class alliance in this case did not modify essential class identities in the direction of fusing them with the democratic demands implicit in hegemonic practices. The same centrality was reinforced in the immediate aftermath of the Russian revolution—as is evident in Zinoviev's slogan of the "bolshevization" of communist parties, where "bolshevization" means "a firm will to struggle for the hegemony of the proletariat." It was only the steadily growing menace of fascism and the incipient cycle of anti-colonial revolutions which began to erode class-based essentialism: in lieu of a manipulative type of class alliance, the interbellum period gave rise to novel political arrangements, extending from "popular front" regimes to Togliatti's "national tasks of the working class" and Mao's "new democracy." "In this new perspective," we read, "hegemony was understood as the democratic reconstruction of the nation around a new class core. This tendency would later be reinforced by the varied experiences of national resistance against the Nazi occupation."[5]

In terms of the study, the crucial break with Marxist essentialism was initiated by Gramsci whose work is portrayed as the decisive "watershed" offering a formulation of the hegemonic link "which clearly went beyond the Leninist category of 'class alliance'." Extricating himself from the legacy of fixed class identities, Gramsci focused on broader social groupings called "historical blocs" whose unity of purpose or "collective will" was fostered by intellectual and moral leadership in a context of cultural and political hegemony. As a corollary, moving beyond simple base-superstructure formulas, his approach perceived ideology not as an abstract system of ideas but as an organic ensemble of beliefs and concrete practices partially embodied in institutions and social structures. Yet, despite these important theoretical advances, Laclau and Mouffe note a persistent ambivalence in Gramsci's work curtailing his pioneering role: namely, a tendency to return to an "ontological" conception of class identity or to ascribe the ultimately unifying power in hegemonic formations to an economically defined class. To the extent that the Gramscian "war of position" still paid tribute to a zero-sum construal of class struggle—they write—it revealed an "inner essentialist core" in his thought "setting a limit to the deconstructive logic of hegemony." The same ambivalence, in their view, was reflected in social-democratic policies of the period, especially in the "planism" of the post-Depression era and also in later technocratic models of state intervention. According to the authors, an exit from this dilemma is impossible unless an effort is made to tackle the "last redoubt of essentialism": namely, traditional "economism" or the doctrine of the foundational status of economics. As they point out, the doctrine is enshrined in three basic theses of classical Marxism—those relating to the neutral or automatic operation of productive forces; the basic unity and growing homogenization of the working class; and the essential link between working class and socialism—theses which singly and in combination are said to be "false" (in light of recent studies showing the impact of the

"politics of production" on economic relations and the attendant pluralism of working class interests). The consequences flowing from the
critique of economism are numerous and affect all facets of the essentialist paradigm; chief among these conclusions are: the "unfixity" of
every kind of social identity; the disappearance of ontologically "privileged subjects"; and the absence of a "logical and necessary relation
between socialist objectives and the positions of social agents in the
relations of production."[6]

Against the backdrop of this historical scenario, the study embarks
on its central and most ambitious task: the theoretical elaboration of a
non-essentialist concept of hegemony as cornerstone of a "radically democratic" political theory. On non-foundational premises, hegemony has
the character of a creative "articulation," that is, of the "political construction" of a social formation out of dissimilar elements. Such a creative articulation is radically at odds with a closed "totality" or a view of
society as a completely intelligible and homogeneous structure—a view
partially operative in Hegelian philosophy and in versions of Marxism.
To clarify their conception of hegemony, Laclau and Mouffe proceed
through a detour: a confrontation with Althusser's structuralist theory
and its aftermath. The most promising feature of Althusser's approach,
they note, was the principle of "overdetermination"—the thesis that
social formations or phenomena are not causally fixed but the result of
a symbolic fusion of plural meanings. As it happened, however, overdetermination remained vague in Althusser's work and was progressively
overshadowed by other structuralist ingredients, especially the claim of
determination by the economy "in the last instance"; as a result of this
claim, symbolic construction functioned merely as a contingent margin
of causal necessity. The theoretical critique of Althusser's model—as
inaugurated by Balibar and continued by spokesmen of British Marxism
(like Hindess and Hirst)—focused on the logical connections among
ingredients of the model and ultimately on the role and status of "structural causality." While promising in many respects, this critique, according to the authors, has so far resulted only in logical disaggregation and
not in a radical reformulation of basic categories. Moving in the latter
direction, the study advances these definitional propositions: "We will
call *articulation* any practice establishing a relation among elements
such that their identity is modified as a result of the articulatory practice. The structured totality resulting from the articulatory practice, we
will call *discourse*." While differential positions articulated within a
discourse are termed "moments," the label *elements* is reserved for differences not discursively structured. Discursive formations are said to
be unified neither logically nor empirically nor transcendentally but

only through an ambivalent symbolic coherence (akin to Foucault's 'regularity in dispersion'). Moreover, discourses are not simply mental phenomena but rather material and behavioral "practices" in a manner bypassing the thought-reality or idealism-realism bifurcation. Most importantly, as articulatory enterprises discourses only selectively structure the social domain without reaching definitive closure; due to their inherent finitude and multivocity, they never exhaust the broader "field of discursivity" with its available surplus of meaning. Hegemony denotes the selective structuring of the social field around distinct "nodal points" seen as privileged discursive accents.[7]

Fleshing out the notion of discursive practices, Laclau and Mouffe comment in some detail on the role of the subject (or subjectivity) in such practices; on the contest or antagonism prevailing between discursive formations; and on the relation between hegemony and democracy. In line with the unfixity of social identities, subjects in their view cannot function as the constitutive origin of social formations—which does not entail the elimination of human agents but rather their construal as "subject positions" within a discursive structure (possibly as nodal points in such a structure). On the level of Marxist analysis, economic classes likewise are only articulated ingredients (possibly nodal ingredients) within a selectively structured social field. Due to their finite and selective character, discursive formations inevitably are in tension with alternative possibilities. In a critical review of Marxist literature, the study sharply demarcates antagonism from such notions as "logical contradiction" and "real opposition" (Realrepugnanz): while the latter are objectively given relations, the former derives precisely from ambiguity and the contestation of givenness. In the authors' words: "Real opposition is an *objective* relation—that is, determinable, definable—among things; contradiction is an equally definable relation among concepts; antagonism constitutes the limits of every objectivity, which is revealed as partial and precarious *objectification.*" Differently phrased, antagonistic relations arise "not from full totalities, but from the impossibility of their constitution." Seen as limit of social formations, antagonism results not merely from the confrontation between different empirical structures, but rather operates as an intrinsic negative potency in every formation challenging its presumed positivity or its objective givenness. According to the authors, this negative potency manifests itself chiefly through a system of equivalence which subverts all positive differences, reducing them to an underlying sameness. "The *ultimate* character of this unfixity (of the social)," they write, "the *ultimate* precariousness of all difference, will show itself in a relation of total equivalence, where the differential positivity of all its terms is dissolved. This is precisely the formula of antagonism, which thus establishes itself as the limit of the social." Yet, just as social positivity can never fully be stabilized, negativity or negative equivalence cannot become a total or all-embracing enterprise (without canceling the very possibility of social articulation). Instead, social formations are predicated on a precarious blend of the "opposed logics of equivalence and difference"—with full integration and total rupture only signaling the extreme ends of a spectrum. This aspect brings into view the relation between hegemony and democracy. Viewed as a social formation, democracy cannot be reduced to total equivalence or a bipolar conflict between self-enclosed camps—despite the possible presence of deep fissures. Differentiating between "popular struggles" (in a Jacobin sense) and "democratic struggles," the study presents the former only as extreme variants within the broader framework of hegemonic democratic relations: "The existence of two camps may in some cases be an *effect* of the hegemonic articulation but not its a priori condition. . . . We will therefore speak of *democratic* struggles where these imply a plurality of political spaces, and of *popular* struggles where certain discourses *tendentially* construct the division of a single political space in two opposed fields. But it is clear that the fundamental concept is that of 'democratic struggle'."[8]

The theme of hegemony and democracy is further explored in the concluding chapter of the study. In the authors' view, the relation between socialism and democratic politics has involved a difficult process of adjustment: namely, the move from an essentialist doctrine—treating the bipolar division of society as "*an original and immutable datum,* prior to all hegemonic construction"—toward a more diversified democratic conception acknowledging the basic "instability of political spaces" and the fact that "the very identity of the forces in struggle is submitted to constant shifts." The last approximation of a factual bipolarity occurred during the French Revolution, with the pervasive opposition between "people" and *"ancien régime."* Since that time, however, the dividing line between social antagonisms has become increasingly "fragile and ambiguous" and its formulation has emerged as the "crucial problem of politics." As discussed in previous chapters, Marxism sought to reconstitute an essential polarity on economic grounds—but without succeeding in translating the distinction of classes into an automatic social-political conflict. According to Laclau and Mouffe, the development of radical democracy has put in question the "continuity between the Jacobin and the Marxist political imaginary," and more generally the assumption of a privileged point of rupture and the "confluence of struggles into a unified political space." Returning to the period of the French Revolution, the study portrays the insurgent "logic of equivalence" as the basic instrument of social change and as the beginning of a long-term "democratic revolution." This process of democratization has gained added momentum in recent decades, due to antagonisms triggered by the so-called new social movements. The targets of insurgency in this case are chiefly the bureaucratization, commodification and growing homogenization of life in advanced industrial societies. In theoretical terms, what these movements bring into view is the specificity of contemporary struggles constituted on the basis of "different subject positions" (in lieu of a fixed or foundational polarity); more generally, they highlight the emergence of a "radical and plural democracy" with a close intermeshing of radicalism and pluralism. "Pluralism is *radical*," we read, "only to the extent that each term of this plurality of identities finds within itself the principle of its own identity. . . . And this radical pluralism is *democratic* to the extent that the autoconstitutivity of each one of its terms is the result of displacements of the egalitarian imaginary."[9]

As the authors recognize, the shift from essentialism to plural struggles does not by itself guarantee a progressive democratic outcome. Pointing to the rise of the "new right" and of neo-conservatism in Western countries, the study detects in our time a new valorization of positive social differences and also of individual autonomy seen as a counterpoint to mass democracy. What this counter-insurgency accentuates—Laclau and Mouffe argue—is the importance of political hegemony and the need to intensify broad-based political struggles in line with the modern process of democratization. Such struggles, they write, should locate themselves fully "in the field of the democratic revolution" and its expanding chains of equivalence; their task, in any case, "cannot be to renounce liberal-democratic ideology, but on the contrary, to deepen and expand it in the direction of a radical and plural democracy." Socialist strategy in the past was ill equipped to shoulder this task, mainly due to its hankering for an "essentialist apriorism"—a hankering manifest in its reliance on privileged subjects ("classism"), on a privileged social basis ("economism"), and on a privileged policy instrument ("statism"). In a condensed form, these preferences surfaced in the attachment to the foundational role of "revolution" (in the Jacobin mould). Overcoming this legacy means to acknowledge the differentiation of contemporary antagonisms and the multiplication of political spaces and avenues: "There is not *one* politics of the Left whose contents can be determined in isolation from all contextual reference. It is for this reason that all attempts to proceed to such determination *a priori* have necessarily been unilateral and arbitrary." Once apriorism is abandoned, socialist strategy has to insert itself into the precarious web of hegemonic democratic relations, particularly into the interplay of positivity and negativity or of the logic of difference and the logic of equivalence—an interplay which is now also phrased as the tension between equality and liberty or autonomy. Disrupting this tension in favor of one constitutive dimension conjures up the peril of a closed society (in the form of either a leftist or a rightist totalitarianism). As the authors conclude: "Between the logic of complete identity and that of pure difference, the experience of democracy should consist of the recognition of the multiplicity of social logics along with the necessity of their (hegemonic) articulation"—an articulation which needs to be "constantly re-created and renegotiated."[10]

II

As should be clear from the preceding synopsis, *Hegemony and Socialist Strategy* is a richly textured, insightful and often provocative work; it is also tightly argued and intellectually uncompromising—in a manner barring easy access. In terms of contemporary labels, the study inserts itself in the broad movement of post-structuralism and postmodernism—but without facile trendiness (and without entirely abandoning structuralist themes, from Saussure to Althusser.[11] Contrary to aestheticizing tendencies or construals, the work clearly demonstrates the relevance of post-essentialism or deconstruction for political theory; in fact, *Hegemony and Socialist Strategy* can and should be viewed as a major contribution to a present-day understanding of democracy. Most importantly, the study counteracts the widespread association of deconstruction with anarchism or with complete social and political randomness. Although devoid of essentialist moorings or ontological fixity, post-structuralist politics—as presented by Laclau and Mouffe—operates in a complex relational web endowed with distinct parameters or constraints, parameters shielding radical democracy from the perils of despotism, totalitarianism, and unmitigated violence.

Although amenable to diverse interpretations, the study (in my view) is basically a political text, offering a splendid example of innovative political theorizing. Apart from its historical resonances, the accent on hegemony involves centrally a revalorization of politics against all forms of reductionism (subordinating politics to other domains). A crucial assault launched in the study is directed at sociologism as well as economism. In a bold formulation—challenging prominent portrayals of sociology as "master social science"—Laclau and Mouffe speak of the "impossibility of society," that is, the inability of the social domain to provide a firm grounding of analysis. As they write, pinpointing a "decisive point" in their argument: "The incomplete character of every totality leads us to abandon, as a terrain of analysis, the premise of 'society' as a sutured and self-defined totality. 'Society' is not a valid object of discourse" since there is "no single underlying principle fixing— and hence constituting—the whole field of differences." What society needs to gain contours is some kind of political articulation, that is, the formulation and establishment of hegemonic political relationship. Reminiscent vaguely of Arendtian arguments the study defines politics as "a practice of creation, reproduction and transformation of social relations," a practice that cannot be located at a "determinate level of the social" since the problem of the political is "the problem of the institution of the social, that is, of the definition and articulation of social relations in a field criss-crossed with antagonisms." Moving beyond Arendt, however, the authors do not accord to politics a stable space or a completely autonomous sphere. In effect, radical democracy in their text is presented as a form of politics which is founded "not upon dogmatic postulation of any 'essence of the social,' but, on the contrary, on affirmation of the contingency and ambiguity of every 'essence,' and on the constitutive character of social division and antagonism. Affirmation of a 'ground' which lives only by negating its fundamental character; of an 'order' which exists only as a partial limiting of 'disorder'."[12]

The attack on the constitutive character of the social domain applies with particular force to economism as it has operated in traditional Marxism. Challenging the presumed determination of the labor process and of class struggle by an abstract "logic of capital," Laclau and Mouffe assert the dependence of the latter on antagonisms linked with a pervasive "politics of production." A number of recent studies, they write, "have analyzed the evolution of the labor process from the point of view of the relation of forces between workers and capitalists, and of the workers' resistance. These reveal the presence of a 'politics of production'" at odds with the notion that capitalist development is the effect "solely of the laws of competition and the exigencies of accumulation." To be sure, attacking economism is not the same as postulating a rigid separation between economics and politics or ascribing a foundational status to the latter. According to the authors, such a view could only be maintained "if political practice was a perfectly delimited field whose frontiers with the economy could be drawn *more geometrico*—that is, if we excluded as a matter of principle any overdetermination of the political by the economic or vice versa." Given that politics is a matter of hegemonic articulation, the relationship between politics and economics cannot be permanently fixed or stabilized and depends on circumstances and prevailing articulatory practices.

'Let us accept instead,' the study asserts, 'that neither the political identity nor the economic identity of the agents crystallizes as differential moment of a unified discourse, and that the relation between them is the precarious unity of a tension. We already know what this means: the subversion of each of the terms by a polysemy which prevents their stable articulation. In this case, the economic *is* and *is not* present in the political and vice versa; the relation is not one of literal differentiations but of unstable analogies between the two terms.'[13]

The dismantling of univocal fixity and the accent on complex relationships lends to the study a quasi-Hegelian or (more properly) post-Hegelian flavor—a circumstance readily acknowledged by the authors. In terms of *Hegemony and Socialist Strategy*, Hegel's philosophy is precariously and ambiguously lodged at the intersection between metaphysics and post-metaphysics—more specifically between a theory of totality and a theory of hegemony (or else between total mediation and hegemonic articulation). In the authors' words, Hegel's work is at once the "highest moment" of German rationalism and idealism and simultaneously "the first modern—that is to say, post-Enlightenment—reflection on society." The ambiguity has to do chiefly with the ability of reason to grasp reality as a whole; differently phrased: with the respective weights assigned to absolute logic and a more opaque and contingent "cunning of reason." Occupying a watershed between two epochs, Hegel is said to represent on the one hand the culmination of rationalism: namely, "the moment when it attempts to embrace within the field of reason, without dualisms, the totality of the universe of differences." On the other hand, however, Hegel's totality or synthesis contains "all the seeds of its dissolution," as the rationality of history can be affirmed "only at the price of introducing contradiction into the field of reason itself." The continued significance of Hegel's thought resides basically in the second dimension: namely, in its midwifing role for a theory of hegemony, opening reflection up to the flux of contingent and not purely logical (or essential) relationships. For Laclau and Mouffe, this is precisely the mark of Hegel's modernity (or postmodernism): in his work "identity is never positive and closed in itself, but is constituted as transition, relation, difference." But if logical relations become contingent transitions, then the connections between them cannot be fixed as moments of an underlying or sutured totality—which means that they are "articulations."[14]

The post-Hegelian quality of the study—or its Hegelianism with a deconstructive twist—surfaces at numerous points and most prominently in the discussion of hegemony and its relation to antagonism. As previously indicated, antagonism denotes not simply a juxtaposition of objective entities (either on a logical or a factual level), but rather involves a process of mutual contestation and struggle. In general philosophical terms, antagonism arises from hegemony's inability to effect social and political closure—that is, from the polysemy and "surplus of meaning" constantly overreaching and destabilizing discursive practices. In language reminiscent of Hegel, the study situates social formations at the crossroads of positivity and negativity, where negativity designates not simply a lack but a "nihilating" potency. "This impossibility of the real—negativity—has attained a form of presence," we read. "As the social is penetrated by negativity—that is, by antagonism—it does not attain the status of transparency, of full presence, and the objectivity of its identities is permanently subverted. From here onward, the impossible relation between objectivity and negativity has become constitutive of the social." The tensional relation between presence and absence resurfaces or is rearticulated as the interplay of two social logics, namely, the logics of equivalence and difference. Here again it is important to notice that, although the two point in opposite directions, neither logic is able to achieve foundational status or complete self-enclosure. In the authors' words: If negativity and positivity exist only "through their reciprocal subversion," this means that "neither the conditions of total equivalence nor those of total differential objectivity are ever fully achieved." Translating the interplay of logics into the more traditional correlation of liberty and equality, another passage asserts: "The precariousness of every equivalence demands that it be complemented/limited by the logic of autonomy. It is for this reason that the demand for *equality* is not sufficient, but needs to be balanced by the demand for *liberty*, which leads us to speak of a radical and *plural* democracy."[15]

The notion of the correlation and interpenetration of social logics presents politics—particularly democratic politics—as an arena of contestation and interrogation, but not as a field of total domination or else mutual destruction. The accent on the relational character of antagonism injects into politics a moral or qualitative dimension, an aspect hostile to the reduction of politics to a simple organism (or mechanism) or else to a naturalistic state of war. If social identities are acquired only through agonal interaction, then it is impossible or illicit either to impose stable identity through a model of integral totality or to foreclose interaction through a system of radical equivalence. Integral closure—the lure of complete social positivity—is chiefly the temptation of the logic of difference. As the authors point out, however, due to its negative potency, antagonism signifies the "limit" of any given social order "and not the moment of a broader totality in relation to which the two poles of the antagonism would constitute differential—i.e., objective—partial instances." The opposite temptation arises from the logic of equivalence: radically pursued, equivalence either totally negates discursive formations and social identities or else polarizes society into two hostile forces of which each operates as the negation of the other. An example of the latter alternative—Laclau and Mouffe observe—can be found in millenarian movements where "the world divides, through a system of paratactical equivalences, into two camps" related only in the mode of negative reversal. More recent instances are terrorism or totalitarian absolutism. By contrast, properly political relations are marked by neither fusion nor fission: social identities are neither objectively given nor totally dissolved, but rather emerge through constant renegotiation (or a process of challenge and response).

> 'Thus, the two conditions of a hegemonic articulation,' the authors state, 'are the presence of antagonistic forces and the instability of the frontiers which separate them. Only the presence of a vast area of floating elements and the possibility of their articulation to opposite camps—which implies a constant redefinition of the latter—is what constitutes the terrain permitting us to define a practice as hegemonic' and more particularly as a democratic practice.[16]

The implications of this relational conception are multiple and significant: only a few can be hightlighted here. Although the study's post-Hegelian thrust is directed chiefly against all forms of integral closure or sutured totality, the proposed remedy or antidote is not random fragmentation. While critical of the pretense of universal principles or discourses, the authors do not simply opt for particularism—which would only entail a new kind of self-enclosure or a "monadic" essentialism. As they indicate, a mere dismantling of totality readily conjures up the peril of "a new form of fixity," namely, on the level of "decentered subject positions." For this reason, a "logic of detotalization" cannot simply affirm "the *separation* of different struggles and demands," just as "articulation" cannot purely be conceived as "the linkage of dissimilar and fully constituted elements." Through a strategy of disaggregation we are in danger of moving "from an essentialism of the totality to an essentialism of the elements" or of replacing "Spinoza with Leibniz." The means for overcoming this danger is provided by the logic of "overdetermination." For, we read, if the sense of every identity is overdetermined, then "far from there being an essentialist *totalization*, or a no less essentialist *separation* among objects, the presence of some objects in the others prevents any of their identities from being fixed. Objects appear articulated not like pieces in a clockwork mechanism, but because the presence of some in the others hinders the suturing of the identity of any of them." Similar considerations apply to the issue of pluralism. Although endorsing a "radical and plural democracy," the study holds no brief for group egotism. In the authors' words, either an absolute pluralism or a "total diffusion of power within the social" would blind us to the operation of overdetermination and to the presence of "nodal points" in every social formation. With slight modifications, relationism or the interpenetration of identities also affects the status of individual autonomy or liberty. Segregated from equality or equivalence, such autonomy only fosters new modes of totalization—which points up the need to reformulate "bourgeois individualism": "What is involved is the production of *another* individual, an individual who is no longer constructed out of the matrix of possessive individualism. . . . It is never possible for individual rights to be defined in isolation, but only in the context of social relations which define determinate subject positions."[17]

Among the most significant contributions of the study are its caveats against total antagonism or against the polarization and militarization of politics. In our violence-prone age when many flirt with theories of radical discord—as an antidote to co-optation—*Hegemony and Socialist Strategy* offers a welcome corrective. In the presentation of Laclau and Mouffe, polarization was the trademark of both Jacobinism and essentialist Marxism; from Lenin's *What is to be Done* to Zinoviev's motto of bolshevization, a military conception of politics dominated the range of strategic calculations. In this conception political struggle is basically a zero-sum game, a game producing a segregation effect in the sense that the hostile camps tend to retreat into the shells of their separate identities. Polar vocabulary was still present—though ambiguously and in modified form—in the Gramscian notion of war of position. For Gramsci, war of position involved the progressive disaggregation of a social formation and the construction of a new hegemony of forces—but along a path which left the identity of the opponents malleable and subject to a continuous process of transformation. Thus, the military imagery was in this case "metaphorized" in a direction colliding with its literal sense: "If in Leninism there was a militarization of politics, in Gramsci there is a demilitarization of war"—although the reformulation reached its limit in the assumption of an ultimate class core of every hegemony. Once the latter assumption is dropped, Gramsci's notion can be metaphorized further in a manner compatible with radical democracy. At this point, the distinction between popular struggles and democratic struggles becomes relevant. While Gramsci still presupposed the division of political space along the lines of popular identities (though granting their constructed character), relinquishing this premise opens the way to a fluid and non-dichotomous concept of hegemony: "We will thus retain from the Gramscian view the logic of articulation and the political centrality of the frontier effects, but we will eliminate the assumption of a single political space as the necessary framework for those phenomena to arise." Democratic struggles are precisely those that involve a plurality of political spaces.[18]

III

While greatly appreciating the depth and rigor of the reviewed study, I cannot refrain from voicing some reservations or critical afterthoughts. These comments are not meant to deprecate the cogency and overall direction of its arguments, but rather to amplify and strengthen the same direction—which is basically that of a viable post-Hegelian political theory. Precisely from an Hegelian vantage, some of the accents of the study appear to me lopsided or skewed. In tracing the genealogy of hegemony, the opening chapter places a heavy—and probably excessive—emphasis on autonomous action and initiative. Thus, in the discussion of Luxemburg, the "logic of spontaneism" is singled out as an important counterpoint to class-based essentialism and the literal fixation of social meanings. Similarly, Sorel's myth of the general strike is held up for its focus on "contingency" and "freedom," in contradistinction to the chain of social and economic necessity. Influenced by Nietzsche and Bergson, Sorel's philosophy is said to be "one of action and will, in which the future is unforeseeable, and hinges on will." Formulations of this kind are liable to inject into the study a flavor of voluntarism which is not entirely congruent with the author's broader perspective. The impression is reinforced in the central portion of the study, namely, in the equation of hegemony with articulation and of the latter with a mode of "political construction from dissimilar elements." The term *construction* seems to place hegemony in the rubric of a "purposive" and voluntaristic type of action (in the Weberian sense)—in a manner obfuscating the distinction between praxis (or practical conduct) and technical-instrumental behavior. Although perhaps inadvertent, the confluence of meanings needs in my view to be sorted out in order to differentiate hegemony more clearly from forms of instrumentalism.[19]

   Once voluntarism is eschewed as remedy for essentialist fixation, the study embarks on hazardous terrain. In fact, its theory of hegemony is lodged at one of the most difficult junctures of Hegelian thought (and of traditional metaphysics in general): the juncture marked by the categories of "freedom" and "necessity," of "determinism" and "contingency." Occasionally, hegemony is portrayed almost as an exit route from necessity and all modes of social determinism. Thus, while Marxist essentialism is said to have banished contingency to the margins of necessity, the relationship is claimed to be reversed in hegemonic articulation—in the sense that necessity now "only exists as a partial limitation of the field of contingency." As the authors somewhat exuberantly add: "If we accept that a discursive totality never exists in the form of a simply *given and delimited* positivity, the relational logic will be incomplete and pierced by contingency. . . . A no-man's-land thus emerges making the articulatory practice possible." Elsewhere, however, this simple reversal is called into question—which opens the road to a complex and fascinating conceptualization of hegemony in terms of an intertwining and mutual subversion of necessity and contingency. Once the goal of final fixation recedes, Laclau and Mouffe observe, a profound ambivalence emerges: at this point "not only does the very category of necessity fall, but it is no longer possible to account for the hegemonic relation in terms of pure contingency, as the space which made intelligible the necessary/contingent opposition has dissolved." What emerges at this point is no longer a simple external delimitation of two contiguous fields, but rather a relationship of mutual interpenetration and contestation. As they write, the relations between necessity and contingency cannot be conceived as "relations between two areas that are delimited and external to each other . . . because the contingent only exists within the necessary. This presence of the contingent in the necessary is what we earlier called *subversion"*—and what, in effect, must be called reciprocal subversion. As a result, the centrality of hegemony is predicated on "the collapse of a clear demarcation line between the internal and the external, between the contingent and the necessary."[20]

What the preceding comments adumbrate is a theoretical relationship which is recalcitrant both to dualism and to monism (in their traditional metaphysical sense). The opposition to dualism is a recurrent theme of the study. Thus, Bernstein's revisionism is chided for embracing a "Kantian dualism" pitting autonomous ethical subjects against economic determinism. Similarly, Marxist orthodoxy is taken to task for harboring a "permanent" and "irreducible" dualism between the logic of necessity and the logic of contingency, with each side being merely the "negative reverse" of the other. Such dualism, the authors note, establishes merely a "relation of frontiers," that is, an external limitation of domains devoid of reciprocal effects. Opposition to dualism is also evident in the notion of discursive materiality and the critique of the thought-reality bifurcation. Yet, at the same time, anti-dualism does not vindicate a simple fusionism or a complete elimination of non-identity. The distinction between "elements" and "moments" in articulatory practices is, in fact, predicated on the persistence of a (non-dualistic mode of) non-identity. If articulation is a practice, we read, "it must imply some form of separate presence of the elements which that practice articulates or recomposes"; it must also exclude the complete transformation of elements into integral moments or components. The same kind of non-identical relationship prevails between social formations seen as articulated discursive chains, on the one hand, and "floating signifiers" constantly exceeding these chains, on the other; and ultimately between discursive practices in general and the "infinitude of the field of discursivity." What comes into view here is a term placed midway between identity and total non-identity, a term which some post-structuralist thinkers have thematized under such labels as *intertwining* or *duality*; Heidegger's *"Zwiefalt"* (two-foldedness) and the Derridean notion of *"différance"* point in the same direction.[21]

In a prominent manner, the notion of intertwining or duality would seem to be applicable to the relation between positivity and negativity or between the logics of difference and equivalence (as these terms are used in the study). As the authors repeatedly affirm, negativity is not simply a void or a logical negation but a nihilating ferment exerting real effects: "The presence of the Other is not a logical impossibility; it exists—so it is not a contradiction." The same thought is expressed in the argument that negativity and positivity exist only "through their reciprocal subversion," and also in the view that antagonism as the negation of a given order operates as the intrinsic limit of that order— and not as an alien force imposing external constraints. Unfortunately, passages of this kind collide with occasional formulations which approximate the interplay to a Sartrean kind of antithesis (of being and nothingness). As Laclau and Mouffe state: "Insofar as there is antagonism, I cannot be a full presence for myself. But nor is the force that antagonizes me such a presence: its objective being is a symbol of my non-being"—where "non-being" is surely an overstatement. Small wonder that on such premises antagonism begins to shade over into total conflict—as happens in a passage which finds the "formula of antagonism" in a "relation of total equivalence where the differential positivity of all . . . terms is dissolved." Flirtation with nothingness is also evident in the statement that experience of negativity is "not an access to a diverse ontological order, to a something beyond differences, simply because . . . there is no beyond." Yet, the fact that negativity is not another objective (or positive) order does not mean that what lies "beyond differences" is simply nothingness. In fact, if differences were related strictly by nothing, the result would be total segregation or equivalence—and by no means the complex web of relationships thematized under the label of *hegemony.* In Heidegger's vocabulary (which, to be sure, has to be employed cautiously), different elements in order to enjoy a relationship are linked on the level of being—a term denoting a non-objective type of matrix in which positivity and negativity, ground and abyss *(Abgrund)* are peculiarly intertwined.[22]

A similar intertwining affects another oppositional pair closely linked with the nexus of presence and absence: the relation of inside and outside, of interiority and exteriority. On this issue, too, the authors are not always entirely clear and oscillate between divergent conceptions. Thus, in presenting every social formation as a "delimited positivity," they affirm that "there is no social identity fully protected from a discursive exterior that deforms it and prevents its becoming fully sutured." The accent on exteriority is further reinforced in a passage dealing with the character of social antagonism. As a witness of the "impossibility of a final suture," we read, antagonism "is the experience of the limit of the social. Strictly speaking, antagonisms are not *internal* but *external* to society; or rather, they constitute the limits of society, the latter's impossibility of fully constituting itself." This formulation, of course, stands in conflict with the notion of limit as a mode of internal subversion or the claim that society is everywhere "penetrated by its limits." Elsewhere, it is true, the study insists explicitly on the "irresoluble interiority/exteriority tension" as a "condition of any social practice," and on the collapse of a "clear demarcation line between the internal and the external." This conception, in my view, is more readily congruent with the emphasis on non-essentialist types of antagonism and on the relational quality of hegemony. The discussion of hegemony contains, in fact, a lucid endorsement of this tensional approach. The hegemonic subject, we learn there, "must be partially exterior to what it articulates—otherwise there would not be any articulation at all." On the other hand, however, "such exteriority cannot be conceived as that existing between two different ontological levels." As a result, to the extent that the term is applicable, exteriority "cannot correspond to two fully constituted discursive formations" or to "two systems of fully constituted differences" (that is, to two domains radically exterior to each other).[23]

The external-internal quandary carries over into the conception of democracy—surely a centerpiece of *Hegemony and Socialist Practice.* In this context, the quandary surfaces as the opposition between democracy construed as a system of radical equivalence and democracy as a social formation intrinsically marked by the tension between equivalence and difference. The first alternative is stressed in the historical narrative tracing the emergence and spreading of "democratic revolution." Referring to the beginning of this process, the study detects a "decisive mutation in the political imaginary of Western societies" at the time of the French Revolution, a mutation which is defined in these terms: "the logic of equivalence was transformed into the fundamental instrument of the production of the social." The same kind of principle is said to govern the subsequent process of democratization: "The logic of democracy is simply the equivalential displacement of the egalitarian imaginary to ever more extensive social relations, and, as such, it is only a logic of the elimination of relations of subordination and of inequalities" and "not a logic of the positivity of the social." Not surprisingly, in order to constitute a viable social order, democracy defined in this manner—as a pure "strategy of opposition"—needs to be supplemented with a "strategy of construction of a new order" bringing into play the "element of social positivity." Actually, however, the construal of democracy as radical equivalence or as expression of a purely "subversive logic" stands in conflict with the conception of "plural democracy" emphasized in the study—a conception in which equivalence and difference, equality and liberty (or autonomy) are inextricably linked. As Laclau and Mouffe state (in a previously cited passage): "Between the logic of complete identity and that of pure difference, the experience of democracy should consist of the recognition of the multiplicity of social logics along with the necessity of their articulation." Against the background of this tensional experience, the pursuit of pure equivalence emerges in fact as a sign of political deformation—provoking the specter of despotism and totalitarianism.[24]

The latter deformation leads me to a final comment. If democracy involves a complex relationship of forces and groupings (recalcitrant to total opposition or essentialist fixation), then antagonism does not necessarily have to have a hostile and mutually coercive character. If hegemony denotes a non-exclusive articulation—fostering an intertwining of exteriority and interiority—then room seems to be made for a more friendly or sympathetic mode of interaction (which, to be sure, cannot entirely cancel negativity and thus an element of equivalence and power). Against this background it appears possible to reinvigorate the Aristotelian notion of 'friendship' seen as a binding matrix of political life—provided political friendship is carefully differentiated from its more utilitarian and instrumental variants. Extending the study's post-Hegelian leanings, it seems likewise feasible and legitimate to view politics as permeated by ethical concerns or by the Hegelian category of

Sittlichkeit. Along the same lines, there may be an opportunity today to rethink the Hegelian state—in such a manner that state no longer signifies a positive structure or totality, and certainly not simply an instrument of coercion, but rather the fragile ethical bond implicit in hegemonic political relations. Democracy under these auspices is still an arena of struggle—but a struggle directed not simply toward domination but toward the establishment of a tensional balance between presence and absence, liberty and equality: that is a struggle for mutual recognition (of differences).

7

RETHINKING THE HEGELIAN STATE

Hegel is not in vogue today; outside of restricted circles or enclaves, his philosophy is no longer the fulcrum of sustained inquiry—not to speak of creative reinterpretation. This situation is not limited to Anglo-American analytical philosophy where Hegel's work has for some time been regarded as outmoded or conceptually *dépassé;* of late, even Continental thinkers—and those attentive to their writings—have come to share this sentiment. In an age of non- or anti-foundationalism, notions like absolute spirit and absolute knowledge are bound to appear as hopelessly obsolete, if not intellectually perverse.[1] A product of holistic speculation, Hegel's opus is seen as the end-point of a long metaphysical tradition or else as the watershed between the past and the dawning age of post-metaphysics, first captured and given voice by Nietzsche. Nowhere is this presumed obsolescence more evident than in Hegel's theory of law (or right) and the state. At a time when a theoretical premium is placed on diversity, contestation and dispersal, the view of the state as an ethical fabric permeated by *Sittlichkeit* is liable to be regarded as a quaint relic of classicism—if not as the emblem of sinister totalitarian designs. From different (philosophical and political) angles, our age thus seems to seal the long-standing dissolution or disintegration of the Hegelian system, a dissolution already witnessed by the first generation of his heirs (including Marx). Yet, perhaps the triumph of posterity is premature. Perhaps, as Heidegger once observed, the problem is not so much the decay or decomposition of Hegel's work as rather the inability of our time to raise itself to the complexity of his insights.[2]

My point here is not to rekindle a Hegelian orthodoxy (if there is such a thing). Neither philosophically nor politically do I see any possibility of neglecting—and even adequately bridging—the vast distance separating us from Hegel's epoch. Philosophically, a long string of initiatives—stretching from Nietzsche over pragmatism to the so-called linguistic turn—have cast doubt on the prospect of finding secure beginnings of thought, whether in reason, consciousness or subjectivity. In social and political terms, our age is segregated from his by the effects of the industrial revolution, the expansion of markets and media networks, and the resulting consolidation and diversification of civil society. In addition, the rise of large-scale bureaucracy and the succession of two world wars have weakened if not eroded confidence in the ethically benign character of the modern nation-state. By itself, however, historical change does not amount to complete disconfirmation—especially in the case of a (self-styled) dialectical philosophy. Thus, the bureaucratization (and militarization) of the contemporary state may belong to those external positivities whose constraint is to be set aside or overcome by the dialectical impulse of spirit—a shift leaving unaffected the status of *Sittlichkeit* as basic social bond. Similarly, the demise or implausibility of the civil service as a viable universal class does not vitiate the search for open-ended human contacts capable of mitigating individual or collective self-enclosure. In the following I intend to sketch or recollect first of all the main features of Hegel's theory of the state, as they are outlined chiefly in his *Philosophy of Right*. Next, I shall discuss some critical rejoinders to Hegel's conception, from Marx and Nietzsche to Popper and Lyotard. By way of conclusion I shall ponder possible ways of rehabilitating and reinvigorating the notion of *Sittlichkeit* and ethical community in the dramatically changed context of a post-metaphysical and post-statist theory of democracy.

I

The notions of an ethical state and of *Sittlichkeit* as concrete social bond are recurrent themes in Hegel's evolving opus—although not always under the same labels or in the same terminological guise. Thus, the emphasis in the early theological writings on popular religious beliefs was meant to invigorate (and purify) community life, in opposition both to the stale positivity of established churches and to the abstract rational principles extolled by Enlightenment thought. Without great difficulty, one can discern here anticipations of the later critique of empirical customs and historical factuality, on the one hand, and of a purely internalized and non-social morality, on the other. In the *Phenomenology of Spirit,* human and social life was presented as in the throes of a protracted learning experience leading from immediate consciousness over reflective self-consciousness to reason (as the consciousness of self-consciousness) and finally to spirit; the latter term at this point was equated with "ethical actuality" *(sittliche Wirklichkeit)* or with "actual ethical being." Although a culmination of the drama of consciousness, spirit or *Sittlichkeit* was said to exhibit its own intrinsic dialectic, namely, a story of conflict and its resolution. On a first, quasi-natural level, spirit designated the prevailing customs of a people and also the rules or habits governing family life. These customs were bound to be contested by the emergence of individual freedom and free inquiry, a process leading to the struggle between rational enlightenment and pure faith or between immanence and transcendence. Only in a final stage was this struggle subdued or overcome in the mode of self-actualized *Sittlichkeit,* that is, in a fully developed ethical and communal life attesting to the reality of absolute spirit.[3]

As we know, Hegel's *Phenomenology* was only a prelude or precursor to his later encyclopedic system—into which it was precariously integrated on the level of subjective spirit or at the transition point leading from the latter to concrete-objective *Sittlichkeit* and the theory of the state. In the *Philosophy of Right,* ethical life appears as the culminating apex of a complex triptych or triadic sequence embracing as its components abstract right (or abstract law), morality and *Sittlichkeit,* with the latter domain being subdivided in turn into family, civil society and the state. The entire sequence is said to reflect the development and self-actualization of human freedom and more particularly of free will—where "will" does not stand in opposition to, but rather forms an integral modality of thought or spirit. As Hegel writes toward the beginning of his treatise: "The grounding of right or law *(Recht)* resides basically in *spirit,* and its precise location and point of origin is the *will* which is *free*—with the result that freedom is both the substance and goal of right and the legal system is the realm of actualized freedom." According to the same paragraph, free will should not be contrasted to spirit (or *Geist*); for "spirit is thought as such, and man is distinguished from animals by virtue of thinking." But "one should not imagine that man is half thought and half will"; rather will is only "a special mode of thinking: namely, thought translating itself into existence" or actualizing itself in reality. Moreover, free will in Hegel's account does not coincide with arbitrariness or a purely contingent disposition. On the contrary, freedom for him always has reference to concrete contexts and thus involves an intermeshing of inside and outside, of ego and alter (or fellow human beings). If one defines freedom as the "ability to do as one pleases," Hegel insists, such a view "can only be taken to reveal a complete immaturity of thought." A purely private disposition divorced from all contexts, he notes, is only "will's *abstract* certitude of its freedom; but it is not yet the *truth* of freedom because the latter has not yet found itself as its content and goal, and consequently the subjective side is still other than the objective." Instead of being the will "in its truth," arbitrariness thus is rather "the will seen as *contradiction.*"[4]

The triadic sequences alluded to above are predicated on the dialectical movement of thought and will: namely, from a stage of immediacy to a reflective withdrawal from immediacy (and thus a moment of division or *Entzweiung*) to a final reintegration of reflexivity and context on a higher level. Thus, free will taken by itself or empirically is the source of abstract right (or law) concerned with objects; by contrast, a reflective will gives rise to the separation of inner and outer worlds and to a sphere of morality opposed to external law; the two moments of givenness and reflexivity are finally reconciled in the idea of *Sittlichkeit* which reveals the actuality of freedom. A similar development occurs inside the field of ethical life itself. The entire dialectic is lucidly explained by Hegel himself, in one of the numerous additions to the main text. Free will, he writes, must first of all give itself some "existence or embodiment" *(Dasein)* and the primary sensual material of such existence are "things, that is, external objects." Thus "the initial mode of freedom is the one which we know as *property*—the sphere of formal and abstract right." However, freedom cannot remain satisfied with the sheer immediacy of existence and thus proceeds to negate this immediacy in the sphere of morality. At this point, "I am free no longer only regarding immediate things but also in the state of sublated (or superseded) immediacy: which means I am free in myself, in my subjectivity." On this level, everything depends on my intentions and purposes, while externality is irrelevant. Yet, internal purposes also demand to be actualized or to be given concrete existence. Consequently, morality, just like purely formal right, now appear as abstractions or abstract moments whose truth is *Sittlichkeit* alone—that is, ethical life seen as "the unity of will as a general concept and particular or subjective will." In turn, the primary embodiment or existence of ethical life is a natural bond, namely, the family united by "love and feeling." Reflective individualization dissolves this primary bond and gives rise to civil society whose members relate to each other as "independent agents" connected only through the "bond of reciprocal need." Reconciliation and reintegration occurs here on the level of the state—the stage of *Sittlichkeit* and of spirit which "yields the enormous unification of autonomous individuality and universal substantiality." The state thus is "freedom in its most concrete form" (subordinate only to the "absolute truth of world spirit").[5]

For present purposes, the most important dialectical phase is the transition from civil society to the state—for it is here that particularity and generality first separate and then coalesce again. Hegel is explicit in presenting individual or subjective particularity as the chief acquisition of modernity and as the feature distinguishing modern from ancient political life. As he states (in the section dealing with morality): "The right of the subject's *particularity*—his right to be satisfied or (differently put) the right of subjective freedom—is the pivot and center of the difference between antiquity and modern times. This right in its infinite scope has been articulated in Christianity and been erected into the general governing principle of a new form of civilization." This aspect is reinforced at a later point (in the section on civil society) in even more dramatic terms. "The creation of civil society," we read there, "is the achievement of the modern age which for the first time has given all the facets of the 'idea' their due." By contrast, the autonomous development of particularity appeared in the ancient world "as the beginning of ethical decay and as the ultimate cause of that world's demise." The reason was that these ancient states were built on "patriarchal and religious grounds" or else on an "intensive but relatively simple *Sittlichkeit*," in any case on a "primitive natural intuition"—with the result that they could not "withstand the disruption *(Entzweiung)* of this condition and the infinite reflection of self-consciousness" and thus "succumbed to the latter as soon as it arose." For instance, Plato in his *Republic* portrayed ethical substance in its "ideal beauty and truth"; however, as regards autonomous particularity—which in his day had begun to "invade Greek ethical life"—he managed to cope with it only "by opposing to it his purely substantial state," while excluding particularity entirely from the structure of the *Republic*. Returning to the contrast between ancients and moderns, Hegel adds that the notion of "the autonomous and inherently infinite personality of the individual," which means the "principle of subjective freedom," could not come into its own in the ethical context of antiquity; rather, the principle "dawned first inwardly in Christian religion and externally (linked with abstract general rules) in the Roman world"—in order to unfold its full potential in modernity.[6]

In the *Philosophy of Right,* modern civil society appears both as an advance over substantial (or unreflective) ethics and as a mode of rupture or diremption requiring further mediation and reconciliation. Basically, civil society is the arena of individual interests and needs, that is, the domain of particularity—although particular, subjective wills remain linked through general rules (but on a purely formal level). As Hegel writes, "the concrete person bent on his (her) particularity as a goal" is one or the first principle of civil society construed as "a totality of wants and a blending of natural necessity and caprice"; but due to the reciprocity of wants and their satisfaction the same society is also governed by "generality" *(Allgemeinheit)* as its second principle. Generality here means the necessary rules and external constraints imposed on individual satisfaction. In Hegel's words: Although in civil society "everyone regards himself (herself) as supreme end and everything else as nothing or immaterial," yet no one can fully pursue or achieve his (her) ends "except by relating to others"—which bestows on the fabric of reciprocal needs the "form of generality" (or universality). Since particularity is inevitably conditioned by generality, he adds, civil society is "the terrain of mediation allowing free play to every idiosyncracy, every talent, every accident of birth and fortune." Seen from the vantage of necessity or generally binding rules, civil society can also be designated as an "external state," that is, as a state based on need and abstract reasoning *(Not- und Verstandesstaat).* More comprehensively viewed, civil society marks the diremption *(Entzweiung)* of ethical life where the particularity of needs and the generality of rules are granted separate existence and develop in opposite directions. In the (well known) formulation of the *Philosophy of Right:* civil society is "the system of *Sittlichkeit* split and lost into its extremes—which constitutes the abstract moment of the idea's actuality." Since the separate existence of particular needs and general necessity is ultimately illusory, however, Hegel also portrays the divided character of civil society as a mode of "appearance" *(Schein)*—in the sense that both particular wills and generality claim to be something which they truly cannot be (namely, separate): the divided relation "constitutes *Sittlichkeit* as a world of appearance— which is civil society."[7]

Correcting and overcoming this divisiveness is the task of the modern state—whose conceptual novelty Hegel emphasizes both vis-à-vis classical substantial ethics and vis-à-vis atomistic or contractarian construals (tied to the domain of civil society). For Hegel, the state is basically the "idea"—and thus free will or human freedom—on the level of fully reflective (not merely intuitive) actuality; differently phrased, it is the actuality of freedom where particular self-consciousness is elevated to, and permeated by, *Sittlichkeit* as the common good. Throughout the *Philosophy of Right,* Hegel takes great pains to differentiate this conception from purely individualistic or contractarian views. As he writes at one point, in the case of *Sittlichkeit* two views are possible and have traditionally prevailed: "either one starts from ethical substantiality or else one proceeds atomistically and builds on the basis of isolated individuals. The latter view is senseless because it leads only to a juxtaposition, whereas spirit is nothing isolated but rather the unity of the particular and the universal." The contrast is underscored in the section on the state. "If the state is confused with civil society and if its end is seen in the security and protection of property and subjective freedom," Hegel affirms, "then the interest of the individuals as such becomes the end of their association, and it follows that membership in the state is something optional." However, the state's relation to the individual—he continues—is "quite different: since the state is objective spirit, it is only as one of its members that the individual attains objectivity, truth and *Sittlichkeit.* The community as such is the true content and aim (of life)." Although in the order of presentation the state follows the discussion of family and society, in actuality public community precedes and renders possible the more limited forms of ethical experience. Neglect of this primacy is the common mistake of contractarian thinkers—including Rousseau, despite the latter's greater depth of insight. Although commendably positing thought and the will as the basic "principle of the state," Rousseau erred in treating will only "in the distinct form of isolated, individual will (like later Fichte)" and in regarding universal will "not as the rational essence of will but only as a 'general will' derived from individual wills in deliberate fashion"—that is, in reducing "the union of individuals to a contract."[8]

While embodying the unity or unification of individuals, the state in Hegel's conception is not simply an undifferentiated collectivity—which would mean a regress to pre-modern substantiality. As he insists, the actuality of freedom accomplished in the state consists in the fact "that personal individuality and particular interests attain their complete development and recognition as rightful, while simultaneously they blend of their own accord into the common (or universal) interest" and even perceive it as their own. Differently put: actuality of freedom means that the common or universal good does not prevail "without attention to particular interests and particular modes of knowing and willing," just as little as individuals live only for particular private ends "without simultaneously embracing the common good and effectively pursuing its aims." While in ancient states particularity was still entirely overshadowed and dominated by community goals, the situation has changed in modernity. The essence of the modern state, Hegel affirms, is "that the universal must be bound up with the complete freedom of particularity and the well-being of individuals"—which means "that the interests of family and civil society must converge in the state just as the commonality of ends cannot be advanced without the knowing and willing participation of particular members whose own rights must be maintained." Thus, in modern states the common or universal good must be furthered "while at the same time subjectivity is fully and vibrantly developed." This consideration leads Hegel to one of the most famous and intellectually most challenging formulations in the *Philosophy of Right*. "The principle of modern states," we read, "has this prodigious power and depth of allowing the principle of subjectivity to unfold completely to the extreme of autonomous personal particularity while at the same time guiding it back into the substantive unity (of the state) and so preserving this unity in the principle of subjectivity itself."⁹

The meshing of particularity and common good is also the hallmark of a properly designed "internal constitution" of the state—a topic on which I shall be very brief due to the dated character of many details. As Hegel notes, only when the two moments (the subjective and the universal) "subsist in their strength can the state be regarded as properly structured and genuinely organized." In large measure, proper structuring involves the differentiation or separation of governmental powers in Montesquieu's sense—though one which remains oriented toward the common good (more strongly than occurs in a system of checks and balances). According to the text, a constitution is rational "insofar as the state internally differentiates its activity along clear conceptual lines, namely in such a manner that each of its powers represents the totality (of the constitution) by maintaining the other moments operative in its own domain." Differentiation in this case is at odds both with a complete fusion or concentration of powers and with their radical segregation or opposition. As Hegel adds: "The principle of the separation of powers contains the essential aspect of *difference* and thus of actualized rationality. However, as construed by abstract reasoning, it signifies (falsely) either the absolute mutual independence of powers or else (one-sidedly) a relation of reciprocal negation and restriction. In this view, the principle turns into hostility and into the fear of each power of the evil machinations of the others." For Hegel, the crucial feature of the principle is that, though differentiated, the powers mutually corroborate each other and coalesce to uphold the unity of the whole. Applying the dialectic of particulars and universals to internal constitutional order, he assigns the determination of general or universal rules to the legislative branch, the subsumption of particular cases and situations under these rules to the administrative branch (including the judiciary), and the reintegration of these functions in a higher mode of subjectivity to the monarchical power. This constitutional arrangement ultimately buttresses Hegel's preference for "constitutional monarchy" as ideal regime or as the regime most congruent with actualized freedom—a preference predicated on that regime's ability not only to balance internal powers but to reconcile and sublate traditional constitutional forms, like monarchy, aristocracy and democracy. "The development of the state to constitutional monarchy," he states, "is the achievement of the modern world where the substantive idea has gained infinite form. The history of this inner deepening of spirit . . . or the story of this genuine formation of *Sittlichkeit* is the content of general world history."[10]

Seen as embodiment of the idea, constitutional monarchy forms the apex of Hegel's conception of the state—a conception whose ethical significance he repeatedly emphasizes. Relevant passages to this effect are widely known and are frequently cited as evidence of Hegel's extreme idealism. Thus, in terms of one of the famous additions to the text, the state is said to be "the ethical totality, the actualization of freedom—just as it is the absolute goal of reason that freedom should be actualized." The state consequently is "spirit-standing-in-the-world and involved in a process of conscious self-realization." According to another, even more provocative formulation, the state is part of "the march of God in the world" and its basis is "the power of reason actualizing itself as will." What is less frequently noted is the undertow of realism in Hegel's work. Thus, in talking about the "march of God in the world" he immediately continues that the reference is not to particular empirical states or particular institutions, but only to the concept of the state. In the *Philosophy of Right* he is quite aware of empirical examples contravening the concept—of the fact that there have been "historically times and conditions of barbarism" where the state was "merely a worldly regime of violence, caprice, and passion." These conditions, he says, are historically attested; but it is a "blind and shallow" view to equate these examples with the concept. More generally, Hegel recognizes the frequent coincidence of state activity with the sheer exercise of domination and violent coercion—but he refuses to identify the description of empirical-historical conditions with the task of philosophical understanding. The state, he writes in a passage ably summarizing his views on the matter, "is no ideal art-work but stands on earth and so in the sphere of caprice, accident, and error; bad behavior thus may disfigure it in many ways. Yet even the ugliest man, or a criminal, or an invalid or cripple is still a living human being; the affirmative moment—life—subsists despite these defects, and it is this affirmative factor which is our theme here" (in the theory of the state).[11]

II

Hegel's *Philosophy of Right* has met with varied reactions over time, often provoking lively polemical attacks; given our distance from its initial composition, the book cannot be properly read and understood without some attention to its *Wirkungsgeschichte*. On a general philosophical level, critical comments have frequently focused on the presumed priority of idealism over realism, of universal over particular categories, and of speculative theorizing over practical engagement. In more specifically political terms, rejoinders have concentrated on the preponderance of public institutions over private-particular initiatives and of collective unity over individual freedom. Less frequently, concerns have been voiced regarding the fragile and precarious status of public *Sittlichkeit* given the internal momentum of civil society. On the whole, scholarly debates have tended to revolve around the balance (or imbalance) of the diverse moments encompassed by ethical life. In Charles Taylor's presentation, Hegel's theory of the state was meant to counteract "two great disruptive forces" which imperil modern society and politics:

> The first is the force of private interest, inherent in civil society and in its mode of production, which constantly threatens to overrun all limits, polarize the society between rich and poor, and dissolve the bonds X of the state. The second is the diametrically opposed attempt to overcome this and all other divisions by sweeping away all differentiation in the name of the general will and the true society of equals.

The latter attempt, he adds, must in Hegel's view issue "in violence and the dictatorship of a revolutionary elite," or in any event in a repressive political regime.[12]

Beyond the issue of proper balancing, more radical critiques have been leveled at the basic design or substance of Hegel's conception. One of the first to raise such substantive-ontological questions was Marx, particularly in his *Critique of Hegel's Philosophy of Right* (and the somewhat later "Introduction" to that study). According to Marx, Hegel's work had failed to implant *Sittlichkeit* concretely in the real life of people, preferring instead to celebrate its abstract-speculative idea (as manifest in the state and its bureaucratic institutions); despite certain rational-progressive features, the proposed public order offered only partial reprieve from past abuses. Applying "transformational criticism"—a strategy first developed by Feuerbach in religious matters—to the public-political domain, Marx portrayed the Hegelian state ultimately as a mode of human self-alienation and self-subjugation, a defect which could only be overcome by a return to its social and economic underpinnings. While acknowledging that the "philosophy of right and of the state" had been given "its most logical, profound and complete expression by Hegel," Marx's review urged the extension of critical analysis to the modern state in its concrete operation, that is, to "the *imperfection of the modern state* itself, the degeneracy of its flesh." Although impressive in its array of abstract categories, what Hegel's work left out of account was chiefly "the *real man*" (or real human being) — and this only because "the modern state itself leaves the real man out of account or only satisfies the *whole* man in an illusory way." What was needed to correct illusory abstractions was a radical "humanization" of *Sittlichkeit* through a focus on the actual contradictions of civil society; only by revolutionizing the latter could state-reason become a universal reason and political rationalization issue in general human emancipation: "A class must be formed which has *radical chains*, a class in civil society which is not a class of civil society . . . (one) which claims no traditional status but only a human status . . . which is, in short, a total loss of humanity and can only redeem itself by a total redemption of mankind."[13]

Despite its important insights and fertile new vistas, Marx's critique cannot in turn escape critical scrutiny of its premises. In large measure, the use of Feuerbach's method — the turn from ideal speculation to the situation of real man — involved mainly a reversal of accents, while leaving the character and meaning of reality basically opaque. In some respects, Marx's arguments even reinforced (on a less subtle level) Hegelian assumptions and the premises of modern philosophy as such. This is evident in the stress on humanization and on man as producer of his material life conditions — an emphasis congruent with modernity's anthropocentric leanings and its infatuation with *homo faber*. More dramatically, the same continuity surfaces in the treatment of the proletariat as universal class — a treatment clearly indebted to the notions of a collective identity (of objective spirit) and of a teleological movement of mankind.[14] By comparison with Feuerbachian modes of reversal, Nietzsche's attack on Hegelianism was more radical and thoroughgoing — because it aimed at the metaphysical underpinnings of Hegel's thought (and of much of Western thought in general). Turning against the thesis of the progressive actualization of spirit or reason, Nietzsche affirmed that history is only "a chaotic pile of rubbish." The same verdict applied to the modern state and its institutions. As Nietzsche observed, in one of his early "Notes": "But a state has no aim; we alone give it this aim or that"; far from embodying a higher purpose or a common *Sittlichkeit,* the state was merely "individual and collective egoisms struggling against each other—an atomic whirl of egoisms." Still more eloquently and zestfully, the same sentiment recurs in the later *Zarathustra*—where the state is portrayed as "the death of peoples" and as "the name of the coldest of all cold monsters." Against the homogenizing and streamlinig ambitions of the state, Nietzsche exhorted his readers to "break the window and leap to freedom"—from the prison of the "new idol": "Only where the state ends, there begins the human being who is not superfluous: there begins the song of necessity, the unique and inimitable tune."[15]

The contest over Hegel's legacy was continued and intensified in our century—sometimes (though not always) in a Nietzschean idiom. On the whole, the dismissal or distrust of public *Sittlichkeit* has been a common feature of theoretical reformulations of the state, both among philosophers and social scientists. Partly under the impact of Nietzsche's attack and partly in response to Marxian initiatives, Max Weber defined the state simply as a means of control—as the (more or less legitimate) locus of the monopoly of force in a given territory. Efforts in our century to reinvest the state with a substantive purpose or collective identity have almost invariably yielded dismal results. Thus, attempts by right-wing thinkers (like Giovanni Gentile) to enlist Hegel's teachings for autocratic aims have paved the way for, or at least aided and abetted, the rise of fascist regimes—with damaging and even disastrous results for the image of Hegelianism in Western (liberal) countries. Scholarly studies stressing the progressive and emancipatory aspect of Hegel's work —like Marcuse's *Reason and Revolution*—were only partially able to undo the damage and to restore Hegel's credit in the political field. For many liberal intellectuals in the West, Karl Popper's verdict has become nearly canonical—to the effect that Hegel was an enemy of the "open society," if not simply a spokesman of Prussian militarism. Among the aspects of Hegel's philosophy allegedly conducive to political closure and even totalitarianism, Popper emphasized the subordination of individuals as particular agents to a higher collectivity and the equation of state-interest (or *raison d'Etat*) with a common *Sittlichkeit.* In his view, holistic construals of politics were theoretically dubious by reflecting an "essentialist" metaphysics rendered obsolete by modern science; and they were practically obnoxious by sponsoring violence and the destruction of freedom. "Only democracy," he insisted, "provides an institutional framework that permits reform without violence, and so the use of reason in political matters."[16]

In recent decades, Popper's indictment of political holism (as a mode of closure) has been corroborated by many thinkers otherwise distant from Popperian empiricism; foremost among these thinkers are contemporary Nietzscheans (or post-Nietzscheans) and especially spokesmen of French post-structuralism. Although anti-holistic and anti-Hegelian themes are pervasive in post-structuralist literature, I shall focus here for the sake of brevity on some works of Jean-François Lyotard. More resolutely than other French authors, Lyotard's writings challenge and denounce unitary conceptions of politics, together with such ancillary notions as the intelligibility of historical evolution and the steady unfolding or actualization of reason. As he affirms in *The Postmodern Condition*, the great unifying or universalist schemes of the past have become obsolete in our time—an age marked by the "crises of narratives," that is, by the erosion of the metaphysical underpinnings of thought and action. In lieu of comprehensive "metanarratives," what is increasingly coming to the fore is the experience of fragmentation, disjunction and "agonal" contestation—and especially the dispersal of traditional philosophical systems into "clouds of narrative language elements." This experience is bound to reshape profoundly both human knowledge and political practice. "The society of the future," Lyotard writes, "falls less within the province of a Newtonian anthropology" (with its unifying assumptions) "than a pragmatics of language particles. There are many different language games—a heterogeneity of elements; they only give rise to institutions in patches—local determinism." In terms of cognitive endeavors, "postmodern" theorizing can no longer be integrated or accommodated in a common framework; rather, it "refines our sensitivity to differences and reinforces our ability to tolerate the incommensurable."[17]

According to *The Postmodern Condition*, the departure from metanarratives means a turn to the "pragmatics" of language or to practical "speech acts"—and away from universal syntactical rules and a shared semantics of meaning. Accentuating the innovative, discontinuous character of pragmatics, Lyotard presents speech acts or utterances basically as "moves" and "countermoves" in a (language) game—where "move" denotes a combative strategy or challenge. This focus, he writes, "brings us to the first principle underlying our method as a whole: to speak is to fight, in the sense of playing, and speech acts fall within the domain of a general agonistics." These arguments carry over from linguistic behavior into the domain of social and political interactions and decisively mark the nature of the "social bond" today. Regarding the latter, the study contrasts contemporary agonistics chiefly with traditional models of integral holism and social harmony—models first inaugurated by the French founders of sociology and later developed and reformulated by functionalist systems theory and cybernetics.

Despite shifts of accent, Lyotard notes, we can discern in this tradition "a common conception of the social: society is a unified totality, a 'unicity' "; this holistic outlook is particularly pronounced in contemporary cybernetic frameworks where all information processes are programmed in advance. Countering these (and related) sociological approaches, the study stresses the central role of language games—in fact, of multiple, heterogeneous games—in supplying the only remaining social bond in a postmodern context. In sharp distinction from unitary schemes, our age is said to witness the " 'atomization' of the social into flexible networks of language games," where each speaker or participant is located at particular "nodal points" of competing communication circuits. Instead of being submerged in social harmony, the "atoms" of society are seen as operating at the "crossroads of pragmatic relationships" and involved in perpetual "moves" and agonal confrontations. "What is needed," Lyotard comments, "if we are to understand social relations in this manner, on whatever scale we choose, is not only a theory of communication but a theory of games which accepts agonistics as a founding principle."[18]

As presented by Lyotard, linguistic and social agonistics is a radical counterpoint to Hegelian philosophy—which is treated as pillar of one of the great metanarratives or legitimating stories of modernity: the story of the dialectic of spirit and its progressive self-actualization. Under the auspices of German idealism, philosophy is said to aim at the unity of knowledge and understanding, as an antidote to their disintegration into separate disciplines. This task, however, can only be accomplished "in a language game that links the sciences together as moments in the becoming of spirit," in other words, "which links them in a rational narration or rather metanarration. Hegel's *Encyclopedia* attempts to realize this project of totalization (which was already present in Fichte and Schelling in the form of the idea of the system)." According to Lyotard, Hegel's dialectic of spirit is couched in terms of narrative knowledge, as a phenomenology of subjective experience or of the life of subjective spirit; but actually the story can only be told as a metanarrative, from the vantage of a universal subject or "metasubject," that is, from the vantage of absolute spirit. With regard to modes of empirical learning and the structure of cultural and political institutions, it is this metasubject which gives voice "to their common grounding" and "realizes their implicit goal; it inhabits the speculative university." Thus, it is only through a transgression of language games, by ascending to the level of a universal subject or metasubject, that Hegel was able to extricate himself from the strife of heterogeneous discourses and perspectives— and ultimately to formulate the vision of a common ethical life in the state. In Lyotard's words: "German idealism has recourse to a metaprinciple that simultaneously grounds the development of learning, of society, and of the state in the realization of the 'life' of a subject, called 'divine life' by Fichte and 'life of the spirit' by Hegel. In this perspective, knowledge first finds legitimacy within itself, and it is knowledge that is entitled to say what the State and what Society are. But it can only play this role by changing levels . . . that is, by becoming speculative."[19]

As Lyotard adds polemically—in language matching Popperian invectives—speculative or transcendental reasoning is far from innocuous in its effects. On Kantian as well as Nietzschean premises, diverse modes of knowledge and language games are seen to be separated by a gulf or "chasm"; only "the transcendental illusion (that of Hegel) can hope to totalize them into a real unity. But Kant also knew," he continues, "that the price to pay for such an illusion is terror. The nineteenth and twentieth centuries have given us as much terror as we can take." In Lyotard's view, speculative thought is vitiated not only by its practical consequences but also by its intrinsic dilemmas and deficiencies—faults which are glaringly evident in our time. Turning to developments in postmodern science, the concluding section of the study finds a decisive shift in contemporary scientific inquiry—namely, from uniformity and stability to the "search for instabilities," from predictable causal processes to the analysis of discontinuity and indeterminacy. What remains in present-day scientific theory, Lyotard notes, are at best "islands of determinism"; in contrast to the harmonious schemes of the past, the accent on conflict and antagonism is today "literally the rule." All these changes augur ill for speculative or "totalizing" paradigms, including the Hegelian vision of synthesis and historical teleology. After the demise of traditional metanarratives the only plausible legitimization of knowledge—he insists—is one based on "paralogy," that is, on the transgression and continuous revolutionary mutation of paradigms. To the extent that unity or consensus are still favored by rationalist approaches, their effect is only the consolidation of conformism: "It is now dissension that must be emphasized."[20]

The preference for agonistics over holism is reinforced in one of Lyotard's more recent studies, appropriately titled *The Contest (Le Différend)*. Elaborating on the study's title, the author distinguishes sharply between "contest" *(différend)* and judicial "litigation" *(litige)*. "In contrast to a litigation," he states, "an agonal contest is a conflict between (at least) two parties which cannot properly be decided due to the absence of a decision rule applicable to both sides of the argument." As he adds, the title of the book suggests that "generally there is no universal rule applicable to diverse modes of discourse"—a circumstance which is traced to the pragmatics of language games and their intrinsic heterogeneity: just as sentences belonging to diverse rule systems "cannot be translated into each other," so the multiplicity of discourse structures produces inter-discursive conflict or contest—one unable to be settled by a higher authority or tribunal. Renewing the attack on holism, Lyotard stresses that universal ideas or categories cannot be objects of cognition or knowledge; the thesis affirming the opposite "might be called 'totalitarism' "—a term carrying connotations both of theoretical deception and practical-political oppression. In an "excursus" specifically devoted to Hegel, the study criticizes the notion of a "speculative discourse" involving a steady unfolding of meaning and culminating in a comprehensive or total knowledge. What this notion entails, Lyotard observes, is a privileging of continuity over discontinuity, of cumulative meaning over its dispersal—a privilege which is "undeniable in Hegelian thought" and which ultimately is rooted in the primacy of the "self" or subjectivity (over otherness). Although acknowledged in the *Phenomenology of Spirit,* plurality of experience is progressively discarded in the course of Hegel's *Encyclopedia*—until at the level of objective and absolute spirit the plural pronoun ("we") is "no longer necessary." This entire ascent, however, is said to be spurious. For, the concept of a supreme or absolute discourse is logically untenable: either this discourse is a discourse like others—in which case it is not supreme; or else it is separate from other discourses—in which case it is not comprehensive (by exempting itself from the whole). Hegel's speculative discourse raised the claim of supremacy; but "the principle of an absolute triumph of one discourse over others is senseless."[21]

III

Seen in conjunction, the preceding criticisms or indictments show Hegelianism to be a troubled and beleaguered paradigm today. Actually, the reviewed attacks are only examples of broader intellectual currents in our time which jointly and from diverse angles lay siege to Hegel's legacy. In my view, a vindication of some Hegelian themes—and especially the theme of *Sittlichkeit*—cannot proceed without awareness of this situation and without attentiveness to some of the major charges or objections. As it happens, not all the reviewed forays are equally weighty or damaging. Thus, the Popperian charge of collectivism and totalitarian repression can be readily countered by pointing to the centrality of freedom in Hegel's theory of the state and his insistence on the linkage of objective reason and public *Sittlichkeit* with particular initiatives (a point previously noted). Similarly, the focus of the young

Marx on humanization is not only compatible with, but essentially predicated on Hegelian premises—and, more generally, premises of the modern philosophy of consciousness—though with a peculiar instrumentalist twist. In Taylor's words, Marx's innovation consisted basically in a "transposition of Hegel's synthesis from *Geist* on to man"; but already in Hegel's thought, *Geist* or spirit could not be actualized or realized without human participation (on both a reflective and practical level). Thus, what Marx's "transposition" amounted to was the production of synthesis through human design or will power—stripped of, or in abstraction from, its ontological moorings. "Man is one with nature," Taylor comments, "because and to the extent to which he has made it over as his expression. The transformation of human society is not aimed at an eventual recognition of a larger order" (as in Hegel) "but ultimately at the subjugation of nature to a design freely created by man."[22]

More troubling and provocative, in my view, is the Nietzschean and post-Nietzschean indictment. As portrayed by Lyotard, Hegelianism is essentially a totalizing metaphysics in which all forms of otherness or non-identity are ultimately integrated or submerged in the maelstrom of absolute spirit and its progressive self-actualization. Against the homogenizing thrust of this vision, Lyotard—like Nietzsche before him—invokes the power of discord, rupture, and discontinuity; in lieu of the consensual harmony of elements, the accent is shifted to contest, dissensus, and agonistics. The motives for this shift are not hard to detect. Philosophically, Lyotard's post-structuralism is a rebellion against the computerization of holism or synthesis, as propounded by contemporary systems theory and cybernetics. On a social and political level, his arguments militate against global ideologies and against the all-pervasive tentacles of the bureaucratic state. In his study of Hegel and modern society, Taylor recognizes the relentless dynamic of integration and homogenization—but as an antipode or counterpoint to Hegel's deeper ambitions. It is clear today, he writes, that the process of homogenization "has swept away traditional bases of identification, traditional modes of *Sittlichkeit*," and further that "the resultant vacuum has been largely filled by national identifications which are frequently divisive and destructive." Although unable to anticipate the full effects of this process, Hegel in his account saw the dismantling of differences as incompatible with a properly constructed ethical and political life; far from endorsing a bland sameness he realized that the latter "would undermine all possible bases of *Sittlichkeit*, would reduce society from an articulated unity to an undifferentiated 'heap' which could only be held together by despotic force."[23]

Taylor's comments can, no doubt, be vindicated by reference to Hegelian texts—but only up to a point. Perhaps, textual vindication in this case tends to overachieve what it seeks to demonstrate: namely, the integral or systematic unity of meaning. As it seems to me, Hegel's arguments are frequently in danger of jeopardizing their own tensional richness and ambivalence in favor of univocity. A case in point is the issue of identity. The phrase (articulated in an early text) that spirit means "the identity of identity and difference" seems to privilege identity while truncating the tensional interplay of sameness and otherness. The same privileging seems to be at work in terms like idea, spirit or reason—to the extent that these terms are meant also to embrace their counter-terms or counterpoints (on the level of full actualization). This consideration applies with special force to the notion of the state and its embodiment in constitutional monarchy. As previously indicated, Hegel's legal and political theory stands in opposition to two antithetical approaches: on the one hand, the mere description of empirical institutions, and on the other, a moralizing utopianism abstracting from the real world. Wittingly or not, the Hegelian state partakes of this precarious ambivalence: identified with concrete institutional features, it is liable to merge into empirical factuality or positivity; yet, removed from such concreteness, it turns into an abstract category if not a reflective chimera. Readers (and non-readers) of Hegel are amply familiar with this intrinsic tension or dilemma—a dilemma highlighted in the well-known and even notorious phrase that "the rational is the real or actual" (and vice versa). As it seems to me, what needs to be remembered at this point is the ontological or metaphysical status of Hegel's claim (in contrast to descriptive or moralizing conceptions): the fact that the state for Hegel is not simply an external givenness nor an inner-moral principle but rather the actualization of human *Sittlichkeit* and the culmination of ethical life—though a culmination necessarily embedded in concrete interactions and social life-forms.[24]

If these considerations are correct, then Hegel's conception of the state cannot simply be attached to, or equated with, the modern state and especially the so-called nation-state. Since his time, the flaws and imperfections of the modern state—the "degeneracy (or putrefaction) of its flesh" (to use Marx's terms)—have become evident in manifold ways. Reduced to an instrument of bureaucratic controls, or else to a vehicle of chauvinist ambitions, the state has increasingly lost its Hegelian sense, approximating instead the external *Verstandesstaat* or else models of collective immediacy (and unfreedom). While implicit in the march of God on earth may be some kind of public *Sittlichkeit*, the latter does no longer find embodiment in statist structures. In this situation, a plausible response may be to retain the impulse of Hegel's dialectic— without clinging to his institutional format. Actually, such a move is quite in keeping with Hegelian motifs. As he observes in the Preface to the *Philosophy of Right,* Plato's political thought was an expression of Greek *Sittlichkeit* at that time—but one which was about to be transcended by freer modes of reflexivity. Though often seen as an "empty ideal," he writes, Plato's *Republic* was "in essence nothing but an interpretation of the nature of Greek ethical life"—a life increasingly infiltrated during that period by "a deeper principle which could appear in it directly only as a longing still unfulfilled" and which he sought to muffle or subdue by clinging to a "particular external form of that same Greek *Sittlichkeit.*" These comments do not have to be limited to classical Greek thought, with its focus on ethical "substantiality," but can readily be extended to the teachings of German idealism—a point frankly acknowledged by Hegel in the same Preface. "As concerns the individual," he states (in a passage not often taken seriously enough), "everyone is in any case a child of his time; and so philosophy too is its own time apprehended in thought. It is just as absurd to fancy that a philosophy can transcend its contemporary world as it is to assume that an individual can overleap his own age, or jump over Rhodes."[25]

Taking Hegel at his word, there is clearly a need today to reconsider the issue of public *Sittlichkeit* and, in that context, to rethink the Hegelian state. As it seems to me, the identification of *Sittlichkeit* with formal state structures is disavowed today by the pervasive instrumentalization of these structures in the hands of bureaucratic, economic, or ethnic elites. At the same time, the format of constitutional monarchy has been rendered implausible—if not entirely obsolete—by advances of the democratic spirit or the deeper principle of universal participation (although this principle remains to a large extent a longing still unfulfilled). Under these circumstances, and still pursuing Hegelian motifs, the remedy cannot simply be found in a revival of private morality or the invocation of abstract ethical maxims—a move which merely reinforces prevailing divisions or modes of alienation (between private and public spheres, between individual and society). One of the important legacies of Hegel's philosophy is the stress on the institutionalization of *Sittlichkeit* and especially on the embodiment or incorporation of public spirit in a universal class—a stress later adapted by Marx on economic premises. Honoring the intent (though not the letter) of this legacy, I see the need for a renewed and more radical adaptation. Under democratic auspices, I believe, embodiment of public spirit can no longer be located in either a bureaucracy or a class but only in plural and heterogeneous groupings cross-cutting social divisions (or inhabiting the margins of such divisions). In our post-metaphysical or non-foundational context, such groups cannot constitute unified collectivities pursuing univocal goals but at best open-ended and shifting alliances dedicated only to a generic and almost non-purposive endeavor: the endeavor of healing the cleavages splitting society along racial, economic and other lines (as well as the cleavage between society and nature). Examples or approximations of such groupings in our time are fraternal organizations, rainbow coalitions, base communities, and especially the so-called new social movements concerned with such issues as ecology, nuclear disarmament, and the dismantling of discriminatory practices. I realize that these are only fledgling institutions vulnerable to exploitation by particular interests. Perhaps, to strengthen social and public ecumenicism, one should think of establishing or reinvigorating cross-cultural communal settings or ashrams, in the Gandhian sense, where people from different backgrounds could live and work together for a period of time. In Gandhi's description, ashrams are multidimensional meeting places bypassing caste, class, and religious barriers; in addition, communal functions or occupations are not distributed in terms of traditional sex or gender roles.[26]

To be sure, notions of this kind seem to collide head-on with postmodern accents on fragmentation, discontinuity, and rupture; clearly, concern with public *Sittlichkeit* does not concur readily with a Nietzschean will to power and particularly with Lyotard's celebration of general agonistics. Yet, the opposition may well be deceptive or misleading. As it seems to me, it is precisely post-metaphysics which militates against complete fragmentation or a self-enclosed particularism. Once foundational premises are dropped (be they located in substances or a generic subjectivity), no element of society can be accorded a stable, self-contained status or the character of univocal fixity. These considerations cast doubt first of all on every type of integral holism or collectivism; but they equally jeopardize the fixity and enclosure of fragments or particulars. However, once fixed separateness is abandoned, all elements or participants of society are seen to be involved in complex relationships—that is, in mutual assessments and reinterpretations—relationships which cannot be confined to the level of conflict or hostility (still wedded to separateness) but must include bonds of sympathy. At this point, democratic theorizing (I believe) gets caught up in Hegel's radical relationism—or in that "bacchanalian revel" of thought in which, as the *Phenomenology of Spirit* states, "no member remains sober" and in whose vortex every part that seeks to isolate itself "immediately dissolves." The same relationism, I would add, can still be invoked as locus of an open-ended public space and thus as emblem of a democratic social bond. No longer buttressed by stable or univocal state structures, public *Sittlichkeit* today must emerge from concrete human interactions cutting across entrenched cleavages and decentering all forms of self-enclosure. This view accords well with Hegel's *Philosophy of Right*, even in its most elevated and high-spirited expressions. As one of Hegel's personal annotations remarks (paraphrasing a poem by Goethe): "What is holy? That which binds humans together—even if it does so only lightly, like the rush a wreath. What is most holy? That which eternally combines and reconciles spirits, fashioning a genuine bond."[27]

8

BLOCH'S PRINCIPLE OF HOPE

Siehe ich mache alles neu.
Rev. 21, 5

Ours is not an age hospitable to utopias—or so it seems. World wars, holocaust, and the threat of nuclear disaster have spawned a pervasive temper of pessimism and despair, or at least a hard-boiled diffidence of broader visions. In Western industrial countries, this temper is aggravated by the upsurge of a realist pragmatism and utilitarianism wedded to robust self-interest and the satisfaction of private wants; transindividual projects—especially projects of a socialist type—are no longer seriously on the agenda. Against this background, the English-language publication of Ernst Bloch's Das *Prinzip Hoffnung* is a startling and perplexing event—akin to the surprise or enigma which, in Bloch's view, lights up the darkness of the "lived moment" propelling it toward future possibilities. Written or sketched for the most part between 1938 and 1947—the darkest phase of our century—Bloch's three-volume study is a sustained and breathtaking paean (easily the most comprehensive ever composed) to human hope and utopian aspirations in all forms and in all times and places. Only the most intensive hope, one may surmise, could have sustained Bloch himself in the successive peregrinations and emigrations of his life: a contemporary and close friend (for a time) of Georg Lukács, he was initially caught up in the socialist fervor unleashed by the October Revolution; forced to leave Germany under the Nazi regime, he returned to East Germany after the war to teach philosophy at Leipzig—until the tightening of repression prompted him to resettle in Tübingen (a move which coincided with the erection of the Berlin Wall). In terms of this life history, the English version of Bloch's opus involves a kind of restitution: conceived during the time of his American citizenship, the volumes extend belated recognition to a prodigal son.[1]

Despite its monumental structure and wide-ranging implications, Bloch's study (in its original German version) provoked only mixed or subdued reactions, especially among Marxist intellectuals. Among orthodox or positivist Marxists his work in general has always been anathema because of its presumed subjectivism, its lack of economic analysis, and its idiosyncratic (expressionistic) style of presentation. Even Western Marxists, however, have tended to remain aloof, treating his writings often as a marginal oddity or at best as a source of occasional insights buried in a welter of opacity. In the words of Martin Jay: "Bloch became and generally remained a scandal and embarrassment to most of his contemporaries in both orthodox and heterodox Marxist circles"; throughout his long life he was "an anomaly, a permanent outsider, the quintessential prophet wandering, as the title of one of his own books put it, 'through the desert.' "[2] After a period of closeness, Lukács soon withdrew from his friend, questioning the Marxist credentials of his utopianism. While sharing the emigré's fate with Adorno and Horkheimer, Bloch never became affiliated with the Frankfurt Institute in exile nor involved in its research program. During his stay in East Germany, his writings soon were criticized for their revisionist leanings and their deviation from official party doctrine. Later, commenting on symptoms of decline in Western Marxism, Leszek Kolakowski bitingly compared Bloch's uncommon ideas with "the fumes of an alchemist's laboratory." Approaching him from the vantage of a communicative rationalism, Habermas (less pejoratively) called him a "Marxist Schelling," chiding Bloch—as well as Schelling—for his attachment both to idealism and a speculative naturalism. "Speaking metaphorically," he wrote, "Bloch's thought takes its bearings from the development of a generally presumed pregnancy in the world rather than attempting to break the social spell cast by current contradictions. The philosophy of nature thus becomes the nature of his philosophy"—a philosophy, moreover, which on a "pre-critical" level is animated by the "breath of German idealism."[3]

To be sure, not all reactions to Bloch have been equally dismissive or reserved;[4] transplanted into novel surroundings, the present English translation may also generate a new and more nuanced appreciation of his work. One precondition for this is a close and patient reading of Bloch's text, a reading bracketing summary labels. In the present context, it cannot possibly be my ambition to comment on the full range of Bloch's encyclopedia of hope—which would vastly exceed the confines of a brief review. Fortunately, Bloch himself has offered clues or guideposts for a focused reading. Apart from elaborating broadly on the theme of hope, the Introduction gives a succinct synopsis or overview of the study's narrative structure, and especially of the five parts or subplots composing the work. After casually exploring everyday wishes and "little daydreams," the study turns in its "second and foundational part"—the part "founding and supporting everything else"—to the "examination of anticipatory consciousness." A main accent in this portion is on hunger as basic human "drive" and on hope as chief "anticipatory affect"; but the central effort revolves around "the *discovery and unmistakable notation of the 'Not-Yet-Conscious.'* "[5] Following a "transitional" interlude dealing with fairytales and other "mirrored" projections, Bloch's path leads, in a fourth stage, to the discussion of utopian blueprints in various fields (from medicine and social life to technology and art) and finally culminates in images of the "fulfilled moment" or the *summum bonum* as revealed in ethical yardsticks, in music, and— most importantly—in religious visions and yearnings from antiquity to the present. Taking my cues from Bloch's outline I shall concentrate first of all on the foundational part of the study and the main features of the so-called ontology of the Not-Yet. Next, I shall shift to the ultimate goal of all utopian longings, giving special attention to Bloch's account of the history of world religious and their respective contributions to the *summum bonum*. By way of conclusion, I mean to assess both the strengths and possible weaknesses or drawbacks of Bloch's arguments, and suggest some reformulations to enhance their continued relevance.

I

"In this book," Bloch announces his overall intention," a particularly extensive effort is made to bring philosophy into the proximity of hope— that is, to a place in the world as inhabited as the most civilized land and as unexplored as the Antarctic." In contrast to all backward looking or merely nostalgic thought, the basic theme of genuine philosophy for

Bloch is the "still unbecome, still unachieved homeland *(Heimat)* as it develops forward and upward in the dialectical-materialistic struggle of the new with the old." *The Principle of Hope* means to "set a signal" for this theme—moreover, a "forward signal" which enables readers to "overtake, not just trot behind." The name or meaning of this signal is "Not-Yet" and it is the chief task of the study "to grasp this meaning thoroughly." To make headway in this task, the foundational chapter takes its departure from anthropological and psychological considerations, and especially from the existential fact *(Dass)* of living with its built-in restlessness and urges: "The nature of our immediate being is empty and hence greedy, striving and hence restless." On the most basic level, the urges of existence may be termed "strivings" or "cravings," namely, cravings to do something or to move somewhere. However, in opposition to animal behavior, human existence is characterized not only by brute cravings but by "felt" or imaginary strivings, that is, strivings moving toward intended or imagined goals; in the latter case, craving gives way to "wishing" and imagining. When craving "passes over into wishing," Bloch notes, "it acquires a more or less definite idea of its target, and in fact as a *better* condition. The intensity of the wish rises precisely with the idea of the better, even perfect state of its fulfilling target." Regarding the underlying motivations of human wishes the chapter at this point examines a number of "drive" theories, and particularly the Freudian theory of instincts and the libidinal unconscious. What Bloch finds unattractive in this theory is essentially the derivative character of libido and the "retrospective" construal of the unconscious (as a storehouse of past images). "From Leibniz's discovery of the subconscious via the Romantic psychology of night and primeval past to the psychoanalysis of Freud," he writes, "basically only the aspect of 'backward dawning' has been described and investigated. Everything present—one thought—is loaded with memory, with past in the cellar of the No-Longer-Conscious; what was not noticed is that there is in the present, indeed in memory itself, an impetus and discontinuity, a brooding and anticipation of the Not-Yet-Become."[6]

Turning from critique to constructive theorizing, Bloch postulates as primary human drive—primary vis-à-vis sexual instincts—the sense of hunger and more broadly the drive of self-preservation. "A man dies without nourishment," he states laconically, "whereas one can live a while without love-making—and even longer without satisfying our power-drive and also without returning to the unconscious" of primeval forefathers. Although termed the "most reliable basic drive," hunger or self-preservation in Bloch's presentation is by no means free from historical change or variability, nor from giving rise to multiple affective modalities or manifestations. Turning against the simple division of affects into modes of appetite and aversion, or inclination and rejection, the chapter proposes the novel distinction between "filled" and "expectant" emotions, that is, affects capable of direct satisfaction and affects governed by long-term wishes or goals. "Filled emotions" (like envy, greed, admiration), we read, "are those whose drive intention is short-term, whose drive-object lies ready, if not in direct individual reach, then at least in the surrounding world. By contrast, *expectant emotions* (like anxiety, fear, hope, belief) are those whose drive intention is long-term, whose drive-object does not yet lie ready, neither in individual reach nor in the surrounding world, and whose beginning and outcome thus still hangs in the balance." According to Bloch, while some expectant emotions (like anxiety and fear) are purely passive, negative or reactive, there is one such affect—the "most authentic emotion of longing and thus of self"—which is actively or positively expectant and governed by the most open-ended and far-reaching drive-intention: the affect of hope. In his words: "Hope, this expectant counter-emotion against anxiety and fear, is *therefore the most human of all mental feelings and only accessible to men, and it also points to the furthest and brightest horizon."* In contrast to other affects, moreover, hope is not restricted to the emotional level, but can also acquire a measure of cognitive intentionality and consciousness—specifically "anticipatory consciousness" —as is evident in more or less conscious daydreams and utopian fantasies or projections: "What hovers beyond the self-extension drive is rather . . . the sphere of the Not-Yet-Conscious, of something never consciously known or actually existing in the past, therefore itself a forward dawning, toward the new. This is the dawning that can envelop even the simplest daydreams; from there it extends into further areas of negated deprivation, and hence of hope."[7]

For Bloch, forward projection or hopeful expectancy is on one level an inner affect or mental state—but it is more than that: anticipatory consciousness is matched and, as it were, borne along by a deep-seated ferment in the outer world or the structure of reality. As he puts it: just as man or human existence is not fully "solid" or self-contained, so there is "much in the world that is still unclosed or unfinished." The two forms of openness are interdependent like two sides of a coin; for "nothing would move inwardly either if the outside world were fully compact." This consideration leads to one of Bloch's central propositions: the notion that reality or "being" is not a static or fixed entity but rather a dynamic potency involved in an ongoing process of development. "Reality," he writes, "is a process; and the latter is the far-reaching mediation between present, unfinished past, and above all: possible future. In fact, everything real passes over into the possible at its forward-processual front, and possible is everything only partially conditioned, everything not yet fully or conclusively determined." To link up this notion of reality more closely with the study's central theme, the chapter introduces a distinction between two types of possibilities or "possible futures": an "objective" possibility captured by cognitive-scientific methods of prediction, and a "real" possibility transgressing the range of the predictable.

> '*Objectively* possible,' we read, 'is everything whose occurrence—on the basis of a partial *knowledge* of existing conditions—can be scientifically expected or at least not be discounted. *Really* possible, by contrast, is everything whose conditions are not yet fully assembled in the sphere of the *object* itself—either because they are still maturing or because new conditions (though mediated with existing ones) emerge for the occurrence of new realities.'

It is in the domain of real possibility that hope or utopian anticipation finds it real-life anchorage, lifting it above mere wishful thinking. Although initially rooted in hunger and expectancy, utopian imagination has in the possibility of "thoroughly mediated newness" its "second and concrete correlate—one lying outside the ferment and effervescence of inner-mental consciousness." Relying on such real-life mediation hope turns from wishing into *docta spes,* into concretely enlightened and "comprehended hope" *(begriffene Hoffnung).*[8]

Based on the distinction between two types of possibility, and also between fixed and evolving reality, Bloch also differentiates between two types of thinking or cognitive attitudes toward the world: a passive-contemplative attitude content with mirroring the world "as it is," and an active-participatory attitude engaged in the open process of reality and deliberately taking the side of hope. "Merely contemplative knowledge," he observes, "necessarily relates to what is finished and past, while being helpless in the present and blind toward the future." On the other hand, the kind of knowledge attuned to the future has "a different mode: one which is not merely contemplative but rather in step with the process, one which is an active partisan in league with evolving goodness; that is, with the humanly worthy in the process." Partisanship of thought at this point is by no means synonymous with a blind optimism or a simple belief in progress—a belief predicated precisely on the predictability and inevitability of a given outcome of history. In line with the category of "real possibility," instead, partisanship here signifies a willingness to labor on behalf of a possible future and to resist militantly its obstruction: "The attitude toward this undecided future—which, however, can be decided through labor and concretely mediated action—is called *militant optimism*." This aspect of militancy or commitment is closely connected in the chapter with several other concepts or categories characteristic of Bloch's outlook: especially the categories of the "front," of the *"novum"* and the *"ultimum."* By being actively engaged on behalf of a possible future, man takes a stand at the forward edge or "front" of both consciousness and reality. In Bloch's words: "Man and process, or rather: subject and object in the dialectical-material process (of the world) are consequently both stationed on the front. And there is no other place for militant optimism than the place opened up by the *category of front."* What happens at the front or emerges as real possibility is newness, novelty or the *"novum"*—a feature Bloch seeks to distance carefully from a Bergsonian *élan vital* with its amorphous or aimless connotations. Although unpredictable in a strict sense, novelty for Bloch is not devoid of *telos* or direction, a direction implanted in the unfolding process of reality itself. Correspondingly, novelty in the end points toward an *"ultimum"*—a stage in which novelty itself is dialectically transcended or suspended *(aufgehoben):* "The newness in the *ultimum* triumphs by virtue of a total leap out of all previous reality—but a leap toward a subsiding newness or toward identity. This category of the *ultimum* is not as unknown as that of the *novum*—since the idea of the 'last things' has always been a topic of those religions which set a time-limit to time itself."[9]

Elaborating further on the preceding passage, Bloch locates the "novelty" of his own approach in the intimate linkage of *novum* and *ultimum:* that is, in the idea that the final stage or highest good of mankind is something new and thus essentially related to the future rather than to a distant past. As he points out: "In the whole course of Judaeo-Christian philosophy, from Philo and Augustine to Hegel, the *ultimum* has been exclusively related to a *primum* and not to a *novum;* as a result, the 'last things' appear simply as the attained return of already completed 'first things' which had been lost or relinquished." This linkage of first and last things or of *primum* and *ultimum* was decisively prefigured in Plato's theory of recollection or *anamnesis, and it was* continued and deepened both in Stoic and in medieval-Christian philosophy. Although tracing the evolving experience of consciousness in his *Phenomenology of Spirit,* Hegel's category of absolute spirit finally submerged process in the timeless circularity of being. "Despite the sharpest lucidity of thought," Bloch comments, "the *ultimum* was here as elsewhere basically defused, in the sense that its Omega recoils back into the Alpha without the potency of the *novum."* The basic model or archetype of all these philosophical conceptions, in his view, is that of a circular movement in which beginning and ending converge, that is, of an "Alpha-Omega" equation within the ring-structure of a "primal being," a being to which process "returns almost like a prodigal son, undoing the substance of its *novum*." Challenging this ring-structure, Bloch attacks traditional conceptions as "prison-formations against real possibility" or as defensive mechanisms seeking to perceive "even the most progressive historical product solely as the recollection or restoration of something once possessed, primally lost." As an antidote to such construals, the chapter invokes terms like "anti-recollection," "anti-circle" and "anti-Hegel," insisting that—wedded to the *novum*—genuine hope cannot possibly be contained within circular or cyclical repetition. From the vantage of the "principle of hope," we are told, the *ultimum* or goal is precisely not a mode of recovery, but rather involves the "blasting open of the *primum agens materiale*"; differently put: the Omega of the goal is not derived from an original or primeval Alpha, but rather "the origin clarifies itself only through the *novum* of the end." As a consequence, the anticipated utopia of freedom takes the form "not of a return but of an exodus—though an exodus into the always intended land promised by process.[10]

To buttress the plausibility or legitimacy of this outlook, Bloch in this context appeals to the legacy of dialectical materialism—a legacy whose antecedents he traces back ultimately to Aristotle's metaphysics. Despite the previous indictment of much of Western or occidental philosophy, Aristotle and his successors are basically exempted from the charge of ontological fixity and actually celebrated as a kind of counterpoint to the mainstream of Western thought. What is chiefly attractive in Aristotle's metaphysics is his definition of matter in terms of *dynamis* or a built-in possibility or tendency—a possibility exceeding the purely mechanical level of material structure. In Aristotle's thought, we read, "matter is by no means limited to the mechanical"; instead, the latter is "for the first time correlated here with the extremely comprehensive concept of *dynamis* or objective-real possibility." Moreover, *dynamis* or possibility operates in Aristotle's metaphysics in two forms: as a more or less inhibiting or structuring nexus of conditions and as an enabling power or potency. In Bloch's words: "Matter is not only 'kata to dynaton' (according to possibility) and thus a conditioning factor relating to the given measure of the possible; rather, it is 'to dynamei on' (being-in-possibility) and therefore the—in Aristotle admittedly still passive—*womb of fertility from which all world-forms inexhaustibly emerge.*" From Aristotle the path of the philosophical counterpoint leads over the Peripatetic school and Arab Aristotelians (like Avicenna and Averroes) to Christian heretical thinkers—especially the "world-creating matter" of Giordano Bruno—and finally to Marx. Even Hegel's philosophy is said to contain traces of Aristotle's concept of *dynamis*—which explains why Marx was able "to place the Hegelian world-spirit so naturally on its feet." In the end it is Marxism, however, which inherited and reformulated decisively the anticipatory thrust of dialectical materialism. In effect, Marxist philosophy is described as a philosophy "of the future—including the future contained in the past"; it is a living philosophy "engaged in the process, in league with the *novum*." And "what is crucial: the principle in whose light the processual-unclosed totality is reflected and promoted is *docta spes* or a dialectical-materialistically comprehended hope."[11]

Recapitulating many of the previous arguments, the conclusion of the "founding" chapter delineates the major dimensions of the ontology of the "Not-Yet" (or "Not-Yet-Conscious"). This ontology, as it now emerges, encompasses the basic categories of the "Not" relating to origins or beginnings, of the "Not-Yet" as characteristic of historical process, and of the "Nothing" or conversely the "All" pertaining to the goal or *ultimum*. The first category points to the fact of immediate existence, the dark unrest of the lived moment. "The facticity of the 'now' is hollow," we read, "it is undefined to begin with, a fermenting *Not*. It is the Not from which everything starts up and begins, around which everything is to be built." According to Bloch, the "Not" is not a thing or a defined presence, but neither is it simply a void; rather, being always the "Not" or negation of something, it is not a pure absence but instead a "not-something" or "not-presence" *(Nicht-Da)*. Ambivalent in its nature, the "Not" cannot be a self-contained entity but is always tensionally related to something. Ontologically speaking, the "Not" is a "lack" of being and its basic impulse is to escape from this lack—which gives rise to human drives, especially the drives of hunger and expectancy, and thus to the ongoing projection of the "Not-Yet." In Bloch's presentation, the "Not" has to be distinguished radically from "Nothing" or nothingness. While the former is enmeshed in the darkness of the moment and its incipient drives, "Nothing" is a pure negativity or mode of annihilation. "Although the Not may be emptiness," Bloch states, "it is also the drive to break out of it; in hunger or privation, emptiness manifests itself precisely as *horror vacui*, as the abhorrence of nothingness by the Not"—or else as directedness toward the "All" or plenary being. As he adds, the dimensions of the sketched ontology are not simply abstract-speculative constructs but rather labels fitted to concrete human affects and real-life events. Thus, the terms "Not," "Not-Yet," and "Nothing" (or "All") are categories "which illuminate in highly condensed terminology the intensively evolving world-substance in its

three principal moments." Differently phrased: they are "real categories" or "regional categories of reality as such" whose interrelation "most
closely approximates the objective-affective content, and thus the qualitative intensity of process-matter in its three basic aspects."[12]

II

Proceeding from these ontological premises, Bloch's study makes its
way slowly through a number of detours and "transitional" terrains—
including fairytales, wishful images, and utopian blueprints—to arrive
finally at visions of the *ultimum* or portrayals of "the fulfilled moment."
Among the various visions discussed in the study's concluding part,
easily the most fascinating and wide-ranging thematic field is occupied
by religion and religious imagery. The attention given to this field and
the tenor of the treatment are particularly noteworthy given the author's
allegiance to Marxism and the latter's frequent identification with a
simplistic atheism. Although not averse to reason or enlightenment,
Bloch shares none of the customary anti-religious biases of modernity—
extending a sympathetic hearing (or the benefit of the doubt) even to
dubious magical or mythical beliefs. In the context of his ontology, religion is a manifestation of man's deepest hopes and utopian longings,
that is, of the tendency of the "Not-Yet" with its goal of plenary being.
While frequently mixed with superstition, illusion or ignorance, he
writes, religious hope is not synonymous with the latter; for, "it was
people in great need who, in protest against their fate, attempted to
change it magically-mythically and turn it for the good. Thus, religious
imagination can by no means be dismissed *in toto* by the achieved
disenchantment of world-views." Despite widespread abuses and debas-
ing practices, religion throughout history elevated mankind above immediate misery and narrow self-concern, propelling it toward the farthest
horizons. In the face of pervasive despair and frustration, "this sighing,
invoking, preaching" characteristic of religion "lived and raised its sight
toward the bright dawn"; and even in the midst of "the (easily identi-
fiable) nonsense of some mythical beliefs" there persisted and arose
perennially "the unanswered question—one fervently pursued only in
religions—about the still enigmatic meaning of life."[13]

    Although rooted in hunger and existential ferment, religion or
religiosity for Bloch is not simply an inner-psychic state, but rather an
expectancy placed at the very edge (and, in a sense, beyond the pale) of
the human condition. Reacting against a shallow humanism—against
the "impudent, cozy-liberal attitude enamored with itself"—Bloch insists
on the radical rupture or breach induced by the religious *ultimum*, a

breach reflected in the biblical words: "For my thoughts are not your thoughts, nor are your ways my ways." Turning to recent philosophy of religion, the chapter fully endorses Rudolf Otto's notion of "numinosity" as hallmark of religious faith. "This remoteness, nay even this dread of the *threshold*," we read, "is part of every religious experience, or it is none"; to this extent Otto is quite right in treating " 'radical otherness' as emblem of the religious object and the 'shuddering numinous' as the aura of holiness." Despite some starkly anti-human overtones, even dialectical theology is invoked at this point as an antidote to complacency. Barthian neo-orthodoxy in particular—represented by some choice statements from the commentary on *Romans*—serves as counterpoint to a reductive immanentism. Against the progressive domestication of the divine, Bloch observes, "Barth appeals to the *Deus absconditus*," the God beyond our cognitive grasp. Despite his tendency to promote religious heteronomy and even a theistic "despotism," Barth's theology has a valid point; at the "grotesque price" of anti-humanism something else is salvaged—"the *humanum*, the *Cur Deus homo* is protected from the trivialization engendered by an all-too sociable liberalism." Thus, notwithstanding its important drawbacks—especially its proclivity to remove the "son of man" as mediator from Christianity itself—Barth's approach is said to harbor a "significant warning or admonition": for it "fanatically defends" a reverence or reverential sphere which "in the subject-relation of religion is so easily lost, right down to the vapid psychologism and priggishness of an educated philistinism." What needs to be done to defuse the illiberalism of a purely negative theology is to rescue or win over its valid core to the side of a "religious or metareligious humanism": For, "only the *deus absconditus* preserves the *problem* of what the legitimate mystery of the *homo absconditus* may be all about."[14]

From Bloch's perspective, thus, humanism is by no means necessarily secular; on the contrary. Precisely when spurious transcendentalisms are demythologized, when (following Feuerbach) religion is seen as a human enterprise or projection—precisely then humanism must be given its broadest contours; differently put: the breach or difference between the divine and the human—a breach no *analogia entis* can fully remove—must ultimately be seen as a difference within man or the human itself. In Bloch's words, "this remains decisive: *radical otherness also holds good for the ultimate humane projections from religion*. It is radical otherness which gives to all the longings for the divinization of man the proper dimension of depth; it is the same otherness which bestows on the hubris of Prometheus its true heaven-storming quality distinguishing it from the flatness of mere individualism and the feeble humanization of the taboo." Rescued from an alien heteronomy and applied to the human domain or *regnum humanum*, numinosity no longer signifies surrender or capitulation to an external power but rather means openness toward the mystery in man—an openness which cannot think highly enough of the human. Shedding its estranging or oppressive quality, religious experience here gains a sense of wonder and appreciation for the miraculous—especially for the explosive-miraculous potency of a hope transgressing man toward his otherness. According to Bloch, the utopian content of all religions, and particularly of messianic expectations, has always been a kind of "homecoming," a desire to be "at home" in existence—but a desire far removed from any cozy comfortableness, any restriction of existence to its "readily surveyable and merely parochial concerns." Rather, homecoming as religious goal means being at home "in the *mystery* of existence."[15]

Seen in a historical perspective, religious evolution does not simply mean secularization or modernization (in the sense of growing disbelief), but rather a process of humanization—a transfer of mystery from distant or alien powers to the heart of human existence or to the core of real life. In Bloch's account, the succession of world-religions reveals increasingly the human face of divine mystery—a circumstance highlighted by the steadily profiled human-ness of religious founders and their growing personal involvement or investment in the revelation of the divine; but the same development does not merely yield an immanent anthropomorphism. Precisely to the extent that the humanity of religious founders has penetrated the divine mystery, he writes, to the same extent man in his "earth-heaven" is charged or infused with "reverence for depth and infinity." Thus, "the growing humanization of religion is not paralleled by any reduction in its sense of awe, on the contrary: the *humanum* now gains the mystery of something divine." The greatest advance in the direction of humanization, according to the study, was initiated by Christianity and the person of its founder, especially through the messianic promise of the "coming kingdom" which ultimately coincides with the *regnum humanum*. In Bloch's words: "Christianity accentuated the mediation between subjective religious experience and the previous taboo of the religious object-side—a mediation which is here called kingdom, the kingdom of God." As he elaborates (somewhat boldly) on scriptural prophesy, the coming kingdom is essentially a reign of freedom—a reign liberated in the end even of God, to the extent that the latter is seen as a separate positivity or a heteronomous-oriental potentate—thus giving rise to a non-repressive community which is more, however, than an immanent construction: "God becomes the kingdom of God, and the kingdom of God no longer contains a god, which means: religious heteronomy and its reified hypostasis are completely dissolved in the theology of the community—but of one which has itself stepped beyond the threshold of *the previously existing creature, of its anthropology and sociology.*" In lieu of a facile continuity, Christian promise points to a "new heaven and new earth," to a "rebirth" of man and a "transfiguration of nature."[16]

To buttress and flesh out the notion of humanization, Bloch offers a detailed narrative of the development of religious beliefs, with a focus on successive world-religions and their founders. In terms of this narrative, the story proceeds basically from belief in distant-alien gods or a passive contemplation of the divine (seen as pre-given) to a growing rapprochement and active-human participation in the divine. "Man," we read, "wants to be close to the powers in which he believes, however much he feels subject to them"; thus, the founders of religion "invest themselves increasingly in radical otherness, turning it into the mystery of a human or humanly mediated context." The story opens in prehistoric times when primitive people worshipped gods seen as "foreign teachers" or alien wanderers. Called Ram among the Celts and Cadmus by the Greeks, such gods were essentially faceless, their names only signaling the shift "from animal to man." While slightly more profiled, even Orpheus and Dionysus were basically pre-human, functioning chiefly as symbols for powerful natural forces and instinctual drives. In comparison with earlier magical and Orphic beliefs, the Olympian gods (as depicted by Homer and Hesiod) were distinctly more human, even anthropomorphic—but at the price of a certain superficiality manifest in their subjection to an inexorable destiny or fate. In Bloch's presentation, only Prometheus and Attic tragedy offered a counterweight to Olympian complacency and a statically fixed fate. Turning from Greece to ancient Egypt and Babylon, the story encounters again complete facelessness and complete submission to heteronomous forces: "The Babylonian and the Egyptian god is considered super-human precisely because he is *inhuman,* animal-headed or star-like." This non-human quality attached even to legendary founders of religion like Thot, who was pictured not as a man but as a god with the head of an ibis. Instead of representing human hopes, Thot personified measurement, numbers, or geometry; clinging to recurrence of the same and a static essence, his message was the extreme concentration of an "extra-human repose." Generally speaking, Egyptian religion for Bloch is the epitome of fixity if not of *rigor mortis.* In his words: "Egypt is not the religion of enigma—as Hegel defined it from the vantage of the Greek sphinx myth—but rather the religion of the *most complete estrangement, of silence and its crystal.*" Babylon with its astral cult bore a close resemblance to this fixity: "As the Nile was dominated by the pyramid, with a corpse at its center, the Euphrates was governed by the stepped tower, dedicated to the seven planets and the houses through which the sun moves."[17]

In comparison with the legendary figures of the Near East, the founders of religion (or a quasi-religious ethics) in China bore a distinctly human face; moreover, their message was no longer the worship of heteronomous forces but the promotion of a type of conduct. Yet, according to Bloch, both Confucius and Lao Tzu retreated entirely behind their message, thus approaching again a kind of anonymity. Confucius was the teacher of the "mean" and of moderate-equitable behavior—a teaching which fitted well into the context of a post-feudal empire in which the emperor symbolized the mean or middle between heaven and earth. Confucianism no longer pays tribute to magical-demonic powers or to astral-mythical constellations; rather it revolves around the balance or harmony between heaven and earth maintained by a concrete empire or *regnum humanum*. As Bloch writes: "Yin and Yang as a whole turn into the earthly and heavenly scales of a great balance— the longed-for universal harmony; and in all this the human world, headed by the emperor, is no longer subjected to nature-gods but only to the *idea of heaven* (which—a specific feature of East Asia—is *no god*)." If Confucius was a subdued or "reticent" founder, Lao Tzu sought to vanish entirely behind his teachings: "The genuine, mystic teacher of Tao appeared by disappearing: Lao Tzu went westward, over the mountain pass, never to be seen again, leaving only his book behind." While Confucius codified proper behavior in the empire, Lao Tzu's message was counter-cultural, averse to established norms, and even hostile to governmental rule; while the former provided a "measure which is easy to keep," the latter counseled "something simple which is hardest to do": namely, a turn to wisdom, a reintegration of self into cosmic harmony, into the "inconspicuous rhythm of the world." Central to Taoism was the emphasis on "non-desiring" and "non-making" and thus on inner tranquility—which, however, was not synonymous with a simple quietism (in the Western sense) but encouraged participation in organic spontaneity. Yet, in counseling integration Taoism also muffled the self-propelled, "extra-natural" character of man: "Again and again the paradox of a pan-human cosmos without human beings breaks through; men disappear in it like all things—indeed like the Tao itself."[18]

The founders with the liveliest human features, in Bloch's account, are five: Buddha, Zoroaster, Moses, Jesus, and Mohammed—a sequence reflecting a steady growth of utopian urgency. Buddha no longer merely pointed to higher principles or to a distant path to wisdom; rather, he sought to exemplify or instantiate his teachings: He "wanted to be nothing but this way and its path, freed from suffering, worldless, prefigured for all men in one." Drawing on Vedic insights and portions of Sankhya philosophy, Buddha chose to personify the path of non-desiring or redemption from desiring and thus to become "the founder-figure— without self-centeredness and without Brahma (or god)—marking the exit route from the suffering of the world caused by the malign impulse of illusion." In his life and his teachings, Buddha proved himself to be a genuine founder, more precisely: as *Tathagata* or the "one who redeems himself." Yet, despite this personal investment, the content of his message in the end demanded his self-effacement or withdrawal—a withdrawal even beyond Lao Tzu's westward mountain pass in the direction of a distant nowhere-land or *Nirvana*. While Taoism still counseled man's integration into a cosmic rhythm, Buddhism even dispelled belief in this rhythm, replacing the latter by an "immense *acosmism*" which was the result of a "thoroughgoing disillusionment or destruction of illusions in this world and in any transcendent world." In contrast to this strategy of retreat, Zoroaster launched himself directly into battle against the forces of the world, more specifically: against the powers of darkness which, from the beginning of time, have sought to defeat or obstruct the reign of light or goodness. With this notion of battle, a world-transforming, historical dynamic entered the arena of religious belief. In Bloch's words: "*History* penetrates into the astral-mythical stasis: the whole world becomes history, namely, the scuffle in which Ormuzd and Ahriman are entangled." Although linked with Babylonian traditions, Zoroaster was no longer a mythical symbol, but a man or "son of man": under the name "Gayomard" or "primal man of light" he was from the beginning at Ormuzd's side. Moreover, as historical figure, Zoroaster foreshadowed a later or final prophet with a messianic calling: "like the Messiah, Saoshyant stands at the end of the days, as lord of the final judgment or the separation of good and evil."[19]

The thrust of a world-transforming dynamic was intensified by Moses. What in Zoroastrism (and later Manichaeism) still remained a cosmic-symbolic battle, turned in Judaism into a concrete historical exodus from distinct modes of oppression. According to Bloch Moses signaled a "leap in religious consciousness"—a leap prepared by an event which was diametrically opposed to former religions of "worldly piety or astral-mythical fate": the event of "*rebellion, the exodus from Egypt*." By sanctifying this event, Moses became the first "*heros eponymos*," the first "name-giving founder of a *religion of opposition*." Compared with near-Eastern and far-Eastern founders, Moses is to Bloch the most personally concrete, the one with the "most profiled human features" who began his career by slaying a taskmaster. Thus, more than elsewhere, "suffering and rebellion stand here at the beginning of faith," marking the religion as a "path into the open." This rebelliousness, however, characterized not only the beginning of Mosaic Judaism but remained a persistent, constitutive trait—leading in the end even to the subversion of the "lordliness" (or heteronomy) of the traditional Yahweh-God in favor of a *regnum humanum*. This subversion was voiced by Job, the preacher Solomon, and in many prophetic sayings where God was not merely revered but measured by the divine yardstick of goodness—and sometimes found wanting. In Bloch's words, through the commitment of Moses the "content of salvation" changed from earlier conceptions: Instead of a fixed essence of the world or a fixed *telos* "there now appears *a promised goal that first must be achieved;* instead of the visible nature-god there appears *an invisible god of righteousness and of the kingdom of righteousness.*" Relying on the phrase from *Exodus* "*Eh'je asher eh'je*" —translated as "I shall be who I shall be"—Bloch attributes to the Mosaic God a future-oriented quality. The phrase, he comments, "places at the very threshold of the Yahweh-phenomenon a god of the end of days, with *futurum* as an attribute of Being." With this shift, the "Omega-god" takes precedence over the "Alpha-god," the *Deus spes* over the *Deus creator* of a supposedly finished and perfect world. This futurism is further underscored by the messianic strand in Judaism, a strand steadily gaining prominence during the last centuries B.C. In messianic expectancy, the promised goal entirely prevails over the "Alpha-god"—to the point of involving even an exodus from existing creation: "Despite his subordination to Yahweh, the Messiah is regarded as nearly equal to him, but as the good God, the helper and goodness in God."[20]

The humanization of faith reached its peak in Jesus of Nazareth— whose life story in its humble details testifies to his historical concreteness. In contrast to embellished legends of founders, Jesus's life shows distinctly anti-mythical traits—among them, in Bloch's view, the trait of personal shyness or aversion to self-apotheosis. "The stable at the beginning and the gallows at the end," he writes, "scarcely fitted into the legendary image of a savior, but shyness is completely alien to it. Likewise the temptations and despondencies of Jesus are uninventable: they say *Ecce homo,* not Attis-Adonis." While distant from pagan myth, Jesus also was at odds with a Yahweh-God construed as alien positivity or potentate. Leaving behind the imperial "throne-room," Jesus put himself as "son of man" into the highest region, making himself more concretely present in this "humanization of his God" than did Zoroaster or Buddha. To be sure, he did not exalt existing man but rather "the utopia of something humanly possible," a utopia whose core and "eschatological fraternity" he exemplified in his life. The ultimate test of this fraternity was the death on the cross—which, Bloch insists, should not be seen as atonement for human sins but as the revenge of the world against Christ's message. "The real Jesus," he writes, "died as a rebel and martyr, not as a paymaster"; his death was the world's reward for the "rebel of love," the "rebel against custom and ruling powers," the "tribune of the final, apocalyptically sanctioned exodus from Egypt." Theologically, what led to his crucifixion was not the claim of being the Messiah (a claim which had gone unpunished previously many times) but rather his insurgency against the existing world with its temporal and religious hierarchies: "Only because the Messiah appeared as the 'son of man' in the pre-cosmic as well as apocalyptic meaning of the term, because he announced a natural catastrophe destroying even Jerusalem and the temple as the instrument and evidence of his triumph, was he treated as a blasphemer and worthy of death." Ultimately, Jesus and his message represented *"eschatology through and through,"* just as his love and ethical teaching can only be grasped in reference to the "coming kingdom," as an "advent" ethics; his Sermon on the Mount, in particular, was "purely adventist" embodying a vision of "impending apocalypse" or "end of the world."[21]

In his apocalyptic urgency Jesus in the end overshadowed and out-distanced his father, the traditional Yahweh seen as "Alpha-God." In dying on the cross out of love Jesus accomplished something of which Yahweh despite his omnipotence was incapable: he embodied an idea and "love of god such as had never been conceived in any god." Thus, Christ's blasphemy consisted not only in his eschatology but in his self-substitution for the "Alpha-god" (though not the God of *"Eh'je asher eh'je"*). Referring to the passage in the gospel of John comparing the "son of man" with the brass serpent held up by Moses in the desert, Bloch sees in the comparison an allusion to the "serpent of paradise" and thus an intimation of Christ's insurgency against a heteronomous demiurge (an intimation historically developed by Ophites, gnostics, and other heretical sects). In essence, Christ's ascendancy and self-substitution heralded the "coming kingdom" as a *regnum humanum:* it replaced theologically divine heteronomy "by Christ's *homousia* or equal-ity to God"; and it operated "democratically and mystically" as the *"per-fection of the exodus god into the god of the kingdom,"* thus as the "dissolution of Yahweh into this glory." In announcing the kingdom, Jesus is also at work in the paraclete or consoler—but in a special way: not simply as the historical, but as the future Christ, the one perform-ing the "leap into the *novum*" of radical otherness: "The paraclete thus becomes the utopia of the son of man—who is no longer utopia when the kingdom is present."

The spirit of utopian hope is operative also in Islam, a religion characterized by a much higher degree of militancy or zealous passion than mainstream Christianity (or Judaism). Apart from prophetic passages in the Koran, utopianism has been sustained chiefly by Islamic mystics—especially through their belief in a final prophet *(Mahdi)* and in an eschatological spirit, called *Chidr* or *al Chadir,* resembling the paraclete. According to Sufi mysticism, the coming kingdom is like "the joy of life after victory in battle," a victory transfiguring all creation and elevating the elect into a divine union or communion.[22]

Concluding his narrative of religious beliefs, Bloch returns to the distinction between Alpha and Omega, between God construed as a fixed or completed entity and the divine as a future promise. As he points out, the distinction coincides with that between a spatial and temporal theology:

> Whereas the god in space, in high altitude, has his perfection essentially as highest *being,* throning as it were above the roof of all world-being, the God of the last days has his being essentially as highest *perfection* which is apocalyptically different from any kind of existing world-being. While the spatial god of astral myth leads to pantheism (the worship of the totality of existing things), the exodus God releases totality out of the existing world-being, chiliastically.

The latter God thus instantiates a future promise: the promise of the kingdom conceived as *regnum humanum*—a conception epitomized by the Christian stress on the son of man over the Alpha-god. The same historical thrust—the focus on the question *Cur Deus homo?*—was later continued by Feuerbach with his "anthropologization of religion," although the latter tended to treat man in turn as a fixed entity rather than an open-ended promise. Feuerbach's move, in order not to be self-canceling, presupposes "a utopian notion of man, not a statically determined one"; it also implies "a *homo absconditus* in the same way as belief in heaven always carried a *Deus absconditus* with it." Just as anthropology contains a religious motive, so atheism properly understood harbors an eschatological hope—an aspect completely missed by the trivial irreligiosity of Enlightenment thinkers (and vulgar Marxists). What is denied by genuine atheism is only the *Jupiter Optimus Maximus* or Alpha-potentate, not the utopian content of the *optimum maximum,* namely, the future kingdom without heteronomy. In Bloch's words: The religious intention of the kingdom "involves atheism (properly understood)"—to the extent that atheism "removes what is meant by God, the *ens perfectissimum,* from the beginning and the world-process and defines it not as facticity but as what it can only be: the highest utopian issue, that of the end" (Omega).[23]

III

A sprawling edifice of vast proportions, Bloch's *Principle of Hope* is clearly an intellectual *tour de force.* After wandering through its many corridors, sidechambers, and secret passageways, the reader is likely to feel stunned if not overwhelmed both by Bloch's magic of words and the depth of his insights. In my view, one of the most attractive features of the work is its rebellious youthfulness and undaunted confidence in future human possibilities. In an age of rampant pessimism, cultural nostalgia and retrenchment, Bloch's study is a breath of fresh air—a large window opening up (especially for Western readers) vistas of a still unfinished history. The half century since the original composition of the work has done nothing to dampen its zest or contagious impact; despite a radically changed context, Bloch's message remains that of an upright posture without servility or arrogance. Equally attractive—and still more intellectually captivating—is the author's portrayal of social development not in terms of a linear disenchantment or secularization, but as a steady concretization of faith. Contrary to the story reiterated from Voltaire to Weber and beyond, social evolution in this view involves not simply the expulsion or exile of religious utopia from human life but rather its instantiation and the correction of a false heteronomy. Strongly and eloquently argued in *The Principle of Hope,* this outlook is not entirely unique to Bloch but has been fleshed out by various philosophers (or philosophers of religion), including Ricoeur. As the latter has observed on numerous occasions, secularization does not necessarily signify the elimination of faith as rather its transfer to the secular city, in the sense of a possible sanctification of the profane or of mundane endeavors. Against this background, disenchantment and desacralization is a double-edged process, involving "not only the dissolution of religion in contemporary culture but also the flowering of an originally biblical theme": namely, "the struggle against the Baals, gods of nature and lords of the earth" and "the preaching of a God who inaugurates and accompanies history more than he consecrates (existing) nature."[24]

Bloch's views on this topic are all the more striking given his Marxist leanings and his pronounced social-political progressivism—a combination which no doubt accounts for his neglect or dismissal in many quarters. Basically, Bloch's religious utopianism is a stumbling block to devotees both of the "Red" and the "Black," that is, both to relentless modernizers wedded to disenchantment and to religious conservatives celebrating the glories of past ages of belief and the untrammeled power of Yahweh (seen as Alpha-god). For the latter, his work means a challenge to established doctrines and beliefs, making it an accomplice of modernism, while the former suspect it for its tendency of mystification. Opposing the pitfalls of both camps, Bloch offers instead a religious faith without obscurantism, a devotion to the numinous without passivity or slavish surrender. As he points out in his comments on the numinous as radical otherness: "Such estrangement is everywhere part of religion, even of religion seen from a utopian perspective and seen utterly without obscurantism. Its *obscurum*—'The Lord said that he would dwell in the thick darkness' (I Kings 8, 12)—is not that of superstition which has pitted too little knowledge against fate, but one of knowledge-conscience *(Wissen-Gewissen)* that finds itself permanently surrounded by the uncanny in the depths and yearns to resolve or mediate it into nothing else but—wonder." Relying on the intrinsic numinosity of human life or existence, Bloch rebukes both the fixation of the divine in past contents and trivial types of irreligion—as promoted by scientism and some forms of Marxism: "As explanation of the world, a merely mechanical materialism has discarded the place of the previous god-hypostasis at its margin—but it has also discarded life, consciousness, process, the switch from quantity to quality, the *novum,* and dialectics as a whole."[25]

Bloch's peculiar status regarding religion—between fundamentalism and disbelief—is paralleled in his ontological or metaphysical stance, as manifest in his opposition both to ontological essentialism (or objectivism) and to anti-metaphysical skepsis. As indicated, his ontology of the Not-Yet seeks to capture the dynamism and unfinished character of being, the openness of the concrete world-process toward novelty and a future promise. In both critiquing metaphysics and revalorizing it on a new plane, his work inserts itself squarely into post-metaphysical trends in our century (from Heidegger to Derrida)—especially trends emphasizing rupture, discontinuity, and non-coincidence (or difference); his stress on wonder and on the centrality of questioning, in particular, resonates with important contemporary efforts to revive Socratic ignorance as an antidote to systemic closure. While appreciating these and many related virtues of Bloch's approach, I feel impelled at the same time to voice some reservations both regarding his ontology and his religious utopianism. Concerning the former, I am uneasy about the stark differentiation between "Not" and "Nothing" (or nothingness)— the first term designating a latent pregnancy or tensional striving and the second a pure negativity or annihilation. As a mode or act of predication, the "not" cannot stand alone but presupposes the ontological category of nothingness (as Heidegger, among others, has repeatedly observed). If "not" is separated from and given precedence over nothingness, both nothingness and all-being tend to become matters entirely of human choice or commitment—which injects into ontology an element of decisionism if not arbitrary bias. If this outcome is to be avoided, if (that is) nothingness and all-being are granted ontological primacy, then the lived moment and its darkness must be characterized not simply by "not" but rather by a "yes" and "no," an affirmation and a negation with the result that the "Not-Yet" cannot simply be a "*not-yet*" in the sense of being the carrier of radical novelty, but instead must signify a genuine ambivalence or a blending of discontinuity and continuity, of newness as well as tradition.[26]

These considerations are relevant on a broader philosophical plane —especially with respect to Bloch's critique of the static quality and circularity of traditional Western philosophy. No doubt, this is difficult terrain and one entirely uncongenial to quick or summary judgments. Surely, recent discussions about foundationalism have amply alerted us to the pitfalls of a rigid essentialism and the perils of ontological reification. Seeking to overcome such dangers, Bloch proceeds to temporalize being and, in particular, to infuse ontology with a futurist quality or an orientation toward the *novum*. While valuable as an antidote to reification, this strategy becomes dubious, however, when pursued unidirectionally—that is, when the future is privileged completely at the expense of other temporal modes. For clearly, the future is only the future of a present or past, just as the past is only the past of a present or future. Against this background, the issue of circularity needs to be reassessed. Particularly in Hegel's case, the charge of static repetitiveness or a purely retrospective Platonism strikes me as odd or vastly exaggerated—given Hegel's emphasis on the experience of mind and the progressive movement of the world spirit in history. On the other hand, Aristotle's portrayal as a distinctly futurist thinker is no less precarious— especially since *dynamis* or real possibility is also described as the "womb of fertility from which all world-forms inexhaustibly emerge" (which suggests not a rupture but a close nexus of past and future). Generally speaking, temporalization or historicization of being cannot simply mean a forward projection—although such projection is surely involved—but only an interplay or circulation of temporal modes whose center is peculiarly at rest; to this extent, ontological thought is always in a sense circular—without being merely static or retrospective. Bloch seems to recognize this point when he depicts the fulfilled moment as one which sets "a time-limit to time," and also in his comments on the Faustian "Stay awhile" *(Verweile doch)* and the mystical "instant" or *nunc aeternum.* In mystical experience, he writes, "an entry into the immediacy of the moment takes place" which is "no longer located in time"; its name therefore is "*nunc stans* or *nunc aeternum,* a name in which the most extreme opposites—moment and eternity—circulate or interchange in perfect dialectical unity."[27]

Apart from ontological dilemmas, there are other—practical and theological—drawbacks connected with a privileging of the future. If past and present are completely devalued, then the future becomes a radical novelty or innovation—which can only happen either through divine intervention or as a result of spontaneous human production or fabrication. The first alternative—associated with an extreme version of dialectical theology—is criticized by Bloch for its heteronomous and even despotic connotations and, in any case, as being at odds with the process of humanization. In the second option, on the other hand, novelty is strictly a human construct—a view which aggravates the technological thrust of our age and completely foils the mystery or wonder of the expected *ultimum.* In discussing technical blueprints and in other passages, Bloch is not averse to celebrating *homo faber* and his accomplishments. Thus, while noting the fragility of human designs, he also points to "the *positive* side of a subject-related value-theory, the side geared to *production:* nothing is any longer ready-made or prepackaged, but rather man builds his house in an inhospitable world according to his own measure."[28] Yet, this cannot be Bloch's last word, given the numinosity of man's measure, its elusive opening toward otherness. Moreover, a constructed future conflicts with the process-character of reality, that is, the central role of *dynamis* or real possibility (in contrast to mere wishful thinking). In line with this processual structure, the future must somehow be prepared—though not strictly determined—by the past, a preparation which is more akin to pregnancy or creative labor than to fabrication. In a sense, the three volumes of *The Principle of Hope* testify eloquently to this preparatory labor of history: in exploring daydreams, fairytales, and religious utopias, Bloch invariably detects future anticipations in past experiences or formulas—which for this reason are not simply false or obsolete.

On a theological plane, the issue of temporalization surfaces in the opposition between the Alpha- and the Omega-god, and the primacy granted to the latter over the former. In Bloch's account, this opposition frequently carries a radically chiliastic, if not Manichean flavor. In discussing Zoroastrian teachings, he notes appreciatively the fervor unleashed by the stark contrast between light and darkness and by the prospect of a destruction of the existing world by the forces of light. This dualistic outlook even carries over into the portrayal of Jesus as the voice of "eschatology through and through." "The world of Jesus," he writes at one point, "was that of Mandaean-Persian dualism, with Satan as the lord of this aeon and the kingdom of light as that of the directly imminent new era. The Messiah here is the bringer of world conflagration" just as the miracle occurs "only *against this world and its irredeemable condition* as interruption." In exploring early Christian beliefs, Bloch gets ensnared and carried away—in my view—by gnostic speculations regarding Christ as the serpent rebelling against the creator-god seen as Satanic ruler of this world. In these and other portions of the study, religious utopianism seems to envisage not so much a transfiguration of nature as rather its destruction and total reconstitution. Contrary to Habermas's allegation of a speculative naturalism, Bloch's outlook at these points seems to champion a radical anti-naturalism—a tendency, it is true, not consistently maintained in his study. Without trying to resolve this issue, I merely want to point here to the extreme ambivalence of his views on nature and its relation to utopia. In some passages, nature or creation seems to be entirely devalued—as when he writes that the apocalyptic "blasting apart" of existing reality reaches in Jesus "its most radical expression": for it insists on "being right away a new heaven and a new earth." In other instances, by contrast, nature (as *natura naturans*) is fully integrated into the process of redemption. Nature, we read in a later passage, is "anything but *passé* or a so-called residuum of the prehistory of man; it is not only the soil of man but also his lasting context." Therefore, with all its "brooding, incompleteness, significance and cipher-status, nature is *not a bygone but rather orient or 'morning-land' (Morgenland)."*[29]

To the extent that it is present in the study, anti-naturalism is closely connected with utopian activism and even eschatological militancy—a militancy not free of gender-related traits. This aspect is revealed in some of the chosen terminology—like the portrayal of forward projection as being "on the front"—and also (more prominently) in the evolution of religious ideas. As presented by Bloch, the exodus from earlier nature-gods is also an emancipation from chthonic or maternal divinities (prevalent particularly in Eastern and far-Eastern mythology). Nor can the reader fail to notice a certain slant in the story of religious founders: the fact that they are all invariably male, with a steady accentuation of the aspect of virile engagement or self-investment. In this respect it is probably no accident that the story terminates with Mohammed whose "virility"—Bloch writes—"is attested by the fact that his most important relic is the weapon, his sword—called *al Fehar*, the 'flashing one'—which is preserved to this day." In his discussion of Islam—but not exclusively there—Bloch seems willing to endorse a militant zeal sometimes bordering on millenarianism. "Seriousness of faith," he writes bluntly, "is orthodoxy; it is a healthy monomania"; and he adds: "Exclusiveness, intolerance in the best sense: all this derives from Moses; there is only El, the goal."[30] In the changed world-context of today, even the religiously committed reader—particularly this reader —must view these lines with deep apprehension if not dismay. In the face of fundamentalist fanaticism in many parts of the globe and of the heightened dangers of military catastrophe, one surely hopes for an alternative, more peaceful path to the kingdom—perhaps along the lines of Gandhian non-violence (ahimsa). In my own conviction, eschatology must be completely shunned as a matter of social or political practice (though not necessarily as a matter of personal faith).[31]For why and how should the spirit of divine fraternity—a synonym for the kingdom—be spread through missionary conquest or holy wars? Or is the son of man really going to appear on a cloud—but a nuclear mushroom cloud? Apocalypse now?

Apart from political considerations (I believe) militant eschatology is also, and more centrally, disqualified by the character of the ultimum, that is, the nature of "El, the goal." In The Principle of Hope this goal is sometimes circumscribed as plenary being, coincidence or identity—in a manner still paying tribute (at least on that score) to German idealism. Thus, referring to the anticipated "solution" of the world-riddle, Bloch presents it as marked by the "figure of identity"—a figure reconciling and even collapsing subject and object and in which "the core of man reveals itself as identical with the world-core." What this account neglects is precisely the unpredictability of the novum, the wondrous quality of the promised future. If the kingdom—as Bloch says—is really an order or regnum humanum, then this order can surely not be reduced to an abstract principle, least of all a principle of identity, but must involve the fruition of the full range of concrete human and natural propensities. Far from being a synonym for coincidence, the kingdom thus must allow for a complex and polymorphous diversity —which obstructs militant chiliastic pursuits. Sensing the drawbacks of a positive identification, Bloch occasionally contents himself with a negative approach to the summum bonum, describing it variously as "anti-pressure," "anti-fate," "anti-death" or (possibly) "anti-labyrinth." No doubt, this approach is preferable to hazardous simplifications or distortions—although it misses the concreteness and non-idealist texture of the promise. Perhaps, to avoid negativism, the only way to match the richness of the ens perfectissimum is through a profusion of terms, an abundant display of the "analogical imagination." Toward the end of his study Bloch resorts to such a cornucopia of terms, leaving behind idealist abstraction: "Happiness, freedom, non-alienation, golden age, land of milk and honey, the Eternally-Female, trumpet signal in Fidelio and Christ-likeness on the day of resurrection: these are so many diverse witnesses and images, but all are set up around that which speaks for itself by still remaining silent."[32]

9

POLITICS OF THE KINGDOM: PANNENBERG'S ANTHROPOLOGY

Faciem tuam requiram ...

Religion is again a lively topic not only in practical-political life but also in social and political thought. The latter development is by far more surprising and intriguing than the practical-political relevance. For some time, political theory had ostensibly settled accounts with, or resolved the status of, religious belief: basically churches and religious movements were classified as one type of interest groups (or input variables) within a comprehensive liberal-democratic model—a model secular in character but not intolerant, within limits, of religious convictions. On the part of organized (especially Protestant) churches, the settlement was widely accepted as a means for securing both internal church autonomy and some influence in the political arena; the social gospel movement in particular saw faith chiefly as a leverage for advancing welfare and progress within secular society. To be sure, the optimism of the liberal settlement was severely challenged, and partly disrupted, by catastrophic events in our century as well as by radical theological criticism—a criticism highlighted in Richard Niebuhr's well-known phrase: "A God without wrath brought men without sin into a kingdom without judgment through the ministrations of a Christ without a cross." Yet, when carried to an extreme, theological criticism had the paradoxical effect of reinforcing the secular-liberal paradigm. Once religion was radically segregated from politics or the city of God from the earthly city, the latter was left entirely to its own devices; purged of all religious and millenarian considerations, social and political theory could return to business as usual.

Seen in this light, the perspective of political theology—as it emerged in Europe in the postwar period—begins to assume distinct contours. As formulated by its proponents, the perspective, I believe, involves neither a simple politicizing of theology nor a theologizing of politics but rather an effort to grasp the peculiar interpenetration of the two cities—to show, that is, how and to which extent political or mundane experience constitutes a challenge to theology, just as the latter represents a challenge to politics and political thought.[1] To be sure, speaking broadly of interpenetration is still a far cry from actually exploring its concrete implications. If mundane experience is really to matter and to constitute a serious challenge to theology, the latter clearly must become attentive to the social and political context of contemporary life as well as to the findings of social-scientific disciplines. By and large, spokesmen of practical or political theology have been hesitant or reluctant to face up to this task implicit in the postulated interpenetration. Against this background, Wolfhart Pannenberg's *Anthropology in Theological Perspective* constitutes an important breakthrough and a milestone in the ongoing rapprochement of the two cities. Impressive in erudition and comprehensive in scope, the study offers nothing less than a compendium of social science literature as seen through the lens of theological exegesis.[2]

In its penetrating insights and careful scholarship, *Anthropology*, in my view, highlights the best potential of practical or political theology; it also attests to its author's status as a theologian and intellectual. Now professor of systematic theology at the University of Munich, Pannenberg has always been deeply concerned with the correlation of immanence and transcendence. While opposing a restrictive or confining immanentism, his writings do not counsel retreat into a non- or other-worldly haven. From Pannenberg's perspective, politics and social-political thought are necessarily overshadowed and called into question by the central message of the gospel: the message of the "imminent kingdom of God." This message, in his view, implies a radical challenge to all

mundane-political institutions and arrangements—but not in the sense
of demoting them to an earthly city divorced from biblical faith. Rather,
without eradicating the difference between the two cities, the gospel
penetrates into the world, providing politics with its hidden sense or
meaning—a sense illuminating the present in light of a future promise.
As Pannenberg observes in one of his more popular writings: "The coming kingdom is not some other-worldly phenomenon; it is the destiny of
present society .... We are not called to choose between concern for the
kingdom and concern for society. Rather, in concern for society we are
concerned for its end and destiny, namely, for the kingdom of God."[3]

For Pannenberg, the correlation of the two cities—their non-dualistic
difference—has never been simply a matter of abstract speculation. In a
sense, all his writings offer detailed and exacting explorations of this
nexus in its various manifestations—including the interplay between
knowledge and faith or the domains of "the visible and the invisible."
This is true even of his more narrowly theological works, such as his
studies on Christology and ecclesiology.[4] In a more pronounced fashion,
the sketched approach is evident in Pannenberg's treatment of ethics
seen as a bridge between reason and revelation; in his discussion of
history as neither a string of contingent events nor as a seamless divine
teleology; and particularly in his comments on the status of science
with their emphasis on a delicate balance of philosophical and theological premises.[5] Without doubt, however, the most ambitious and captivating illustration of this outlook can be found in his *Anthropology*
(first published in German in 1983 and translated into English in 1985).
Traversing virtually the entire range of the human and social sciences,
the study seeks to demonstrate the relevance of faith and theology at the
very frontiers of contemporary social-scientific debates. In the words of
the (German) Preface, the study's focus is not on a specialized religious
"sub-system" of society but on the "religious dimension of human reality in its structural uniqueness." For, Pannenberg adds, unless human
reality "in its full breadth" is marked by religious motifs, "religion as a
specialized theme of human behavior and social organization is liable
to drift into an isolation heralding its final obsolescence."[6]

Given the sprawling, multifaceted character of *Anthropology in
Theological Perspective,* I shall not recapitulate here the full range of its
arguments. Instead, I shall concentrate on three major themes particularly relevant to political theology: namely, first, the question of human
nature and of man's position in the world; secondly, the issue of politics
and the interrelation of polity and faith; and thirdly, the status of religion
and the church in the context of secular society. By way of conclusion,
I shall add some afterthoughts and critical queries.

I

The question of human nature is clearly central to Pannenberg's *Anthropology*—as befits the etymological roots of the term. Contrary to Anglo-Saxon usage, the term in the study encompasses basically all the human disciplines or sciences of man, from human biology and psychology to history; among these disciplines, however, philosophical anthropology (in the European sense) occupies a foundational status by pinpointing crucial theoretical premises. Attention to this perspective is by no means a novel feature in Pannenberg's opus; in fact, one of his earliest publications—entitled *What Is Man?*—probed relevant literature in this field and its implications for contemporary theology. As the opening lines of that book boldly asserted: "We live in an age of anthropology. One of the principal goals of contemporary thought is a comprehensive science of man; many different scholarly disciplines are united in this goal." According to Pannenberg, the focus on the sciences of man was predicated on a decisive theoretical shift or sea-change in the modern era—a shift which progressively displaced metaphysics, as foundational discipline, in favor of anthropology. Crucial to this displacement, in turn, was the growing centrality of man in modern thought—the fact that man was no longer a mere microcosm within the cosmos or a subordinate ingredient in the universe but the constitutive agent of the world: "The fundamental change that man's consciousness has experienced in recent times is expressed in this: man is no longer willing to fit into an order of the world or of nature, but wants to rule over the world .... The world is no longer a home for man; it is only the material for his transforming activity." As a result, the question of human nature in our time can "no longer be answered in terms of the world: it has been turned back upon man himself"—which accounts for the significance of the sciences of man.[7]

Instead of relying on traditional dogmatic views of human nature (deriving from the Greeks or scholasticism), *What Is Man?* turned to recent philosophical anthropology, and especially to the teachings of Max Scheler, Arnold Gehlen, and Helmuth Plessner regarding man's basic "world openness" or man's "eccentric" position vis-à-vis the world and himself. "In anthropology," Pannenberg observed, "the newly discovered, unique freedom of man to inquire and to move beyond every given regulation of his existence is called his 'openness to the world' "— an expression intended to capture the central feature that "makes man a man, distinguishes him from animals, and lifts him out above non-human nature in general." Man's openness was demonstrated, first of all, by his relative freedom from ecological or environmental constraints.

While each type of animal is limited to an environment that is species-specific and fixed by heredity, man can be said to "have a world" in the sense of being flexible or malleable with regard to environmental conditions. This flexibility was also evident in the relatively non-specialized character of many human organs and also in the fact of man's "premature birth," a fact which allows man to experiment with environments during a long period of maturation. Human openness was further and particularly manifest in the unbounded character of human drives and instincts. Whereas animal instincts are basically context-dependent and triggered only in the presence of appropriate objects, human drives exceed contextual stimuli and are directed into the open "toward something undefined." It was chiefly at this point that *What Is Man?* detected the possibility of a theological interpretation. For, if all instincts aim at the goal of fulfillment and if human drives are essentially open-ended or infinite, then the fulfillment of human strivings presupposed a non-mundane or infinite target or objective: "Man is infinitely dependent. Thus, in everything that he does in life he presupposes a being beyond everything finite, a vis-à-vis upon which he is dependent. Only on this basis can his imagination form conceptions of this being. Our language has the word 'God' for this entity upon which man is dependent in his infinite striving."[8]

        Arguments of a similar kind are fleshed out in greater detail—and also in a more nuanced manner—in Pannenberg's *Anthropology*. The Introduction, entitled "Theology and Anthropology," carefully explicates the underlying motivations of the study. In Pannenberg's presentation, the importance of anthropology is due both to secular philosophical trends and internal theological considerations. Regarding the former, the concentration on the sciences of man—he writes—reflects "both the general intellectual climate of modernity and the development of this climate as it found characteristic expression in the course of modern philosophy. . . . The focus of modern philosophy on man as subject of all experience and of philosophical reflection itself could not fail to exert its impact on theology." Apart from secular trends, the inner-theological impulse for the focus derives from "the fact that Christian theology relates to the salvation of man," that is, from the theological preoccupation with the "human person." In modern times, this preoccupation has increasingly taken the form of a man-centered outlook in the sense that God was conceived "as a presupposition of human subjectivity and thus in terms, or from the vantage point, of humanity and no longer of the world. Not the natural world as such but man's experience of the world and of his existence in it supplied repeatedly the premise for discussing the reality of God." Pannenberg is not unaware of some dubious corol-

laries of this outlook, especially the tendency toward religious subjectivism and privatization. Commenting on social developments during
the last two centuries he observes: "The state became religiously neutral, while the choice of religious confession became the private affair of
individuals or free groups of individuals. . . . The trend toward segmen-
tation and privatization of religion is one of the dominant currents in
modern history, and it explains the prominent role which pietism
acquired in the modern history of religious devotion." Reinforcing and
compounding privatization is the lure of anthropocentrism or human
self-enclosure. The focus on man, the Introduction concedes, has no
doubt conjured up

> the peril of an anthropocentric constriction of theology. Schaeder
> and especially Karl Barth saw this danger and saw it correctly: it is
> the danger that man in his theologizing is concerned only with
> himself instead of with God and thus misses the core of theology.
> . . . By narrowly focusing on individual salvation (especially under
> the influence of pietism), theologians have largely forgotten that
> not human religious experience but the divinity of God must
> occupy first place in theology.[9]

Notwithstanding these perils and reservations, Pannenberg underscores the inescapable importance of anthropology for theological argumentation, mainly because of its foundational status as successor to
metaphysics. If religion wishes to be more than private or subjective
belief—he insists—theology has to place itself on the terrain of modern
secular thought, which is the terrain of the scrutiny of human nature in
the sciences of man. Accordingly, he adds, Christian theology in the
modern age "must provide itself with a foundation in general anthropological studies. This is not a question of a perspective which one may or
may not adopt. No one is free to choose the problem context in which he
wishes to insert his contribution—no matter what form this contribution may take. This applies also to Christian theology in view of the
state of discussion as it has developed in modern times." In turning to
anthropology, moreover, theology—according to Pannenberg—must
become seriously engaged in the ongoing inquiries of the human sciences, without dogmatically prejudging their findings. Thus, in lieu of
a "dogmatic anthropology" which presupposes the reality of God on
biblical grounds, the Introduction opts for a "fundamental-theological"
approach as guidepost for the entire study: Such an anthropology "does
not argue from dogmatic data and presuppositions, but rather turns its
attention directly to the phenomena of human existence as investigated

in human biology, psychology, cultural anthropology or sociology—with the goal of interrogating the findings of these disciplines in terms of their religious and theological implications." Theological appropriation of the human sciences most decidedly does not mean a simple borrowing from, or loose invocation of, anthropological research. Instead, the goal is one of "critical appropriation"—which means the attempt to lay "theological claim" to the phenomena described in the anthropological disciplines: "To this end, the secular description is accepted as merely a provisional account of the human condition—an account which needs to be deepened by showing a further, theologically relevant dimension embedded in the anthropological findings."10

Pursuing cues contained in the earlier book on human nature, Pannenberg's *Anthropology* turns its attention first to philosophical anthropology—in line with the study's overall strategy of moving from the most general or foundational discipline to steadily more concrete modes of human science. As in the previous book, the focus of the discussion is again on the contrast between human "world openness" and the contextual and environmental "boundedness" of animal behavior. In Pannenberg's words, "philosophical anthropology shares with behaviorism and German behavioral research the principle that human beings must be interpreted in terms of their corporeality and particularly of their bodily and hence observable behavior"; it differs, however, from behavioral approaches by recognizing "man's special position in the domain of animal life. Scheler and Gehlen pinpointed this position with the concept of 'openness to the world', while Plessner preferred the term 'eccentricity'—although he meant to express the same content (only with a critical proviso and with the goal of more precise delimitation)." In Scheler's case, the notion of "openness" sought to capture the fact that man is no longer tied to species-specific drives and contexts but "free from environments" *(umweltfrei)*. In contradistinction to animals, man's instinctual apparatus is not closely linked with immediate environmental stimuli; rather, his instincts or drives can roam freely beyond given contexts or else be "voluntarily inhibited" from reacting to environmental conditions. While for Scheler openness was biologically unlimited and only precariously counterbalanced by spirit, Plessner viewed man as a structural correlation of biological centeredness and "eccentricity"—the latter term designating man's ability to assume a distance to the world and himself; though culminating in reflection and self-consciousness, eccentricity was simultaneously conditioned by man's instinctual and physiological malleability. In a similar vein, Arnold Gehlen translated Scheler's notion of openness into the thesis of a structural brokenness or "evolutionary inhibition," a thesis according to which man appears basically as a "deficient being" *(Mängelwesen)*. Reflecting the fact of "premature birth," deficiency denotes chiefly man's biological and instinctual non-specificity, that is, the "hiatus" existing between external contexts and inner drives—a hiatus which, in Gehlen's view, could only partially be bridged through cultural artifacts.[11]

In developing the theological implications of these teachings, *Anthropology* takes a detour via Johann Gottfried Herder—a name only briefly alluded to in the earlier book. In several of his writings, Herder had articulated views which anticipated recent philosophical anthropology, including the notion of the context-dependence of animal behavior and of man's inferiority to animals regarding "the intensity and reliability of his instincts." In his study on the origin of language (of 1772), Herder had portrayed the human infant as "the most orphaned child of nature. Naked and bare, weak and in need, shy and unarmed," man initially faces nature's vicissitudes. Yet, instinctual weakness and unreliability in Herder's view were not merely a sign of deficiency but also the emblem of man's higher destiny or calling: namely, the calling to find his proper habitat beyond nature. This destiny, in turn, was not a sudden gift but rather presupposed a slow process of maturation and human self-perfection—a process which could reach fulfillment only in man's gradual assimilation to God in whose image he was shaped. In Pannenberg's words: "Animal instincts are replaced in Herder's account by a divinely supplied direction of human life. Seeing that their instinctual life had retrogressed, God did not abandon human beings to a complete lack of orientation from which they would have to rescue themselves without transhuman support. Rather, according to Herder, God implanted in man's heart a direction to be followed in his self-perfection, and this direction is the cultivation of God's image in man." Such cultivation, one should note, was seen neither as the mere unfolding of innate capacities nor as the result of external intervention, but rather as a complex learning process or "education of mankind" in which social traditions, inborn reason, and divine providence peculiarly interact. "In Herder's fully developed anthropology," Pannenberg adds, "the idea of the image of God has the function of pinpointing the unfinished state of man's humanity in such a way as to counter the difficulty that the fulfillment of human destiny cannot be thought as the deed of those in whose life it is to become reality. . . . On the other hand, the goal of humanity must be seen also as something which characterizes the uniqueness of man's natural existence; for only in this way can the goal be understood as fulfillment of man's destiny."[12]

According to *Anthropology*, Herder's suggestive insights must be supplemented and refined—but are not rendered obsolete—by recent anthropological arguments. In focusing on human openness and eccentricity, Scheler as well as Plessner and Gehlen can be said to "approximate Herder's ideas in the context of the modern discussion of philosophical anthropology." At the same time, recent arguments and formulations need to be complemented and deepened through recourse to Herder's notion of human maturation and self-perfection; this can be done if the focus is placed on the direction and goal of world-openness and on the trans-natural anchor of human eccentricity. Can human self-transcendence be interpreted theologically as a movement toward a divine image, and world-openness accordingly as openness to God? Pannenberg asks, and he responds: "Even when moving beyond all experience or conception of sensible objects, man continues to be 'eccentric', that is, related to something other than himself—but now to an Other beyond all the objects of his world, an Other that simultaneously embraces this entire world and thus ensures the possible unity of human life in the world, despite the diversity and heterogeneity of mundane influences." According to the study, the otherness encountered at this point cannot merely be a general-neutral horizon of all objects and phenomena—which would be a vacuous concept. Rather, when reaching out to the comprehensive horizon encompassing all objects of direct or possible perception, man is said to relate himself "eccentrically to a pre-given *reality*, and thus this outreach affirms implicitly the divine reality." On the other hand, the path of self-perfection can also be disrupted or reversed in the direction of human self-encapsulation and self-enclosure oblivious of the divine image—a self-enclosure which, in Pannenberg's view, is the origin of human sinfulness and perversion: "Where the opposition of the ego to otherness becomes total and where everything else is reduced to a means of the ego's self-assertion, at that point the ego's rupture with itself and its constitutive eccentricity becomes acute." Self-assertion at this juncture turns into self-centeredness and egotism—which spells doom for man's higher destiny.[13]

II

Issues of politics and political theory surface in *Anthropology* chiefly in the context of a discussion of social institutions. After having first sketched the core features of philosophical anthropology, and after next having traced their repercussions in the fields of social psychology and psychoanalysis, the study finally (in its third part) turns to cultural anthropology, political sociology, and historiography, in an effort to portray concretely the "shared world" of human beings—which is basically a world of shared cultural meanings partially embodied in institutions.

In Pannenberg's presentation, "culture" is neither the result of individual creativity nor an external-collective constraint but rather a fabric of meanings constituted in and by language—a language which, in turn, is not merely performative utterance but has a transindividual, playful, and partly mythical character. In terms of the opening lines of the chapter on institutions, the unity of culture is "based on a shared consciousness of meaning which founds and permeates the order of the social world and originally was represented in communal play. The universal medium of this shared consciousness—which provides the basis for the eccentric identity of individuals—can be found in language which itself has the form or structure of play." Adapting (in part) the distinction between *langue* and *parole*, Pannenberg views language and cultural meaning not simply as individual inventions—despite the importance of utterance for the actualization of language. Although the articulation of meaning in a given situation, he notes, depends on performative utterances, the meaning present in language antedates and over-reaches individual expression. The same can be said of the consciousness of meaning in its relation to the cultural context: "this consciousness, too, is not adequately grasped when it is presented purely as human activity." The most concrete and enduring manifestation of shared meaning resides in social "institutions" defined as regularized forms of human coexistence: "Only by means of institutions regulating coexistence does shared consciousness of meaning produce the kind of common 'life-style' which Rothacker rightly treated as the mark of cultural unity at a given point of social development."14

Pannenberg's discussion of institutions and their theoretical status ranges broadly over recent sociological and anthropological literature— a treatment of which I can give here only a brief synopsis. Basically, his approach seeks to steer a middle course between—or find an alternative to—functional or objectivist theories of institutions, on the one hand, and intentional or actor-based explanations, on the other. According to functionalism, social institutions are fixed and durable patterns of behavior designed to meet basic human needs or else broader societal requirements; in the second perspective, by contrast, institutions are traced essentially to individual motivations and reciprocal expectations between individuals. In Pannenberg's view, both accounts are lopsided, though for opposite reasons: functionalism is defective because of its proclivity to reification (and even quasi-religious mystification) of contingent arrangements; actor-based explanations, in turn, fall short of grasping the durability of institutionalized role patterns. Moving beyond these theoretical models, *Anthropology* ascribes the autonomy and durability of social institutions to the matrix of shared cultural meanings in a society, a matrix which, in turn, is anchored in a common language seen as "primeval institution" *(Urinstitution)*. "The precedence of institutions over individual intentions," we read, "derives from the pre-givenness of experienced and linguistically articulated fabrics of meaning," that is, from their capacity to embody "lasting meaning frames of human coexistence." Far from denoting reified structures, however, these meaning frames are regularly linked with concrete interactions or with "reciprocity of human behavior in concrete, recurring life-situations and in continuing or enduring relationships." Actually, having outlined the general features of institutions, the study proceeds to differentiate between two major types: one in which shared meaning takes precedence over interactions and where individuals are chiefly members of a community; and another in which meaning and interaction are subordinate to individual goals. While the latter type prevails in the domains of economic production and legal relations, the former is exemplified by family, nation, polity, and church.[15]

The theme of politics or the polity inserts itself directly into the sketched theory of institutions. In line with the preceding typology, the polity (or the state) emerges basically as a communal or community-focused institutional setting—although community here coincides by no means with a reified collectivism. As Pannenberg points out, the communal character of politics was strongly emphasized in classical philosophy: according to Aristotle man is by nature a political creature, which means that, viewed in his essence or ideal-ethical potential, man finds his *telos* or fulfillment in the polity. This view, it is true, was contradicted already by the ancient Sophists who construed the state as a mere conventional arrangement between self-seeking individuals—a construal which was later continued and fleshed out in modern liberal thought with its stress on the contractual basis of political life. As in the case of institutional theory in general, Pennenberg prefers to seek a middle course between these conflicting conceptions. "Human nature," he writes, "is not social or political in the sense that the individual possesses no independence in relation to society and its institutional structures, whether family or state. On the other hand, the independence of individuals vis-à-vis family and state is not based on a complete neutrality toward all forms of human community. Rather," he adds, in a passage underscoring the political-theological tenor of his arguments, "their independence is due to the fact that the institutional structure of human community has itself a religious foundation to which individuals can appeal even against the concrete forms of their shared world. Only at this level is it possible to resolve the antagonism between individual and institutional social order."[16] The religious foundation invoked in this passage is specifically the Christian religion with its simultaneous emphasis on individual autonomy and dignity in the sight of God, and on the integration of individuals into the (mystical) "body of Christ" and into the future "kingdom." By virtue of this emphasis, the Aristotelian—and later Stoic—notion of a mundane polity acquired greater religious depth, while at the same time being shielded against collectivist dangers.

As Pannenberg realizes, there has long been an anti-Aristotelian strand in Christian thought. Once the accent is placed on man as the "image" or counterpart of a transcendental God, all secular communities and institutions tend to be relativized and reduced to external settings devoid of intrinsic significance; by the same token, individual believers are radically "emancipated" from the polity. To the extent that the existence of state or polity is acknowledged, its function tends to be limited to a punitive or negative role: the role of counteracting and controlling human sinfulness. According to *Anthropology*, this negative outlook—with its focus on *coercere malum*—has a long tradition in Christian thought, stretching from the Church Fathers (specifically Irenaeus) to Reformation theology. Nevertheless, control of sin was never the exclusive concern of Christian faith; from the beginning, negative coercion was supplemented and counterbalanced by a more positive or constructive conception: the notion of the polity as part of a divinely ordained scheme designed to assist man on his path toward salvation. In classical terminology, political institutions could be said to be grounded in, and the goal of, human nature—although "nature" in this case did not mean a naturalistic fact and certainly not a primeval condition exempt from sin but rather the receptacle of a promise or the stage of divine redemption.

'Amidst all the sinful perversion of human political relations,' Pannenberg observes, 'the divine will to order and justice asserts itself again and again, using as means to its ends even men's desire for power and mutual jealousy. The political 'nature' of man is thus not a remnant untouched by sin, left over from an originally perfect creation, but is part and parcel of human destiny which, like creation as a whole, finds its fulfillment only in the future and can only then be fully known.'

Against this background, Aristotle's natural teleology is transformed into a religious eschatology, just as his notion of political "autarchy" is anchored in a divine plan: "The aporias in the Aristotelian idea of autarchy or self-sufficiency . . . point beyond the earthly polis, which

Christians regard only as a provisional form of man's political calling—
a calling which reaches its completion only in the kingdom of God,
following the cessation of all domination of man over man."[17]

According to Pannenberg, this modified or transformed Aristotelianism was present in St. Augustine's teachings—despite the latter's
strong preoccupation with human sinfulness and his denunciation of
the decadence of secular (Roman) civilization. This is particularly
evident in his doctrine of "peace," where earthly peace was seen as
adumbration of heavenly peace and *pax Romana* as anticipation of *pax
Christi*. "In Augustine's teaching on earthly and heavenly peace," we
read, "the role (of the polity) is explained in such a way that the Aristotelian idea of man's political vocation is sublimated and absorbed into
it. With this teaching Augustine moves beyond the construal of the
state simply as God's response to sin aimed at the control of evil." From
Augustine's perspective, peace was a universal ontological category in
the sense that all things and creatures are destined to seek a state of rest
or repose. Accordingly, man was impelled by his nature to cultivate a
sociable communion and peaceful coexistence with his fellow human
beings: "Thus the political destiny of man appears as an application of
the idea of peace beyond the range of individual life to human communities." Genuine peace, for Augustine, is founded on mutual harmony
(concordia): the harmony among household members in the family and
among citizens in the state—an idea which does not exclude a non-
repressive kind of hierarchy or authority structure. Such harmony, in
turn, is the result of just and loving relations between members of a
community, relations where each participant grants to all others their
due or what properly belongs to them. Since, however, man owes to God
reverence and worship, harmony cannot prevail where God is not granted
his due. Accordingly, a purely secular society or a polity devoid of worship cannot achieve genuine peace; its earthly order does no longer anticipate the divine kingdom. This thought explains Augustine's polemical
argument (directed chiefly against Cicero) that in the absence of true
worship no human polity can claim to be just.[18]

While praising Augustine's general differentiation between the two
cities, Pannenberg voices a number of caveats—which are indicative of
the more political bent of his political theology. Although not disdain-
ful of the Aristotelian legacy, Augustine's treatment of the secular polity
is said to be too cursory to match the classical example. Moreover, in his
correlation of *civitas terrena* and *civitas Dei*, the former is almost
completely subordinated to the latter—with the added difficulty that
civitas Dei is largely a synonym for the Church. What is missing in
Augustine is an awareness of the theological significance of the polity

itself, in contradistinction to religious or ecclesiastic institutions: "He did not bring out the fact that the political order, as distinct from the Church, stands in a special relationship, even if a broken one, to the future kingdom of God. This is so because the latter has itself a political character inasmuch as, in contrast to any domination of man over man, it will accomplish the proper task of political order: the establishment of justice and peace." Augustine's de-emphasis or denigration of the political order stands insofar in stark opposition to the Byzantine "theology of the empire" with its effort to provide a positive theological interpretation of a political community molded by Christian faith. To this extent, *Anthropology* continues, "the Aristotelian thesis of man's political vocation is qualified by Augustine far more than it need have been in the direction of a distantiation from the concerns of this world." The entire argument should not be misconstrued as a rejection of the distinction between the two cities or as an uncritical glorification of the state. As Pannenberg repeatedly emphasizes, existing polities are only distant reminders of their true potential, only shadowy "stand-ins" or "place-keepers" *(Platzhalter)* of the promised kingdom. Stripped of its linkage with worship, he agrees thus far with Augustine, the state cannot properly claim allegiance: "The legitimacy crisis of the secular state is not solely a question of public morality and appropriate political reforms: it has deeper roots in the loss of the religious foundation for moral obligation and the authority of law."[19]

III

The significance of religion or religious faith, one should note, does not coincide with, and is not exhausted by, the legitimation of political order. In line with his comments on the origin of culture and language, Pannenberg ascribes to religion a "constitutive" role in human life—a role reflected in the fact that religion has for its topic "the unity of the world as such in relation to its divine source and its possible perfection from the same source." Against the backdrop of this unity, religion thematizes "the meaning of human life and the meaningful order of human coexistence. In the words of the young Schleiermacher, religion grapples with the universe." In a sense, both religion and politics aim at unifying human experience by embedding it in a coherent fabric of meaning. However, while the polity requires religious or theological legitimation for its viability, religion—operating on a deeper, more constitutive level—does not require political support or justification. "Since political rule has for its task the unification and ongoing integration of society," Pannenberg observes, "it must derive its legitimacy from the religious foundations that make reality intelligible as an ordered and meaningful whole. It can therefore be claimed that the modern secular state lacks legitimacy since it is cut loose from religious moorings." On the other hand, religious faith is not necessarily tied to specific political arrangements and its function is not limited to the aim of buttressing or supporting a given regime. In fact, when seen merely as a functional requisite for the maintenance of a given social order or particular forms of government, religion is alienated from its central purpose and "already hopelessly corrupt."[20]

According to *Anthropology*, religion and politics are closely intertwined but by no means synonymous or readily congruent. Precisely the commonality of their aim—to unify the meaning of experience—may entail mutual antagonism or conflict. In Pannenberg's words, given the close proximity of their concerns, religion and political rule "may easily be at loggerheads. Political power *can* be a manifestation of the unifying rule of almighty God over the world: in that case, it can radiate messianic glory and allow human beings to share in the blessings of divine order. On the other hand, however, political power can pretend to be itself the fulfillment of human destiny: in that case, it becomes God's competitor; in Christian eyes, the state then assumes features of the Antichrist." The two possibilities are closely related to the "eccentric" character of human existence, or rather to the connection between centeredness and eccentricity. While in the first case the center of human life is projected into openness beyond mundane arrangements, the second option restricts and muffles eccentricity through complete integration of individuals into the secular order. The inevitable result of the latter option is a stifling collectivism and, in extreme cases, political tyranny and totalitarianism. The two alternatives also shed light on the Aristotelian conception of man as political animal: only when suffused with religious faith does this conception properly capture man's higher vocation. "Human beings," we read, "are indeed destined for social life, and only in a social community can they live in conformity with their calling. Their vocation is thus in fact political—but it cannot be fully or definitively realized in any mundane political order. The only communal order in which the destiny of individuals could be fully achieved is the kingdom of God which transcends all possibilities of political integration through human power."[21]

To some extent, the eccentricity of human life and the difference between the two cities are endemic to all modes of religious belief; however, they have been accentuated in Christianity due to the combined emphasis on a transcendent God and on individual salvation. In Christianity, Pannenberg notes, the anthropological justification of political order (provided in Greek thought) and the Jewish "dualism of

Yahweh-faith and monarchy" were welded together "in the conviction that the destiny of individuals is never completely exhausted by the polity—which only has the provisional function of ensuring a peaceful human coexistence. Human salvation, by contrast, can only be expected in the coming kingdom of God." In the Christian tradition, anticipation of the latter kingdom in the present world can occur not so much through political citizenship as rather through participation in the "sacramental and symbolic communion of the church." Accordingly, the discrepancy of the two cities in traditional Christianity took mainly the form of a tension between state and church or between political and ecclesiastic institutions. This tension or mutual contestation, it is true, has been largely suspended in the modern age due to the division of Christianity into competing churches. In the wake of religious wars and confessional conflicts, institutionalized faith ceased to be the warrant of the future *pax Christi,* with the result that the state—now the secular state divested of religious underpinnings—emerged as the sole arbiter and peacemaker in human affairs. Deprived of its close linkage with the political realm, religion underwent a growing process of political neutralization and privatization, until at the end it was leveled into the liberal framework as a variant of interest-group politics. Under these circumstances, a revitalization of faith—necessary for the coherent viability of the polity—presupposes a rethinking of the correlation of the two cities and also a rethinking and regeneration of the role of the Church in secular society. This reassessment is particularly important in light of present tendencies toward a secularization of some churches, on the one hand, and toward a purely internal fundamentalism, on the other.[22]

Pannenberg's comments on the role and regeneration of the Christian Church (or churches) are relatively brief and cursory in *Anthropology;* however, his remaining opus is replete with trenchant observations on the topic. Particularly telling passages are contained in *Theology and the Kingdom of God*—some of which deserve to be mentioned here. "Because the Church has in so many ways narrowed her vocation and deviated from her hope," we read there, "many responsible people wonder out loud if the Church has not become obsolete. Theology is challenged by the sad appearance of the empirical Church as a hangover from another historical period. The appropriate response to this challenge is to be found in a new emphasis upon the Church as an eschatological community pioneering the future of all mankind." According to Pannenberg, the "sad appearance" of the Church (or churches) is due both to theoretical confusions and to structural deficiencies. Regarding the former, he points primarily to the tempting conflation of Church and kingdom: "Sometimes the Church has been identified with the kingdom;

at other times it has been said that the Church is the present form of the kingdom, as distinguished from the kingdom's future fulfillment. The second confusion is as bad as the first." All too often these modes of conflation have historically served the purposes of "ecclesiastic officials" who pretend or like to think "they are in possession of the truth, or at least that they possess the ultimate criterion of the truth." At this point, the problem of theoretical confusion shades over into structural deficiencies which revolve chiefly around ecclesiastic and theological authoritarianism. Until authoritarian elements of the past are overcome, Pannenberg insists, the Church will be unable "to make the contributions that are desperately needed in our world." Liberal secularism, against this background, may have served a benign purpose: by exposing dogmatic authoritarianism, its impact may be "a blessing that enables the Church to see itself more clearly as a pilgrim community on the way to meeting the future of God's coming kingdom. This awareness may bring about a new Christian unity without uniformity."[23]

In *Anthropology* a similar argument is developed with reference to Paul Tillich's notion of a "theonomous" culture and polity—where "theonomy" stands in contrast both to an alienating-authoritarian heteronomy and a man-centered or secular autonomy. What encourages and supports Tillich's vision, Pannenberg notes, is the fact that in our ecumenical age Christian churches "have largely risen above the dogmatism that, together with clerical claims to power, was chiefly responsible for the division of past centuries." This development in his view is not simply a matter of external adaptation but derives from a deeper and more nuanced understanding of Christian revelation and faith— with the result that "the basic modern idea of tolerance is today deeply rooted in Christian consciousness itself and has even altered Christian attitudes to non-Christian religions." As a consequence, the ongoing and urgently needed revitalization of the religious foundations of societies and polities should not—and hopefully will not—entail "a relapse into the intolerance of religious wars from which the modern state emerged." Moreover, theonomy should not be misconstrued as a subordination of the polity to the Church, nor as an indiscriminate amalgamation of the two cities. Rather, Pannenberg adds, theonomous renewal can only occur "under the auspices of the differentiation between church and state"—a difference, though, which "does not signify a segregation of the two domains nor religious neutrality of the state but which expresses the Christian understanding of the polity as a provisional order of this world. It is precisely this provisional character which allows the institutional order of society to be grasped as representation or manifestation of the divine order and of God's will to justice."[24]

IV

Pannenberg's *Anthropology* clearly constitutes a major contribution to contemporary theology as well as to the dialogue between theology and the human and social sciences. Given the growing specialization and proliferation of academic learning, the study's interdisciplinary range amounts to a sheer *tour de force*. Seen in conjunction with Pannenberg's broader opus, *Anthropology* surely is a high-water mark in recent practical and political theology with its emphasis on the differentiated linkage between religion and polity, knowledge and faith. Viewed in historical perspective, this opus signals an important emendation both of liberal Protestantism and of the Barthian (and Bultmannian) break with secularized eschatology: while abandoning trust in the providential progress of secular society, Pannenberg's approach does not simply opt for a fundamentalist inwardness, but recovers the public dimension of faith. Without shallow utopianism, the focus on the coming kingdom rescues both politics from despair, and religion from privatization and social irrelevance.

Despite these and related merits, the study's arguments are not free from quandaries and unresolved ambiguities. A major quandary emerges from the book's title (and overall tenor): Does an "anthropology in theological perspective" not necessarily entail a "theology in anthropological perspective" or an anthropocentric theology? As Pannenberg recognizes, the danger of anthropocentrism has been prominently pinpointed by Barth and others in their critique of the progressive theology of the nineteenth century. As indicated, his response to this line of criticism is to refer to the intellectual "problem context" in the modern age, that is, to the growing philosophical concentration on "man as the subject of all experience." Yet, one may query to which extent escape from some of the ills of modernity is possible through recourse to this central modernist idea. Pannenberg's comments on the issue are somewhat pale and elusive. "Modern anthropology," he writes, "reflects this growing independence of modern man from the confessionally conflicting systems of Christian theology and thus from any explicitly religious themes. This shows how ambivalent a procedure it would indeed be to try to base a Christian dogmatics and theology on anthropological conceptions which arose from the progressive abandonment of Christian dogma." As he adds, in a passage which hardly lessens the difficulty of the procedure: the fact that modern anthropology has historically been characterized by "a certain (nonreligious) tendency" should "merely teach theologians not to accept indiscriminately the findings of a non-theological anthropology as basis for their work, but rather to appropriate them in a critical manner."[25]

What renders the procedure clearly hazardous is the postulated linkage of man and God. Even a critical appropriation of secular anthropology does not necessarily vindicate a theological interpretation—at least not on the level occupied by the anthropological and social sciences (which is the level of empirical knowledge). Pannenberg himself acknowledges the problem of this interpretive move. In translating the concepts of world-openness and eccentricity into openness toward God, he queries: "Is this step justified? In this open-ended transcendence of themselves and all objects of their experience, are human beings not simply related to an encompassing general horizon?" The reply that— when reaching out "to the most general horizon"—man relates himself "eccentrically to a pre-given *reality*" and thus "implicitly affirms the divine reality," surely requires further corroboration and further elaboration on the notion of reality.[26] As it seems to me, Scheler's and Plessner's anthropology perhaps does not preclude, but it also does not simply insure a theistic interpretation. Conversely, the same anthropology does not exclude a non-theistic construal—as is illustrated in the work of Albert Camus (which in turn is indebted to Nietzschean teachings). Perhaps, a non-theistic interpretation today even has some theological advantages. Perhaps, it is important to expose oneself fully, with Camus, to the godlessness of a secularized age and its secular anthropology—in order to grasp the need and urgency of the coming kingdom (a need muffled by a theologized reading).

Quite apart from such quandaries of exegesis, the study faces difficulties in the domain of anthropology itself. In its successive chapters, the study's focus is on such disciplines as psychology, cultural anthropology, sociology, and historiography—in a manner seemingly oblivious of the deep ferment presently beleaguering all the human and social sciences. As it happens, humanist anthropology (especially when identified with anthropocentrism) is today under siege both in philosophical and social-scientific discourse. To some extent, Schelerian humanism or personalism was already questioned by Heidegger in his *Letter on Humanism*. More recently, the centrality of man and the modern category of subjectivity have been the target of relentless structuralist and post-structuralist critique. In his *The Order of Things*, Michel Foucault probed the historical genealogy or archaeology of the human sciences, challenging precisely the foundational status of some of the disciplines singled out by Pannenberg, including psychology and sociology. In Foucault's view, the humanist outlook of traditional social sciences has for some time (specifically since the turn of the century) been eroded by the rise of a number of counter-sciences in the same fields, notably by ethnology and linguistics. "The idea of a 'psychoanalytic anthropology', and the idea of a 'human nature' reconstituted by ethnology," he wrote, "are no more than pious wishes. Not only are they able to do without the concept of man, they are also unable to pass through it, for they always address themselves to that which constitutes his outer limits. . . . From within language experienced and traversed as language, in the play of its possibilities extended to the furthest point, what emerges is that man has 'come to an end'." Elsewhere Foucault called for an awakening from the "confused sleep of (Hegelian) dialectics and of (philosophical) anthropology," adding: "The breakdown of philosophical subjectivity and its dispersion in a language that dispossesses it while multiplying it within the space created by its absence is probably one of the fundamental structures of contemporary thought."[27]

Even bracketing Foucault's anti-humanism, one can hardly ignore the effects of his (and related) arguments on the problem context in our time, especially on the role of anthropological premises. These effects, I am afraid, are not always fully pondered in *Anthropology*. A case in point is the status and function of language. As mentioned, Pannenberg occasionally ascribes to language a foundational role, depicting it as the primeval institution *(Urinstitution)* in society, an institution in which shared cultural meanings are anchored. In other passages, however, *Anthropology* leans in the direction of the independence and priority of thought vis-à-vis language, a notion supported in part by cognitive psychology and some studies on language acquisition. "According to Piaget," we read, "a child's development of thought processes through sensorimotor interaction with the environment clearly precedes the acquisition of language, and this argument merits our assent. This means for us that the emergence of religious themes also precedes the acquisition of language and is constitutive for such acquisition." In *What Is Man?* this option of the priority of mind shades over into a frankly instrumental conception of language as a human tool. Referring to "the service that language performs for man," Pannenberg asserts: "Man, so to speak, spins a network of words and relations between words as the means for representing the interconnection of diverse things in reality. He . . . becomes lord of the world through an artificial world that he spreads out between himself and his surroundings."[28] From a post-structuralist perspective, of course, such assertions are highly dubious and even scarcely intelligible. For, given language's character as a primeval institution and as a network of interrelated symbols, how can there be an external or transcendental signified prior to language—whether that signified be mind, man, or God? This consideration casts doubt on the incipient foundationalism of some of Pannenberg's arguments (evident, for example, in the ascription of a constitutive role to religious belief).

Closely related with the question of language is the status of the individual agent and human subjectivity. On the whole, the thrust of *Anthropology* is directed against the privatization of faith, as it has emerged in the wake of post-Reformation individualism, and toward a strengthening of shared meanings and communal bonds. Simultaneously, however, Pannenberg seeks to preserve individual autonomy as an antidote to social conformism. While underscoring human openness, *What Is Man?* does not abandon individual subjectivity. "Even where a person breaks through into the open," we are told, "the ego is always in it. The person who thinks he can move beyond his self only lives in a dream world; wherever he might move, he brings his self with him." In *Anthropology*, the concern with subjectivity is evident in the stress on "self-consciousness" and on the process of individual identity formation. "The ego," Pannenberg concedes, "does not enjoy complete independence from the Thou or from the broader social life-context represented by immediate reference groups. Rather, the ego proves to be dependent on its social context for the determination of its own identity; and thus the question must be faced from the very beginning: is human eccentricity perhaps to be defined as sociality?" Contextual dependence, however, does not seem to cancel a certain ontological primacy of autonomy. The question, Pannenberg adds, should not be misconstrued in the sense that individuals could be "collapsed into their role in a social life-context" whose collective outlook would grant to them "no independent and inviolable worth." The issue of individual identity, in his view, can lay claim to "universal relevance"—even though, outside of modern Western society, few other cultures have raised this issue "into an open question for individuals themselves." Somewhat later the identity theme is given a theological interpretation— through the argument that "the transcendence of selfhood beyond its social situation corresponds to the relationship to God implicit in the original trust which already transcends its ties to the mother. . . . Because selfhood is ultimately grounded in the relation to God, persons can be free vis-à-vis their social situation."[29]

A minimal question at this point concerns the mutual congruence of these assertions. More importantly, one may ask whether the remedy for modern ills (like privatization) can be found in the arsenal of modern-liberal categories. The precariousness of this procedure surfaces particularly in connection with the power-claims of modern anthropocentrism, especially the claims to dominion over nature. In *What Is Man?* these claims are cast in theological garb—which does not reduce their stridency: "The unity of the whole of reality, which man progressively carries out through his intellectual and technological dominion over the world, does not have its basis in ourselves, but only in God." The same view is echoed and further underscored in *Anthropology* through reference to the canons of scientific inquiry.

> 'It seems in fact,' we read, 'that there is a connection between man's relation to God and his increasing mastery over the natural conditions of his existence. Only by virtue of the fact that, in his eccentric self-transcendence, man moves beyond the immediately given to the broadest, most encompassing horizon of all things—only in this manner is man able to grasp an individual object in its uniqueness as distinguished from other objects. . . . This process of defining the distinctness of things has become the basis for all human mastery over nature.'

As an afterthought, it is true, Pannenberg notes a possible discrepancy between such mastery and a genuinely theonomous culture. The modern principle of human autonomy, he concedes, guarantees nature "far less protection against limitless human exploitation than does Christian anthropology." Once individual freedom is defined as "unlimited power of self-disposition," the man-nature balance is deeply disturbed; to this extent the modern aspiration to unrestricted control over nature "has in fact been shaken and unsettled by the ecological crisis."[30]

The questionable status of man and human autonomy puts in jeopardy, or at least casts a new light on, another central thesis of *Anthropology:* the thesis of the essential linkage of man and God. If man is indeed conceived in the image of God—as Pannenberg claims (I believe correctly)—then perhaps we need to reconsider this image so as to avoid its contamination with modern notions of intentional subjectivity and mastery. Such contamination, I fear, is dangerously courted in the depiction of religion as source of the "unity of meaning" in the world and in the portrayal of political power as possible manifestation of "the unifying rule of almighty God." Several leading thinkers in our time—from Benjamin to Levinas—have urged a disengagement of faith from facile anthropomorphisms, that is, a recognition of the radical otherness of God or of the difference of His face (a difference which does not preclude mutual access). This seems to me timely advice. In a century ravaged by two world wars and attempts at Holocaust, how can we remain insensitive to the otherness and virtual incommensurability of the divine image—an image we cannot hope to approximate except through a difficult process of dislocation? Pannenberg occasionally recognizes this discrepancy, especially in some comments bordering on negative theology. "Every conceptual determination of the infinite by such notions as world-ground, absolute being, or God," he notes at one point, "is in fact itself finite and therefore able to be transcended and negated, just as are other finite ideas." Unfortunately, such comments do not affect his general conception of anthropology. The otherness of the image of God, in my view, also has repercussions on the coming kingdom. Precisely in light of Pannenberg's critical comments on the empirical church, this kingdom needs to be thoroughly cleansed of connotations of wilful sovereignty and imperial rule—in favor of a conception stressing non-domination and mutual engagement (and perhaps the friendship of God and man).[31]

In my assessment, *Anthropology* is particularly persuasive where its theonomous arguments—undogmatically presented—take precedence over traditional metaphysical categories and legacies. This precedence is strongly manifest in the concluding section of the study, devoted to a discussion of history seen as a process propelled by purposive actions but uncontrolled by a human teleology. "Seen in conjunction with human agency and the undeniable importance of action for the self-preservation and expansion of human life," Pannenberg observes, "man's personal autonomy may too readily be construed as 'self-constitution'"—a construal which neglects the theonomous character of history and the unpredictable working of the spirit in the world. The working of the spirit, however, is manifest in the cultivation of community or a shared form of life—a community which "transcends and overcomes the isolation of individuals" through mutual understanding and love. Despite the possibility of a corruption or perversion of communal life through selfishness or collective self-enclosure, harmony and community—Pannenberg adds—"do remain marks of the true spirit," provided they anticipate or foreshadow, however dimly, the coming kingdom. By embodying universal peace and reconciliation—a reconciliation far removed from uniformity and conformism—Christ can be said to be the incarnation of the spirit and the realized image of God. But, *Anthropology* concludes, Christ is this realized image "not just for himself alone" but as head of his body, the Church of believers. The correspondence between human life and God's image is fulfilled ultimately in the "community of God's kingdom—a kingdom whose messianic king is Christ the 'servant' and in which all dominion of man over man will be abolished."[32]

APPENDIX

HEIDEGGER, HÖLDERLIN, AND POLITICS

Not long ago I was privileged to participate in a conference organized in honor of Albert Hirschman, that eminent economist, sociologist, anthropologist, and student of politics; one of Hirschman's challenging books is entitled *Essays in Trespassing*.[1] The following pages also are intended as such an essay in trespassing. Dealing simultaneously with "Heidegger, Hölderlin, and Politics" means to move across significant academic and intellectual boundaries, chiefly the dividing lines between philosophy, poetry, literary criticism, and political thought; one might also add the demarcation between past and present. The objective of my trespassing effort, I want to emphasize, is not simply to produce an indistinct amalgam of ingredients—which would involve not so much the transgression as the erasure of boundaries; my goal is rather to highlight both the distinctness and the mutual correlation of the respective domains.

Before proceeding I need to qualify my undertaking in several ways. My presentation shall not range broadly over Heidegger's entire opus— which would not only be foolhardy but actually impossible (given the present state of this opus). Nor shall I attempt to comment on all of Heidegger's numerous writings devoted to Hölderlin. My focus is going to be more restricted: I intend to concentrate chiefly on one relevant publication, namely, Heidegger's lecture course entitled *Hölderlin's Hymnen "Germanien" und "Der Rhein" (Hölderlin's Hymns "Germania" and "The Rhine")*. Originally presented at the University of Freiburg during the winter semester of 1934/35, the course (or its text) has recently been published as part of the ongoing edition of Heidegger's collected works, the so-called *Gesamtausgabe*.[2]

There are several reasons—good reasons, I believe—for focusing on the mentioned lecture course. Heidegger's courses—particularly those offered between 1923 and 1944—were for the most part previously unpublished and are only now slowly being made available to the public. Thus, there is the freshness and excitement of a new encounter with Heidegger's thought as one after another of these volumes appear in print. There is a better reason, however, which has to do with the author himself. Despite the mountain of pages he has written, I think one should realize that Heideger was first and foremost not a writer of books or treatises but a teacher. The testimony of eye witnesses fully concurs on this point. All his students—even those who later drifted away from him—are unanimous in extolling the spellbinding character of his lectures and the intense fascination of his oral presentations. In his recently published *Heideggers Wege*, Hans-Georg Gadamer ascribes to his teacher a "nearly dramatic appearance, a power of diction, a concentration of delivery which captivated all his listeners." He also recounts how, in his lectures, Heidegger was able to transform Aristotle (among other classics) from a "scholastic" mummy into a living presence or a speaking "contemporary"—thus providing a dynamic illustration of what Gadamer later was to call *"Horizontverschmelzung"* (fusion of horizons). Hannah Arendt has been no less eloquent on this aspect. In an essay written on the occasion of Heidegger's eightieth birthday she observed: Even before any of his major publications had appeared, his "name traveled all over Germany like the rumor of the hidden king. . . . The rumor about Heidegger put it quite simply: Thinking has come to life again; the cultural treasures of the past, believed to be dead, are being made to speak, in the course of which it turns out that they propose things altogether different from the familiar, worn-out trivialities they had been presumed to say. There exists a teacher; one can perhaps learn to think."[3]

There is another general consideration which, in my view, recommends the lecture courses to our attention: their discursive and maieutic character. More so than polished texts, the courses offer a glimpse of Heidegger at work, that is, into the laboratory of his thought. Precisely because they were addressed to students rather than a nondescript audience, the courses are more attuned than his books to the need of sustained or progressive learning; they also tend to be more argumentative, more ready to unpack complex notions, and also to confront opposing views in a critical fashion. (These and related advantages, I feel, completely outweigh certain drawbacks endemic to lecture courses, such as an occasional repetitiveness or a tendency to recapitulate discussed topics.) Regarding the specific lecture course of 1934, there is an additional motivation for my choice: the fact that it follows on the heels of a notorious episode or debacle in Heidegger's life, namely, his service as Rector of the University of Freiburg from April 1933 to February 1934. As is well known this episode has placed a heavy onus, perhaps an indelible stain, on Heidegger's public record—a stain which some interpreters like to present as evidence of a permanent commitment to fascism. In these pages I shall not enter into a discussion of this unfortunate interlude and of the dense emotional aura surrounding it.[4] The issue I want to raise, from a political angle, is rather whether the Hölderlin course of 1934 still reflects the sentiments of 1933 or whether, on the contrary, it manifests a profound disillusionment with, and turning away from, the National-Socialist regime—a regime which, during the same months, was steadily tightening its grip on the nation.

Yet, I do not propose to tackle this issue directly or frontally but in a more roundabout way. Clearly, the chosen lecture course is not an ordinary political tract or pamphlet, a tract amenable to straightforward political (or ideological) exegesis. The central topic of the course are two poems or hymns by Hölderlin dating back to the year 1801. Thus, the questions I need to face initially are of a literary character— and seemingly far removed from politics: Why does Heidegger turn to poetry, and particularly to Hölderlin's poetry, at this time? Differently and more elaborately put: What is for him the meaning of poetry (Dichtung) and why does he choose Hölderlin to illustrate this meaning?

I

The status of poetry in Heidegger's philosophy is a complex problem which resists brief summary; one way to facilitate access is to stress the distance from customary aesthetic assumptions (and from modern subjectivist aesthetics in general). Contrary to common-sense beliefs, poetry for Heidegger is not simply the production of nice-sounding strings of words, nor a purely decorative exercise designed to engender aesthetic delight. Broadly speaking, poetry in his treatment has ontological status: it is a prominent or eminent mode of the epiphany of being— where being does not designate a given object (whose presence could be empirically determined), but rather an ongoing happening, a process of advent and retreat, of disclosure and concealment. Since it is not a fixed entity, being needs to be continuously re-created and re-enacted— although not in the sense of a willful fabrication. Poetry participates in this continuing enactment or "constitution of being" (Stiftung des Seins) by putting it into words—although again not in a direct fashion, but through the medium of poetic language which simultaneously reveals and conceals. In the lecture course of 1934, Heidegger calls poetry also the "original voice or language of a people" *(Ursprache)* because such language permits the constitution of the being of a people—namely, by opening up a historical space for its deeds and accomplishments as well as for its failures and catastrophes.[5]

Given this conception of poetry, what is the significance of Hölderlin, and especially of his later hymns? From Heidegger's perspective, Hölderlin's work is exemplary or prototypical precisely with regard to the constitution of being. Repeatedly he portrays Hölderlin as the "poet's poet"—not only in the ordinary sense (of distinguished or outstanding poet) but in the deeper sense that his work constitutes the very being or meaning of poetry. To illustrate this meaning the lecture course invokes Hölderlin's poem "As On a Holiday . . ." *("Wie wenn am Feiertage . . .")* which contains these lines: "Yet, it behooves us, poets, to stand bareheaded beneath God's thunderstorms" *("Doch uns gebührt es, unter Gottes Gewittern, Ihr Dichter! mit entblösstem Haupte zu stehen").* As the course comments: "The poet captures God's lightning in his words and inserts these lightning-filled words into the language of a people. Rather than voicing his inner experiences he stands 'beneath God's thunderstorms.' "[6]

However, Heidegger ascribes to Hölderlin a further, more specific significance or role: namely, as a "German poet" or as "poet of the Germans" —although, I should add right away, this phrase must not be taken in a restrictive-ethnic, and not even in a directly referential, sense. Hölderlin is poet of the Germans not merely because he happens to be born among Germans but, more radically, because his poetry "constitutes" the "being" of Germans by opening up a historical possibility for them—albeit a possibility they tend to ignore. The Preface to the lecture course describes Hölderlin as a poet "whom the Germans have yet to face (in the future)." In a later passage Hölderlin is portrayed as "the poet who poetically invents the Germans" or more elaborately as "the poet, that is, the founder *(Stifter)* of German being because he has farthest projected the latter, that is, propelled it ahead and beyond into the most distant future." In which sense or direction has Hölderlin projected this possibility? Heidegger states the answer repeatedly. "He was able," he writes, "to unlock this far-future distance because he retrieved the key out of the experience of the deepest need or agony: the experience of the retreat and (possible) return of the gods." Using a slightly different formulation the Preface notes that—leaving behind our "historicist pretentions"—Hölderlin has "founded the beginning of a different history, a history revolving around the struggle and decision regarding the advent or flight of God."[7]

I intend to return to this issue or struggle later; for the moment I just want to let these phrases linger or resonate. As indicated, the lecture course does not deal with Hölderlin's entire opus but concentrates on two of his later hymns—dating from the period when his mind was slowly beginning to drift toward darkness. Heidegger in his lectures offers a detailed exegesis of the two hymns—which I cannot fully recapitulate here. Nor shall I attempt to give a descriptive account of the content of these poems (if such a thing were at all possible). At this point I simply want to pick out a few lines or stanzas to convey the general flavor. In the first hymn, for example, there occur these lines which are addressed by an eagle to a priestess named Germania: "It is you, chosen, all-loving one who have grown strong to bear a difficult fortune (ein schweres Glück)." And the hymn concludes thus: " . . . on your holidays, Germania, when you are priestess and when defenseless (wehrlos), you provide counsel to kings and nations." Finally, some lines from "The Rhine" about half-gods, sons of gods (Göttersöhne), poets: "For ordinary man knows his home and the animal knows where to build, but these carry the wound in their inexperienced souls of not knowing where to turn."[8]

II

While I cannot retrace here Heidegger's entire commentary, I can and need to review some of his major arguments regarding these poems. First, a few words on the reading of poetry or poetic texts. In addition to providing a substantive analysis, the lecture course also offers numerous observations on exegesis or literary interpretation in general—observations which seem directly relevant to contemporary literary criticism. As Heidegger emphasizes, poetry—and Hölderlin's poetry in particular—cannot simply be explained or decoded in terms of historical influences, environmental conditions, and least of all in terms of personal biography. Despite their obvious importance, historical settings in his view cannot be used as a shortcut to interpretation—a shortcut predicated on the assumption that historical periods are more directly accessible to understanding than texts and that the latter can therefore readily be deciphered in terms of the former. Perhaps, he retorts, we may sometimes have to interpret a period or social context in light of its leading texts. Heidegger is more adamant in his critique of psychological or biographical approaches to exegesis. Poetry, he insists, is not the outpouring of inner feelings, the expression of personal sentiments or experiences—the teachings of traditional (modern) aesthetics to the contrary notwithstanding. Summarizing the traditional outlook the course remarks: Inner feelings are here claimed "to find tangible outer expression—for instance, in a lyrical poem. These processes and sentiments in the poet's 'soul' can then be further analyzed with the help of modern 'depth psychology.' Along these lines one can compare writers of different genres as (psychological) types—such as epic, lyrical, or dramatic writers; depth psychology thus turns into typological analysis." As Heidegger bitingly comments: "Expression is also the barking of a dog. ... This conception places poetry *ab limine* under auspices where even the slightest possibility of real understanding hopelessly disappears."[9]

Contrary to this subjective-expressive view Heidegger finds the essence of poetry in complete surrender or exposure. Following Hölderlin's suggestion in "As On a Holiday," he writes: Instead of articulating inner feelings the poet "stands 'beneath God's thunderstorms'—'bare-headed', defenselessly surrendered and abandoned." When Hölderlin occasionally speaks of the "soul of the poet," the phrase (he notes) does not designate a "rummaging in inner psychic feelings" nor an "experiential core somewhere inside," but rather refers to the "utmost exile of naked exposure." For both Hölderlin and Heidegger, thunderstorm and lightning are the peculiar "language of the gods" which poets are meant to capture "without flinching" and to transplant into the language of a people. As the lecture course elaborates, the "language of the gods" is not a direct mode of speech but rather a set of indirect "winks," cues or traces. Poetry, from this perspective, is "the transmission of these winks to the people"; seen from the angle of the latter, it is the attempt "to place the being of a people under the aegis of these winks"—an attempt which does not mean their transformation into "observable objects or intentional contents. It is precisely by enduring and transmitting the "winks of the gods," that poetry is said to contribute to the "constitution of being."[10]

Together with the subjective-expressive approach, Heidegger also rejects the definition of exegesis as a reconstruction of the *mens auctoris* (author's intention). In his view, the author's mind—provided it could be uncovered—is not a reliable or authoritative guide; actually, it is the poem which constitutes the author as author or poet, rather than the other way around. In reading a poem, he observes, we cannot take refuge in the author's intent as a fixed point; instead, we are drawn into the torrent of the poetic language, into the "cyclone" *(Wirbel)* of the poetic saying. As this observation indicates Heidegger, in criticizing the subjective or mentalist conception, does not simply opt for a textual objectivism or autonomy, that is, for the timeless, aesthetic essence of a text or opus—such as a "Sophocles in itself, a Kant in itself," or a poem in itself. Rather, interpreting a text requires dynamic participation and involvement on the part of the reader—who, in turn, is not a sovereign master. This means: the reader must be willing to undergo the same surrender that the poet endured; he must himself be ready to enter the cyclone of the poetic word. Thus, Heidegger stresses the need to "participate" in poetry, the need to be drawn into the "power sphere *(Machtbereich)* of poetry" and to let poetry exert its leavening and transforming impact on human life.[11]

III

To be sure, in offering his exegesis of Hölderlin's poems, Heidegger does not himself speak as a poet but as a thinker or philosopher; his interpretation is a distinctly philosophical endeavor or labor. Repeatedly the lecture course portrays the relation between thinking and poetry *(Dichten und Denken)* as a relationship marked by both distance and proximity— that is, as a relationship of two enterprises whose boundary is both a connecting link and a line of demarcation. In Heidegger's view, thinking and poetry are neither synonymous nor are they worlds apart; as he notes (in another context), they "dwell close together on high mountain tops separated by an abyss." The lecture course, in any event, is not merely a poetic paraphrase or a literary exercise; instead, it deliberately pursues the task of philosophical penetration, an effort guided by the need for "lucid sobriety" *(heller Ernst)* as distinguished from calculating wit or academic pedantry.

> 'If any poet,' Heidegger writes, 'demands for his work a philosophical approach, it is Hölderlin; and this not only because as poet he happened to be "also a philosopher"—and even one whom we confidently can place next to Schelling and Hegel. Rather: Hölderlin is one of our greatest, that is, most impending *thinkers* because he is our greatest *poet.* The poetic understanding of his poetry is possible only as a philosophical confrontation with the manifestation of being achieved in his work.'[12]

Judged in strictly philosophical terms, the lecture course is significant not only because of its analysis of Hölderlin's poems but also—in equal measure—because of the light it throws on Heidegger's own perspective and on the development of his thought. The reader acquainted with *Being and Time* will encounter many themes familiar from that work—especially the theme of the ontological status of *Dasein,* of man as the "witness of being" whose *Dasein* is lodged in the existential tension of "thrownness" and "project" *(Geworfenheit* and *Entwurf).* There are also comments on "being-toward-death" as well as on *Mitsein* and authentic "co-being." As the lecture course states: "Being directly touches and concerns us—we cannot even exist without being entangled in being. But this being or existence of ours is not that of an isolated subject but rather a historical co-being or togetherness as being-in-a-world." In line with the earlier work, the course also contains significant passages on the meaning of time—particularly the distinction between ordinary time seen as the "mere flux of successive nows" and genuine time as the advent or manifestation of being.[13]

In addition to these more familiar topics the course at various points moves beyond the perimeters of *Being and Time* in the direction of Heidegger's subsequent works. Thus, the portrayal of *Dasein* as a "linguistic event" *(Sprachgeschehnis)* and as "dialogue" *(Gespräch)* foreshadows arguments more fully developed in *On the Way to Language*. "Only where language happens," the lectures state, "can being and nonbeing disclose themselves; this disclosure and concealment, however, is who we are." Similarly, the description of genuine time as a "waiting for the *Ereignis*" may be said to adumbrate later discussions of this mode of ontological happening (sometimes translated as "appropriation" or "appropriating event"). A prominent feature of the lecture course is also the recurrent reference to "creators" or "creative agents" *(die Schaffenden)*—a topic which, as we know, became crucial in some of Heidegger's writings during the immediately following years. In particular, the subdivisions of "creators" into poets, thinkers, and "founders of states" *(Staatsschöpfer)* is a striking anticipation of an argument familiar from "The Origin of the Work of Art" (of 1935-36); the same could be said about passages dealing with the role of conflict or "agon" *(Streit)* as precondition of ontological "harmony" *(Innigkeit)*.[14]

IV

I shall not prolong this review of philosophical themes; instead, I want to turn to another boundary: that connecting poetry and thinking with politics. I intend to approach this boundary on two levels: a more overt and a more latent or subterranean level. First, let me draw your attention to some overtly political passages in the lecture course. There are a great number of these—some quite forthright and brazen if placed in the context of 1934. The opening pages of the course refer to a fragment from Hölderlin's late opus which reads: "About the highest I shall be silent. Forbidden fruit, like the laurel, however, is most of all the fatherland. This (fruit) everyone should taste last." And Heideger comments:

The fatherland, our fatherland Germany—forbidden most of all, removed from everyday haste and busy noise . . . . With this we already indicate what our focus on "Germania" does not mean. We do not wish to offer something usable, trendy or up-to-date and thereby advertise our lecture course—which would convey the pernicious impression as if we wanted to garner for Hölderlin a cheap timely relevance. We do not seek to adapt Hölderlin to our time, but on the contrary: we want to bring us and those after us under the yardstick of the poet.

Our fatherland, forbidden most of all—surely strange words at a time of patriotic and chauvinistic frenzy.[15]

But there is more to come. Commenting on Hölderlin's portrayal of Germania—as a priestess or else as a dreamy maid "hidden in the woods" —Heidegger compares this image with a famous national monument: the statue of Germania in the Niederwald forest. This monument, he notes, depicts "a massive woman *(ein Mordsweib)* with flowing hair and a giant sword. By contrast, Hölderlin's Germania is by today's standards 'unheroic.' " What makes things worse is the reference to a "defenseless" Germania offering counsel to nations. Thus, Heidegger adds mockingly, Hölderlin "is apparently a 'pacifist,' one who advocates the defenselessness of Germany and perhaps even unilateral disarmament. This borders on high treason." A little later, during a discussion of the expressive view of poetry, the course directly attacks one of the regime's most representative poets or literary figures: Erwin G. Kolbenheyer. In a speech held at various German universities the latter had claimed that "poetry is a necessary biological function of a people." Heidegger retorts: "It does not take much brain to realize: this (description) applies also to digestion—which likewise is a biologically necessary function of a people, especially a healthy one." The same discussion contains a dig at Alfred Rosenberg, the regime's star ideologist, and at the doctrine of racial biologism or biological racism. The expressive view, Heidegger insists, is mistaken regardless of whose sentiments are involved: whether these sentiments are those of a single individual or a "collective soul," whether (with Spengler) they reflect the "soul of a culture" or (with Rosenberg) they express a "racial soul" or the "soul of a people." Regarding fascist biologism, another passage should also be mentioned. In light of his stress on "earth" and "homeland," Heidegger has sometimes been assailed as harboring a sympathy for the ideology of "blood and soil" *(Blut und Boden)*. Alluding to the practice of literary criticism of his time—to the "dubious arsenal of the contemporary science of literature" —the lecture course states: "Until recently everyone was looking for

the psychoanalytic underpinnings of poetry; now everything is satu-
rated *(trieft)* with folkdom and with 'blood and soil'—but nothing has
really changed."16

Here, for good measure, are a few more stabs at pet fascist conceptions or slogans. Advocating a view of philosophy as perpetual questioning, Heidegger writes, in mock self-criticism: "Questioning? But no:
the decisive thing is clearly the answer. That much every pedestrian or
man on the street understands, and since he understands it, it must be
right and the whole outlook is then called 'folkish science' or 'folk-
related science' " *(volksverbundene Wissenschaft,* the official aim of every
discipline at the time). Or again, a little later, Heidegger finds a linkage
between the fascist view of culture and bourgeois "culture industry."
"Only small times," he observes, "when the whole *Dasein* decays into
fabrication—only such times officially cultivate the 'true, good, and
beautiful' and establish appropriate state ministries for this cultivation." This confusion is compounded by the mistaken assumption folk
culture could be enhanced "through the expanded institution of profes-
sorships for folk science and primeval history." Elsewhere, Heidegger
displays his chagrin over ongoing developments in academia and education in general. His turn to Hölderlin, he insists, does not reflect an
attempt to salvage a national heritage or to "utilize (the poet) in a direct
political manner"—things "which no doubt we shall encounter abun-
dantly in the coming years, following the completed political integration *(Gleichschaltung)* of the humanities." In a sardonic vein—pondering
future prospects of philosophy—the lecture course notes at one point
that "it now appears as if thinking will soon be entirely abolished."17

While criticizing the political winds of the time (I should add)
Heidegger does not depict his own preoccupation with Hölderlin as a
simple retreat from politics or as an abandonment of the political arena
as such. On the contrary, the lectures explicitly present this concern as a
kind of counter-politics or as signaling a radical change of political
course. "Since Hölderlin has this hidden and difficult meaning to be
the poet's poet and the poet of the Germans," we read, "therefore he has
not yet become a guiding force in the history of our people. And since he
is not yet this force, he should become it. To contribute to this task is
'politics' in the highest and most genuine sense—so much so that who-
ever makes headway along this line has no need to talk about 'politics'."18

V

What alternative course or direction does this counter-politics suggest?
We approach here, I believe, the deeper or less overt significance of

Hölderlin in the context of 1934—and, more broadly, in the context of our age. Heidegger delineates this significance by elaborating on the "basic mood" *(Grundstimmung)* of the two poems "Germania" and "The Rhine," a mood which underlies and permeates the poetic saying in these hymns as a whole. By "mood," one needs to emphasize right away, Heidegger does not mean an inner-subjective feeling or psychological sentiment. Readers of *Being and Time* cannot be misled on this point, which is reiterated in the lecture course: "mood" in Heidegger's usage is a kind of ontological "tuning" or "attunement"—the attunement of *Dasein* and being, or the mode in which being is revealed/concealed in a *Dasein* or (as here) in poetry. As he says, "mood" *(Stimmung)* denotes "least of all the merely subjective or the so-called interior of man"; rather, it means "the original exposure into the vastness of beings and the depth of being."[19]

Turning first to "Germania," what—in Heidegger's exegesis—is the basic mood or tuning pervading the poem? According to the lecture course, this tuning derives from a fundamental, though subterranean event of our age: the flight or disappearance of the gods. Hölderlin's hymn begins with these lines: "Not them, the blessed ones who once appeared, the images of gods of old, them I may no longer call. . . ." However, this non-calling is not simply an act of resignation, least of all a sign of abandonment or indifference; rather: non-calling is a synonym for the patient endurance of a loss, for a long-standing and profound suffering. This means: the tuning or mood of "Germania" is essentially one of "mourning" *(Trauer)*. Yet, in the treatment of both Hölderlin and Heidegger, mourning is not identical with mere emotional sadness or melancholy, and certainly not with a plaintiff anxiety or distress. Rather, as a mode of attunement, mourning has a sober and almost serene quality; in Heidegger's words, it is not a psychological but a "spiritual" (or ontological) category. Occasioned by the loss of gods, the mourning pervading "Germania" is in fact a "hallowed" or "sacred mourning" *(heilige Trauer)*. Moreover, mourning here does not signify a breach or simple farewell. As in the case of a loved one, the experience of the loss of gods actually nurtures and strengthens the bond of love and the desire for reunion. As Heidegger notes: "Where the most beloved is gone, love remains—for else the other could not at all have gone (as the beloved)." Thus, mourning here is both acceptance of the loss—a refusal to cling—and a determined waiting for reconciliation, an expectant readiness for the return of the gods.[20]

The theme of mourning is further elaborated in the second hymn "The Rhine" whose focus is on the role of half-gods or demi-gods—namely, as exemplary mourners. In Hölderlin's presentation these demi-gods are directly guided by a divine mission or destiny *(Schicksal)* and thus are able to chart a course for human life; they include the great streams or rivers (like the Rhine) which create a path for human habitation, and also the poets who carry the gods' lightning to men. In Heidegger's commentary, half-gods are basically "over-men and under-gods" *(Übermenschen und Untergötter)*. "When thinking about the being of man, he observes, we necessarily point beyond man toward a higher region; in thinking about gods, on the other hand, we inevitably fall short and remain at their threshold. Hence the importance of half-gods as mediators and place-keepers of the "in-between" realm. Standing directly under divine mandates, half-gods are particularly vulnerable and exposed; being specially attuned to the withdrawal (and possible return) of the gods, their existence is marked by intense suffering and endurance. In effect, their suffering is the emblem of their mediating and creative role. Thus, as in the case of "Germania," the basic mood or tuning of "The Rhine" is one of hallowed mourning, occasioned by the flight of the gods. In Heidegger's words: "The manner in which the being of half-gods—the mid-point of being as a whole—is disclosed is suffering. This great and alone decisive kind of suffering, however, can pervade *Dasein* only in the form of that mood which manifests simultaneously the fugitive and approaching power of God and the exposed plight of human life: the mood of sacred mourning and expectant readiness."[21]

VI

One should mark this well: mourning—sacred mourning—as the central mood of Hölderlin's hymns and also of Heidegger's entire lecture course. How incongruous—in 1934, and still today. How much disillusionment and personal agony must have preceded and nurtured this mood in the case of both Hölderlin and Heidegger. How far removed, how radically distant is this outlook from the ebullient self-confidence of the fascist regime in 1934, from the mood of national "resurgence" *(Aufbruch)* at the inception of the "Thousand-year *Reich*."[22] (1934, one may recall, was the year of the mammoth Party Congress in Nuremberg which, in a celebrated film, has been glorified as "triumph of the will.") How distant is this outlook also from our own contemporary life—from our own ebullient self-confidence in the unlimited blessings of technological progress.

Mourning, sacred mourning—about what? About the god-lessness of our age, about the withdrawal and absence of the gods. I should add right away that mourning of this kind is not simply a call for moral or spiritual renewal or for a mobilization of religious faith; least of all is it a call for a strengthening of church institutions or confessional ties. Godlessness here is not a question of the vitality of established churches or of inner-personal belief. Instead: it has to do with the absence of gods from our civilization and our existence as a people, that is, from our way of life or way of being. It has to do with our relegation of the divine to a decorative status on holidays, to the status of folklore at religious festivals. As Heidegger emphasizes: "The issue is not how an empirically given people handles its traditional religion or denominational faith. Rather, at stake is the genuine advent or non-advent of God in the life of a people out of the agony of its being."[23]

The stress on a common "way of life" (or ontological condition) highlights another dimension of the key mood of the two hymns: the reference to a "homeland" or "fatherland." For Hölderlin and Heidegger, mourning is not an isolated individual experience or subjective state of mind; rather, it is a mourning "in" and "with the homeland" *(Heimat)* or "with the native earth" *(heimatliche Erde)*. However, homeland here does not simply denote a natural habitat or an empirical-ecological setting; nor is it a mere abstraction or speculative-metaphysical idea. As interpreted in the lecture course, homeland is rather the site of an ontological mediation—the name for a concrete promise, namely, for a potential dwelling place of the gods. Properly speaking, mourning is possible only on the basis of such a promise. For, how could one talk of their withdrawal or advent if gods lived in an immutable realm separated from humans by an unbridgeable gulf? And how could one sense or experience their loss if human life were invariably wretched? Mourning thus necessarily involves a transgression of traditional metaphysics (predicated on the juxtaposition of two separate worlds).

VII

Let me slowly come to a close. I have explored Heidegger's exegesis of Hölderlin's hymns and also some of their overt and covert political implications. I do not wish to leave the impression that I find all of Heidegger's arguments equally persuasive. Some passages still carry overtones of a youthful exuberance *(Sturm und Drang)* which required further seasoning; some details also are not entirely congruent, in my view, with the overall direction of his thought. Thus, I find dubious Heidegger's persistent reference to "the people" *(Volk)* in the sense of a homogeneous entity or totality. Precisely his non-objectivist ontology and his stress on ontological difference should have suggested to him a greater differentiation or heterogeneity among people (perhaps along the lines of Arendt's notion of 'plurality'). Appeals to the people or a bland populism are particularly problematic if the people—here the German people—are assigned an eminently poetic or historically creative role; surely subsequent years and decades must have disabused Heidegger of such hopes. Together with the concept of the people, I would also question the notion of the state as used in the lecture course, especially in the portrayal of founders of states, as exemplary historical agents; too heavily burdened with modern metaphysical weight, the state does not seem an adequate vehicle for Heidegger's thoughts.[25] Finally, I find disconcerting the excessive emphasis on conflict and agon *(Streit, Feindseligkeit)*—an emphasis which renders harmony *(Innigkeit)* extremely precarious if not impossible. In the exegesis of "The Rhine," this emphasis is actually so strong and pervasive that Heidegger almost omits to comment on a crucial theme in Hölderlin's poem: the impending "wedding feast of gods and men." In this instance the experiences of subsequent years and the outbreak of the war seemed to have a remarkable effect. When Heidegger again offers a lecture course on Hölderlin (in winter of 1941-42), his focus and the basic tuning of his course is precisely this wedding feast *(Brautfest)*.[26]

Yet, I wish to end on a different note: by returning to 1934. In the midst of fascist triumphalism, Heidegger's lecture course is pervaded by overwhelming grief. What is the significance then of Hölderlin in Heidegger's perception? Who is this poet as reflected in the two hymns and in the lectures? He is, simply put, a caller in the desert, a voice in the wilderness of our age—or, as Heidegger says, a "first fruit" or "first born" *(Erstling)* liable to be sacrificed. What does the voice proclaim? Mostly this: prepare the ground, make straight the paths—for a possible return of the fugitive gods, and thus for a possible reconciliation or wedding feast.[27] Not that through our attitude or activity we could somehow halt their flight or force or fabricate their reappearance; but our grief and expectation may at least serve as an invitation or solicitation encouraging their return. Mourning thus is preparatory for a different age: for a way of life which would again be suffused with lightning and poetic imagination, a life in which young men could again see visions and old men dream dreams. This is also the meaning of the fatherland as a hallowed or promised land. Heidegger concludes the lecture course by once again invoking the fragment with which he began: "About the highest I shall be silent. Forbidden fruit, like the laurel, however, is most of all the fatherland. This (fruit) everyone should taste last."

NOTES

INTRODUCTION

1. Michel Foucault, *The Order of Things* (New York: Vintage Books, 1973), p. xxiv.

2. Regarding anti-foundational pluralism see also my "Pluralism Old and New: Foucault on Power," in *Polis and Praxis* (Cambridge, MA: MIT Press, 1984), pp. 77-103.

3. In recent Western experience a similar attitude was reflected in the life and work of Martin Luther King. Regarding the relation between India and the West compare Wilhelm Halbfass, *India and Europe: An Essay in Understanding* (Albany: SUNY Press, 1988)—which appeared after the chapter was written. The latter is also true of Bhikhu Parekh, *Gandhi's Political Philosophy* (Notre Dame: University of Notre Dame Press, 1988).

4. See Jürgen Habermas, *The Philosophical Discourse of Modernity: Twelve Lectures,* trans. Frederick Lawrence (Cambridge, MA: MIT Press, 1987). For a work in many ways paralleling Habermas's approach see Alan Megill, *Prophets of Extremity: Nietzsche, Heidegger, Foucault, Derrida* (Berkeley: University of California Press, 1985). For an alternative account of the discourse of modernity compare William E. Connolly, *Political Theory and Modernity* (Oxford; Blackwell, 1988).

5. See Eric Voegelin, *Order and History,* vol. 5: *In Search of Order* (Baton Rouge: Louisiana State University Press, 1987).

6. See Bernhard Waldenfels, *Ordnung im Zwielicht* (Frankfurt-Main: Suhrkamp, 1987); Ernesto Laclau and Chantal Mouffe, *Hegemony and Socialist*

Strategy: Towards a Radical Democratic Politics, trans. Winston Moore and Paul Cammack (London: Verso, 1985).

7. See *Hegel's Philosophy of Right,* trans. T. M. Knox (London: Oxford University Press, 1967); Jean-François Lyotard, *The Postmodern Condition: A Report on Knowledge,* trans. Geoff Bennington and Brian Massumi (Minneapolis: University of Minnesota Press, 1984). In bypassing *Gemeinschaft* and *Gesellschaft,* my proposal also seeks to cut a path through the contemporary debate between "communitarianism" and "liberalism"; on this debate see Amy Gutmann, "Communitarian Critics of Liberalism," *Philosophy and Public Affairs,* vol. 14 (1985), pp. 308-322, and John R. Wallach, "Liberals, Communitarians, and the Tasks of Political Theory," *Political Theory,* vol. 15 (1987), pp. 581-611.

8. See Ernst Bloch, *The Principle of Hope,* trans. Neville Plaice, Stephen Plaice, and Paul Knight, 3 vols. (Cambridge, MA: MIT Press, 1986); Wolfhart Pannenberg, *Anthropology in Theological Perspective,* trans. Matthew J. O'Connell (Philadelphia: Westminster Press, 1985); Martin Heidegger, *Hölderlins Hymnen "Germanien" und "Der Rhein"* (1934-35; *Gesamtausgabe,* vol. 39; Frankfurt-Main: Klostermann, 1980). Particularly in view of the contemporary preoccupation with Heidegger's National-Socialist period, it seems fair to look also at the "other side" of his intellectual and political development.

9. Jacques Derrida, *Margins of Philosophy,* trans. Alan Bass (Chicago: University of Chicago Press, 1982), pp. ix, xxiii.

CHAPTER 1

1. See Karl Jaspers, *The Origin and Goal of History,* trans. M. Bullock (New Haven: Yale University Press, 1953), also *The Future of Mankind,* trans. E. B. Ashton (Chicago: University of Chicago Press, 1961); Friedrich Nietzsche, *Ecce Homo: How One Becomes What One Is,* trans. R.J. Hollingdale (New York: Penguin Books), p. 127 ("Why I Am A Destiny," section 1).

2. See E. Vernon Arnold, *Roman Stoicism* (Cambridge: University Press, 1911), and Max Pohlenz, *Die Stoa* (Göttingen: Vandenhoek and Ruprecht, 1940).

3. See e.g. M. H. Carré, *Realists and Nominalists* (London: Oxford University Press, 1946); R. I. Aaron, *The Theory of Universals* (London: Oxford University Press, 1952); and I. M. Bochénski et al., *The Problem of Universals* (Notre Dame: University of Notre Dame Press, 1956). The unifying factors mentioned above must be supplemented by the institutions of the Catholic Church and by the use of Latin as common language among scholars and intellectuals. In emphasizing the doctrine of universals, and later nominalism, I shortchange the medieval theory of *analogia entis* (with its linkage of universals and particulars).

4. The following statements from the *Communist Manifesto* are still instructive: "The bourgeoisie, by the rapid improvement of all instruments of production, by the immensely facilitated means of communication, draws all

nations, even the most barbarian, into civilization. The cheap prices of its commodities are the heavy artillery with which it batters down all Chinese walls, with which it forces the barbarians' intensely obstinate hatred of foreigners to capitulate. It compels all nations, on pain of extinction, to adopt the bourgeois mode of production. . . . The bourgeoisie has subjected the country to the rule of towns. It has created enormous cities, has greatly increased the urban population as compared with the rural, and has rescued a considerable part of the population from the idiocy of rural life. Just as it has made the country dependent on the towns, so it has made barbarian and semi-barbarian countries dependent on the civilized ones, nations of peasants on nations of bourgeois, the East on the West." See Karl Marx and Frederick Engels, *The Communist Manifesto* (New York: International Publishers, 1948), p. 13.

5. Jürgen Habermas, *Knowledge and Human Interests,* trans. Jeremy J. Shapiro (Boston: Beacon Press, 1971), pp. 312-313. The Appendix actually was Habermas's inaugural address at the University of Frankfurt in 1965.

6. Habermas, "A Postscript to *Knowledge and Human Interests,*" *Philosophy of the Social Sciences,* vol. 3 (1975), pp. 157-189. Compare also "Some Difficulties in the Attempt to Link Theory and Practice" in Habermas, *Theory and Practice,* trans. John Viertel (Boston: Beacon Press, 1973), pp. 13-24; and my "Critical Epistemology Criticized" in *Beyond Dogma and Despair* (Notre Dame: University of Notre Dame Press, 1981), pp. 246-269.

7. See "What is Universal Pragmatics?" in Habermas, *Communication and the Evolution of Society,* trans. Thomas McCarthy (Boston: Beacon Press, 1979), pp. 1-3, 6, 9, 12-14, 26. Referring to structural linguistics Habermas observes (pp. 14, 20) that "it is the great merit of Chomsky to have developed this idea (i.e., of universal capabilities) in the case of grammatical theory"; at the same time, toning down the "essentialist" claims of linguistics, he states that Chomsky's "maturationist" assumption (regarding the correlation of depth grammar and mental development) "seems to me too strong"—a point which leads him in the direction of Piaget's developmental psychology. Although acknowledging an affinity with "transcendental hermeneutics" as proposed by Karl-Otto Apel, Habermas differentiates his approach by pointing to the distinction between a (Kantian) constitution of experiences and the generation of utterances and also to the at least quasi-empirical status of reconstructive analysis (pp. 23-25).

8. See the essays on "Moral Development and Ego Identity" and "Historical Materialism and the Development of Normative Structures" in *Communication and the Evolution of Society,* pp. 69-94, 95-129; also *Legitimation Crisis,* trans. Thomas McCarthy (Boston: Beacon Press, 1975), esp. Part 3, pp. 95-117, and *Moralbewusstsein und kommunikatives Handeln* (Frankfurt-Main: Suhrkamp, 1983), esp. pp. 53-125.

9. Habermas, *The Theory of Communicative Action,* vol. 1: *Reason and the Rationalization of Society,* trans. Thomas McCarthy (Boston: Beacon Press, 1984), p. 137. The latter claims were hedged in by various caveats but not aban-

doned in the study. As Habermas added, with reference to the rational structure of communicative action: "If the requirement of objectivity is to be satisfied, this structure would have to be shown to be *universally valid* in a specific sense. This is a very strong requirement for someone who is operating without metaphysical support and is also no longer confident that a rigorous transcendental-pragmatic program, claiming to provide ultimate grounds, can be carried out." The universalistic aspirations are still maintained in the more recent study on the "discourse of modernity." Through modern forms of communication, Habermas states, "processes of opinion and consensus formation get institutionalized which depend upon diffusion and mutual interpenetration no matter how specialized they are. The boundaries are porous; each public sphere is open to other public spheres. To their discursive structures they owe a (barely concealed) universalist tendency. . . . The European Enlightenment elaborated this experience and adopted it into its programmatic formulas." See Habermas, *The Philosophical Discourse of Modernity: Twelve Lectures*, trans. Frederick Lawrence (Cambridge, MA: MIT Press, 1987), p. 360.

10. Johann Gottlieb Herder, *Auch eine Philosophie der Geschichte zur Bildung der Menschheit* (1774; Frankfurt-Main: Suhrkamp, 1967), p. 106. To be sure, Herder was not *simply* a defender of particularism against universalism, or of immanence against transcendence—as Gadamer persuasively shows in his "Postscript" (pp. 146-177). Compare also my "Abeunt studia in mores: Berlin on Vico and Herder" in *Twilight of Subjectivity* (Amherst, MA: University of Massachusetts Press, 1981), pp. 257-263.

11. Richard Rorty, *Philosophy and the Mirror of Nature* (Princeton: Princeton University Press, 1979), pp. 379-382; Mary Hesse, *Revolutions and Reconstructions in the Philosophy of Science* (Bloomington: Indiana University Press, 1980), p. 173.

12. This point has been forcefully made by Agnes Helles, "Habermas and Marxism," in John B. Thompson and David Held, eds. *Habermas: Critical Debates* (Cambridge, MA: MIT Press, 1982) pp. 21-41. As she points out, even assuming universal structures, their presence does not necessarily have motivating force, but actually may stifle practice.

13. Rorty, "Habermas and Lyotard on Postmodernity," in Richard J. Bernstein, ed. *Habermas and Modernity* (Cambridge, MA: MIT Press, 1985), pp. 165-166. As he adds (pp. 170, 173): if Bacon—the "prophet of self-assertion"—had been taken more seriously (instead of Descartes and Kant), "we might not have been stuck with the canon of 'great modern philosophers' who took 'subjectivity' as their theme" and might have seen that canon "as a distraction from the history of concrete social engineering which made the contemporary North American culture what it is now, with all its glories and all its dangers."

14. Jean-François Lyotard, *The Postmodern Condition: A Report on Knowledge*, trans. Geoff Bennington and Brian Massumi (first French ed. 1979; Minneapolis: University of Minnesota Press, 1984), pp. xxiii-xxv. I could have chosen as

illustrative example also some facets of the work of Michel Foucault (especially aspects stressing rupture and discontinuity); but for present purposes Lyotard's approach seems particularly forthright and instructive.

15. *The Postmodern Condition,* pp. 4-5, 9-10. As Lyotard adds (p. 88, notes 34 and 35), speech acts for him are placed in the domain of the *"agon"* (or joust) rather than that of rational communication. The term "agonistics" is traced to "Heraclitus's ontology," the dialectic of the Sophists and also to Nietzsche's observations in "Homer's Contest."

16. *The Postmodern Condition,* pp. 11-13, 15-17. The term "nodal points" is adopted from the vocabulary of systems theory.

17. *The Postmodern Condition,* pp. 29, 31-32, 38-41, 46-47. As Lyotard observes (p. 43): "The principle of a universal metalanguage is replaced by the principle of a plurality of formal and axiomatic systems capable of arguing the truth of denotative statements; these systems are described by a metalanguage that is universal but not consistent" (that is, ultimately by ordinary language).

18. *The Postmodern Condition,* pp. 53-56, 59-61. As Rorty comments soberly: "Lyotard argues invalidly from the current concerns of various scientific disciplines to the claim that science is somehow discovering that it should aim at permanent revolution, rather than at the alternation between normality and revolution made familiar by Kuhn. To say that 'science aims' at piling paralogy on paralogy is like saying that 'politics aims' at piling revolution on revolution. No inspection of the concerns of contemporary science or contemporary politics could show anything of the sort." See "Habermas and Lyotard on Postmodernity," in Bernstein, ed., *Habermas and Modernity,* p. 163.

19. Lyotard, *Le Différend* (Paris: Editions de Minuit, 1983) pp. 8-10.

20. *Le Différend,* pp. 10-11, 17, 27-29, 199-200. The study differentiates sharply between dialogue and agonal contest. There is a contest, we read (p. 46), "between the defenders of agonistics and the proponents of dialogue. How can this contest be settled? The latter say: through dialogue; the former: through the agon. If these positions are insisted upon, then the contest is perpetuated and becomes a kind of metacontest: a contest over a manner of settling the contest regarding a certain definition of reality."

21. In *The Postmodern Condition,* Lyotard repeatedly places linguistic rules and the "social bond" on a contractual basis—which would seem to locate agonistics in the tradition of modern contractarianism (pp. 10, 43, 66). The same study also stresses the distinction between power and "terror" (pp. 46, 66)—but without clarifying their difference. As one may recall, Sartre's *Being and Nothingness* formulated a strictly conflictual model of the social bond—on entirely subject-centered and intentionalist premises. For critical assessments of Lyotard's political theory see Stuart Sim, "Lyotard and the Politics of Antifoundationalism," *Radical Philosophy,* No. 44 (1986), pp. 8-13; Seyla Benhabib, "Epis-

temologies of Postmodernism: A Rejoinder to Jean-François Lyotard," *New German Critique,* vol. 33 (1984), pp. 103-126; David Ingram, "Legitimacy and the Postmodern Condition: The Political Thought of Jean François Lyotard," *Praxis International,* vol. 7 (1987-88), pp. 286-305.

22. Gadamer, "The Universality of the Hermeneutical Problem," in *Philosophical Hermeneutics,* trans. and ed. David E. Linge (Berkeley: University of California Press, 1976), pp. 15-16 (translation slightly altered). For the German version see Gadamer, *Kleine Schriften I: Philosophie, Hermeneutik* (Tübingen: Mohr, 1967), p. 111.

23. Gadamer, "Replik," in Karl-Otto Apel et al., *Hermeneutik und Ideologiekritik* (Frankfurt-Main: Suhrkamp, 1971), pp. 289, 301-302, 317. I do not deny a certain vacillation in Gadamer's arguments—especially the fact that his emphasis on dialogue may privilege a consensual model (over agonal contest). For a fuller discussion of this issue see my "Hermeneutics and Deconstruction: Gadamer and Derrida in Dialogue," in *Critical Encounters* (Notre Dame: University of Notre Dame Press, 1987), pp. 130-158.

24. Martin Heidegger "The Origin of the Work of Art," in *Poetry, Language, Thought,* trans. Albert Hofstadter (New York: Harper & Row, 1971), pp. 44, 48-50. A similar correlation is outlined in the Schelling lectures of 1936 between the dimensions of "ground" and "existence": "Ground is what sustains self-disclosing appearance and maintains it in its grasp. Existence, on the other hand, is self-transcendence and manifestation—a movement which is based on the ground and explicitly confirms the latter as its ground. Ground and existence belong together; only their linkage renders possible their separation and strife—which in turn yields a higher concord." See Heidegger, *Schellings Abhandlung Über das Wesen der menschlichen Freiheit (1809),* ed. Hildegard Feick (Tübingen: Niemeyer, 1971), pp. 137-138.

25. Maurice Merleau-Ponty, *The Visible and the Invisible,* ed. Claude Lefort, trans. Alphonso Lingis (Evanston: Northwestern University Press, 1968), p. 263; *Signs,* trans. Richard C. McCleary (Evanston: Northwestern University Press, 1964), pp. 119-120. Merleau-Ponty in the latter context recommends a method which consists "in learning to see what is ours as alien and what was alien as our own" (p. 120). Compare also Heidegger, *Identity and Difference,* trans. Joan Stambaugh (New York: Harper & Row, 1969), and *Vorträge und Aufsätze* (3rd ed.; Pfullingen: Neske, 1967), vol. 2, pp. 23-24.

26. Bernhard Waldenfels, *Ordnung im Zwiellcht* (Frankfurt-Main: Suhrkamp, 1987), pp. 10-11, 29, 39, 43-46. For a more detailed discussion see Chapter 5 below.

27. Ernesto Laclau and Chantal Mouffe, *Hegemony and Socialist Strategy: Towards a Radical Democratic Politics,* trans. Winston Moore and Paul Cammack (London: Verso, 1985), pp. 93, 105-111, 122-129, 188. For a more detailed discussion see Chapter 6 below.

28. Merleau-Ponty, *Signs*, p. 139; Eric Voegelin, *Order and History*, vol. 4: *The Ecumenic Age* (Baton Rouge: Louisiana State University Press, 1974), p. 305. For some contemporary formulations of cross-cultural understanding, akin to "universal hermeneutics," see Alasdair MacIntyre, *Whose Justice? Which Rationality?* (Notre Dame: University of Notre Dame Press, 1988), esp. pp. 389-403, and David Tracy, *Plurality and Ambiguity: Hermeneutics, Religion, Hope* (New York: Harper & Row, 1987).

CHAPTER 2

1. Cited in Raghavan Iyer, *The Moral and Political Thought of Mahatma Gandhi* (2nd ed.; London: Concord Grove Press, 1983), p. 4.

2. Raghavan Iyer, *The Moral and Political Writings of Mahatma Gandhi*, 3 vols. (Oxford: Clarendon Press, 1985-1988). Volume I deals with "Civilization, Politics, and Religion"; volume II with "Truth and Non-Violence"; and volume III (forthcoming) with "Non-Violent Resistance and Social Transformation."

3. Iyer, *The Moral and Political Writings of Mahatma Gandhi*, vol. 2 (Oxford: Clarendon Press, 1986), pp. 150, 475.

4. Karl Marx, "Theses on Feuerbach," Thesis XI; in Robert C. Tucker, ed., *The Marx-Engels Reader* (New York: Norton, 1972), p. 109. For general background compare Guy Claxton, *Wholly Human: Western and Eastern Visions of the Self and Its Perfection* (London: Routledge & Kegan Paul, 1981); Raghavan Iyer, ed., *The Glass Curtain Between Asia and Europe* (London: Oxford University Press, 1965); Charles A. Moore, ed., *Philosophy and Culture: East and West* (Honolulu: University of Hawaii Press, 1962); Sidney L. Gulick, *The East and the West* (Rutland, VT: Tuttle, 1962); Barbara Ward, *The Interplay of East and West* (New York: Norton, 1957).

5. Iyer, *The Moral and Political Thought of Mahatma Gandhi*, pp. 234-238. The citations are from Gandhi, *The Story of My Experiments with Truth*, trans. Mahadev Desai (Ahmedabad: Navajivan, 1956), p. xii; and *Harijan* (weekly paper), August 1939. The term *Gita* in the text refers to the *Bhagavad Gita*.

6. Gandhi, *Hind Swaraj* (1909; re-ed. Ahmedabad: Navajivan, 1938). Compare Ramashray Roy, *Self and Society: A Study in Gandhian Thought* (New Delhi: Sage Publications, 1985), pp. 34, 36-44. For the notion of "enframing" *(Gestell)* see especially Martin Heidegger, *The Question Concerning Technology and Other Essays*, trans. William Lovitt (New York: Harper & Row, 1976).

7. Iyer, *The Moral and Political Thought of Mahatma Gandhi*, pp. 17, 34, 101-102. Compare also Pyarelal, *Mahatma Gandhi: The Last Phase*, vol. 2 (Ahmedabad: Navajivan, 1958), p. 137. Obviously, Gandhi's reservations apply chiefly to "orthodox" or economistic construals of Marx and less to neo-Marxist reformulations or perspectives.

8. *The Diary of Mahadev Desai*, vol. I (Ahmedabad: Navajivan, 1953), p. 109; cited in Iyer, *The Moral and Political Thought of Mahatma Gandhi*, pp. 18-19. As Iyer elaborates (p. 18): Gandhi was "not a rationalist—he distrusted reason too much for that—and he placed a religious reliance upon faith on the ground of the inadequacy of any man's personal experience and mental faculties. In the last analysis, Gandhi stands outside the modern tradition of political reasoning because of his unwillingness to follow a strictly logical route in coming to conclusions." In a similar vein, Bhikhu Parekh observes: "Although he (Gandhi) valued and stressed the importance of reason, he felt that it could not by itself yield conclusive moral principles, for it was always possible to criticize and disagree with whatever principles another man advanced. Not only was reason inherently skeptical and inconclusive, but Gandhi thought that it was also inherently incapable of generating *moral* principles. For him reason was nothing more than the capacity for logical reasoning governed by the formal criteria of logical consistency. It, therefore, presupposed something other than and prior to itself upon which to exercise its powers of analysis." See Parekh, "Gandhi and the Logic of Reformist Discourse," in Bhikhu Parekh and Thomas Pantham, eds., *Political Discourse: Explorations in Indian and Western Political Thought* (New Delhi: Sage Publications, 1987), pp. 287-288.

9. M.S. Deshpande, ed., *Light of India* (Sangli: Deshpande, 1950), p. 277; quoted in Iyer, *The Moral and Political Thought of Mahatma Gandhi*, p. 7.

10. Parekh, "Gandhi and the Logic of Reformist Discourse," pp. 278-279. As Parekh adds (p. 279): "For Gandhi, to lose oneself in their service was to lose oneself in the *Brahman*. True religion consisted in active social service, and *moksha* consisted in selfless absorption in the 'ocean of humanity', wishing nothing for oneself that others cannot have and struggling to wipe every tear from every eye."

11. Parekh, "Gandhi and the Logic of Reformist Discourse," p. 285.

12. Parekh, "Gandhi and the Logic of Reformist Discourse," p. 277; also Parekh, "Some Reflections on the Hindu Tradition of Political Thought," in Thomas Pantham and Kenneth L. Deutsch, eds., *Political Thought in Modern India* (New Delhi: Sage Publications, 1986), pp. 27-28.

13. As Parekh writes: "Like all great reformers, Gandhi was allowed the right to *dissent* from his tradition because he had proved his *loyalty* to it. . . . Gandhi challenged Hindu institutions and practices largely on the ground that they were excrescences or corruptions of 'original' or 'pure' Hinduism. This form of reasoning implied that the original Hinduism, however defined, was Gandhi's final court of appeal. . . . While reforming it, he also reaffirmed it at a deeper level." See Parekh, "Gandhi and the Logic of Reformist Discourse," pp. 290-291.

14. Iyer, *The Moral and Political Thought of Mahatma Gandhi*, p. 20. See also *Young India*, October 12, 1921; quoted in Indira Rothermund, "Gandhi's *Satyagraha* and Hindu Thought," in Pantham and Deutsch, *Political Thought in Modern India*, p. 298.

15. *Young India,* March 16, 1925, and July 30, 1931; see also Gandhi, *The Story of My Experiments with Truth,* p. 4. As Thomas Pantham points out, the notion of the "manyness of reality" was influenced by the Jain doctrine of *anekantavada* according to which "reality is not one-dimensional but multidimensional. Accordingly, different truth claims may refer to different aspects of the same reality." See Pantham, "Habermas' Practical Discourse and Gandhi's *Satyagraha,*" in Parekh and Pantham, *Political Discourse,* p. 303. Compare in this context also Heidegger, "On the Essence of Truth," in *Martin Heidegger: Basic Writings,* ed. David F. Krell (New York: Harper & Row, 1977), pp. 117-141.

16. Albert Schweitzer, *Indian Thought* (Boston: Beacon Press, 1936), p. 186; quoted in Rothermund, "Gandhi's *Satyagraha* and Hindu Thought," p. 301.

17. Iyer, *The Moral and Political Writings of Mahatma Gandhi,* vol. 2, p. 642. In another letter written half a year earlier he observed (p. 640): "The first *mantra* of the *Ishopanishad* says that God pervades the universe and it is man's duty to surrender his all to God in the first instance. There is nothing which he can call his own; having made the surrender man is to take out of it what he may require for his legitimate needs but not a whit more."

18. Pantham, "Habermas' Practical Discourse and Gandhi's *Satyagraha,*" p. 303. Pantham also cites these Gandhian comments (p. 304): "The appeal of reason is more to the head, but the penetration of the heart comes from suffering. It opens up the inner understanding of man. Suffering is the badge of the human race, not the sword." See also *Young India,* October 12, 1921, and February 9, 1925; cited in Iyer, *The Moral and Political Thought of Mahatma Gandhi,* pp. 282, 290. The interlacing of reason and sensibility is ably summarized by Parekh when he writes that Gandhi's mode of discourse "was rational but not narrowly 'rationalistic' in nature. . . . It acknowledged the power of reason, but also recognized its limitations. At the same time, it was religious but not 'superstitious' or based on 'blind faith'. It emphasized not the dogmas and revealed truths, but the 'experimental' insights of great seers and saints, and subjected them to the test of reason." See Parekh, "Gandhi and the Logic of Reformist Discourse," p. 289.

19. *Modern Review,* October 1916; cited in Iyer, *The Moral and Political Thought of Mahatma Gandhi,* pp. 179-180.

20. Ashis Nandi, "Oppression and Human Liberation: Towards a Post-Gandhian Utopia," in Pantham and Deutsch, *Political Thought in Modern India,* p. 353. As Nandi adds (p. 354): "All his life, Gandhi sought to free the British as much as the Indians from the clutches of imperialism and the Brahmans as much as the Untouchables from the caste system. Such a position bears some similarity with certain forms of Marxism and Christianity. Father G. Gutierrez represents both these ideological strains when he says: 'One loves the oppressors by liberating them from the inhuman condition as oppressors, by liberating them from themselves. But this cannot be achieved except by resolutely opting for the oppressed, i.e., by combating the oppressive classes. It must be real and

effective combat, not hate'." The reference is to Gustavo Gutierrez, *A Theology of Liberation* (New York: Orbis Books, 1973), p. 276.

21. Gandhi, *Democracy: Real and Deceptive,* ed. R. K. Prabhu (Ahmedabad: Navajivan, 1961), p. 32; quoted in Pantham, "Beyond Liberal Democracy: Thinking with Mahatma Gandhi," in Pantham and Deutsch, *Political Thought in Modern India,* p. 399. Pantham's essay offers an excellent discussion of Gandhi's relation to Western liberalism and capitalism.

22. Iyer, *The Moral and Political Writings of Mahatma Gandhi,* vol. 2, p. 562. The "Satyagraha Ashram" near Ahmedabad existed from 1915 to 1933.

23. *Harijan,* April 20, 1947, reprinted in *Mainstream,* March 21, 1987 (pp. 7-10); see also S. Narayan, ed., *The Selected Works of Mahatma Gandhi* (Ahmedabad: Navajivan, 1969), vol. 6, p. 325; and A. K. Saran, "Gandhi and the Concept of Politics: Towards a Normal Civilization," *Gandhi Marg* (February 1980), pp. 680-681. I am indebted for these references to Thomas Pantham, "On Modernity, Rationality and Morality: Habermas and Gandhi" (unpublished ms.).

24. See Leo Strauss, "An Introduction to Heideggerian Existentialism," in Thomas Pangle, ed., *The Rebirth of Classical Political Rationalism: An Introduction to the Thought of Leo Strauss* (Chicago: University of Chicago Press, 1989), pp. 27-46. As Strauss adds in the same context: "Heidegger is the only man who has an inkling of the dimensions of the problem of a world society. . . . The East has experienced being in a way which prevented the investigation of beings and therewith the concern with the mastery of beings. But the Western experience of being makes possible, in principle, coherent speech about being. By opening ourselves to the problem of being and to the problematic character of the Western understanding of being, we may gain access to the deepest root of the East."

25. Iyer, *Parapolitics: Toward the City of Man* (New York: Oxford University Press, 1979), pp. vii, 32. See also Nandi, "Oppression and Human Liberation," in Pantham and Deutsch, *Political Thought in Modern India,* p. 358; and his *Traditions, Tyranny and Utopias* (Delhi: Oxford University Press, 1987), especially the chapters "Towards a Third World Utopia" and "From Outside the Imperium: Gandhi's Cultural Critique of the West," pp. 54, 161.

CHAPTER 3

1. Jürgen Habermas, *Der philosophische Diskurs der Moderne: Zwölf Vorlesungen* (Frankfurt-Main: Suhrkamp, 1985), p. 32 (hereafter abbreviated as *Diskurs);* trans. by Frederick Lawrence as *The Philosophical Discourse of Modernity: Twelve Lectures* (Cambridge, MA: MIT Press, 1987), p. 21 (hereafter abbreviated as *Discourse;* in this and subsequent citations I have slightly altered the translation for purposes of clarity).

2. *Diskurs,* p. 120; *Discourse,* p. 97.

3. I have discussed some of the other thinkers included in the study else-where (in a manner deviating from Habermas's exegesis); compare my "Plural-ism Old and New: Foucault on Power," in *Polis and Praxis* (Cambridge, MA: MIT Press, 1984), pp. 77-103, and "Hermeneutics and Deconstruction: Gadamer and Derrida in Dialogue," in *Critical Encounters* (Notre Dame: University of Notre Dame Press, 1987), pp. 130-158. See also Dallmayr and Gisela J. Hinkle, "Foucault *in memoriam* (1926-1984)", *Human Studies*, vol. 10 (1987), pp. 3-13.

4. *Diskurs*, pp. 13, 26-27, 29, 31; *Discourse*, pp. 4, 16-18 (the last passage is omitted in the English translation).

5. *Diskurs*, pp. 33, 37, 40-42; *Discourse*, pp. 21-22, 26, 28-30. As Habermas adds: "No matter how forcefully interpreted, the ethos of polis and early Christianity can no longer furnish the standard which could guide an inter-nally divided modernity." *Diskurs*, p. 43; *Discourse*, p. 31.

6. *Diskurs*, pp. 44, 46; *Discourse*, pp. 31-34.

7. *Diskurs*, pp. 51-52; *Discourse*, pp. 38-39. Compare *Hegel's Philosophy of Right*, trans. with notes by T. M. Knox (London: Oxford University Press, 1967), p. 161 (par. 260; translation slightly altered).

8. *Diskurs*, p. 33; *Discourse*, p. 22. The applauding comment was quoted above. In a similar vein the study states: "With the concept of the absolute . . . Hegel is able to grasp modernity on the basis of its own principle. In doing so he shows philosophy as the power of synthesis which overcomes all positivities produced by (abstract) reflection." This does not prevent Habermas from claiming that Hegel "misses the essential goal for a self-grounding of modernity: namely, to conceive positivity in such a manner that it can be overcome by relying on the same principle through which it is generated—the principle of subjectivity." See *Diskurs*, pp. 41, 49; *Discourse*, pp. 29-30, 36.

9. *Diskurs*, pp. 35, 53; *Discourse*, pp. 24, 39-40.

10. *Diskurs*, pp. 49, 54, 56-57; *Discourse*, pp. 36, 40, 42-43.

11. Regarding public religiosity one might fruitfully compare Hegel's com-ments on the topic in *Philosophy of Right* which steer a difficult but fascinating course between established (or "positive") religion and a strict separation of church and state; see *Hegel's Philosophy of Right*, pp. 165-174 (par. 270).

12. Martin Heidegger, *Hegels Phänomenologie des Geistes* (*Gesamtausgabe*, vol. 32; Frankfurt-Main: Klostermann, 1980), p. 52. Heidegger presents Hegel's philosophy as an "onto-theo-logy," because Hegel's "idea" or "spirit" *(logos)* is also the designation for the essence of being which coincides with God (pp. 140-141). The lectures caution against approaching Hegel with the "methods of an *ab ovo* defunct Hegelianism" (p. 121). Compare also Heidegger, *Hegel's Con-cept of Experience*, trans. J. Glenn Gray and Fred D. Wieck (New York: Harper & Row, 1970).

13. See *Hegel's Philosophy of Right*, p. 156 (par. 258). While applauding Rousseau's philosophical treatment of the topic, Hegel in the same context (p. 157) criticizes the French thinker for taking "the will only in a determinate form as the individual will" and for regarding "the universal will not as the absolutely rational element in the will, but only as a 'general' will which proceeds out of individual wills as out of conscious wills."

14. Habermas in this context assigns a broad philosophical significance to the Young-Hegelian movement: "We remain until today in the theoretical state which the Young Hegelians initiated by distancing themselves from Hegel and philosophy as such . . . Hegel inaugurated the discourse of modernity; but only the Young Hegelians have established it permanently. For they extricated the idea of an immanent-modern critique of modernity from the weight of Hegel's concept of reason." See *Diskurs*, p. 67; *Discourse*, p. 53.

15. *Diskurs*, pp. 71, 93; *Discourse*, pp. 56, 74. Referring to Hegel and the two Hegelian schools Habermas adds: "Three times the attempt to tailor reason to the program of a dialectic of enlightenment miscarried. In this situation Nietzsche had the option either of subjecting subjective reason once again to an immanent critique—or else of abandoning the program altogether. He opted for the second alternative, thus renouncing the task of a renewed revision of reason and *bidding farewell* to the dialectic of enlightenment." See *Diskurs*, p. 106; *Discourse*, pp. 85-86.

16. *Diskurs*, pp. 105-109; *Discourse*, pp. 84-88.

17. *Diskurs*, pp. 110-114; *Discourse*, pp. 88-92.

18. *Diskurs*, pp. 115-118; *Discourse*, pp. 92-95.

19. *Diskurs*, pp. 116-120; *Discourse*, pp. 93-97.

20. Habermas completely neglects a major *motif* of Nietzsche's break with Wagner: the latter's linkage of Christianity with anti-Semitism. On this point see Peter Bergmann, *Nietzsche: "The Last Antipolitical German"* (Bloomington: Indiana University Press, 1987), pp. 144-145. I recognize that Nietzsche's position toward Christian faith, and religion in general, was complex and ambivalent— but not much more so than that of many other modern thinkers. Henry Aiken's cautious comments are at least worth pondering: "Despite Zarathustra's claim or prophecy that 'God is dead', neither he nor his creator is, in the root sense, irreligious. In one sense Nietzsche, like James, '*suffered* from incredulity', and it is this fact which distinguishes him from all the dime-a-dozen atheists and agnostics for whom disbelief in the existence of God is hardly more momentous, and no different in essential meaning, than disbelief in the existence of centaurs." See Henry David Aiken, "An Introduction to *Zarathustra*," in Robert C. Solomon, ed., *Nietzsche: A Collection of Critical Essays* (Notre Dame: University of Notre Dame Press, 1980), p. 125.

21. *Diskurs*, pp. 116-118; *Discourse*, pp. 93-95. For an alternative interpretation see my "Farewell to Metaphysics: Nietzsche," in *Critical Encounters*, pp. 13-38.

22. See Friedrich Nietzsche, *The Birth of Tragedy,* in *The Birth of Tragedy and The Genealogy of Morals,* trans. Francis Golffing (Garden City, NY: Anchor Books, 1956), pp. 25-26.

23. These comments occur in Section 197, entitled "The Hostility of the Germans to the Enlightenment." See Nietzsche, *The Dawn* (1881), in Walter Kaufmann, ed., *The Portable Nietzsche* (New York: Viking Press, 1968), p. 85; also *Twilight of the Idols* (1888) in the same collection, pp. 479, 481 (section on "Reason in Philosophy").

24. For an extended commentary on these fragments see Martin Heidegger, *Nietzsche,* vol. 1: *The Will to Power as Art,* trans. David F. Krell (New York: Harper & Row, 1979), and *Nietzsche,* vol. 3: *The Will to Power as Knowledge and as Metaphysics,* trans. Joan Stambaugh, David F. Krell, and Frank A. Capuzzi (New York: Harper & Row, 1987). Compare also *The Joyful Science* (1882), in *The Portable Nietzsche,* p. 101 (section 319).

25. *Diskurs,* pp. 121-124, 126-127; *Discourse,* pp. 97-103.

26. *Diskurs,* pp. 158-163; *Discourse,* pp. 131-136.

27. *Diskurs,* pp. 169-176; *Discourse,* pp. 141-148.

28. *Diskurs,* pp. 165-166, 177-180; *Discourse,* pp. 138-139, 148-152. Here as elsewhere Habermas distinguishes between an "objective" (natural) world, an inter-subjective or "social" world, and a "subjective" (inner) world. The validity claim of "truth" is juxtaposed to the claims of "rightness" and "truthfulness."

29. *Diskurs,* pp. 123-124, 167-168, 181, 188-189; *Discourse,* pp. 99, 139-141, 152-153, 158-160.

30. *Diskurs,* p. 122; *Discourse,* p. 98. Habermas's claim in the same context that Heidegger was never really "touched by the genuine experiences of avant-garde art" is contradicted by the philosopher's documented attachment to Cézanne, Klee and other modern artists. The charge of a "classicist aesthetics" also fails to take into account Heidegger's lectures on "The Origin of the Work of Art" (of 1935-36); see Heidegger, *Basic Writings,* ed. David F. Krell (New York: Harper and Row, 1977), pp. 149-187.

31. As Habermas states: "Quite likely the *Kehre* was in reality the result of the experience of National Socialism, that is, the experience of an historical event that in a sense *happened* to Heidegger." See *Diskurs,* p. 185; *Discourse,* p. 156. My point is not to deny the role of politics but to question the juxtaposition of inner-philosophical and external-political motives and the subordination of the former to the latter.

32. See Heidegger, *Sein und Zeit* (11th ed.; Tübingen: Niemeyer, 1967), pp. 115-116 (par. 25) and pp. 263-264 (par. 53). In contrast with Sartre's approach, Heidegger's notion of "project" *(Entwurf)* should be seen in close connection with "thrownness" *(Geworfenheit)*—not merely as separate categories, but as

two sides of the same coin. On the non-subjectivist character of *Being and Time* see Friedrich-Wilhelm von Herrmann, *Subjekt und Dasein: Interpretationen zu "Sein und Zeit"* (2nd ed.; Frankfurt-Main: Klosterman, 1985). Heidegger's early subjectivism is not confirmed (as Habermas claims) in "What is Metaphysics?" or "Vom Wesen des Grundes"; on the contrary. The latter essay presents man as a "being of distance" *(Wesen der Ferne)*, linking the capacity for "listening into the distance" with the possibility of authentic co-being; see "Vom Wesen des Grundes" in Heidegger, *Wegmarken* (Frankfurt-Main: Klostermann, 1967), pp. 70-71.

33. *Sein und Zeit*, p. 118 (par. 26). A little bit later (p. 120) Heidegger adds: "Alone-ness is a deficient mode of co-being, its possibility a proof for the latter." The thematization of co-being is followed by a discussion of language as speech (par. 34)—a treatment which in striking ways anticipates later speech-act theory. The alleged parallelism between Husserl and Heidegger is borrowed from Theunissen's *The Other* (who corrected himself in part in a postscript to the original study); see Michael Theunissen, *The Other: Studies in the Social Ontology of Husserl, Heidegger, Sartre, and Buber*, trans. Christopher Macann (Cambridge, MA: MIT Press, 1984), pp. 367, 413 (note 9). For a critical discussion of Theunissen's approach and an alternative interpretation of co-being see "Egology and *Being and Time*" and "Heidegger and Co-Being" in my *Twilight of Subjectivity* (Amherst, MA: University of Massachusetts Press, 1981), pp. 56-71. Regarding the theory of language in *Being and Time* compare "*Dasein* and Speech: Heidegger" in my *Language and Politics* (Notre Dame: University of Notre Dame Press, 1984), pp. 117-120.

34. I have tried to flush out some of these remarks in his lectures on Hölderlin held in the winter of 1934 (less than a year after his resignation as Rector); see "Heidegger, Hölderlin and Politics" in *Heidegger Studies*, vol. 2 (1987), pp. 81-95 (reprinted below as Appendix).

35. See Heidegger, *Identität und Differenz* (Pfullingen: Neske, 1957), pp. 17-20; also *Diskurs*, pp. 162, 172-173; *Discourse*, pp. 135, 144-145.

36. *Diskurs*, p. 181; *Discourse*, pp. 152-153. The equation of being or the "truth" of being with freedom is clearly stated in "On the Essence of Truth" (1930), in Heidegger, *Basic Writings*, pp. 117-141; in *Vom Wesen der menschlichen Freiheit: Einleitung in die Philosophie* (1930), ed. Hartmut Tietjen (*Gesamtausgabe*, vol. 31; Frankfurt-Main: Klostermann, 1982); and also in *Schellings Abhandlung Über das Wesen der menschlichen Freiheit* (1936), ed. Hildegard Feick (Tübingen: Niemeyer, 1971). For a more detailed discussion see my "Ontology of Freedom: Heidegger and Political Philosophy," in *Polis and Praxis* (Cambridge, MA: MIT Press, 1984), pp. 104-132.

37. See *Diskurs*, pp. 128, 163, 167; *Discourse*, pp. 104, 136, 139-140; also Heidegger, *Hegels Phänomenologie des Geistes*, p. 143. Habermas's dismissal of recollective thinking is parallel to his dismissal of Hegel's "absolute spirit." In my view, Heidegger's philosophy is not opposed to science but only to the reduction of philosophy to science (or to the prevalent scientific paradigm).

38. *Diskurs*, pp. 182-183; *Discourse*, pp. 153-154.

39. *Diskurs*, pp. 346, 353-354, 356, 361-363; *Discourse*, pp. 296, 302-305, 309-312.

40. *Diskurs*, pp. 28-30, 177, 346-347; *Discourse*, pp. 17-19, 149, 296-297. The different spheres or dimensions of the model are discussed in *Diskurs*, pp. 361-368; *Discourse*, pp. 310-316. In another passage Habermas contests that the interactive life-world in his model is composed of subjects or individuals—speaking instead of "communicative agents" or "subjects capable of speech and action." See *Diskurs*, pp. 397-398; *Discourse*, p. 343.

41. *Diskurs*, pp. 374-376; *Discourse*, pp. 321-323. As Habermas writes: "As little as we can renounce the *supposition* of a purified speech, as much must we make do in real life with 'impure' speech." See *Diskurs*, p. 376; *Discourse*, p. 323.

42. *Diskurs*, p. 372; *Discourse*, p. 320. The statement neglects that the meaning of confirmation and pragmatic experience also changes with changing meaning-horizons. Habermas's treatment of the relation of meaning-discovery and validation (especially in his attacks on Heidegger and others) tends to reduce discovery to a mere antichamber whose opacity or noises cannot affect the process of validation. This outcome is hardly obviated by the concession that meaning-constitution "retains the contingent potency of genuine innovation." See *Diskurs*, p. 373; *Discourse*, p. 321.

43. *Diskurs*, pp. 348-349, 379; *Discourse*, pp. 298-299, 320. Habermas's distinction at this point between agents as "authors" and "products" of historical contexts replicates the division between "producer" and "product" castigated in the case of Heidegger, Castoriadis and others. See *Diskurs*, p. 370; *Discourse*, p. 318.

44. *Diskurs*, p. 397; *Discourse*, pp. 342-343.

45. *Diskurs*, pp. 399-401, 405-407; *Discourse*, pp. 344-347, 349-352. The study actually sketches a three-tiered schema of coordination ranging from the habitual life-world over formal life-world structures to segregated systems or subsystems; see *Diskurs*, p. 407; *Discourse*, pp. 351-352. For a more detailed discussion of Habermas's ambivalent view of the life-world see my "Life-World and Communicative Action" in *Critical Encounters*, pp. 90-94.

46. *Diskurs*, pp. 368, 378, 393, 396, 403, 407; *Discourse*, pp. 316, 325, 339, 342, 348, 352. In the absence of ontological or "essentialist" assumptions it is unclear how "excess" or "preponderance" is to be defined. In a later passage the life-world is presented as a vulnerable domain "in need of protection"—which again presupposes an essentialist conception. See *Diskurs*, p. 413; *Discourse*, p. 413.

47. Compare Habermas, "Die Moderne—ein unvollendetes Projekt," in *Kleine politische Schriften I-IV* (Frankfurt-Main: Suhrkamp, 1981), pp. 444-464. For an elaborate attack on the "extremism" of Nietzsche's heirs see Allan Megill, *Prophets of Extremity: Nietzsche, Heidegger, Foucault, Derrida* (Berkeley: University of California Press, 1985).

48. *Diskurs,* pp. 355-358; *Discourse,* pp. 304-307.

49. *Diskurs,* pp. 41-42, 54, 79, 94, 164-165, 178, 345-346; *Discourse,* pp. 29-30, 40, 63, 74, 136-137, 149, 295-296.

50. As Habermas asserts, the participant in discourses is as individual "wholly autonomous only on the condition" that he remains bound or "embedded in a universal community"; *Diskurs,* p. 401; *Discourse,* pp. 346-347. But as Hobbes would have asked: who stipulates or secures this condition (beyond the sphere of definitional fiat)? According to a later passage, the communicative model is said to explain why "critique and fallibilism even reinforce the continuity of traditions" and why "abstract-universalistic methods of discursive will-formation even solidify the solidarity of life-contexts." See *Diskurs,* p. 402; *Discourse,* p. 347.

51. Jacques Derrida, *Writing and Difference,* trans. Alan Bass (Chicago: University of Chicago Press, 1978), p. 80. In its concluding pages Habermas's study actually advances arguments reminiscent of Foucauldian or post-structuralist themes: especially the themes of micro-powers and of group resistances to centralized state control; *Diskurs,* pp. 420-423; *Discourse,* pp. 361-365. For an elaboration of the Derridian sense of community see Drucilla Cornell, "The Poststructuralist Challenge to the Ideal of Community," *Cardozo Law Review,* vol. 8 (1987), pp. 989-1022.

CHAPTER 4

1. Eric Voegelin, *Order and History,* vol. 5: *In Search of Order* (Baton Rouge: Louisiana State University Press, 1987), p. 1.

2. *In Search of Order,* pp. 13-14. The diagnostic and therapeutic aims of Voegelin's work are sensitively underscored by Jürgen Gebhart in his "Epilogue" to the volume (p. 110): "He intended to call forth islands of order amidst the disorder of the age, thus reminding us of Kant's famous 'island of truth surrounded by the wild and stormy ocean, the actual abode of delusion.' The symbolism of the philosophical inquiry in itself may become the nucleus of some communion of existential concern in terms of a social field of existential order."

3. *In Search of Order,* pp. 13-16. As Voegelin states, summarizing his position (p. 16): "There is a consciousness with two structural meanings, to be distinguished as intentionality and luminosity. There is a reality with two structural meanings, to be distinguished as the thing-reality and the It-reality. Consciousness, then, is a subject intending reality as its objects, but at the same time a something in a comprehending reality; and reality is the object of consciousness, but at the same time the subject of which consciousness is to be predicated."

4. *In Search of Order,* pp. 17-18.

5. *In Search of Order,* pp. 19-22.

6. *In Search of Order*, pp. 24-26. Some of the statements regarding the "questioner" and his quest seem to carry autobiographical overtones, particularly the passage (p. 25) which describes the effort at resymbolization as "the story of his experience of disorder, of the resistance aroused in him by the observation of concrete cases, of his experience of being drawn into the search of true order by a command issuing from the It-reality, of his consciousness of ignorance and questioning, of his discovery of the truth, and of the consequences of disorder unrestrained by regard for the order he has experienced and articulated."

7. *In Search of Order*, pp. 27-32. In Voegelin's view, the diversity of historical symbolizations involves basically a greater or lesser degree of compactness and differentiation. Thus, he speaks (p. 32) of "the diversification of compactness through the language of the myth, through mythospeculative constructions of the cosmogonic type, and through pneumatically differentiated mythospeculations; the further diversification of differentiated types of consciousness through the experiential accents on either the divine irruption of the *pneuma* or on the noetic quest in response to a divine movement; the diversification of these various types in a plurality of ethnic cultures;" and the like.

8. *In Search of Order*, pp. 33-37.

9. *In Search of Order*, pp. 37-44.

10. *In Search of Order*, pp. 48-51, 53.

11. *In Search of Order*, pp. 54-99.

12. *In Search of Order*, pp. 62-64, 67-69. According to a note in the text, the commentary on Hegel was to be followed by another section on Hegel which, however, was not written. Regarding the "God-is-dead" movement see also Voegelin's essay "Response to Professor Altizer's 'A New History and a New but Ancient God?'" in *Journal of the American Academy of Religion*, vol. 43 (1979) pp. 769-772.

13. *In Search of Order*, pp. 70-74, 86-91.

14. *In Search of Order*, pp. 92-94, 99-102.

15. *In Search of Order*, pp. 28, 102. Regarding Plato see also Voegelin, *Order and History*, vol. 3: *Plato and Aristotle* (Baton Rouge: Louisiana State University, 1957), Part I, reprinted as *Plato* (Baton Rouge: Louisiana State University, 1966), and "Reason: The Classic Experience," *Southern Review*, vol. 10 (1974), pp. 237-264.

16. *In Search of Order*, pp. 104-106.

17. *In Search of Order*, pp. 6-7, 100. See also Voegelin, *The New Science of Politics* (Chicago: University of Chicago Press, 1952), p. 122.

18. *In Search of Order*, p. 97 (italics mine). Regarding Emmanuel Levinas compare his *Totality and Infinity*, trans. Alphonso Lingis (Pittsburgh: Duquesne University Press, n.d.).

19. *In Search of Order,* p. 74; see also *Order and History,* vol. 1: *Israel and Revelation* (Baton Rouge: Louisiana State University Press, 1956), pp. 1-2, and *Order and History,* vol. 4: *The Ecumenic Age* (Baton Rouge: Louisiana State University Press, 1974), p. 186. The affinity with Gadamer and Heidegger, and also with Whitehead and William James, is noted by Gebhardt in his "Epilogue" to *In Search of Order,* pp. 111, 115. A thinker not mentioned by Gebhardt is Karl Jaspers whose concept of the "encompassing" *(das Umgreifende)* is echoed in Voegelin's references to a "divinely designed comprehending reality *(periechon)* of all living beings" (p. 95). I am aware that the rapprochement of Voegelin and Heidegger conflicts with the former's harsh critique of "fundamental ontology" and of Heidegger as an "ingenious gnostic" in *Science, Politics and Gnosticism* (Chicago: Regnery, 1968), pp. 46-48.

20. *In Search of Order,* pp. 30-31, 79-84, 92, 100-102. Regarding the "fourfold," the opening sentences of *Order and History* speak of the "quaternarian structure" of reality comprising God and man, world and society in a "primordial community of being." See *Israel and Revelation,* p. 1. For a discussion of some of the mentioned Heideggerian themes compare Joseph J. Kockelmans, *On the Truth of Being: Reflections on Heidegger's Later Philosophy* (Bloomington: Indiana University Press, 1984), esp. pp. 99-72, 94-141.

21. *In Search of Order,* pp. 10, 17, 103. The citation from "The Beginning and the Beyond" is taken from Sandoz's Introduction. The notion of sacrality stands in clear conflict with the claim of a progressive secularization and "linguistification of the sacred" as advanced by Jürgen Habermas in *The Theory of Communicative Action,* vol. 2: *Lifeworld and System: A Critique of Functionalist Reason,* trans. Thomas McCarthy (Boston: Beacon Press, 1987), pp. 77-111.

22. Regarding Martin Buber's distinction see his *I and Thou* (Edinburgh: Clark, 1937). As is well-known, the notion of embodiment or embodied consciousness was used by Merleau-Ponty and Gabriel Marcel precisely in an effort to circumvent the subject-object polarity.

23. Voegelin, *In Search of Order,* pp. 103-104. For a contemporary discussion of thinghood see Heidegger, *What is a Thing?,* trans. V. B. Barton & V. Deutsch (Chicago: Regnery, 1967); and regarding nothingness, his "What is Metaphysics?" in Heidegger, *Basic Writings,* ed. David F. Krell (New York: Harper & Row, 1977), pp. 95-112.

24. *In Search of Order,* pp. 5, 10-11. The last cited passage is taken from "The Beginning and the Beyond"; both this passage and the statement in the letter of 1943 (to Alfred Schütz) can be found in Sandoz's Introduction.

25. *In Search of Order,* pp. 23, 33, 37, 39, 99.

26. *In Search of Order,* pp. 29, 93-96 98, 106. The distinction between the "god of the Beginning" and the "god of the End" evokes the opposition between the "Alpha-God" and the "Omega-God" elaborated by Ernst Bloch. For an interpretation of the *Timaeus* stressing more the ambiguity and multivocity of the

cosmos see Hans-Georg Gadamer, "Idee und Wirklichkeit in Platos Timaios," in *Gesammelte Werke,* vol. 6: *Griechische Philosophie* II (Tübingen: Mohr, 1985), pp. 242-260.

27. Voegelin, *In Search of Order,* pp. 50, 52: see also his *Science, Politics and Gnosticism,* pp. 23-25. In Tucker's edition, the passage in question reads: "When you ask about the (initial) creation of nature and man, you are abstracting, in so doing, from nature and man. You postulate them as *non-existent,* and yet you want me to prove them to you as *existing.* Now I say to you: give up your abstraction and you will also give up the question. Or if you want to hold on to your abstraction, then be consistent, and if you think of man and nature as *non-existent,* then think of *yourself* as non-existent; for you too are surely nature and man. (But then, as non-existent) don't think, don't ask me—for as soon as you think and ask, your *abstraction* from the existence of nature and man has no meaning." See *The Marx-Engels Reader,* ed. Robert C. Tucker (New York: Norton, 1972), p. 78 (insertions in brackets are mine added for the sake of clarification). To be sure, Marx's argument does not at all vindicate the claim of human "self-creation"—given the complete obscurity of the meaning of "self" and "creation." In a way, Voegelin's comments on the "beginning of the beginning" underscore the difficulty.

28. *In Search of Order,* pp. 64, 103. The label "gnosis" or "gnosticism"—familiar from Voegelin's earlier writings—is applied in the text not only to Hegel, but also to Ficino and to all kinds of "metastatic" movements: those seeking escape from the world as well as those seeking to radically change if not destroy the world (pp. 33, 37, 53, 63). This broad or summary usage has been criticized by students of the history of gnosis, including Hans Jonas, *Gnosis und spätantiker Geist* (Göttingen: Vandenhoeck and Ruprecht, 1954) and Hans Blumenberg, *The Legitimacy of the Modern Age,* trans. Robert M. Wallace (Cambridge, MA: MIT Press, 1983), pp. 123-220. In my view, Voegelin's text gives little room to the notion of human "freedom" and its role in modernity—a fact which accounts at least in part for deficiencies of his Hegel-interpretation.

29. Martin Heidegger, *Hegel's Concept of Experience,* trans. J. Glenn Gray and Fred D. Wieck (New York: Harper & Row, 1970), p. 130. Heidegger (p. 50) also describes the path of consciousness as an *"itinerarium mentis in Deum"*—a phrase Voegelin traces to St. Bonaventura (*In Search of Order,* p. 81). For some of Voegelin's earlier attacks on Hegel see *Science, Politics and Gnosticism,* pp. 67-80 (where the *Phenomenology* is described as the *"magnum opus* of the murder of God." p. 67), and "On Hegel: A Study in Sorcery," *Studium Generale,* vol. 24 (1971), pp. 333-368.

CHAPTER 5

1. See Jürgen Habermas, *The Philosophical Discourse of Modernity: Twelve Lectures,* trans. Frederick Lawrence (Cambridge, MA: MIT Press, 1987), and his

"Modernity versus Postmodernity," *New German Critique*, vol. 22 (Winter, 1981), pp. 3-14; also Kenneth Baines, James Bohmann and Thomas McCarthy, eds., *After Philosophy: End or Transformation?* (Cambridge, MA: MIT Press, 1987), and Jacques Derrida, "The Ends of Man," in *Margins of Philosophy*, trans. Alan Bass (Chicago: University of Chicago Press, 1982), pp. 109-1360. For the portrayal of postmodernism as farewell from or "incredulity toward metanarratives" see Jean François Lyotard, *The Postmodern Condition: A Report on Knowledge*, trans. Geoff Bennington and Brian Massumi (Minneapolis: University of Minnesota Press, 1984), pp. xxiii-xxiv.

2. The impression of a linear progression is conveyed by Lyotard when he writes: "Thus the society of the future falls less within the province of a Newtonian anthropology (such as structuralism or systems theory) than a pragmatics of language particles." See *The Postmodern Condition*, p. xxiv.

3. Bernhard Waldenfels, *Ordnung im Zwielicht* (Frankfurt-Main: Suhrkamp, 1987).

4. Waldenfels was born in 1934 and is presently professor of Philosophy at the University of Bochum. Apart from the subsequently discussed writings, the following works also should be noted: B. Waldenfels, *Das sokratische Fragen: Aporie, Elenchos, Anamnesis* (Meisenheim: A. Hain, 1961); B. Waldenfels, J. M. Broekman, and A. Pažanin, eds., *Phänomenologie und Marxismus*, 4 vols. (Frankfurt-Main: Suhrkamp, 1977-79), trans. by J. Claude Evans, Jr., as *Phenomenology and Marxism* (London: Routledge and Kegan Paul, 1984); R. Grathoff and B. Waldenfels, eds., *Sozialität und Intersubjektivität* (Munich : Fink Verlag, 1983); Alexandre Métraux and B. Waldenfels, eds., *Leibhaftige Vernunft: Spuren von Merleau-Pontys Denken* (Munich: Fink Verlag, 1986); also Merleau-Ponty, *Die Struktur des Verhaltens*, trans. B. Waldenfels (Berlin: W. deGruyter, 1976).

5. Waldenfels, *Das Zwischenreich des Dialogs; Sozial-philosophische Untersuchungen im Anschluss an Edmund Husserl* (Phaenomenologica, vol. 41; The Hague: Nijhoff, 1971). Compare also Michael Theunissen, *Der Andere: Studien zur Sozialontologie der Gegenwart* (Berlin: deGruyter, 1965), trans. by Christopher Macann as *The Other* (Cambridge, MA: MIT Press, 1984), and Alfred Schutz, *Collected Papers*, vol. I: *The Problem of Social Reality*, ed. Maurice Natanson (Phaenomenologica, vol. 11; The Hague: Nijhoff, 1967).

6. Waldenfels, *Das Zwischenreich des Dialogs*, pp. 58-59, 63.

7. *Das Zwischenreich des Dialogs*, pp. xiii, 51, 54, 62, 132. In delineating his approach, Waldenfels (p. 55, note 186) drew a parallel with "a similar attempt undertaken by Emmanuel Levinas"—although the parallels with Schutz and Gadamer were perhaps more clearly evident.

8. Waldenfels, *Der Spielraum des Verhaltens* (Frankfurt-Main: Suhrkamp, 1980), pp. 7-8, 16.

9. *Der Spielraum des Verhaltens*, pp. 8-10. Countering the charges of relativism or historical perspectivalism, Waldenfels noted that rejection of uni-

versal rationality does not mean endorsement of its opposite (pp. 25-26): "Just as between concrete languages we can have a *translation* between different cultures—a translation which establishes a kind of unity within difference, without reducing differences to mere moments or phases of a total process. From this angle, the *one* life-world emerges as nothing more nor less than a web or a chain of separate worlds—worlds which criss-cross and intersect in many ways but which (except for partial purposes) cannot be ordered hierarchically or teleologically with a view toward a comprehensive totality. The question whether there is *one* rationality or rather specific forms or fields of rationality has many consequences to which I can here only allude; thus, the problem arises how we can formulate a critique of everyday life without resorting to the concept of an ideal or fully integral world. Such a critique would have to inhabit the margins of concrete life-worlds instead of occupying an imaginary center."

10. Waldenfels, *Phänomenologie in Frankreich* (Frankfurt-Main: Suhrkamp, 1983), p. 13. The chapter on Levinas was actually written by Stephan Strasser. Coincidentally, the same year saw the publication of Alan Montefiore's *Philosophy in France Today* (Cambridge: at the University Press, 1983), a book which contains a series of essays by French authors rather than offering a comprehensive exegesis.

11. *Phänomenologie in Frankreich,* pp. 548-550. Drawing on cues provided by Heidegger and the later Merleau-Ponty the study counsels not the elimination of man but rather a thought attentive to the "chiasm" or margin of man—that is, a thought focused on "the small ridge which *both* separates and unites human culture and non-human nature. The *sens sauvage* refers to and eludes man simultaneously; anthropology is ruptured—but without dissolution of man into nothingness" (p. 562, note 118).

12. Waldenfels, *In den Netzen der Lebenswelt* (Frankfurt-Main: Suhrkamp, 1985), pp. 8-9, 27, 32.

13. *In den Netzen der Lebenswelt,* pp. 11, 93, 107, 116-117, 175.

14. Waldenfels, *Ordnung im Zwielicht* (Frankfurt-Main: Suhrkamp, 1987), pp. 10-11.

15. *Ordnung im Zwielicht,* pp. 20, 22, 29-31, 40, 47.

16. *Ordnung im Zwielicht,* pp. 54, 56, 66, 76.

17. *Ordnung im Zwielicht,* pp. 89, 98, 100, 111. In opposition to the traditional notion of "sufficient reason" Waldenfels formulates at this point a "principle of insufficient reason" (p. 112).

18. *Ordnung im Zwielicht,* pp. 119, 123-124, 129, 132-133.

19. *Ordnung im Zwielicht,* pp. 144-148, 151, 154-155, 158-159, 169. Waldenfels discusses in this context also the issue of relativism. While acknowledging the "relativity of validity conditions," that is, of frames of reference or thematic fields, he also emphasizes the relatedness produced through agonal responsiveness (pp. 163-167).

20. *Ordnung im Zwielicht*, pp. 175-176, 180-182, 186, 189, 191-193, 200.

21. *Ordnung im Zwielicht*, pp. 29, 39. The accent on this leap or rift differentiates Waldenfels' perspective not only from a consensual rationalism but also from a Gadamerian "fusion of horizons"; but Gadamer's name is rarely (if ever) mentioned in the study.

22. *Ordnung im Zwielicht*, pp. 41-43.

23. *Ordnung im Zwielicht*, pp. 43-46.

24. *Ordnung im Zwielicht*, pp. 46-48, 121. For insightful comments on passion and suffering see also p. 195. For a similar reorientation of action theory compare my "Praxis and Experience" in *Polis and Praxis: Exercises in Contemporary Political Theory* (Cambridge, MA: MIT Press, 1984), pp. 47-76.

25. *Ordnung im Zwielicht*, pp. 157-158. As Waldenfels adds (p. 159-160), the pre-beginning opens a future "which exceeds our plans and predictions. It likewise cannot be located on the temporal axis as what comes later; rather, it belongs to the present as something that is *now imminent or impending* and thus eludes our grasp." Differently phrased, pre-beginnings are "inscribed into the body of the present like a birth mark."

26. *Ordnung im Zwielicht*, pp. 52, 67, 160, 167, 175, 196. At another point (p. 55), Waldenfels chides Habermas's portrayal of "dramaturgical action" as self-presentation for ignoring the dramatic play or scene itself: "If dramaturgical action together with dramaturgical speech is reduced to self-expression, not much is left of the soil in which speech *(lexis)* and action *(praxis)* originate." For a critique of the principle of "universalization" and of Kohlberg's theory of moral development (from convention to "pure ethics") see pp. 105-106.

27. *Ordnung im Zwielicht*, pp. 78-80. That Waldenfels does not take lightly the issue of relativism emerges from these comments (p. 162): "The idea of truth and goodness—which since Plato's time recurrently overshadows concrete reality —fulfills two functions which one cannot lightly abandon. On the one hand, the idea operates as intensifying *ferment* producing tension and heightened aspirations; if this function is canceled without replacement, we face the prospect of a leveling indifference which could induce a cultural deep-freeze. On the other hand, the idea together with its heirs serves as *court of appeal* against pure arbitrariness, whim or power, against everything that relies on mere facticity. Here our joyful deconstructionists sometimes take the easy path, by thinking only of destruction rather than transformation." For a similar attempt to link ethics with ethos see my "Ethics and Recollection" in *Twilight of Subjectivity* (Amherst: University of Massachusetts Press, 1981), pp. 250-254. Compare also Agnes Heller, *The Power of Shame* (London: Routledge and Kegan Paul, 1985) and *Beyond Justice* (Oxford: Blackwell, 1987).

28. *Ordnung im Zwielicht*, p. 97. Waldenfels acknowledges the closeness of contingent ordering and cosmological thought in the case of an open-ended

notion of cosmos (p. 96) and with regard to the role of concrete exemplars or paradigmata (p. 148).

29. *Ordnung im Zwielicht,* p. 194.

CHAPTER 6

1. Ernesto Laclau and Chantal Mouffe, *Hegemony and Socialist Strategy: Towards a Radical Democratic Politics,* trans. Winston Moore and Paul Cammack (London: Verso, 1985).

2. *Hegemony and Socialist Strategy,* pp. 1-4. In critiquing a class-based essentialism, Laclau and Mouffe locate themselves plainly in "a post-Marxist terrain"—which does not imply a summary dismissal of Marxism. As they emphasize (p. 4): "If our intellectual project in this book is *post*-Marxist, it is evidently also post-*Marxist*." Moreover, the critique of essentialism extends beyond traditional Marxism to other discursive frameworks or "normative epistemologies" (p. 3): "Political conclusions similar to those set forth in this book could have been approximated from very different discursive formations—for example, from certain forms of Christianity, or from libertarian discourses alien to the socialist tradition—none of which could aspire to be the truth of society."

3. *Hegemony and Socialist Strategy,* pp. 7, 14, 18.

4. *Hegemony and Socialist Strategy,* pp. 37, 40. According to the authors, Bernstein's revisionism also supported a gradualist type of reformism—but only for contingent reasons. Basically, the two strategies or approaches do not coincide (p. 30): "Thus, in attempting to identify the precise difference between reformism and revisionism, we must stress that what is essential in a reformist practice is political quietism and the corporatist confinement of the working class."

5. *Hegemony and Socialist Strategy,* pp. 51, 56, 61-62.

6. *Hegemony and Socialist Strategy,* pp. 65-67, 69, 75-77, 85-87.

7. *Hegemony and Socialist Strategy,* pp. 95, 97-98, 105, 108-112. As the study adds (p. 113): Since "all discourse is subverted by a field of discursivity which overflows it, the transition from 'elements' to 'moments' can never be complete. The status of the 'elements' is that of floating signifiers, incapable of being wholly articulated to a discursive chain. . . . It is not the poverty of signifieds but, on the contrary, polysemy that disarticulates a discursive structure. That is what establishes the overdetermined, symbolic dimension of every social identity. Society never manages to be identical to itself, as every nodal point is constituted within an intertextuality that overflows it. *The practice of articulation, therefore, consists in the construction of nodal points which partially fix meaning; and the partial character of this fixation proceeds from the openness of the social, a result, in its turn, of the constant overflowing of every discourse by the infinitude of the field of discursivity."*

8. *Hegemony and Socialist Strategy,* pp. 115-117, 122-129, 132-133, 137.

9. *Hegemony and Socialist Strategy,* pp. 151-152, 155, 164, 166-167.

10. *Hegemony and Socialist Strategy,* pp. 171, 176-177, 179, 182-184, 186-188. Compare also their comment (p. 192): "The de-centering and autonomy of the different discourses and struggles, the multiplication of antagonisms and the construction of a plurality of spaces within which they can affirm themselves and develop, are the conditions *sine qua non* of the possibility that the different components of the classical ideal of socialism—which should, no doubt, be extended and reformulated—can be achieved."

11. The distance from structuralism is expressed in these comments: "When the linguistic model was introduced into the general field of human sciences, it was this effect of systematicity that predominated, so that structuralism became a new form of essentialism: a search for the underlying structures constituting the inherent law of any possible variation. The critique of structuralism involved a break with this view of a fully constituted structural space. . . . The sign is the name of a split, of an impossible suture between signified and signifier." See *Hegemony and Socialist Strategy,* p. 113. The authors refer in this context explicitly to Jacques Derrida, "Structure, Sign and Play in the Discourse of the Human Sciences," in *Writing and Difference,* trans. Alan Bass (Chicago-London: University of Chicago Press, 1978), p. 280.

12. *Hegemony and Socialist Strategy,* pp. 111, 122, 153, 193. As they add, the prevalence of politics also injects instability into the distinction of public and private spheres, leading to a pervasive politicization of life (p. 181): "What has been exploded is the idea and the reality itself of a unique space of constitution of the political. What we are witnessing is a politicization far more radical than any we have known in the past, because it tends to dissolve the distinction between the public and the private, not in terms of the encroachment on the private by a unified public space, but in terms of a proliferation of radically new and different political spaces."

13. *Hegemony and Socialist Strategy,* pp. 79, 120-121.

14. *Hegemony and Socialist Strategy,* pp. 94-95. The repercussions of traditional rationalism are found in Hegel's theory of the "state" and especially in his conception of the bureaucracy as "universal class" (p. 191). The assessment of Hegel relies strongly on A. Trendelenburg, *Logische Undersuchungen* (first ed. 1840; 3rd ed., Hildesheim: Olms, 1964).

15. *Hegemony and Socialist Strategy,* pp. 129, 184. Another passage (p. 130) phrases the two logics in the vocabulary of linguistics, associating the logic of difference with the "syntagmatic pole" of language (the sequence of continuous combinations) and the logic of equivalence with the "paradigmatic pole" (relations of substitution).

16. *Hegemony and Socialist Strategy,* pp. 126, 129, 136. Elsewhere the danger of the two social logics is seen in their transformation from a "horizon" into a "foundation" (p. 183).

17. *Hegemony and Socialist Strategy,* pp. 87, 103-104, 142, 182-184. Regarding universalism compare these comments (pp. 191-192): "The discourse of radical democracy is no longer the discourse of the universal. . . . This point is decisive: there is no radical and plural democracy without renouncing the discourse of the universal and its implicit assumption of a privileged point of access to 'the truth,' which can be reached only by a limited number of subjects."

18. *Hegemony and Socialist Strategy,* pp. 59, 69-70, 137. For a critique of the "foundational" treatment of power or domination in political life see p. 142. As it seems to me, Foucault's later writings point in a similar direction; compare my "Pluralism Old and New: Foucault on Power" in *Polis and Praxis: Exercises in Contemporary Political Theory* (Cambridge, MA: MIT Press, 1984), pp. 77-103, and my "Democracy and Postmodernism," *Human Studies,* vol. 10 (1986), pp. 143-170.

19. *Hegemony and Socialist Strategy,* pp. 12, 37-38, 85, 93. For a differentiation of "praxis" from Weberian categories of action theory compare my "Praxis and Experience" in *Polis and Praxis,* pp. 47-76.

20. *Hegemony and Socialist Strategy,* pp. 86, 110-111, 114, 142. Another passage presents the external demarcation of the two categories under the image of a *"double void"* (p. 131).

21. *Hegemony and Socialist Strategy,* pp. 12-13, 25, 34, 47, 93, 108-110, 113. Compare Martin Heidegger, "Moira," in *Vorträge und Aufsätze* (3rd ed.; Pfullingen: Neske, 1967), vol. 3, pp. 36-38, 45-48, also *Identität und Differenz* (Pfullingen: Neske, 1957); and Jacques Derrida, *Margins of Philosophy,* trans. Alan Bass (Chicago: University of Chicago Press, 1982). For the notion of "intertwining" see Maurice Merleau-Ponty, *The Visible and the Invisible,* trans. Alphonso Lingis (Evanston: Northwestern University Press, 1968), pp. 130-155.

22. *Hegemony and Socialist Strategy,* pp. 125-126, 128-129. Compare also Heidegger, *On Time and Being,* trans. Joan Stambaugh (New York: Harper and Row, 1972).

23. *Hegemony and Socialist Strategy,* pp. 111, 125, 127, 135, 142.

24. *Hegemony and Socialist Strategy,* pp. 155, 188-189. The tensional view is also endorsed in the assertion (p. 189) that the "project for a radical democracy" must "base itself upon the search for a point of equilibrium between a maximum advance for the democratic revolution in a broad range of spheres, and the capacity for the hegemonic direction and positive reconstruction of these spheres on the part of subordinated groups." In part the authors' ambivalence stems from a mingling of two conceptions of politics: namely, politics as "polity" (or political regime) and politics as "policy." For this distinction see Ernst Vollrath, "The 'Rational' and the 'Political': An Essay in the Semantics of Politics," *Philosophy and Social Criticism,* vol. 13 (1987), pp. 17-29, and my "Politics and Conceptual Analysis: Comments on Vollrath," pp. 31-37.

CHAPTER 7

1. I do not deny a resurgence of interest in Hegel's work among some philosophers—except to note that many of these efforts remain academic (or removed from ongoing philosophical debates). Most noteworthy in this context are Charles Taylor, *Hegel* (Cambridge: University Press, 1975); Stanley Rosen, *G. F. W. Hegel: An Introduction to the Science of Wisdom* (New Haven: Yale University Press, 1974); and Robert C. Solomon, *In the Spirit of Hegel* (New York: Oxford University Press, 1983). Richard Bernstein once observed that Anglo-American analytical philosophy was moving by its own internal momentum to a Hegelian position—an assessment which was probably too summary or optimistic; see his *Praxis and Action: Contemporary Philosophies of Human Activity* (Philadelphia: University of Pennsylvania Press, 1971), pp. 24 (note 21), 233.

2. Martin Heidegger, *Hegels Phänomenologie des Geistes* (*Gesamtausgabe*, vol. 32; Frankfurt-Main: Klostermann, 1980), p. 57.

3. G. F. W. Hegel, *Phenomenology of Mind*, trans. J. B. Baillie (2nd ed.; London: Allen & Unwin, 1964), pp. 457-461.

4. *Hegel's Philosophy of Right*, trans. T. M. Knox (London: Oxford University Press, 1967), paragraphs 4 (with addition) and 15, pp. 20, 27, 226-227 (in the above and subsequent citations I have changed the translation slightly for purposes of clarity).

5. *Hegel's Philosophy of Right*, paragraph 33 (addition), pp. 235-236.

6. *Hegel's Philosophy of Right*, paragraphs 124, 182 (addition), 185, pp. 84, 123-124, 266. As Hegel adds (paragraph 185, addition, pp. 267-268): "Plato wished to exclude particularity from his state, but this is no help—for exclusion of this kind would contravene the infinite right of the 'idea' to allow freedom to the particular. It was first in Christian religion that the right of subjectivity arose, together with the infinity of self-awareness, and while granting this right, the whole order must at the same time retain strength enough to put particularity in harmony with the unity of ethical life."

7. *Hegel's Philosophy of Right*, paragraphs 181, 182 (with addition), 183, 184, pp. 122-123, 267. One should note at this point the ambivalent correlation of *Schein* and *Erscheinung* in Hegel's philosophy.

8. *Hegel's Philosophy of Right*, paragraphs 156 (addition), 256, 258, pp. 155-157, 261.

9. *Hegel's Philosophy of Right*, paragraphs 260 (with addition), pp. 160-161, 280.

10. *Hegel's Philosophy of Right*, paragraphs 272, 273, pp. 174-176. Hegel's view of the separation of powers differs from a mechanical system of "checks and balances" in which each power relates to the others only in the mode of competition or hostility. As he states (paragraph 272 with addition, pp. 175,

286): "To take the merely negative as starting point and to elevate ill will and mistrust to the level of first principle, and then on the basis of this premise slyly to construct dikes whose efficiency in turn necessitates counter-dikes against them—this is characteristic of negative reasoning *(Verstand)* and in sentiment of the outlook of the rabble .... The truth is that the powers are to be distinguished only as moments of the concept. If instead they subsist independently in abstraction from one another, then it is clear as day that two autonomous units cannot constitute a whole but must give rise to strife, whereby either the whole is destroyed or else unity is restored by force."

11. *Hegel's Philosophy of Right,* paragraphs 258 (addition), 270, pp. 171, 279. Compare also Hegel's critique of Haller's empirical-historical treatment of the state, and especially of the latter's contention that domination is part of the "unalterable, eternal ordinance of God"; paragraph 258, p. 159.

12. Charles Taylor, *Hegel and Modern Society* (Cambridge: University Press, 1979), p. 131. In a similar vein, countering charges of an oppressive "statism," Pelczynski observes that, in the view of some critics, "a traditional patriarchal society, a feudal monarchy or a modern collectivist, highly regulated state would all seem happily to fit Hegel's conception of an ethical order. But to think that would be to ignore the peculiar modern dimensions of *Sittlichkeit* represented by abstract right and morality. ... To count as true *Sittlichkeit* the ethical order in our own epoch must be shot through with personal rights and spheres of autonomy, and be acceptable to individual conscience; it must (in other words) incorporate the principles of particularity and subjectivity." See Z. A. Pelczynski, "Political Community and Individual Freedom in Hegel's Philosophy of State," in Pelczynski, ed., *The State and Civil Society: Studies in Hegel's Political Philosophy* (Cambridge: University Press, 1984), p. 69. The notion of a balance of universality and particularity is corroborated in Andrew Vincent, *Theories of the State* (Oxford: Blackwell, 1987), p. 143; also in Shlomo Avineri, *Hegel's Theory of the Modern State* (Cambridge: University Press, 1972), pp. 176-184.

13. Karl Marx, *Critique of Hegel's "Philosophy of Right",* ed. Joseph O'Malley (Cambridge: University Press, 1970), pp. 136-137, 141-142 (translation slightly altered). The citations are actually from "A Contribution to the Critique of *Hegel's Philosophy of Right:* Introduction" (1843-1844). As O'Malley comments (p. Li): "In terms reminiscent of Hegel's early doctrine of the simultaneous development of religious and political alienation, Marx declares that the modern political state exists as the religious sphere of human life in opposition to the mundane sphere of civil society; it is the religion of popular life, the heaven of its universality in opposition to the earthly existence of its actuality."

14. Only in a few passages did Marx touch at the roots of modern metaphysics, for example, in the statement: "Hegel's chief mistake consists in the fact that he conceives of the contradiction in appearance as being a unity in essence, i.e. in the Idea; whereas it certainly has something more profound in its essence, namely, an essential contradiction." See *Critique of Hegel's "Philosophy of Right",* p. 91.

15. Walter Kaufmann, ed., *The Portable Nietzsche* (New York: Viking Press, 1968), pp. 39-41, 160-163.

16. Karl Popper, *The Open Society and Its Enemies* (rev. 5th ed.; London: Routledge and Kegan Paul, 1966), vol. I, p. 4. Compare also Anthony Quinton, "Karl Popper: Politics without Essences," in Anthony de Crespigny and Kenneth Minogue, eds., *Contemporary Political Philosophers* (New York: Dodd, Mead & Co., 1975), pp. 147-167.

17. Jean-François Lyotard, *The Postmodern Condition: A Report on Knowledge*, trans. Geoff Bennington and Brian Massumi (Minneapolis: University of Minnesota Press, 1984), pp. xxiii-xxv.

18. *The Postmodern Condition*, pp. 11-12, 15-17.

19. *The Postmodern Condition*, pp. 33-35.

20. *The Postmodern Condition*, pp. 53-56, 59-61, 81. The linkage of Hegel and "terror" actually occurs in the essay "Answering the Question: What is Postmodernism?" which is attached as an Appendix to the study. In Lyotard's account, the main example of a contemporary rationalist defense of consensus is Habermas's theory of communicative action. Curiously, despite the distance between the two authors, Habermas also has taken Hegel to task for stressing holism (or the unity of the state) at the expense of particular initiatives or the will of "free and equal individuals." See Jürgen Habermas, *The Philosophical Discourse of Modernity: Twelve Lectures*, trans. Frederick Lawrence (Cambridge, MA: MIT Press, 1987), pp. 39-40.

21. Lyotard, *Le Différend* (Paris: Editions de Minuit, 1983), pp. 8-10, 17, 139-142, 199.

22. Taylor, *Hegel and Modern Society*, pp. 143, 145. As he adds (p. 145): while acknowledging his debt to Hegel, Marx "naturally released all the indignation of the radical Enlightenment at his conception of the state. The Hegelian synthesis is denounced as one achieved in thought only, masking the effective diremption of the real. In the polemic Marx inevitably distorted Hegel, speaking at times as though he was somehow concerned with 'abstract thought' alone, and was not also the protagonist of another kind of praxis. But the debt is undeniable and comes through Marx's text even when he is not engaged in acknowledging it."

23. *Hegel and Modern Society*, pp. 131-133. A central political motivation of Lyotard's critique is the memory of Auschwitz, and the impossibility of integrating the latter into an unfolding teleology of meaning; see especially *Le Différend*, pp. 145-154.

24. The phrase regarding the "identity of identity and difference" occurs particularly in the so-called *Differenzschrift* of 1801; see Hegel, *Differenz des Fichte'schen und Schelling'schen Systems*, ed. G. Lasson (Leipzig: F. Meiner, 1928). The thesis that "the rational is the real" is formulated in the "Preface" to

the *Philosophy of Right* where Hegel elaborates: If "the idea passes for 'only an idea', for a mere fancy or opinion, then philosophy rejects such a view and shows that nothing is actual except the idea. Once this is granted, the important thing is to apprehend in the appearance of the temporal and transient the substance which is immanent and the eternal which is present." See *Hegel's Philosophy of Right*, Preface, p. 10,

25. *Hegel's Philosophy of Right*, Preface, pp. 10-11.

26. For Gandhi's description of the ashram at Kochrab see Raghavan Iyer, ed., *The Moral and Political Writings of Mahatma Gandhi*, vol. 2: *Truth and Non-Violence* (Oxford: Clarendon Press, 1986) pp. 562-564. Akin to ashrams are some forms of *kibbutzim*, particularly if members are gathered from different classes and nationalities. On the whole, the ideas of the so-called utopian socialists are in my view not entirely obsolete.

27. Hegel, *Phenomenology of Mind*, p. 105, and *Grundlinien der Philosophie des Rechts*, ed. Eva Moldenhauer and Karl M. Michel (*Werkausgabe*, vol. 7; Frankfurt-Main: Suhrkamp, 1970), paragraph 132, p. 249. (The annotation is not contained in Knox's English translation.) For some of the above arguments I am indebted to Ernesto Laclau and Chantal Mouffe, *Hegemony and Socialist Strategy: Towards a Radical Democratic Politics* (London: Verso, 1985).

CHAPTER 8

1. Ernst Bloch, *The Principle of Hope*, trans. Neville Plaice, Stephen Plaice, and Paul Knight, 3 vols. (Cambridge, MA: MIT Press, 1986). The first German edition appeared in 1959. For a condensed narrative of Bloch's life (1885-1977) and works see "Translators' Introduction," pp. xix-xxxiii; also Erhard Bahr, *Ernst Bloch* (Berlin: Colloquium Verlag, 1974) and Wayne Hudson, *The Marxist Philosophy of Ernst Bloch* (New York: St. Martin's Press, 1982).

2. Martin Jay, *Marxism and Totality: The Adventures of a Concept from Lukács to Habermas* (Berkeley: University of California Press, 1984), p. 174.

3. See Leszek Kolakowski, *Main Currents of Marxism*, vol. 3: *The Breakdown*, trans. P. S. Falla (Oxford: Oxford University Press, 1978), p. 422; Jürgen Habermas, "A Marxist Schelling," in *Philosophical-Political Profiles*, trans. Frederick G. Lawrence (Cambridge, MA: MIT Press, 1983), p. 76; also Rugard O. Gropp et al., *Ernst Blochs Revision des Marxismus* (Berlin: Aufbau, 1957).

4. As Jay notes: "Paradoxically, he came to be honored more by theologians than by Marxists who remained resistant to the indigestible religious elements in his thought." See *Marxism and Totality*, p. 175. Regarding theological appraisals see especially Jürgen Moltmann, "Messianismus und Marxismus," in *Über Ernst Bloch* (Frankfurt-Main: Suhrkamp, 1968), pp. 42-60.

5. Bloch, *The Principle of Hope*, vol. 1, p. 11.

6. *The Principle of Hope,* vol. 1, pp. 6, 9-10, 45-46. Bloch thus opposes to Freud's backward looking unconscious a forward looking or anticipatory unconscious. (In the above and subsequent citations I have changed the translation slightly for purposes of clarity.)

7. *The Principle of Hope,* vol. 1, pp. 65, 74-75, 77.

8. *The Principle of Hope,* vol. 1, pp. 9, 195-197. Compare also the section on "layers of the category of possibility," pp. 223-249.

9. *The Principle of Hope,* vol. 1, pp. 198-203.

10. *The Principle of Hope,* vol. 1, pp. 18, 203-205.

11. *The Principle of Hope,* vol. 1, pp. 9, 206-208. In line with the two Aristotelian modes of *dynamis* Bloch distinguishes between a "cold stream" and a "warm stream" of Marxism (p. 209): the former involving a "science of conditions" as well as a "science of struggle," the latter exemplifylng the "liberating intention and materialistically humane, humanely materialistic real tendency." Regarding the development of Aristotelianism compare also Bloch, *Avicenna und die Aristotelische Linke* (Frankfurt-Main: Suhrkamp, 1963).

12. *The Principle of Hope,* vol. 1, pp. 306-307. In this "concise ontology," Bloch elaborates (p. 307), the "Not" characterizes the "intensive, ultimately interest-based *origin* of everything," while the "Not-Yet" reflects the "*tendency* in the material process toward the manifestation of its content"; the "Nothing" or "All" finally refers to the "*latency* in this tendency, in a negative or positive sense and chiefly at the most advanced front of the material process."

13. *The Principle of Hope,* vol. 3, p. 1202.

14. *The Principle of Hope,* vol. 3, pp. 1194-1195.

15. *The Principle of Hope,* vol. 3, pp. 1195-1196.

16. *The Principle of Hope,* vol. 3, pp. 1196-1197. As Bloch emphasizes in this context (p. 1198), the "otherness" of religiosity necessarily separates the coming kingdom from merely human designs or constructed utopias: "As little as religious selfhood coincides with the existing human creature, and as little as religious homecoming has in common with positivism's smug contentment in empirical circumstances, just as little does the religious idea of the kingdom, in its intended scope and intent, coincide fully with any social utopia." In fact, "social history and social utopia—even an attained classless society—are separated from the *summum bonum* of the religious-utopian kingdom by the leap or rupture implicit in the explosive intention of rebirth and transfiguration."

17. *The Principle of Hope,* vol. 3, pp. 1197, 1204, 1216-1218.

18. *The Principle of Hope,* vol. 3, pp. 1220-1221, 1223, 1225-1226, 1230. In a striking passage, Bloch alerts to the linkage between the Taoist aversion to "making" and the feminine or matriarchy (p. 1228): "In the aversion to

mechanical-abstract fabrication, there speaks unmistakably chthonic memory, belief in the giving and guarding earth-mother; long-lost matriarchy continues to reverberate in the maxim of non-making, as spontaneity in repose. And it is not fortuitous that Lao Tzu's life-Tao thus reproduces and sublimates images from the earlier matrilineal period in China: for Tao is the ancient name for an animal-shaped world-mother."

19. *The Principle of Hope*, vol. 3, pp. 1242-1243, 1249-1252. As Bloch elaborates, Zoroaster's teachings were later radicalized by the Mesopotamian sect of the Mandaeans and especially by Mani, the founder of Manichaeism. In Manichaean doctrine, he notes (p. 1247), Babylonian astrology turned into a "cosmic alchemy," that is, the struggle to distill pure gold out of the metal of the world or to liberate goodness from the shackles of evil.

20. *The Principle of Hope*, vol. 3, pp. 1231-1234, 1236-1238. According to the Cabbalist Isaac Luria—Bloch adds (p. 1237)—creation itself can be seen as an exile: *"bereshit"* (the beginning) was the beginning of an imprisonment, a "contraction" of God initiating the "captivity of Israel."

21. *The Principle of Hope*, vol. 3, pp. 1259-1260, 1262-1264.

22. *The Principle of Hope*, vol. 3, pp. 1265-1266, 1268, 1273, 1277-1278.

23. *The Principle of Hope*, vol. 3, pp. 1199, 1284-1285, 1292. As he adds (p. 1200): "Even in its secularized form, and all the more so in its utopian-total sense, the kingdom remains a *messianic front-region even without any theism.* . . . Atheism is therefore so far from being the enemy of religious utopia that it constitutes its precondition: *without atheism there is no room for messianism."* See also Bloch, *Atheismus im Christentum: Zur Religion des Exodus und des Reichs* (Frankfurt-Main: Suhrkamp, 1968).

24. Paul Ricoeur, *Political and Social Essays,* ed. David Stewart and Joseph Bien (Athens: Ohio University Press, 1974), p. 186.

25. Bloch, *The Principle of Hope,* vol. 3, pp. 1197, 1199.

26. The problem of decisionism or arbitrary bias also affects Bloch's psychology—where one is not always sure (for example) why "expectant emotions" are privileged over "filled emotions," and among the former why "hope" takes precedence over other types (like anxiety or fear). Some recent philosophers (like Heidegger and Sartre) have focused precisely on "dread" and "nausea" to illustrate the transcendental openness of human existence.

27. *The Principle of Hope*, vol. 3, pp. 1300-1301. Compare also the statement (vol. 1, p. 292): "No flowing can be conceived or dialectically understood without the 'now' in the midst of time, a point which is not even itself time but rather the 'peculiar something', in Plato's words, out of which the time (and not merely our conception of it) of the real temporal stream arises and in which movement is united with restless rest."

28. *The Principle of Hope,* vol. 3, p. 1331.

29. *The Principle of Hope,* vol. 3, pp. 1269-1270, 1306-1307, 1353. Although close to "process theology" in many ways, Bloch has not sufficiently elaborated (in my view) the possibility of non-static analogies between nature and the divine. For a general discussion of analogical thinking in its relation to radical otherness see David Tracy, *The Analogical Imagination* (New York: Crossroad, 1986).

30. *The Principle of Hope,* vol. 3, pp. 1274, 1276.

31. At least at this point Bloch's principle of hope needs to be supplemented by the "principle of responsibility" as articulated, e.g., by Hans Jonas in *The Imperative of Responsibility: In Search of an Ethics for the Technological Age* (Chicago: University of Chicago Press, 1984).

32. *The Principle of Hope,* vol. 3, pp. 1285, 1297, 1310-1311, 1352, 1375. Compare in this context Sheehan's perceptive comments: "A philosophical effort to name the unnamable while leaving metaphysics behind might conceive of itself as an 'atheology.' This would be a mode of discourse—or better, a silent attunement to one's own movement—that recognizes that the theos of traditional metaphysics and Christian theology is hardly adequate to the mystery inscribed in that movement. Atheology is a refusal of all claims to know already that the world is grounded in self-identical cognition. It radically calls into question the ontology of coincidence." See Thomas Sheehan, *Karl Rahner: The Philosophical Foundations* (Athens: Ohio University Press, 1987), p. 316. Compare also Mark Taylor, *Erring: A Postmodern A/Theology* (Chicago: University of Chicago Press, 1984).

CHAPTER 9

1. For an introduction to contemporary "political" or (more broadly) "practical" theology see Charles Davis, *Theology and Political Society* (Cambridge: Cambridge University Press, 1980); Dermot Lane, *Foundations for a Social Theology* (New York: Paulist Press, 1984); Dennis McCann and Charles R. Strain, *Polity and Praxis: A Program for American Practical Theology* (New York: Winston, 1985); Johann Baptist Metz, *Faith, History and Society: Toward a Practical Fundamental Theology* (New York: Seabury Press, 1980); Don Browning, ed., *Practical Theology* (New York: Harper & Row, 1983).

2. Wolfhart Pannenberg, *Anthropology in Theological Perspective,* trans. Matthew J. O'Connell (first German ed. 1983; Philadelphia: Westminster Press, 1985). Hereafter cited as *Anthropology.*

3. Pannenberg, *Theology and the Kingdom of God,* ed. Richard John Neuhaus (Philadelphia: Westminster Press, 1969).

4. Pannenberg, *Grundzüge der Christologie* (Gütersloh: G. Mohn, 1964); *Jesus—God and Man,* trans. Lewis L. Wilkins and Duane A. Priebe (Philadelphia: Westminster Press, 1968); *The Church,* trans. Keith Crim (Philadelphia: Westminster Press, 1983).

5. Pannenberg, *Theology and the Philosophy of Science*, trans. Francis McDonagh (Philadelphia: Westminster Press, 1976); *Human Nature, Election, and History* (Philadelphia: Westminster Press, 1977); *Ethics*, trans. Keith Crim (Philadelphia: Westminster Press, 1981).

6. Pannenberg, *Anthropologie in Theologischer Perspektive* (Göttingen: Vandenhoeck & Ruprecht, 1983), p. 7.

7. Pannenberg, *What Is Man?*, trans. Duane A. Priebe (first German ed. 1962; Philadelphia: Fortress Press, 1970), pp. 1-3.

8. *What Is Man?*, pp. 3, 10. Regarding philosophical anthropology see especially Max Scheler, *Die Stellung des Menschen im Kosmos* (Bern: Francke Verlag, 1927); Arnold Gehlen, *Der Mensch: Seine Natur und seine Stellung in der Welt* (1940; 8th ed., Frankfurt-Main and Bonn: Athenäum, 1966); Helmuth Plessner, *Conditio Humana* (1961; republished, Pfullingen: Neske, 1964); also my "Social Role and 'Human Nature': Plessner's Philosophical Anthropology," in *Beyond Dogma and Despair* (Notre Dame: University of Notre Dame Press, 1981), pp. 69-93.

9. Pannenberg, *Anthropology*, pp. 12-16. In the above and subsequent citations I have partially altered the translation for purposes of clarity.

10. *Anthropology*, pp. 15, 19-21.

11. *Anthropology*, pp. 35-42.

12. *Anthropology*, pp. 45, 60. The reference is to Johann Gottlieb Herder, *Essay on the Origin of Language*, in J. J. Rousseau and J. G. Herder, *On the Origin of Language*, trans. J. H. Moran and A. Gode (New York: Ungar Publ., 1967); also to Herder, *Outlines of a Philosophy of the History of Man*, trans. T. Churchill (New York: Bergmann Publ., 1966).

13. Pannenberg, *Anthropology*, pp. 69, 85.

14. *Anthropology*, pp. 397-398. The reference is to Erich Rothacker, *Probleme der Kulturanthropologie* (1942; second ed., Bonn: Bouvier, 1948).

15. Pannenberg, *Anthropology*, pp. 399-414. The functionalist position is identified chiefly with the work of Durkheim, Malinowski and Parsons, while the intentionalist outlook is ascribed to Gehlen and symbolic interactionism.

16. *Anthropology*, p. 446.

17. *Anthropology*, pp. 449-450. In these passages, Pannenberg evidently seeks to steer a course between or beyond the orthodox Calvinist position of a *corruptio naturae* and the Thomistic notion of a wounded but redeemable nature *(vulnera naturae)*.

18. *Anthropology*, pp. 450-452. Curiously, *Anthropology* devotes little or no space to the political conception of Thomas Aquinas. In my view, once Aristotle's stress on contemplation (of the divine) as supreme human *telos* is taken

seriously, the Aristotelian *polis* does seem to allow for the kind of openness Pannenberg seeks in Christian, especially Augustinian, theology.

19. *Anthropology*, pp. 452-453, 472. The status of Augustine in the context of political theology, and especially the danger of a dualistic bifurcation of the two cities, are discussed in greater detail and with subtlety in Pannenberg, *Human Nature, Election, and History*, pp. 67-71.

20. *Anthropology*, pp. 473-474.

21. *Anthropology*, pp. 475-476.

22. *Anthropology*, pp. 477-482.

23. Pannenberg, *Theology and the Kingdom of God*, pp. 75, 77-78, 93, 101.

24. *Anthropology*, p. 483. The reference is to Paul Tillich, *Religionsphilosophie* (Stuttgart: Kohlhammer, 1962).

25. Pannenberg, *Anthropology*, p. 18.

26. *Anthropology*, p. 69.

27. See Michel Foucault, *The Order of Things: An Archaeology of the Human Sciences* (first French ed. 1966; New York: Vintage Books, 1973), pp. 379, 383; *Language, Counter-Memory, Practice: Selected Essays and Interpretations*, trans. Donald F. Bouchard and Sherry Simon (Oxford: Blackwell, 1977), pp. 38, 42. Compare also my *Twilight of Subjectivity* (Amherst: University of Massachusetts Press, 1981), pp. 21-37.

28. Pannenberg, *Anthropology*, p. 350; *What Is Man?*, p. 20.

29. *What Is Man?*, p. 56; *Anthropology*, pp. 164-165, 241.

30. *What Is Man?*, p. 62; *Anthropology*, pp. 76, 79.

31. *Anthropology*, p. 70. The otherness of God and its implications for "prophetic" utterance are recognized even by a "post-structuralist" frequently unsuspected of religious leanings: Jacques Derrida. As he observed in an interview: "I mean that deconstruction is, in itself, a positive response to an alterity which necessarily calls, summons or motivates it. Deconstruction is therefore vocation— a response to a call . . . . I concede that the style of my questioning as an exodus and dissemination in the desert might produce certain prophetic resonances. It is possible to see deconstruction as being produced in a space where the prophets are not far away." See Richard Kearney, *Dialogues with Contemporary Continental Thinkers* (Manchester: Manchester University Press, 1984), pp. 118-119. Compare also James Bernauer, "The Prisons of Man: An Introduction to Foucault's Negative Theology," *International Philosophical Quarterly*, vol. 27 (1987), pp. 365-380.

32. Pannenberg, *Anthropology*, pp. 528-532.

APPENDIX

1. Albert O. Hirschman, *Essays in Trespassing: Economics to Politics and Beyond* (Cambridge: Cambridge University Press, 1981).

2. Martin Heidegger, *Hölderlins Hymnen "Germanien" und "Der Rhein"*, ed. Susanne Ziegler (*Gesamtausgabe*, vol. 39; Frankfurt-Main: Klostermann, 1980); hereafter abbreviated *Hölderlins Hymnen*.

3. Hans-Georg Gadamer, *Heideggers Wege* (Tübingen: Mohr, 1983), pp. 14, 118; Hannah Arendt, "Martin Heidegger at Eighty," in Michael Murray, ed., *Heidegger and Modern Philosophy: Critical Essays* (New Haven: Yale University Press, 1978), pp. 294-295.

4. I have addressed some aspects of this episode in my "Ontology of Freedom: Heidegger and Political Philosophy," *Political Theory*, vol. 12 (May, 1984), pp. 204-234; reprinted in slightly revised form in my *Polis and Praxis* (Cambridge, MA:MIT Press, 1984), pp. 104-132. The text of Heidegger's "Rektoratsrede" of May 1933 has recently been republished, together with a retrospective epilogue written by Heidegger in 1945; see Hermann Heidegger, ed., *Die Selbstbehauptung der deutschen Universität* (Frankfurt-Main: Klostermann, 1983).

5. *Hölderlins Hymnen*, pp. 20, 33, 64, 216-217.

6. *Hölderlins Hymnen*, p. 30. For the English version see *Friedrich Hölderlin: Poems and Fragments*, trans. Michael Hamburger (Ann Arbor: University of Michigan Press, 1967), p. 375 (translation slightly altered). For a more general assessment of Hölderlin's poetry by Heidegger see "Hölderlin und das Wesen der Dichtung," in Heidegger, *Erläuterungen zu Hölderlins Dichtung*, ed. Friedrich-Wilhelm von Herrmann (*Gesamtausgabe*, vol. 4; Frankfurt-Main: Klostermann, 1981), pp. 33-48.

7. *Hölderlins Hymnen*, pp. 1, 220.

8. *Friedrich Hölderlin: Poems and Fragments*, pp. 405, 407, 410 (translation slightly altered).

9. *Hölderlins Hymnen*, pp. 6-7, 26-28. With a clear political edge Heidegger adds (p. 28): "If anything deserves the much abused label 'liberal', it is this conception. For, on principle and from the outset, this conception distances itself from its own thoughts and beliefs, reducing them to mere objects or targets of opinion. Poetry in this manner becomes an immediately given phenomenon among other phenomena—a phenomenon which is further characterized by the equally non-committal designation as 'expressive manifestation' of an inner soul."

10. *Hölderlins Hymnen*, pp. 30-33.

11. *Hölderlins Hymnen*, pp. 19, 45, 58-59, 145. Repeatedly the lecture course also comments on the status of metaphors in poetry—a theme which is important

because of the connection between "metaphors" and "meta-physics." Thus, refer-ring to the first stanza of "As On a Holiday" Heidegger states (pp. 254-255) that these lines do not offer a "poetic comparison such as an 'image' or a 'metaphor'." For, in a poetic comparison, "what is compared with what? Typically a process in nature with a spiritual-mental experience. But what do we mean by 'nature' and by 'spirit'? . . . No matter how we construe these terms, what is the point of a comparison if the poet insists that nature itself educates the poet?"

12. *Hölderlins Hymnen*, pp. 5-6, 8. See also Heidegger, *What is Philoso-phy?*, trans. William Kluback and Jean T. Wilde (New Haven: College and Uni-versity Press, 1956), p. 95.

13. *Hölderlins Hymnen*, pp. 55, 61, 173-175. As Heidegger insists (pp. 73, 174), the "ownness" *(Jemeinigkeit)* of *Dasein* and of individual death does not nullify the ontological character of co-being. Accentuating the aspect of "thrown-ness" in every project, the course establishes a close linkage between "being" and "suffering," associating genuine human existence with the need continuously to "undergo" its own calling *(Leiden seiner selbst,* p. 175).

14. *Hölderlins Hymnen*, pp. 51, 56, 69-71, 117-118, 123-128, 144, 275.

15. *Hölderlins Hymnen*, p. 4; see also *Friedrich Hölderlin: Poems and Fragments*, p. 537 (translation slightly altered).

16. *Hölderlins Hymnen*, pp. 17, 26-27, 254. Regarding Heidegger's invoca-tion of "blood and soil" in his so-called "Rektoratsrede" of May 1933, compare the sensible comments of Graeme Nicholson in his "The Politics of Heidegger's Rectoral Address," in *Proceedings: Heidegger Conference* (18th Annual Meet-ing, University of Wisconsin-Stevens Point, May 1984), pp. 212-213.

17. *Hölderlins Hymnen*, pp. 5, 41, 99, 221. In another context (p. 210), Heidegger attacks the portrayal of Christ as *"Führer"*—a portrayal, he says, which is "not only an untruth but also, what is worse, a blasphemy vis-à-vis Christ."

18. *Hölderlins Hymnen*, p. 214.

19. *Hölderlins Hymnen*, p. 142.

20. *Hölderlins Hymnen*, pp. 80-82, 95. As Heidegger adds (p. 95): "Sacred mourning is ready to renounce the old gods; yet—what else does the mourning heart desire but this: in relinquishing the gods to preserve immaculate their divinity and thus, through a preserving renunciation of the distant gods, to remain in the proximity of their divinity. The not-being-able-to-call the old gods, the acceptance of the loss, what else is it—it is nothing else—but the only possible, resolute readiness to wait for the divine." Together with Hölderlin, incidentally, Heidegger (p. 84) interprets the term "sacred" or holy in the sense of "unselfish"—something which radically transcends the domains of both indi-vidual or general interest (or utility).

21. *Hölderlins Hymnen*, pp. 165-166, 182. For an attempt to find a more overt political meaning in "The Rhine" see Johannes Mahr, *Mythos und Politik in Hölderlins Rheinhymne* (Munich: Fink Verlag, 1972).

22. Heidegger was well aware of the mentioned incongruence or contrast. As he writes (*Hölderlins Hymnen*, p. 80): "The flight of the gods must first become an experience and this experience must push *Dasein* into a basic mood in which a historical people as a whole endures the plight of its godlessness and brokenness. It is this basic mood which the poet seeks to implant in the life of our people. Whether this happened in 1801, and whether in 1934 it has not yet been perceived and grasped—this is not the issue since dates are immaterial at such a watershed."

23. *Hölderlins Hymnen*, p. 147.

24. *Hölderlins Hymnen*, pp. 88, 90, 104, 122-123.

25. In this respect some of Heidegger's later works contain an important self-correction. Thus, a lecture course held in summer of 1942 contrasts the "polis" construed as an ontological site to the modern conception of "the state." See Heidegger, *Hölderlins Hymne "Der Ister"*, ed. Walter Biemel (*Gesamtausgabe*, vol. 53; Frankfurt-Main: Klostermann, 1984), pp. 100-101.

26. See Heidegger, *Hölderlins Hymne "Andenken"*, ed. Curd Ochwadt (*Gesamtausgabe*, vol. 52; Frankfurt-Main: Klostermann, 1982), pp. 76-78, 188.

27. In Heidegger's words: "The task is to take seriously the long-standing flight of the gods and in and through this seriousness to anticipate their return —which means: to participate in the preparation of their renewed advent and thus to refashion the earth and the land anew." See *Hölderlins Hymnen*, pp. 146, 220-221.

INDEX

abnormality, 105
absolutism, 114, 129
action, 58, 61, 66, 107, 205
  instrumental, 58, 61
  communicative, 67-69, 113, 224, n.9, 248 n.20
activism, 60, 80
Adorno, Theodore W., 159
aesthetics, 50-52, 54, 59, 65, 116, 209, 211
agnosticism, 81, 93
agon, 34, 214, 220
agonistics, xvi, 11-12, 16-17, 140-153, 156, 225 n.15, 225 n.20
ahimsa, xiii, 28, 32, 34-35, 181
alienation, 155
alterity, 86
Althusser, Louis, 121, 125
amoralism, 113-114
anamnesis, 79, 164
anarchism, 117, 125
anoia, 79
anomie, 52
antagonism, 20, 98, 122-123, 126, 128-130, 133-135, 151, 193, 197, 244 n.10
anthropocentrism, xvi, 40, 86, 115, 188, 201, 203

anthropology, xvii, 73, 149, 170, 175, 183-184, 186-190, 200-201, 204
  cultural, 189, 191, 201
  dogmatic, 188
  philosophical, 186, 189-191, 202, 253 n.8
anthropomorphism, 76, 169, 200,204
anti-discourse, 41, 48
anti-dogmatism, 54
anti-dualism, 133
anti-foundationalism, 101, 116, 137
anti-Hegel, 165
anti-humanism, 49, 59, 69, 168, 202
anti-modernism, 59, 70
antinomy, 71
antiquarianism, 49
anti-rationalism, 50, 55, 62
anti-recollection, 165
anti-universalism, 9-10
Apartheid, 27
Apel, Karl-Otto, 9, 223 n.7
Apollo, 53, 96
apriorism, 124
appropriation, 214
archaeology, 118, 201
Arendt, Hannah, 126, 208, 219
argumentation,17, 34, 51, 109

aristocracy, 145
Aristotle, 3, 110, 114, 135, 165-166,
    178, 193-197, 208, 253 n.18
art, 4, 42-43, 46, 49-50, 54-55, 59, 65,
    113, 160
    modern, 49
articulation, 121, 126-129, 131
art-work, 17
ashram, 35-36, 156
atheism, 167, 175
atheology, 252, n.32
atomization, 150
atonement, 174
attunement, 217
Augustine, St., 164, 195-196, 254 n.19
Austro-Marxism, 119
autarchy, 194
authoritarianism, 199
authority, 195
autonomy, 40-42, 58, 61, 65, 107, 124-
    125, 130 183, 192-194, 199, 203-205
Averroes, 165
Avicenna, 165
Axelrod, P. B., 119

Bacon, Francis, 25, 64, 224 n.13
Balibar, Etienne, 121
Barth, Karl, 168, 188, 200
Bataille, Georges, 41, 49, 55, 59, 64,
    113
becoming, 85, 87
beginning, 75-76
behavior, 99-100
behaviorism, 189
being, ix, 21, 33, 37-38, 56-59, 71, 75,
    82, 85-87, 92-94, 133-134, 161-165,
    173-175, 177-178, 187, 209-214,
    217-219, 230 n.24
    absolute, 205
    lack of, 166
    of people, 210, 212
    plenary, 166-167, 181
being-with, 60
Benjamin, Walter, 104, 204
Bergson, Henri, 85, 131, 164

Bernstein, Eduard, 118-119, 132
Berkeley, George, 64
biologism, 215
biology, 186, 189
Bismarck, Count, 54, 118
bloc, 120
    historical, 120
Bloch, Ernst, x, xvi, 158-182, 238 n.26
bolshevization, 119-120, 130
Bourdieu, Pierre, 105
Brahman, 30
Bruno, Giordano, 166
Buber, Martin, 89, 98
Buddha, 33, 171-173
Buddhism, 32, 77, 172
Bultmann, Rudolf, 200
bureaucratization, 124, 138

Cadmus, 170
Camus, Albert, 201
capitalism, 27-28, 118, 230 n.21
    advanced, 119
    organized, 118
Carneades, 8
Cartesianism, 12, 60, 101, 112
caste, 31, 36
    system, xiii, 25, 36
Catoriadis, Cornelius, 235 n.43
Charlemagne, 3
chiasm, xv, 18
Chomsky, Noam, 6, 223 n.7
Christianity, 30, 52, 77, 85, 141, 168-
    169, 175, 197-198, 229 n.20, 232 n.20
Christology, 185
church, 193-195, 196-199, 205, 219, 222
    n.3, 231 n.11
Churchill, Winston, 29
Cicero, 195
civilization, 27, 37-38, 141, 219, 223
    n.4
    modern, 27-28, 36
    Western, 28, 36
class, 120
    working, 118-120
    universal, 138, 147, 155, 244 n.14

classicism, 137
classism, 124
co-being, 60-61, 172, 256 n.13
collectivism, 35, 152, 156, 193, 197
collectivity, 143, 148, 156
colonialism, xii
communication, 6-7, 11, 88, 98-100,
    109, 150, 225 n.15
  linguistic, 98
  theory of, 6
communitarianism, 222 n.7
community, 17, 68, 72, 75, 143, 169-170,
    193-195, 199, 205
  non-repressive, 169
  political, 196
  social, 197
competence, 7, 41, 63
  cognitive, 56
  communicative, 7
  linguistic, 6-7
  rule, 7
comprehensibility, 6
conflict, 15, 109, 197
conformism, 205
Confucius, 171
consciousness, xvi, 4, 40, 47-49, 57,
    67-69, 75-77, 79-83, 87-88, 94, 97-101,
    138-139, 162-164, 177, 186, 192
  absolute, 94
  anticipatory, xvi, 160, 162
  existential, 80
  intentional, 82
  modern, 49
  moral, 7
  reversal of, 94
  transcendental, 89, 107
consensus, 10, 15, 17-19, 34, 46-47,
    64-65, 67-68, 109, 151
constellation, 18
constitution, 144
contemplation, 62
contest, ix, xii, 11, 13-18, 148, 152
  agonal, 15, 19
contestation, xv-xvi, 14-15, 128, 132,
    137, 149, 198
contextualism, 66

contingency, xv, 8, 20, 115, 131-132
contractarianism, xvi, 4, 48, 64, 143,
    225 n.21
conversation, 40
corporation, 114
cosmopolis, xii, 1-3, 20, 38
cosmopolitanism, xii
cosmos, 106, 186
counter-discourse, xiii-xiv, 48, 63-64,
    69-70
counter-enlightenment, xiv, 55
counter-politics, 216
creation, 77, 84
criticism, 211
  literary, 207, 211, 215
culture, xv, 5, 18, 22, 26, 56, 67-68,
    103-104, 192, 196, 199
  Eastern, 24, 36
  European, 27, 29
  industry, 216
  Oriental, 24
  Western, 24, 29, 95
  world, 1
Curzon, Lord, 24
cybernetics, 11-12, 149, 153

decisionism, 58, 61, 178, 251 n.26
deconstruction, xiii, 39, 97, 116-117,
    125, 254 n.31
democracy, xv, 9, 20, 35, 116, 122-125,
    134-138, 145
  mass, 124
  new, 120
  plural, 124, 128, 130, 135
  radical, 123, 125-126, 130, 245 n.17
democratization, 124, 135
demythologization, xvi
Derrida, Jacques, x, xiv, xvii, 41, 64,
    70-72, 102, 133, 177, 254 n.31
Desai Mahadev, 28
Descartes, René, 4, 12, 40-41, 56, 107,
    224 n.13
despotism, 125, 168
determinism, 13, 28, 111, 119, 132,
    149, 151

detotalization, 129
development, 8
  cognitive, 8
  normative, 8
dharma, 31-32
dialectic, 10, 80, 93, 150, 155, 177, 202
  of enlightenment, 48-49, 64, 232
    n.15
  of spirit, 10, 12, 150
dialogue, xv, 9, 16-18, 98, 104, 109,
  225 n.20, 226 n.23
difference, xv, 18-20, 71, 87, 123, 125-
  128, 133-135, 144, 153-154, 168, 177,
  185, 204
  ontological, 56, 62, 87, 219
Dionysus, 50, 52-53, 62, 70, 96, 170
discontinuity, 153, 156, 177-178
discourse, ix, 5, 14-16, 34, 39-41, 48-52,
  58-59, 64-66, 69-72, 109, 117-119,
  121-122, 126-129, 150-152
  absolute, 152
  modern, 52, 58, 64, 70-71
  of modernity, 221 n.4, 224 n.9, 232
    n.14
  Nietzschean, 70-71
  practical, 7
  rational, 54, 71
  speculative, 152
discursivity, 122, 133, 243 n.7
disenchantment, 167, 176-177
disobedience, 34
  civil, 34
disorder, x, xv, 79, 83-84, 89, 90-91,
  108, 126
dissensus, 15
distance, 82
  reflective, 80, 82, 88
dogmatism, 54, 199
dogmatomachy, 85, 93
domination, 2, 27, 35-38, 52, 128, 145,
  195-196
dualism, 89, 132, 180
Durkheim, Emile, 253 n.15
dynamism, 177

eccentricity, 189, 191, 197, 201, 203
ecclesiology, 185
ecology, 156
economics, 119-120
economism, 28, 92, 120-121, 124-126
economy, 40, 121
ecumenicism, 32
egocentrism, 72, 107
Egypticism, 53
Einstein, Albert, 23
element, 121, 133, 243 n.7
emancipation, 10, 12, 26, 36, 50, 68,
  147, 180
embodiment, 98-101, 114, 140
empiricism, xi, 64, 89, 149
empowerment, 35
enlightenment (also Enlightenment),
  xii-xiv, 2, 4, 8, 12, 39-42, 44, 47-51,
  54, 63, 68-70, 104, 139, 167, 175,
  224 n.9
epistemology, 3, 51, 54, 57-61, 66-67
epoché, 98
experience, xvii, 5, 16, 33, 47-49,
  53-54, 87, 100
  hermeneutical, 16
experimentalism, 54
equality, 128, 135-136
equivalence, 122-125, 128, 129, 133-135
  negative, 123
eschatology, 81, 181, 194, 200
essence, 173, 193, 212
essentialism, 53, 117, 120, 124-126, 129,
  131-132, 177-178, 243 n.2, 244 n.11
ethics, 4, 42-44, 51, 54, 65-68, 101,
  113-114, 142, 171, 185
  advent, 174
  communicative, 6-7, 100
  discourse, 7
  substantial, 142
ethnocentrism, 8-9
ethnology, 201-202
ethos, 114
event, 90, 96-98, 111-113, 115
  threshold, 108
evolution, 7, 119, 149, 176
  social, 176

existence, 86, 88, 91, 161-162, 166, 169,
177, 186-188, 190, 197, 204, 214,
226 n.24
existentialism, 37, 60, 85
exteriority, 134-135
externality, 140

fabrication, 179
facticity, 166, 176
faith, xvii, 28-29, 32, 40, 46, 185, 196,
199-200
Christian, 196
fallibilism, 54
family, 44, 139-140, 143-144, 193, 195
fanaticism, 181
Fanon, Frantz, 35
fascism, 97, 120, 209
fatalism, 31
Faust, 179
feudalism, 4
Feuerbach, Ludwig, 146-147, 168, 175
Fichte, Johann Gottlieb, 40, 46, 58,
60, 80, 143, 150-151
field, 105
Foucault, Michel, xi, xiv, 41, 71, 102,
118, 122, 201-202, 225 n.14, 226 n.51,
245 n.18
foundationalism, 9, 53, 58, 85, 178, 202
fragmentation, xvi, 16, 118-119, 129,
149, 156
freedom, 35, 40, 445-48, 59. 62, 101, 107,
119, 131-132, 139-148, 152, 165, 169,
182, 186, 204, 234 n.36, 239 n.28
radical, 101
subjective, 141
Freud, Sigmund, 107, 161, 250 n.6
friendship, 135
front, 164, 180
functionalism, 192
fundamentalism, 177, 198
futurism, 174

Gadamer, Hans-Georg, x, 16-17, 86,
208, 224 n.10, 226 n.23, 238 n.19,
239 n.26, 240 n.7

Gandhi, Mahatma, x, xii-xiii, 23-24,
26-38, 156, 181, 249 n.26
Gebhart, Jürgen, 236 n.2
Gehlen, Arnold, 186, 189-191
Gemeinschaft, xvi
genealogy, 117, 131, 201
generality, 142
Gentile, Giovanni, 148
Gesellschaft, xvi
gnosis, 79
gnosticism, xiv, 78, 81, 93, 180, 239
n.28
Goethe, Johann Wolfang, 157
Goffman, Irving, 105
goodness, 106, 114
gospel, 183
social, 183
grammar, 6
generative, 6
Gramsci, Antonio, 23, 120, 130-131
Gutierrez, Gustavo, 229 n.20

Habermas, Jürgen, xiii, 2, 4-11, 15-16,
39-79, 96, 100, 103, 113, 180
Handke, Peter, x
Hegel, Georg F. W., xiii-xvii, 26, 40-49,
59, 62-65, 69-71, 78-82, 93-94, 101,
113, 127, 131, 135-157, 164-166, 170,
178, 202, 213, 231 n.8, 232 n.14, 237
n.12, 244 n.14, 246 n.1
Hegelianism, 127, 148, 152-153, 231
n.12
hegemony, 19, 116-128, 131-134
Heidegger, Martin, ix-x, xiv, xvii,
17-18, 27, 37, 41, 49, 55-64, 67, 70-71,
86-87, 92, 94, 115, 133, 138, 177-178,
201, 207-220, 230 n.24, 233 n.30,
235 n.42, 251 n.26
Hellenism, 3
Heraclitus, 13
Herder, Gottfried, 2, 8-9, 190-191, 253
n.12
hermeneutics, 2, 5, 10, 16-17, 86, 99,
113
ontological, 86

symbolic, 101
transcendental, 9, 223 n.7
universal, 16
Hesiod, 82, 87, 170
Hesse, Mary, 9
heteronomy, xvii, 40, 58, 62, 71, 107, 168-169, 173-176
Hinduism, xiii, 30-32, 77, 228 n.13
Hirschmann, Albert, 207
historicism, 78
historicity, 87
historiography, 191, 201
history, 117, 172, 176, 185-186, 205, 216
Hobbes, Thomas, 64
Hölderlin, Friedrich, 42-43, 50, 56, 207-220
holism, 11-12, 14-16, 19, 106, 148-153, 156
Homer, 82, 170
hope, 162-163, 165, 169
comprehended, 166
Horkheimer, Max, 159
humanism, xvi-xvii, 4, 167-168, 201
humanization, 147, 152, 168-170, 173, 179
Hume, David, 4, 64, 110
Husserl, Edmund, 18, 56-60, 89, 97-99, 102

idealism, 12, 57, 79, 113, 122, 127, 145-146, 159
German, 150-151, 155, 160, 181
transcendental, 43, 49
identity, xii, xv, 6, 18-20, 50, 62, 68-70, 93, 118-119, 121-127, 129-133, 154, 164, 181, 192, 203
class, 120
collective, 147-148
ego, 7, 68, 223 n.8
political, 127
social, 121-122, 128-129, 134
ideology, 55, 120, 124
critique of, 55
illiberalism, 168
imagination, 79, 113, 167, 187, 220

analogical, 182
immanence, x, xiv, xvi-xvii, 18, 71, 77, 89-90, 139, 184, 224 n.10
immanentism, 86, 90, 168, 184
immediacy, 140
imperialism, 229 n.20
in-between, 98-99, 103, 110-111
individualism, xvi, 35, 41, 130, 168, 203
possessive, 130
individuality, 141
individuation, 52-53
industrialization, 27, 37
institution, 191-194, 202
primeval, 193, 202
social, 191
instrumentalism, 131
intentionality, xiv, 75-76, 79-82, 86, 89-90, 99-101, 111-112, 162, 236 n.3
interaction, 60, 63-66, 98, 100, 110, 128
interactionism, 99
symbolic, 253 n.15
intercorporeity, 107
interiority, 134-135
interpretation, 211, 213
intersubjectivity, 45, 60, 66, 97-98, 109
intertwining, xv, 18-19, 97
intuitionism, 63
Irenaeus, 194
irrationalism, 29, 51, 54, 59, 69-71, 96
Islam, 175, 181
It-reality, xiv, 75-79, 81-84, 89-91, 94, 236 n.3
Iyer, Raghavan, 23, 28, 35, 38

Jacobinism, 123, 130
James, William, 232 n.20, 238 n.19
Jaspers, Karl, 2, 238 n.19
Jay, Martin, 159
Jesus, 171, 173-174, 180
Judaism, 172-173, 175
judgment, 40, 42, 51, 65
aesthetic, 51
judiciary, 145

justice, 31, 194, 196, 199
  proportional, 106

Kant, Immanuel, 4, 9, 14, 40-42, 56-57,
  63-68, 80, 107, 110-111, 119, 132, 151,
  212, 223 n.7, 224 n.13
karma, 31
karma yoga, 25-26, 33
Kautsky, Karl, 118
kenosis, 33
Kierkegaard, Søren, 47, 57, 60
kingdom, 174-175, 181, 183-185, 194,
  198-200, 205
  coming, 174, 185, 201, 205, 250 n.16
  of God, 169, 184, 195-198
knowledge, 5, 11, 25, 29, 40, 58, 163,
  200
  absolute, 80-81, 93
  critical, 6
  scientific, 102
Kohlberg, Lawrence, 7, 242 n.26
Kolakowski, Leszek, 159
Kolbenheyer, Erwin G., 215
Kuhn, Thomas, 225 n.18

Labriola, Antonio, 119
labor, 5, 71, 179
Lacan, Jacques, 41
Laclau, Ernesto, x, xv, 19-20
language, 5, 11, 15, 66-67, 74-76, 79,
  83, 86-88, 93, 99-100, 104, 149, 192-
  193, 196, 202-203, 212-214
  game, 10-16, 22, 100, 149-152
  poetic, 210
Lao Tzu, 171-172
Left Hegelianism, 49, 92
legitimacy, 197
legitimation, 12, 112
Leibniz, Gottfried W., 4, 87, 111, 129,
  161
Lenin,V. I., 120, 130
Leninism, 119, 130
Levinas, Emmanual, 86, 101, 204, 240
  n.7

liberalism, xi, 117, 168, 222 n.7, 230
  n.21
liberty, 125, 128, 130, 135-136
life-world, 5, 22, 48, 57, 61, 66-69, 72,
  97, 102-103
linguistics, 88, 99, 201, 223 n.7
localism, 10
Locke, John, 64
logocentrism, 28, 64, 107
logos, xi, 3, 8, 63, 106
Lukács, Georg, 159
luminosity, xiv, 75-76, 79, 82, 89-90,
  236 n.3
Luxemburg, Rosa, 118, 131
Lyotard, Jean-François, xvi, 2, 10-15,
  138, 149, 151-153, 156

Malinowski, Bronislaw, 11
Manichaeism, 172,179, 251 n.19
Marcel, Gabriel, 238 n.19
Marcuse, Herbert, 148
margin, xii, xvi-xvii, 26, 36, 108, 115,
  132
Marx, Karl, 4, 25, 28, 69-71, 92, 138,
  146-148, 152, 154, 166, 248 n.22
Marxism, 4, 11, 27-28, 99-101, 117-118,
  121, 123, 126, 130-132, 159, 166-167,
  177, 229 n.20, 243 n.2, 250 n.11
  classical, 120
  orthodox, 118
  Western, 159
materialism, 27-28, 92, 177
  dialectical, 165
matter, 165
Mead, George Herbert, 58
meaning, x, xv, 16, 18, 20, 63, 67, 97,
  105, 108, 110-112, 149, 152-153, 167,
  192-193, 196-197, 203-204, 209, 216
  cultural, 191, 202
  incarnate, 101
  intentional, 100
  social, 131
  surplus of, 122, 128
  universal, 16
mediation, 127, 142

Merleau-Ponty, Maurice, x, xii, xv,
18-21, 97, 99, 101-102, 107-109, 111,
238 n.19, 241 n.11
Messiah, 174, 180
messianism, 50
metadiscourse, 10
metalanguage, 225 n.17
metanarrative, 10, 96, 149-150
metaphysics, xi, 10, 14-15, 28, 42, 51,
55-56, 62, 70, 86-87, 95, 112, 127, 132,
148, 165, 177, 186-188, 219, 247 n.14
overcoming of, 87
metaxy, xiv-xv, 77, 79-80, 82-90, 92
militancy, 175, 180
millenarianism, 181
mobilization, 219
modernism, 39, 108, 112, 177
modernity, xiii-xiv, xvi, 14, 27-29, 36,
39-45, 48-58, 63-64, 67-70, 81, 90,
96, 104, 107, 127, 144, 150, 167, 187,
200, 221 n.4, 224 n.9, 231 n.8
modernization, xiii, 7-8, 27-29, 43,
67-69, 169
Mohammed, 171, 180
moksha, 25-26, 30
moment, 121, 133, 243 n.7
fulfilled, 160, 178
lived, 158
monarchy, 145, 198
constitutional, 145, 154-155
monism, 132
monotheism, 92
Montesquieu, 144
moralism, 144
morality, 42, 139-141
Moses, 171-172, 181
Mouffe, Chantal, xv, 19-20
mysticism, 63, 175
mystification, 177, 192
mythology, 50, 180

Nandi, Ashis, 23, 35, 38
narrative, 12-13, 90
National Socialism, 209, 222 n.8, 233
n.31

naturalism, 54, 159, 180
nature, xii, xv, xvii, 3, 5, 18-19, 40,
53, 56, 65, 87, 103-105, 115, 156, 159,
176, 185-186, 190, 194-195, 203-204
human, 4, 106, 186-189, 193, 202
state of, 4
necessity, 132, 142
negation, 166, 178
negativity, 123, 128, 133-135, 166, 178,
181
neo-conservatism, 124
neo-Hegelianism, 97
neo-Kantianism, 97
neo-Platonism, 81, 93
neo-utilitarianism, 64
neutralization, 198
Newton, Isaac, 149
Niebuhr, Richard, 184
Nietzsche, Friedrich, xiv, 2, 9-12,
40-41, 48-56, 59, 63-64, 69-71, 96,
131, 137-138, 147-153, 156, 201, 225
n.15, 232 n.15
nihilism, 54, 96, 114
nivritti, 25
nominalism, 2, 8
non-action, 33
non-being, 133, 214
non-identity, 70, 93, 133, 153
non-meaning, 20
non-order, xv, 115
non-reason, 71, 97, 103
non-theism, 32
non-violence, xiii, 28, 34, 181
normality, 105
nothingness, 133-134, 166, 177-178
novum, 164-165, 177
numinosity, 168-169, 177, 179

objectivism, 25, 49, 58, 61, 102, 212
objectivity, 143
oblivion, 81, 93
imaginative, 81
obscurantism, 29, 54, 74, 177
ontology, ix, xiv, xvi, 25, 62, 84, 93, 101,
160, 166-167, 177-178, 219, 250 n.12

fundamental, xiv, 57, 86, 238 n.19
  participatory, 93
  practical, ix
onto-theology, 93
openness, 189, 191, 197, 201
optimism, xiii, 163, 183
  militant, 164
order, x, xv, 20, 73-74, 77-79, 83-87,
  89-93, 95-96, 101-108, 112-116, 126,
  133, 186, 194-195, 199
  contingent, 102, 109, 112
  divine, 197
  genesis of, 113
  political, 95, 196-197
  public, 146
  social, 101, 106, 197
  universal, 197
orthodoxy, 119, 181
  Marxist, 119, 132
other, x, 18
otherness, x, xvii, 33, 43, 49-52, 55,
  70-72, 86, 91, 103-104, 107, 110-111,
  115, 153-154, 169, 179, 191, 204-205,
  250 n.16
  radical, 168, 170, 174, 177, 252 n.29
Otto, Rudolf, 68
overdetermination, 121, 126, 129-130

Pannenberg, Wolfhart, xvii, 184-205
Pantham, Thomas, 23, 34
pantheism, 175
paradigm, 13, 15, 64, 66
  shift of, 64-66, 72
paralogy, 10, 13, 15, 151, 225 n.18
parapolitics, 38
Parekh, Bhikhu, 23, 29-31
Parmenides, 82, 87
parochialism, xii, 29
parousia, 78, 81-82, 86, 90, 94
Parsons, Talcott, 11, 253 n.15
particularism, 129, 156, 224 n.10
particularity, 16, 45-47, 141-144, 247
  n.12
Pascal, Blaise, 28, 65
peace, 195-196

periagoge, 72, 81, 94
personalism, 201
personality, 67-68
pessimism, 158,176
phenomenology, 56, 60, 97, 99-102,
  107, 150
  existential, 101
  hermeneutical, 57, 62
  social, 105
  transcendental, 97
Philo, 164
philosophy, xi, xvii, 2, 20, 25, 39,
  45-49, 55-59, 73-74, 93, 121, 127, 137,
  155, 159-160, 164-166, 207, 209, 216
  analytical, 137
  Christian, 164
  classical, 193
  of consciousness, 56, 58, 64-66, 71,
    88, 100-102, 153
  dialectical, 138
  German, 79-80, 96-97
  Greek, 3, 37, 77, 106
  of history, 49, 113
  Indian, 23
  of language, 2
  modern, 65, 147-148
  moral, 7
  practical, 33
  of religion, 168
  Western, 2, 21, 23-25, 27, 178
Piaget, Jean, 6-7, 202, 223 n.7
pietism, 188
Plato, xiv, 3, 12, 46, 72, 78, 81, 83-87,
  89-92, 104, 141, 242 n.27
Platonism, 70, 79, 178
Plekhanov, Georgi V., 119
Plessner, Helmuth, 186, 189, 191, 201
pluralism, xii-xiii, 17, 121, 124, 130,
  221 n.2
plurality, 220
poetry, 207, 209-216
polarization, 130
polis, xii, xvi, 1, 3, 44
politics, 117-119, 124-126, 135, 146-149,
  169, 173, 184-185, 191, 193, 196-197,
  200, 207, 214, 216

democratic, 128
of production, 126
polity, 193-194, 196, 198-200
polytheism, 92
Popper, Karl, 138, 148-149, 151
populism, 92, 220
positivism, xi, 86, 90, 250 n.16
  logical, 4
positivity, 122-125, 128, 132-135, 138-
  139, 154
possessivism, 27, 36
possibility, 163, 165
  objective, 163
  real, 163, 165, 178-179
post-empiricism, 9
post-enlightenment, 127
post-Hegelianism, 127, 129, 131
post-humanism, 96
post-metaphysics, 95, 117, 127, 137, 156
postmodernism, xiii-xiv, 9-10, 39-41,
  49, 55, 95-96, 104, 125-127, 226 n.21,
  240 n.1, 248 n.20
postmodernity, 14, 39
post-structuralism, 2, 95-97, 100, 109,
  116, 125, 149, 153
power, xv, 5, 11, 13-15, 19, 25, 35, 48,
  71, 76, 106, 116, 135, 165, 194, 197
  drive, 161
  political, 197, 204
  separation of, 144
practice, ix, xv, xvii, 9, 19, 31, 34
  discursive, 133
  political, 149
  social, 19,134
pragmatics, 6, 9-12, 14, 149, 152
  universal, 6-7, 9, 67
pragmatism, 138, 158
pravritti, 25-26
praxis, 5, 31-33, 40, 46, 62-64, 131
pre-Socratics, 87
pre-understanding, 57
primitivism, 103
privatization, 188, 198-200, 203
productivity, 40, 46
progressivism, 176
proletariat, 4, 118-120

Prometheus, 168, 170
property, 140, 143
Protestantism, 200
psychoanalysis, 161, 191
psychologism, 168
psychology, 6, 99, 186, 189, 201
  behavioral, 99, 111
  cognitive, 202
  depth, 212
  developmental, 6, 223 n.7
  Gestalt, 99, 105
  social, 191

quietism, 171

racism, 215
radicalism, 124
Rai, Lala Rajput, 29
ramarajya, 38
rationalism, xii-xiii, 2, 4, 8, 13, 28,
  37-40, 46, 48-49, 53-54, 65-66, 109,
  113, 127, 159, 242 n.21
  communicative, 159
  enlightenment, 8, 48, 50
  modern, 54
  Western, 37
rationality, 4, 8, 40, 49-51, 53, 56,
  63-66, 69, 96, 100-103, 106, 127, 144,
  147, 241 n.9
  communicative, 7, 41, 67
  instrumental, 55
  material, 103, 106
  responsive, 105
  substantial, 42, 106
rationalization, 8, 52, 68, 103
realism, 122, 145-146
reality, 75-77, 79, 82-85, 87-90, 133,
  140, 147, 162-164, 167, 179, 185-187,
  190-191, 197, 201-203
reason, xi-xii, xv, 3-4, 16-17, 28, 32-34,
  40, 43-46, 48-58, 62-66, 69-71, 96-97,
  102-106, 110, 114, 127, 138-139, 145,
  149, 154, 167, 228 n.8
  absolute, 45, 47

communicative, 67
modern, 58
practical, 42, 54, 65
purism of, 68
theoretical, 54, 58
universal, 17, 147
recollection, 56, 79, 82, 113, 164-165
reconciliation, 42-45, 49, 53-55, 69-70, 99, 141-142, 205, 217, 220
reconstruction, 6-7
rational, 6, 67
reductionism, 28, 125
Reformation, 4, 39, 41, 194
reification, 25, 178, 192
relationism, xvi, 130, 156
relativism, 16, 78, 114, 241 n.19, 242 n.27
relevance, 105-106
religion, 44-46, 52, 168-171, 173, 176-177, 183-185, 188, 196-198, 200, 204, 231 n.11
Christian, 194
traditional, 219
world, 169-170
remembrance, 79, 82, 87, 93
Renaissance, 4, 41
resistance, xiii,79, 91
revelation, 85-86, 199
reversibility, xv, 18
revisionism, 118-119, 132, 242 n.4
revolution, 1, 117, 120, 124
democratic, 124, 135
French, 123, 135
industrial, 138
informational, 1, 11
October, 159
Ricoeur, Paul, 86, 101, 106
right, 139
abstract, 139-140
Right Hegelianism, 40, 46, 48-49, 62, 64
rightness, 6-7, 65, 67, 106, 233 n.28
Romanticism, 2, 8-9, 50, 54-55, 161
Rosenberg, Alfred, 215
Rothacker, Erich, 192
Rousseau, Jean-Jacques, 27, 64-65, 143, 232 n.13

Roy, Ram Mohan, 32
rupture, 114-115, 123, 153, 156
Russell Bertrand, 64

Sandoz, Ellis, 74, 85
salvation, 188, 194, 197
Saran, A.K., 29
Sartre, Jean-Paul, 101, 133, 233 n.32, 251 n.26
sarvodaya, 35
satya, 25, 32
satyagraha, xiii, 32-34
Saussure, Ferdinand, 125
Scheler, Max, 186, 189, 191, 201
Schelling, Friedrich W. J. von, 42-43, 63, 150, 159, 219
Schiller, Friedrich, 43, 49, 63
Schleiermacher, Friedrich D. E., 196
scholasticism, 99, 186
Schutz, Alfred, 97, 240 n.7
Schweitzer, Albert, 33
science, 4, 9-11, 40-42, 53-55, 65, 67, 76, 113, 185
empirical, 5
folk, 216
human, 200-201
of man, 186-188
modern, 10, 148
natural, 80
postmodern, 11, 151
reconstructive, 6
social, 200-201
scientism, 54, 101, 177
secularism, xvi, 199
secularization, xvi, 169, 176, 198
self, x, 18, 152, 203
self-consciousness, 47, 93, 141-142
self-reflection, 6, 56, 63
semantics, 6, 149
semiotics, 99
Sextus Empiricus, 8
Sittlichkeit, xvi, 44, 114, 136-143, 145-148, 152-157, 247 n.12
skepticism, 64
socialism, xi, 117, 120, 123, 244 n.10

sociality, 203
society, xvi, 3, 56, 67-68, 126, 143,
    153-156, 185, 193
  civil, xvi, 44, 64, 138-139, 141-147,
    247 n.13
  European, 27
  modern, 146
  post-industrial 95
  secular, 183, 185, 198, 200
  Western, 72, 203
sociologism, 125
sociology, 170, 189, 201
Socrates, 23, 31, 53, 83, 91
solipsism, 57, 60, 72
Sophocles, 212
Sorel, Georges, 118-119, 131
space, 83, 87
speculation, 82
  metastatic, 78
speech, 6-7, 58, 66, 68
  act, 65
  ideal, 100
Spengler, Oswald, 215
Spinoza, Benedict, 129
spirit, 40, 46-47, 62, 70, 138-139, 143,
    145-147, 150, 154, 189
  absolute, 43-47, 64, 71, 137-139, 150,
    152-153, 164, 234 n.37
  objective, 44-45, 48, 143, 147
  world, 141, 166, 178
spontaneism, 131, 171
state, xv-xvi, 40, 42-48, 136-139, 141,
    143-148, 151-157, 188, 193-198, 220,
    231 n.11, 257 n.25
  external, 142, 154
  modern, 142, 144-146, 154, 199
  secular, 196-197
Stoicism, xii, 2-4, 164, 194
Strauss, Leo, 37
strike, 119
  general, 119, 131
structuralism, 18, 99-101, 121, 240 n.2
struggle, 128, 136
  democratic, 123, 131
  popular, 123, 131
subjectivism, 43, 51-54, 57-61, 159, 188

subjectivity, xi, 18, 40-47, 50-52, 56-60,
    64-66, 70-72, 80, 84, 87-88, 97, 106,
    112, 138, 144-145, 156, 187, 201-204,
    246 n.6, 247 n.12
  modern, 107
  transcendental, 57, 101
substantiality, xvi, 141-143, 155
subversion, 132-134
suffering, 33-34, 173, 229 n.18, 256
    n.13
swadeshi, 32,35
swaraj, 32, 35
symbol, 76, 80, 87
symbolization, 77, 82-84, 88, 91, 237 n.7
syndicalism, 118-119
synthesis, 69, 104, 153
system, 68-69, 72-74, 85
  scientific, 80

Taoism, 77, 171-172, 250 n.18
tapas, 33-34
Taylor, Charles, 146, 153-154
technology, xii, 4, 37, 40, 56, 72, 160
teleology, 102, 110, 113, 151, 185, 194,
    205
temporality, 86
temporalization, 179
text, 75
theism, 32
theology, xvii, 85, 92, 168-170, 184-188,
    196, 198, 200
  Christian, 187-188
  dialectical, 86, 168, 179
  negative, 86, 168, 204
  political, xvii, 184-185, 195, 200
  practical, 184, 252 n.1
  process, 252 n.29
  progressive, 200
  Reformation, 194
theonomy, 199
theory, 32, 100
  of action, 110-111
  critical, 4, 9, 99-100
  political, 116, 121, 125, 131, 183-184,
    191

systems, 11-12, 149, 153
Theunissen, Michael, 97, 234 n.33
thing-reality, xiv, 75-76, 80-84, 87, 89, 236 n.3
Thom, René, 13
Thomism, 3
threshold, 115, 168, 173
Tillich, Paul, 199, 254 n.24
tolerance, 199
topology, 110-111
totalitarianism, 28, 106, 125, 135, 148, 197
totalitarism, 14, 152
totality, 43-46, 69, 118, 121-122, 126-129, 132, 136, 142-145, 150, 175, 219
totalization, 150
tradition, xiii, 31, 36, 43, 48-49, 68, 95-96, 101, 108, 112-114, 137, 150, 178, 190, 228 n.13
traditionalism, xii, 29, 108, 112
transcendence, x, xiv, xvii, 18, 71, 77, 86, 89-90, 139, 184, 224 n.10
transcendentalism, 168
truth, 5-7, 24, 28, 32-37, 46, 54, 59, 63-67, 74-79, 82-83, 87-88, 90-92, 112, 117, 140, 199, 233 n.28
ontological, 16, 25
propositional, 58, 63
truthfulness, 6, 65-67, 233 n.28
turn, 15
linguistic, 14-15, 66, 138
ontological, 56
typification, 105

ultimum, 164-165, 167
understanding, 5-6, 16-18, 57
universal, 2-3, 8, 18
universalism, xii, 2-4, 8-10, 15-17, 36, 68, 224 n.10, 245 n.17
agonal, 20
lateral, 18
universality, 45-46, 142
universalization, 242 n.26

univocity, 154
unreason, 96
untouchability, 30-31, 36
untruth, 90-91
utilitarianism, 4, 64, 158
utopia, 158, 165, 173-176, 180
utopianism, 68, 112, 154, 159, 175-177, 180, 200

value spheres, 113
validity, 6, 67
claims, 6-7, 51, 65-67, 113
violence, 28, 34-35, 125
Voegelin, Eric, xiv, 20, 73-94
Voltaire, 8, 40, 176
voluntarism, 131

Wagner, Richard, 49-50
Waldenfels, Bernhard, x, xv, 18, 96-115
war, 120
of position, 120, 130
Weber, Max, 8, 114, 131, 148, 176, 245 n.19
Whitehead, Alfred North, 238 n.19
will, 139-140
general, 143, 146
to power, 33, 48, 51-52, 55, 156
Winch, Peter, 102
Wittgenstein, Ludwig, 13-14, 58, 66, 102, 105
world, 57, 61, 63-67, 186
external, 86
objective, 58, 60-61, 64-65
social, 65
subjective, 65

Young Hegelianism, 40, 46-49, 56, 59, 62-64

Zinoviev, Gregori E., 119, 130
Zoroaster, 171-173, 179